D0947293

FINDING FREEDOM

America's Distinctive Cultural Formation

John Harmon McElroy

Southern Illinois University Press
Carbondale and Edwardsville

Printed in the United States of America

Designed by Joanne E. Kinney

Production supervised by Natalia Nadraga

Library of Congress Cataloging-in-Publication Data

McElroy, John Harmon.
    Finding freedom.

    Includes index.
    1. United States—Civilization.   2. National
characteristics, American.   3. Liberty.   I. Title.
E169.1.M157   1989   973   88-26547
ISBN 0-8093-1515-7   CIP

The paper used in this publication meets the minimum
requirements of American National Standard for Information
Sciences—Permanence of Paper for Printed Library Materials,
ANSI Z39.48-1984. ∞

for Laurie, Helen, Lisa, and John
with the same love you feel
and will feel for your children

CONTENTS

Acknowledgments

Without incurring any responsibility for the ideas or information in this book, a number of persons have helped me during its composition, and of these I wish especially to thank Sylvia Teresita Alonso, Kevin and Lisa Button, Clark Cahow, Paul Carter, Larry Evers, John Hope Franklin, Frances Kelley, Richard J. Kopec, C. Townsend Ludington, Onyria Herrera McElroy, Robert Mirandon, H. D. Morrison, George C. Myers, Jean-Claude Robert, Herbert Smith, and Juan Villegas; and, for his friendship as well as his help, Gerald McNiece. I acknowledge also students I have taught at the University of Arizona, Adam Mickiewicz University in Poland, the Federal University of Santa Catarina in Brazil, and the University of Salamanca in Spain for their help in the shaping of my ideas about American culture; as well as public audiences before whom I have lectured on that subject in Arizona under the auspices of the Arizona Humanities Council, academic audiences in six states of Brazil to whom I spoke under the auspices of the Commission for Educational Exchange Between the United States of America and Brazil, and the members of the Argentina Association of American Studies and their guests whom I addressed at their annual meeting in Buenos Aires in 1986.

Necessary Preliminary Observations

Culture may be defined as a unique set of simple beliefs formed and communicated over generations of time through behavior. It is the set that is complicated, not the beliefs themselves, which have to be simple in order to remain coherent over time. And it is the set that is unique, not every belief in it.

No culture is unique in the sense that none of its belief-behaviors exists in any other culture. Every culture belongs to a configuration of overlapping cultural phenomena whose ramifications include all human societies. For example, although the culture of the United States of America is unique in having a set of belief-behaviors that no other culture exactly duplicates, regional and ethnic cultures exist within it whose sets of belief-behaviors largely overlap, without being identical to, the culture of the United States, and the culture of the United States exists with other distinctive cultures as a part of the more extensive phenomenon known as Western culture. To claim to be studying a particular culture is to claim a certain focus of interest.

What gives a culture its authority to represent right behavior and to compel behavior in any given generation is its connection with the actions of previous generations. Belief-behaviors peculiar to one or two generations do not make a culture. Only ideas that have been sanctified by being acted upon continuously from generation to generation are cultural beliefs. (In this work, the reference to a generation as a period of time indicates thirty years.)

A culture, as such, has inertia. Normally, after beliefs and behaviors have validated each other during several generations and have come to form a cultural set, they persist in that form unchanged, even though the conditions that originally produced the set may alter or disappear altogether. Understanding the distinctiveness of the conditions under which a culture forms is therefore necessary for understanding the distinctiveness of its set of belief-behaviors. A culture is something that both was and is, and the use of the term *cultural formation* as a synonym for *culture*

particularly calls attention to the historical character of culture by suggesting something formed in the past which retains that form in the present.

By providing a justifying sense of participation in correct, continuing
behavior (correct because continuing) and by conferring an identity that
is both historical and social, cultures satisfy deep, undeniable human needs.
So strong is the urge to participate in a historically sanctified configuration
of belief-behaviors that human beings have been known to prefer death
to violation of their culture's norms; and so pervasively normal to the
participants in a cultural formation is the set of its belief-behaviors that they
are unaware of the distinctiveness of the set until they journey outside the
continuum of its reality.

Because every culture judges itself by its own standards, every culture
considers itself superior to every other culture. The rule is universal and
applies to the culture of the United States no less than to any other cultural
formation.

This book proposes to identify, through appropriate comparisons,
the primary historical conditions that produced the distinctive cultural
formation of the United States of America. It does not undertake to describe
regional or ethnic subunits of American culture or to examine American
culture as a subunit of any larger cultural configuration. In carrying out
this purpose, no statement made about another culture should be mistaken
for a systematic description of it. The only cultural formation systematically
under consideration is that of the United States.

A comparative, historical method is best suited to discovering what is
distinctive about any cultural formation that one hopes to understand
objectively, and Brazil, Canada, and Spanish America provide the most
relevant comparisons for studying the cultural formation of the United
States because the historical conditions under which these cultures formed
as colonies of European imperial powers in the Americas resemble the
formative historical conditions of American culture more closely and more
categorically than those of any other culture. Certainly, the historical conditions of cultural formation in Europe have been essentially unlike those
that have pertained to the United States of America.

The general finding of this study, after applying this method, has been
that the cultural formation of the United States of America is the least
European of the four major continental cultures of the Americas. Long-
lasting and comparatively unique demographic and geographic conditions
existed in central North America, where the United States developed, to
make the people of this region of the Americas less oriented toward Europe
and European cultural beliefs and behaviors than were the peoples of
Brazil, Canada, or Spanish America. One notices, for instance, that Canada

continued its allegiance to a European monarchy until 1982; that Brazil instituted a European-style monarchy of its own after gaining its independence from European dominion; and that Spanish America has, like Europe, many separate nations.

It is also appropriate here at the outset to say something about the use of the terms *America* and *American* in this book. Anyone who lives in any nation of either South or North America is of course an American in the same way that anyone of any nation of Asia is an Asian or any nation of Europe is a European. However, the continental name *American* applies to the people of the United States of America in an additional way since this nation's name incorporates the continental name—a right of choice won through being the first Americans to revolt against European imperialism. The only natural reference to the people of the United States of America is therefore as Americans; and *America* is as inevitable an abbreviation of the name their revolutionary ancestors gave their country as *the United States* is.

American culture began in the continental wilderness that existed in central North America in the seventeenth century. In offering no sign of civilization (i.e., cities) throughout its vast reaches, this wilderness, whose ancient forest had started growing after the last ice age, ten thousand years before, had for the Europeans who first explored it and for those who, a hundred years later, committed themselves and their descendants to living in it, a forbidding psychological oldness. It was a continental presence that intimidated Europeans by invoking Europe's deep antiquity—the racial memory of the time before civilization in Europe. The voyage across the Atlantic to this wilderness in the sixteenth and seventeenth centuries was for Europeans not just a journey across three thousand miles of saltwater but a journey backward through some six thousand years to a condition of space and time like that before the beginning of their civilization. This fundamental consideration about the cultural formation of the United States—its beginning in an awareness of a condition of oldness that had to be transformed and made new (i.e., civilized) if large numbers of persons of European descent were to live in it—is discussed in this study through the use of the terms *Stone Age, Stone Age wilderness, Stone Age reality,* and *Stone Age space-time continuum.*

FINDING FREEDOM

America's Distinctive
Cultural Formation

CHAPTER

1

EUROPEAN AND AMERICAN CULTURE

The extracontinental imperialism of Europe that began with the Portuguese and Spanish voyages of the late 1400s initiated the development of the modern cultures of Brazil, Canada, Spanish America, and the United States by bringing populations of Europeans and Africans into permanent contact with the original peoples of the two American continents. Given the diverse character of the new populations that began to be constituted in different places in the Americas after 1500, plus the radically non European geography of most of the American continents and their much greater land areas in comparison to the continent of Europe, it was impossible to perpetuate European culture intact anywhere in the Americas. The divergences of Jamaican, Canadian, and United States cultures—all supposedly equal heirs to the English language and the English tradition of law—illustrate the primary effect of conditions in the Americas on cultural developments there after the first permanent European settlement was established by Columbus in 1493 in the Caribbean.

The enormous, free migration of people from Europe to the Americas during the last five centuries, the much smaller, forced migration from Africa to these continents during the first four of these centuries, and the still smaller, free migration from Asia during the last two centuries have cumulatively been the largest movement of human beings in history. The differences in the kind of immigration that Canada, the United States, Spanish America, and Brazil received, the different numerical distributions of these immigrants in the Americas, their various relationships to the differently distributed and enculturated original peoples of the Americas, and the varying geographical conditions in the two American continents where they settled have been the principal conditions for the differentiated cultural formations that have come into being in these continents during the past five hundred years.

EUROPEAN AND AMERICAN GEOGRAPHIES

Geography provides no sufficient explanation of differences in cultural formations. No single factor does. But it must be considered one of the primary influences on cultural formations. Where people live affects how they can behave, and this in turn affects what beliefs they can pass down from generation to generation through behavior to form a culture. The behavior associated with group consciousness and extracontinental imperialism in European culture, for example, has a fundamental origin in European geography.

Europe is a quite small, uniquely peninsular continent. Only Australia has a smaller area, and no other inhabited continental landmass except Australia has the general access to the sea that Europe has because of its intensely peninsular geography. Most of Europe is less than 250 miles from saltwater. Furthermore, this continent is unique among the continents of the world in being broadly attached to another, much larger continent (Asia) and in being within eyesight of yet another, also much larger continent (Africa) across two narrow straits of seawater. No other continent in the world except Europe has been easily accessible from two much larger continents. These fundamental geographical facts have had an effect on what has happened culturally in the continent of Europe.

Europe's central landform is the five-hundred-mile-wide peninsula bounded by the Baltic and North seas, the Atlantic Ocean, and the Mediterranean and Black seas. This long central peninsula, whose axis runs between the city of Gomel and the mouth of the Garonne River, accounts for nearly one-third of Europe's area. It attaches to the pre–Ural plain of eastern Europe at the Baltic republics, Byelorussia, and the Ukraine. Curving out to the north from that plain in a connected series are the Kola, the Finnish, and the Scandinavian peninsulas; and attached to the southern half of the main peninsula are the Balkan, the Italian, and the Iberian peninsulas. These six smaller peninsulas, along with the large European islands in the Mediterranean and the big islands of Britain, Ireland, and Iceland, comprise slightly more of Europe's area than the long central peninsula, the remainder of this continent being the wide plain in front of the north–south-running Ural Mountains, which mark the division between Europe and

Asia. Thus, because two-thirds of Europe's territory is either peninsular or insular—a geographical condition which encouraged the development of separate tribes within these islands and almost islands—and also because Europe is unique in being accessible over land and across narrow straits to both of the world's two largest continents—a geographical condition which invited repeated tribal migrations and other sorts of invasions from Asia and Africa—this comparatively small but physically rich continent has acquired over the millennia an extraordinarily large number of competing national groups.

Europe's density of population is in the same category as Asia's, and its density of nations is much higher than that of any other continent. In 1985, Europe had 177 million people for each million square miles of its area; Asia had 171 million people per million square miles. (By comparison, Africa, North America, and South America had between 38 and 46 million persons per million square miles; Australia, 5.) Without counting Monaco, Andorra, and Liechtenstein as nations or considering the various European parts of the Union of Soviet Socialist Republics as separate nations, the average number of nations in Europe per million square miles is just over seven. In Africa there are 4.3 nations per million square miles; in Asia, South America, and the North American mainland, 1.9, 1.7, and 1.1. In other words, Europe has a density of population that is the same as Asia's and a density of nations much higher than any other continent. This distinctive combination of high population density and high density of nations can at least partly be explained in terms of Europe's unique peninsular geography and its unique proximity to two continents much larger than itself. This high density of both people and national groups, which no other continent but Europe exhibits, has been a fundamental condition of its continental culture. That is to say, Europeans have culturally thought and behaved as they have because there have historically been a great many of them having a great many different tribal origins—oftentimes outside of the continent—competing with each other in an attractively rich but comparatively restricted peninsular geography.

Europe's peninsularity, which is what puts most of its land area within 250 miles of saltwater, and its unique density of both population and competing groups have made this comparatively small continent the only one known to history with a number of nations that have used sea power to establish and maintain immense overseas empires for long periods of time. That unique cultural behavior began ten centuries ago, with the permanent settlement of the big mid-Atlantic island of Iceland by seafarers from the Scandinavian peninsula who, around the year 982, also permanently settled the mammoth ice-capped island off northeastern North

America (Greenland) and, soon afterward, briefly inhabited the largest island in the estuary of North America's St. Lawrence River. By the twelfth century, however, this initial extracontinental imperialism by European mariners had subsided. It resumed on a spectacular scale in the late fifteenth century with the activities of seafarers from the Iberian peninsula, who in the early seventeenth century were vigorously joined in the cultural behavior of creating enormous overseas empires by seafaring peoples from the coastlands and islands of west-central Europe. Navigators from the Italian peninsula played prominent parts in both the fifteenth-century and the seventeenth-century phases of this second, sustained extracontinental imperialism by sea.

In the sixteenth century, large-scale extracontinental imperialism was also launched from Europe by land, eastward from the pre–Ural plain into northern Asia, a conquest that eventually led this group of imperially minded Europeans to the Pacific Ocean and across the fifty-mile-wide Bering Strait into North America and down the west coast of this third continent as far as northern California. Because this eastern European nation conquered a vast empire contiguous to Europe (the entire northern half of Asia), it still retains control over it and has a land area reminiscent of the size of the British empire at its height. During the last forty years (1945–85), the deeply enculturated imperialist behavior of the USSR, which is really not a country in any normal sense of the word but a domestic empire of nations occupying more than one-seventh of the world's total land surface, has even caused it to project its deeply enculturated imperialist behavior into the center of the central European peninsula and overseas into several regions of Africa, southeast Asia, and the Caribbean Sea by creating in those areas of the world a series of so-called national governments that are directly dependent on it, while Europe's other extracontinental imperialist nations during this same forty-year period have all ceased to create new colonies for themselves, have given up their former colonies, and have restricted their political power to their own national territories in Europe. Only the ruling class of this final European imperialist state, the hugest "country" the world has ever seen, persists in carrying on this fading tradition of European cultural behavior. (When one excludes the uninhabited continent of Antarctica from consideration, the far-flung borders of the Soviet Union encompass more than one-sixth of the land surface of Earth, without taking into account the colonies it has created since the end of World War II in Europe, Asia, Africa, and the Americas; the imperial character of the Soviet Union is attested in its insistence that two of its Union Republics—the Ukraine and Byelorussia—be given separate voting rights as nations in the United Nations, so that the USSR is the only "country" in the world with three votes instead of one in the UN General Assembly.)

In the Americas, too, geography has of course had a fundamental effect on cultural behavior. Most of Canada, for instance, the second-largest nation in the world (3.8 million square miles, an area equal to the entire continent of Europe), is largely uninhabited and virtually unchanged from what it was around the time of the first permanent European settlements within its borders because its vast boreal mainland, subarctic inland sea (mistakenly named a bay by its European discoverers), and arctic archipelago (one of whose islands is larger than Great Britain, Austria, Hungary, and Switzerland combined) are in a heavy grip of ice for most of the year. This geography makes large-scale population and internal development of most of Canada extremely difficult. Because so much of its territory lies in frigid northern latitudes, Canada's population, which is quite small in relation to its size, has remained concentrated within one hundred miles of its southern border.

Similarly, Brazilians, whose nation is 87 percent the size of Europe (3.3 million square miles), have been restricted in their behavior by the forbidding geography of their heartland, the Amazon. This river basin contains an estimated two-thirds of all the river water on the planet, and some part of it is always in flood. The Amazon rain forest is almost as large as the forty-eight contiguous states of the United States; and the two-hundred-mile-wide estuary of the Amazon River, which the Brazilians rightly call "the river sea," embraces an island larger than Switzerland. Even as far inland as a thousand miles from the Atlantic Ocean, the Amazon River is still so wide in places that the curvature of the Earth prevents a person looking through a telescope from seeing across it from one bank to the other. Today, as in the past, most Brazilians live on or not far from the long Atlantic coast of their nation. Only a small fraction of Brazil's population lives in the silent, tree-dimmed solitudes of the Amazon Basin.

Brazilians think of the city of São Paulo, even though it is only twenty-five miles from the ocean, as being in "the interior" because the two dimensions of Brazil's cultural space have historically been the coast, which has been the primary focus of Brazilian life, and the rest of the national territory, which is "the interior." Brazilians, during the formative centuries of their culture, were usually more content with the familiar, easy beauty near the Atlantic beaches of their country than with the harsh areas far from the coast. For geographical reasons, theirs has been a littoral culture, just as Canada's has been a border culture. In terms of Brazilian culture, therefore, if you are out of sight of the sea you are in "the interior." However, one finds in the speeches of the eighteenth-century Brazilian patriot "Tiradentes" (Joaquim José da Silva Xavier), two and one-half centuries after the European settlement of Brazil, and in statements by other leaders down to the present, a recurring call for Brazilians to move away from the seaboard and to occupy the lands of their huge country that are far from the smell of the sea. And, gradually, with increasing momentum, Brazilians in the twentieth century have been changing their cultural beliefs and behavior and doing that.

The United States of America, whose national territory (3.6 million square miles) is 95 percent the size of the continent of Europe, has been historically an inwardly oriented culture in comparison to Canada and Brazil. At its center is the greatest expanse of arable land in either of the two American continents: an immense river basin having a mostly temperate climate, much rich topsoil, and none of the torrential, soil-leaching annual rainfall that characterizes the jungle that covers the Amazon Basin. Most of this great central river drainage of North America, comprising one-half the United States, has been developed. Moving into the center of a big continent, to possess and develop it, constitutes one of the principal ways in which the cultural behavior of Americans has historically differed from that of Brazilians, Canadians, and Spanish Americans, none of whom had a heartland in which they could behave that way from generation to generation. (The extremely elongated geography of Spanish America prevents it from having a central heartland, though its area, 4.4 million square miles, is 13 percent larger than the continent of Europe.) Except for the United States, the major continental cultures in the Americas have all looked outward to Europe. Only the people of the United States from an early moment in their cultural history looked inward to the creation of a new cultural space for themselves, and only they developed a way of thought and behavior from generation to generation based on that mental habit, because only their cultural ancestors had a geographical opportunity, in combination with motives that persisted for generations, for occupying a continental interior that was developable and habitable on a large scale by a new population.

Europe's proximity to and connection with the far larger continents Africa and Asia and the incursions of tribal groups from those continents into Europe fostered an extraordinary number of groups contending for space in Europe, as did also its uniquely peninsular, and often mountainous, geography. Tribal migrations and the resulting hostilities between settled groups and groups on the move characterized life in Europe both before and during the early centuries of the Christian era. (The pagan tribes called Saxons and Angles, for instance, invaded Britain in the late fifth century AD.) Europe's long history of tribal migration and conflict provided the basis for its modern nations. Like the modern nations of Africa, these often do not represent an actual assimilation of groups. Yugoslavia, for instance, though considered a single European nation today, recognizes in its laws five major "nationalities" and many other groups having autonomous language rights. The Soviet Union, which includes all of eastern Europe as well as all of northern Asia, is a patchwork throughout its enormous area of nearly one hundred nationalities whose multiplicity of national languages employs five different alphabets. Four of these (the Cyrillic, the Latin, the Georgian, and the Armenian alphabets) occur in the European part of the Soviet Union. Each of the fifteen union republics of the Soviet Union, ten of which are in Europe, has its own official language. The same point can also be illustrated from western Europe. In Spain, besides Basque, Catalan, and Castilian (the three languages still spoken by many people and employed in written literature), Leonese, Valenciano, and Galician were likewise in use as popular and literary languages through the nineteenth century. Similarly, in Great Britain in the nineteenth century, the national languages of the Scots, Irish, and Welsh were in wide use in addition to English, and still have not entirely vanished from literary or popular use.

In American cultural history, nationalism has meant the voluntary creation of a unified space almost as large as all of Europe (3.6 million square miles compared to Europe's 3.8 million square miles) by an expanding population of self-selected European immigrants and their descendants. This individualistically constituted (as opposed to tribally constituted) population represented a radically new kind of population in human history. No nation before the settlement of the United States in the seventeenth and eighteenth centuries had ever had a rapidly growing population predominately comprised of the descendants of individuals who had chosen to emigrate to it as individuals, free of the kind of governmental screening that characterized European emigration to Brazil, Canada, and Spanish America during the formative centuries of their cultures. In the United States, this new kind of population organized itself over and over again into new geopolitical units called states through a process like that legislated in 1787 in the Northwest Ordinance, a law as fundamentally expressive of American cultural thought and behavior as the Constitution of the United States.

In the cultural history of Europe, nationalism has meant frequent wars among a multiplicity of tribally originated nations constantly striving for advantageous alliances against hereditary enemies, and it has also often meant the subordination of weak nations to powerful nations in the ever-shifting power realignments that so frequently redefined the borders between groups. Because of Europe's tribal past, history to a European has been a matter of evening old scores. The United States has no such past.

History for Americans has been a going-back, by a new kind of self-selected population and their American-born descendants, to a beginning in the Stone Age and starting the process of civilization over again, without any tribal past to determine their behavior. In consequence, Americans have a radically different sense of history than have Europeans.

Europe's repeated invasions by migratory groups and their competition for space within the continent produced in European culture a belief that disunity and hostility are normal, until peace (that is, dominance) is imposed through armed force or the threat of using force. Other cultural modes of thought and behavior that Europe's intensely tribal past have produced can also be identified: the belief in and practice of giving elites within groups special privileges (the necessity of concentrating autocratic power in the military leaders of a group engaged for many years in migrations in alien territory); the belief in and practice of group rights and differentiated privileges (the prerogatives of conquerors over those they conquer); the concept of unarmed serfs fixed as property to inheritable land and subservient to armed lords, and other extreme inequalities in the distribution of wealth (the claims of victorious tribal leaders and their principal military subordinates to the lion's share of the spoils of conquest, including the labor of conquered peoples); and, the assertion of the idea of inheritable qualities of superior leadership (the natural pretensions to permanent superiority of tribal military leaders after alien lands have been conquered and divided up).

As group militarily contended with group for booty and dominion in Europe during the twenty centuries of the Christian era and as far back as recorded history goes in Europe, the leaders of victorious groups at times contracted marriages of mutual advantage among the leading families of the groups they dominated, in order to secure their loyalty and to enhance the legitimacy of their dominion. Marriage was also an important part of the constant need for military alliances in the nearly continuous history of conflict among the many competing groups in European history. From this behavior emerged a cultural belief in hierarchies of political and social authority and responsibility throughout the continent. Established through military prowess, this cultural tradition was institutionalized and perpetuated in the idea of superior bloodlines. Evidence of the importance of the institutions of caste and kingship in European culture—institutions that helped to preserve intact the migratory groups who entered Europe and gave legitimacy to their division of conquered spoils—are the vestigial ten monarchies still observable in modern Europe, a number nearly equaling the eleven current monarchies of Asia.

In contrast to the tribally based population of Europe, individuals and families formed the population of the United States. In what became the United States of America, groups were constituted by the consent of the individuals who organized them to accomplish some necessary task or to establish a community structure for the common good of collections of individuals. Participation in such deliberately constituted groups served the interests of the individual. Sometimes emigrants to America from Europe who were strangers to each other organized themselves for mutual benefit even during the ship passage to America.[1]

Crossing the Atlantic by ship was a kind of confirmation of the belief in equality. It made European emigrants to America conscious of confronting the same physical circumstances and of having the same need for comfort and safety as the other Europeans who had selected themselves to go to America to live. Conditions in the United States during the centuries of its colonial period reinforced this sense of equality by making cooperation by consent a fundamental necessity of survival and progress. Authority could not be established or maintained in America by invoking Europe's aristocratic and group-centered culture because aristocrats and already-structured groups generally did not emigrate to America and there were no competing national groups within American society. A historian of the population of the ancient wilderness of central North America and the process of self-selecting individuals repeatedly creating communities from it has summed up the fundamental behavior that characterized American society from generation to generation as follows: "The new settlers were in most locations strangers to each other upon arrival, but they were obliged to learn quickly to work together;" and, "The first impulse of every new settlement, before land was cleared, cabins built, or stockade raised, was to hold a town meeting in which every man old enough to bear arms voted by majority rule for regulations governing social conduct, assignment of community tasks, and mutual defense."[2]

In America, groups were not the focus of an allegiance that absorbed and preempted the concerns of the individual, as they were in the culture that arose from Europe's tribal past, because America was populated predominately by self-seeking individuals rather than by generations-old, already-structured groups intending to maintain their group identity. The hierarchical, authoritarian, group mentality of European cultural behavior

---

1. Philip Taylor, *The Distant Magnet: European Emigration to the U.S.A.* (London: Eyre & Spottiswood, 1971), p. 137.

2. Dale Van Every, *Forth to the Wilderness: The First American Frontier 1754–1774* (New York: Arno Press, 1977), p. 305; by the same author, *A Company of Heroes: The American Frontier 1775–1783* (New York: Arno Press, 1977), pp. 14–15.

is illustrated in the response to the American Revolution by some Highland Scots who emigrated as clan groups to the Carolinas under the authority of their hereditary military chieftains after being defeated in Scotland by the forces of the English king. One would suppose that such persons would readily join in a war against the British monarchy. But such was not always the case. Under the leadership of their hereditary chiefs, some of the Highland Scots in the Carolinas remained loyal to the monarchy that had caused them to abandon their homeland because their quarrel with the English king had not been over whether a king should rule them but over which king it should be. When it came to a revolution to abolish royal authority, their European culture prevailed because their group mentality as a clan was founded on the cultural idea of a hereditary leader of legitimate, supposedly superior blood.

The satisfaction of individual desires, not the desire to maintain a European group structure, was the overarching motive for most of the migration to America from Europe in the seventeenth and eighteenth centuries, when American culture was formed. The same motive continued to characterize migration to America from Europe in the nineteenth and twentieth centuries. Satisfying the individual—in terms of comfort, safety, happiness, equality of liberty—was the principal reference of cultural thought and behavior in what became the United States of America. American culture did not develop a group-centered mentality because, almost from the beginning, it was made up of a mixture of persons from a wide variety of European groups (nations) who frequently intermarried with persons from some other European ancestry according to their individual feelings.

Only during the first seventeen years after the first permanent colony of Englishmen settled in Virginia in 1607 was the European population on the Atlantic coastal plain of North America mainly of one European nationality. After 1624 it became increasingly mixed. The Dutch established a colony at the mouth of the Hudson River in that year, and in 1638 Swedes established another colony in the Delaware River valley in what eventually became parts of New Jersey, Pennsylvania, and Delaware, about half of whose settlers were Finns because Finland was then dominated by the Swedish crown. In the mid-1660s English sea power eliminated these embryonic rivals but not their populations, which remained largely in place under British rule. And even as the numbers of individuals and families from England emigrating to the Atlantic coastal plain of North America increased, so too did the numbers of persons from other nations of Europe and the non-English parts of Britain because the imperial government of

England generally followed a policy of allowing non-English Europeans to settle there. Thus, before 1640, in the Atlantic coastal plain, there were Danes, Frenchmen, Portuguese Jews, Spanish traders, Bohemians, Poles, Germans, and Italians, as well as persons from the four national groups of the British Isles and other places in Europe.[3]

Between 1660 and 1770, as the American population increased from seventy-five thousand to well over two million, the proportion of English blood in that predominately European-descended population steadily decreased. The historian Gary B. Nash in his often-cited study *Red, White, and Black: The Peoples of Early America* estimates that, not long before the American Revolution began in 1775, "roughly half of the inhabitants of the Thirteen Colonies had no English blood in their veins."[4] There was reason, therefore, for the complaint of the patriotic Englishman living in Philadelphia and writing to his brother in England in 1770 that he had experienced some difficulty in locating in that largest American city, where a declaration of American independence was soon to be made, "twenty native Englishmen to celebrate St. George's day."[5]

Subordination by rank, discipline, differentiated privileges and responsibilities according to rank, and habitual respect for established authority as such are modes of thought and behavior characteristic of armies. They are also modes of thought and behavior characteristic of the aristocratic culture that developed in Europe from its long history of tribal migration and warfare. And English culture was as hierarchical and as authoritarian in its formation as any of the group-minded cultures on the mainland of Europe because the peopling of the British Isles took place in the same way as the peopling of the rest of Europe. The creation of the United Kingdom of Great Britain and Ireland was a matter of invasions, conquests, and military domination of one group by another, just as the creation of the nations on the mainland of Europe was. Britain's insularity could make no appreciable cultural difference until the navy created by English

3. Marcus Lee Hansen, *The Atlantic Migration 1607–1860: A History of the Continuing Settlement of the United States* (Cambridge: Harvard University Press, 1941), pp. 38–39.

4. Gary B. Nash, *Red, White, and Black: The Peoples of Early America,* second edition (Englewood Cliffs, NJ: Prentice-Hall, 1982), p. 200.

5. Quoted in Carl and Jessica Bridenbaugh, *Rebels and Gentlemen: Philadelphia in the Age of Franklin* (Westport, CT: Greenwood Press, 1978; reprint of 1942 edition), p. 260. Evidence for the diminishing proportion of English-descended Americans is reported by the "Committee on Linguistics and National Stocks in the Population of the United States," American Historical Association, *Annual Report* 1, 1931, pp. 124–25, 310.

nonarchs in the sixteenth century became strong enough to convert the North Sea and the English Channel from often-used pathways of invasion into impassable moats of defense. By that time, however, Europe's basic modes of cultural thought and behavior were firmly fixed in the British Isles.

No such history pertained to the thirteen colonies ruled by Britain on the Atlantic coastal plain of North America. They achieved independence from Europe between 1775 and 1783 in a radically non-European way. They joined together voluntarily, not just in a mutually advantageous military alliance but in a permanent, national political union. It is also remarkable that not one of the thirteen stayed out of the fight to renounce European dominion. It was not just a voluntary union. It was a unanimous union. Pro-British, monarchical factions existed in every one of the thirteen colonies but were not strong enough in any of them to prevent even a single colony from participating in the revolutionary movement whose Continental Congress issued in 1776 the declaration that a new kind of sovereignty of the people had come into being in North America, deriving from a century and a half of self-selecting emigration to America from many parts of Europe. The policy of the British government on how its colonies in central North America were populated was its worst imperial mistake because it unwittingly created a population united in rejecting the European cultural tradition of powerful aristocratic rulers, hierarchies of privilege, hereditary kingship, and subordination by social rank. The liberal-minded Prussian and professional soldier who became the drillmaster of the national army of the newly proclaimed United States of America during its war against British dominion quickly came to know the fundamentally non-European mentality of the troops he instructed in military discipline. Baron von Steuben wrote to a friend in Europe of his experience with the common soldiers of America: "The genius of this nation is not in the least to be compared with the Prussians, the Austrians, or French. You say to your soldier, 'Do this,' and he doeth it, but I am obliged to say, 'This is the reason that you ought to do that,' and then he does it."[6]

Typical of the mentality of European culture, representation in the British parliament in the seventeenth century was structured according to group interests: towns, nobility, bishops, universities, country gentry, merchants, artisans. The political revolt in England in the 1640s that executed the reigning king did not abolish monarchy but only changed the British constitution so that future British kings had to recognize that certain

6. Quoted in James Thomas Flexner, *Washington: The Indispensable Man* (New York: New American Library, 1979), p. 118.

groups represented in Parliament were more powerful than the crown. And the British parliamentary act of 1688 called the "Bill of Rights" had nothing to do with individual rights. It simply limited the rights of the crown, first by forbidding the crown from ever being given to a Roman Catholic, and second by declaring that the kings of Britain could never maintain an army without the consent of the groups represented in Parliament.

It makes little sense to invoke the British constitution of the seventeenth and eighteenth centuries or its theoreticians as the model from which the political culture of the United States of America took shape. Unlike the British constitution, the Constitution of the United States has never made nobility of birth, religious conformity, or ecclesiastical rank a qualification for holding a government office or appointment. Nor has the Constitution of the United States ever established a national church regulated and financially supported by the national government, as has been, until recently, the case in Britain. The age-old principle of the British constitution "one state—one church" has characterized not only British political culture until recently but the political order generally found in the history of European nationalism. (The mystique of the State as ultimate authority that has been so important to European thought is alien to American culture. What Americans have instead of the State is the mystique of the Constitution, a written, contractual agreement among themselves.) In the United States, religious belief has been an individual matter; but in Britain and other parts of Europe, it has historically been a matter of state. The ruling aristocracies of Europe commonly saw in the idea "one state—one church" a principle useful to group discipline and hierarchical control. And the conversion of pagan tribes in Europe to Christianity during the first millennium of the Christian era was often effected in group aggregates simply by converting the group leader, who then decreed the conversion of his followers in the same way that tribes in Africa and Oceania in the nineteenth century were converted to Christianity. In Europe's group-minded, hierarchical culture, tribal leaders were followed and obeyed in the matter of personal religious faith as in other things that were culturally seen as important to tribal coherence and power. In American history, there is not one instance of a religious war; but there are many in European history because religion in that continent has been a matter of state. Fifty years after the American Revolution, an American resident in London observed that the English regarded the state churches of Italy, France, Spain, Turkey, and all the rest of the world, as abhorrent; but "having got the truth themselves," they felt it was imperative to have "a religious establishment" and legally fortify it with exclusive privileges. In 1828, according to this informant, the "prevalent opinion" in England was that the United States had no religion because it had no state church.[7]

The European principle "one state—one church" remained a part of the British constitution for half a century after the end of the American Revolution. Not until 1828–29 did British constitutional law free governmental positions of religious qualifications; not until 1854 and 1856 were Catholics and other non-Anglicans admitted to Oxford and Cambridge universities; and, not until 1877 were persons who did not conform to the state-established Church of England granted equal access with Anglicans to fellowships, professorships, and headships in the English universities.[8]

Down to 1911, the British government's House of Lords had real power under the British constitution, including final say over whether bills for funding the government would become law; and membership in this branch of the government, consisting of bishops of the state church, whom the king as head of the state appointed, and nobly born peers of the realm, was entirely nonelective and for life. Simple rank in the hierarchy of the church and the nobility established this right to wield political power in government. To this day, in fact, established social and ecclesiastical rank determines membership in the House of Lords, but since the constitutional reform of 1911 the House of Lords of the British government has had virtually no power. In that same momentous year in which the British constitution became more like the American constitution, persons elected to the House of Commons were for the first time given a stipend. Prior to 1911, election to Commons carried no salary, thereby making it almost certain that only persons of considerable financial means would ordinarily serve in it; and those who were elected frequently turned out to be the sons, sons-in-law, brothers, brothers-in-law, nephews, and uncles of the nonelective, entitled, life members of the House of Lords. The so-called House of Commons in the sixteenth, seventeenth, eighteenth, and nineteenth centuries, despite its name, always had a large proportion of British noblemen and their relatives among its members.

An American of long acquaintance with European affairs in the early twentieth century, Raymond Leslie Buell, who was to have a distinguished

7. James Fenimore Cooper, *Gleanings in Europe: England* (Albany: State University of New York, 1982), p. 240.

8. David Thomson, *England in the Nineteenth Century (1815–1914)* (Harmondsworth, England: Penguin, 1950), pp. 58–62.

career as a diplomatic representative of the United States in Europe, observed of the British constitution as it stood in the 1920s:

> To Americans, the system of Church and State which prevails in
> England seems anomalous. The government has assigned to the
> Church valuable revenues, and the Anglican faith is the official
> religion of the realm. The Archbishops of Canterbury and York,
> together with a number of bishops, sit in the House of Lords and
> are appointed for life by the government. The organization of the
> Anglican church is based on acts of Parliament. In 1919 the Church
> of England Assembly (Powers) Act was passed. This act authorizes a
> clerical assembly to pass resolutions which bind the church if
> approved by Parliament. It was under this act that the revision of
> the Prayer Book [of the Church of England] was attempted. . . . a
> revision was finally approved by church authorities. . . . [and]
> submitted to Parliament for final approval. . . . The debate drew
> forth expressions of strong emotion—men were in tears. It aroused
> tremendous interest throughout the country. . . . On December 15,
> 1927 the Commons rejected the Prayer Book. A House composed of
> Baptists, Methodists, Jews, Agnostics, as well as Anglicans, decided
> the liturgical future of the Anglican church. The bishops, sorely
> grieved that their work had been in vain, made a few changes and
> again submitted the measure, but the Commons once more rejected
> it on June 14, 1928. The incident has increased the sentiment in
> England for disestablishment—for the complete separation of
> Church and State. While this might deprive the church of certain
> revenues, a disestablished church could control its own destiny.[9]

Anyone who considers American culture a transatlantic projection of English culture, especially in matters of political belief and behavior, should seriously contemplate this telling example of English constitutional history from the 1920s.

In European culture, equality of liberty has been in some measure a group mentality. Apart from certain equalities of law that applied to all individuals without regard to social rank, equality in European history has also been the equality of peers within hierarchies of group privilege. Superior caste and conformity to a state religion could confer liberties of great personal advantage. Such matters of group membership have never figured in the history of America's national government. Representation in the United States Congress under the American constitution has been

9. Raymond Leslie Buell, *Europe: A History of Ten Years* (New York: Macmillan, 1929), pp. 150–53.

constructed on the basis of the equality of individuals and of states as units of population and geography: first, on states each having an equal number of representatives as units of geography and, second, on each state's population having an equal representation per standard unit of population. This structure expresses the general American belief that equality of liberty should not be qualified by social rank, religious conformity, or place of residence. In the British constitution, privileged, unequal representation by locale, by tradition, by social class, by "interests," by religion has had a longer history than have American political institutions founded on equality of liberty. One can only suppose that among the causes of the gradual reform of the British constitution during this and the previous century in the direction of the American cultural belief in equality of liberty has been the example of the Constitution of the United States of America itself. British constitutional reforms have not, however, gone so far as to abolish the monarchy or the House of Lords or to disestablish the Church of England as the state religion. These venerable parts of the British constitution persist, even though they are now mere shadows of their former realities. Their *pro forma* existence and the British public's nostalgic tolerance of their expensive maintenance bespeak a long cultural history of privilege and rank far different from the political culture of the United States.

Equality in the history of England, as in the history of Europe generally, started at the top, among a class of military leaders who claimed an equal right with each other and their hereditary leader. The Communist party leaders in the Soviet-bloc countries in eastern and central Europe, who practice "democracy from the top" and who now rule three-fifths of Europe's territory and two-fifths of its population, are throwbacks to this idea and to the hoary European idea of "one state—one church." The discipline of obedience to the Communist party as a "vanguard" that leads "the masses"—the language of Soviet Marxism-Leninism—is an idea the leader of any of the armed migratory tribes in Europe's ancient past could have accepted. And, as one European historian has noted, the last absolute monarchs to rule in Europe "would have found nothing strange in the cult of personality" in the countries taken over by Communist parties since 1917.[10] The cult of personality, that is, autocratic dictatorship, has weakened since the death in 1953 of the Soviet tyrant Stalin, but the group mentality of communism, with its hierarchies of privilege and its concentration of power at the top, does not inspire confidence in a new future in Europe characterized by equality of liberty for all individuals. Rather, this militant political system is chillingly reminiscent of Europe's blood-drenched tribal

10. Anthony Wood, *Europe: 1815–1945* (New York: David McKay, 1964), p. 475.

past. What is encouraging, however, is that three-fifths of the population of Europe now lives under a multiparty democratic system of government. And the inherent human longing for equality of liberty—as opposed to "freedom" under the absolutely rationalized, total-planning-from-the-top "democracy" of Soviet government—is certainly evident among the eastern European nations of the Soviet Union who are now entering their third generation of life under one-party communist government, as well as among the captive nations of central Europe, whose governments have been structured by the leadership of the Communist Party of the Soviet Union into a "fraternal" system of internationally hierarchical power.

CHAPTER

2

SELF-SELECTING EMIGRANTS

The first permanent European settlement in the thirteen colonies that became the United States of America was in 1607, and 176 years later, at the end of the American Revolution in 1783, Britain recognized the independence of the United States. The first permanent European settlement in Brazil was in 1532, but Brazil did not become independent of Portugal until 290 years later; European settlement in mainland Spanish America began with the conquest of Mexico between 1519 and 1522, and three centuries were to pass before independence came to mainland Spanish America (a much longer period elapsed before it came to Spain's island colonies in the Caribbean); Canada, settled permanently by the French in 1608, one year after the permanent settlement of the United States by the English, who in 1760 conquered Canada and added it to their empire, did not gain complete control of its constitution from Britain, thereby becoming fully sovereign, until 1982.

Thus, the United States completed in 1959 a period of national sovereignty equal in length to the 176 years of its history from 1607 to 1783 when it was not a sovereign nation. But Brazil and mainland Spanish America will not complete a period of full sovereignty in their histories equal to the years of their dependence on Europe until early in the twenty-second century, and Canada not until the middle of the twenty-fourth century.

The United States was not, then, just the first nation in the Americas to become independent of Europe. It is more important to notice that it did so far earlier in its history than any other part of the Americas. This is a basic difference in cultural behavior. The difference becomes all the more striking in observing that Canada and the United States, the only two major continental cultures of the Americas with a shared language, are the most extremely opposed in terms of their years under European rule versus their years of independence. The reason Americans sought and gained complete political independence from Europe so much sooner in their history than did Brazilians, Canadians, and Spanish Americans in theirs, can be traced to the distinctive population history of the United States.

Not only do the differences in the proportion of dependence on Europe in the histories of Brazil, Canada, Spanish America, and the United States indicate their varying orientations to European culture (approximately 375 years of dependence for Canada, 300 years for mainland Spanish America, 290 years for Brazil, and only 175 years for the United States), but the ways in which they each obtained their sovereignty also represent significant variants of cultural behavior.

Canadian sovereignty was attained over a long span of time by a process of parliamentary negotiation centered in Europe. The process did not even begin until 1867, nearly one hundred years after the American Declaration of Independence, when the British Parliament acted on a petition by Canadians and passed a bill granting Canada a political organization having some semblance of national unity. This act of the British Parliament—the British North America Act of 1867—forms the basis of the Canadian constitution to this day. Like the British constitution on which it is modeled and from which it has directly developed in a deliberate, slow gestation, the Constitution of Canada is not a definitive single document entirely written, ratified, and amended through elected bodies of representatives of the Canadian people; rather, it is an accumulation of laws that legal tradition and the authority of constitutional lawyers, judges, parliamentarians, legislators, and diplomats in Canada and in England have devised, construed, enacted, and negotiated as the Constitution of Canada. And throughout this prolonged, complicated, tradition-conscious process of gradual constitutional evolution, Canadians have regarded the kings and queens of Britain as having natural and ultimate authority over their country's political life.

Before 1982, the Canadian constitution could not be amended in Canada in all of its parts. Only in 1981—one-half century after other nations in the British Commonwealth had asked for and received full control of their constitutions—did the Canadian government request the same thing of the British government: to give it sole and exclusive sovereign authority to amend its own constitution. And the act of the British government granting this request, the Constitution Act of 1981, is now a part of the Canadian constitution. But it became constitutional law for Canada only when it was signed in 1982 by the reigning British monarch, who still retains under its provisions the title Queen of Canada. This act, passed in London in 1981 by the British Parliament and signed in Ottawa the next year by the British monarch, because it finally gave Canada complete control over the Constitution of Canada 115 years after the British Parliament established the basis of Canada's constitution in the British North America Act, may be said to have completely ended British dominion in Canada. What Canadians referred to in 1982 as "the patriation of the Canadian constitution" was the Canadian equivalent of the Battle of Yorktown in 1781, which effectively ended British authority in the United States of America; yet the face of the British monarch continues to be printed and stamped on Canadian money; the British monarch remains the head of state of Canada with authority to appoint officers in its government; and "God Save the Queen" is still sung in Canadian schools.

The deference to Britain by which Canada gained its sovereignty bespeaks a basic difference between Canadian and American culture. It can best be illustrated by the following facts: not until 1923 did Canada sign a treaty without a British countersignature; not until 1927 did Canada appoint an ambassador on its own authority; not until 1947 did Canadians become citizens of Canada—prior to that year their passports identified them as "British subjects born in Canada" or "British subjects naturalized in Canada"; not until 1949 did the decisions of Canada's highest court cease to be subject to review and approval by the British government in London; and not until 1965 did Canada adopt a national flag. As an official Canadian government pamphlet published in 1982 to inform Canadians about what their government had negotiated with the British government for them explains: "Canada [before 1982] was the only sovereign country in the world that still had to turn to the Parliament of another country to amend the most important parts of its own Constitution."[1] In other words, Canada until that year was not fully sovereign.

Brazil attained sovereignty in 1822 when the crown prince of Portugal asserted it in a vocal declaration made on the banks of a Brazilian river to a retinue of his followers. Historians believe he acted on the advice of his father, the king of Portugal, who had left him in Brazil as his regent with the counsel that, should the Brazilians appear determined to make themselves independent of Portugal by force, he should declare himself in favor of independence. That way the royal house of Portugal might have

1. *The Constitution and You* (Ottawa: Minister of Supply and Services of Canada, 1982), p. 8.

some chance of continuing to reign in Brazil in the person of Dom Pedro and his descendants. In 1822, support for Brazilian independence was strong among the educated minority of Brazilians who were not slaves. The idea of creating a Brazilian monarchy was seen as a good way to go about it, especially by the numerous titled noblemen in the upper class, provided that a constitution was written for the monarchy by representative Brazilians. Consequently, three months after Dom Pedro delivered his *grito* beside the Ypiranga River in what is now metropolitan São Paulo, he was crowned, with Brazilian approval, as Pedro I, Emperor of Brazil; and after that, a constitutional assembly produced a constitution that finally met with his approval. (Dom Pedro vetoed the first constitution presented to him because it did not give him enough power as emperor.) The constitutional Brazilian monarchy, thus institutionalized in 1824 after only minor military opposition from the imperial Portuguese garrisons in Brazil, hereditarily endured for sixty-five years. In 1889, a bloodless coup forced the Brazilian-born emperor Dom Pedro II from the Brazilian throne, and a new constitution was written, giving the nation a republican form of government. Only Brazil among the major continental cultures in the Americas achieved sovereignty this way, by creating a monarchy.

The Spanish-American mainland gained its sovereignty piecemeal in a series of wars between 1809 and 1824. (Spanish imperial rule on the Caribbean islands of Hispaniola and Cuba did not end until 1865 and 1898.) In Mexico, the revolt against Spain was effected finally not by war but by negotiated withdrawal of Spanish troops and the proclamation of a Mexican monarchy after a revolution in Spain frightened the Spanish viceroy and Mexican monarchists into making this change six years after Spain's garrison forces in Mexico crushed the initial armed revolt. Indeed, all of the initial revolts against Spanish authority throughout mainland Spanish America were put down by royal troops. The revolutionaries nonetheless persisted for fourteen years and eventually gained the military victories that brought independence and republican government. The same would probably have happened eventually in Mexico as well, for three years after his coronation as Emperor of Mexico, the makeshift monarch of that country was deposed by armed Mexicans and a republican form of government instituted.

A culturally significant behavior during mainland Spanish America's revolt against Spain was the tendency of military commanders to "pronounce" the independence of a city or a region on their personal authority and to engage on their own initiative in other fundamental political activities, such as single-handedly writing national constitutions. In other words, military chiefs in Spanish America behaved sometimes as though no distinction existed between military command and political authority, the latter seemingly being in their minds indistinguishable from the former. In their pretensions to autonomous political power, military commanders sometimes acted like protomonarchs who would tolerate no opposition to their wills. The egalitarian spirit of political compromise and majority rule had little place in the governments of the proliferation of nations that sprang up in Spanish America after the unifying power of the Spanish throne was eliminated.

During most of the 150 years since that event, in most of the many nations of Spanish America, to control the government one has had first to control the army because, in effect, in that culture, military authority was governmental authority. Dissension among *caciques* (political bosses), *jefes* (political leaders), and *caudillos* (military strongmen), following independence from Spain, contributed not only to the formation of sixteen separate nations but to much political instability within those nations. Bolivia offers the extreme example of 185 "revolutions" (changes of political authority) since 1825. But there have cumulatively been a great many coup d'états, "revolutions," uprisings, and "pronouncements" of changes of government in the other fifteen Spanish-speaking nations of mainland North and South America during this same period. When dissension broke out among the Spanish conquerors of the Americas in the sixteenth century, the Spanish king could send troops to bring order to the division of the spoils of conquest. But no supreme military power existed to impose unity among the leaders of the far-flung independence movements in the Spanish empire in North and South America in the early nineteenth century. And the political history of Spanish America since then—especially its separation into many nations, which is the only replication of the political map of Europe in the Americas, and its persistent history of the resort to military force to determine political power—suggests a cultural connection with the mentality and behavior of the fractious sixteenth-century conquistadors of Spanish America.

Like Spanish America, the United States of America also fought a war to gain its independence from Europe. But it was a war controlled by an elected legislature. A congress, elected from all of the voluntarily unified thirteen American colonies, directed the American Revolution. This non-European cultural behavior was the real American Revolution. The "Continental Congress"—as the legislature that directed the American Revolution significantly called itself—derived its authority from a constitution called the Articles of Confederation drawn up by the Congress and ratified in the states by elected legislatures. The war that made good the Declaration of Independence written and signed by the Congress in 1776 had a single commander in chief commissioned by and responsible to the Congress.

Four years after the war's end, when the congressionally created, state-ratified constitution under which it had been waged proved unworkable, a new constitution was peaceably written by another national assembly of elected delegates, and a major political transition was achieved without any of the violent divisiveness among military chieftains that marred the attainment of independence from Europe in Spanish America. The new constitution that was written for the United States in 1787 by a specially elected national convention was debated in specially elected conventions in the American states, and only after it had been ratified by three-fourths of them the next year did it take effect as the Constitution of the United States of America. This Constitution still remains in effect today and is the single most important expression of America's cultural distinctiveness.

INDIGENOUS AND IMMIGRANT POPULATIONS OF THE AMERICAS

The differences in cultural beliefs and behavior observable in when and in how the United States, Spanish America, Brazil, and Canada achieved their independence from Europe can be related to differences in their population histories. Brazil, Canada, and Spanish America all acquired populations after 1500 that in various ways had the group consciousness typical of European cultural history. The United States did not.

Some information on the indigenous populations of the Americas before 1500 is necessary for an understanding of the cultural developments in these continents after 1500. At the beginning of the emigrations to the Americas from Europe and Africa five centuries ago, the American continents were probably less populated than either Europe or Africa. Colin McEvedy and Richard Jones in their *Atlas of World Population History* estimate that the total population of the American continents before 1500 was perhaps one-tenth of Europe's and Africa's estimated 127 million (eighty-one million in Europe, forty-six million in Africa),[2] though some historical demographers say the Americas had not many million fewer people in the late fifteenth century than Africa and Europe combined. Estimates of the population of the Americas immediately before Columbus's first voyage vary greatly, from a low of 8.4 million to a high of 112 million, because of different assumptions that are made to interpret the scanty available data. The "small population" school of thought favors a figure somewhere below fifteen million; the "big population" school, a figure somewhere in excess of fifty million. A range of difference of sixty million

2. Colin McEvedy and Richard Jones, *Atlas of World Population History* (London and New York: Penguin, 1978), pp. 19, 207.

in the estimates put forth by "big population" advocates, as opposed to a variance of only six million among "small population" advocates, somewhat tends to diminish the credibility of the "big population" school. The mean between the upper and lower extremes of these two kinds of interpretation would give a population of thirty-two to thirty-three million American Indians at the time of Columbus's first voyage in 1492, which is probably too high a figure but may actually have been the case.[3]

All historical demographers are in agreement, however, that a massive die-off from disease, mainly smallpox and measles, began among American Indians with the advent of European settlement and that this devastation of the indigenous American population continued for more than a generation until American Indians developed some immunity to the diseases introduced by the mere presence of the Europeans. Advocates of the "big population" school claim a die-off in the range of 90 to 95 percent of American Indians during several generations, which is unheard-of even in the well-documented epidemiological history of the virulent Black Death that ravaged Europe in the fourteenth century, though certainly the disruption of normal food supplies in the largest concentrations of Indian populations, caused by Europeans forcing many Indians to work in mining instead of agriculture, must have appreciably increased mortality from disease in those areas. These concentrations were heaviest in southern North America, the central Andean uplands of South America, and the civilized regions between those principal centers of pre-1492 American population and civilization: in other words, in Spanish America. In several regions of these civilized parts of the Americas, the population in 1500 was certainly in the millions. In central and northern North America, in the Amazon, in the Brazilian Highlands, and in southern South America, however, the pre-1492 populations were not civilized, were scattered rather than concentrated, and were considerably smaller.

In 1600, approximately three-quarters of a century after the earliest Spanish and Portuguese colonies were established on the North and South American mainlands and around the time of the beginning of French and English settlements in North America, the population of the Americas was still almost entirely Indian. The distribution of this population and its proportional size in relation to subsequent distributions of immigrants from Europe and Africa during the next three hundred years were crucial differentiating factors in the cultures that were to develop in Brazil, Canada, Spanish America, and the United States.

3. William Donovan, *The Native Population of the Americas in 1492* (Madison: University of Wisconsin Press, 1976), surveys opinions on this question.

In Canada in 1600, there were perhaps two hundred thousand Indians, and during the following two centuries, no European population developed there that was anywhere near that size and no African population at all. European emigration to Canada by the end of 150 years of French rule had amounted to only twenty thousand, despite France's large population, which stood at twenty-four million in 1760 when Britain conquered Canada and incorporated it into the British empire. During the formative centuries of its culture, Canada had, by far, the lowest number of European immigrants of any post-1492 cultural area of the Americas, even though the population of France exceeded by a great deal that of any other extra-continental maritime power in Europe. The smallness of this population in relation to the powerful warrior nations of Indians to the south and to the west of the French settlements in the St. Lawrence Valley well down into the eighteenth century contributed to preventing Canadians from viewing the wilderness where these Indians lived as something they might appropriate for themselves and widely develop. A garrison mentality thus became part of Canadian cultural thought and behavior early in its history, and Canada has been during most of its history essentially a borderland whose cultural center was elsewhere (for the first 150 years of its history in France and for the next 225 years in England). The special provision that the Canadian Constitutional Act of 1981 makes for the continuation of government should an invasion prevent a regularly scheduled election reflects the borderland mentality of Canadian culture.

During the first five generations after its European settlement (1608–1763), Canada had the only population in the Americas that was almost purely European. Except for a small amount of interbreeding with Indians, it was uniformly French and Roman Catholic. In short, Canada was then a small, homogeneous projection into northern North America of France as it had been before the Protestant Reformation. Then, in 1760, with the fall of Montreal, following hard on the heels of the fall of Quebec, occurred the most momentous single event of Canada's cultural history: the Conquest—as it is referred to in Canadian history books—of this little piece of pre–Reformation France in the St. Lawrence Valley by France's hereditary enemy England. This conquest was a replication in North America of a primary feature of Europe's cultural history: one group conquering another to acquire dominion over its population and settlement in its territory.

Twenty years after the Conquest, the first large, non-French, non–Roman Catholic element was added to Canada's population. This immigration was not from Europe. It came from the former British colonies in central North America after they had won independence for themselves. These immigrants were as group-minded and European-oriented in their thinking as were the French-speaking, Roman Catholic Canadians they joined. They were forty thousand of the staunchest monarchists and the loyalest imperialists of the British empire, who had fought and sacrificed mightily to preserve the authority of the kingship of George III in central North America. They preferred giving up living there to living under a nonmonarchical, non-European, nonimperial government. They moved to Canada in order to remain a part of a European empire under the rule of a European king. By the time this migration of forty thousand English-speaking monarchist-imperialists from the republic of the United States (about 1 percent of the American population at that time) had joined the seventy-five thousand French-speaking Canadians around 1800, a long-lasting, fundamental cultural change had been wrought in Canada. From then on, for the whole of the nineteenth century and much of the twentieth century, the beliefs and behavior of Canadian culture would be shaped not only by a strong consciousness of being a border outpost on the marches of European empire but also by the problem of what should be the respective communal rights of two demographically equal and separate groups, each of which identified itself in terms of its adherence to one or the other of two of western Europe's competing national groups. Ever since then, French-speaking and English-speaking Canadians have referred to themselves as different races, and the thinking of these groups has basically been oriented toward the past rather than toward the future. Their respective allegiances to France and Britain were set for them by a hated conquest of French Canada by Britain in 1760 and a hated revolution against British monarchism and imperialism by American republicans in 1775.

Canadian cultural beliefs are still group-minded in the same way that European culture is group-minded, doubts about the rightness of the American Revolution still linger in Canada, and the face of the reigning British monarch still appears on Canadian money. But the historical cultural belief of all Canadians, whether French-speaking or English-speaking, that Canada was only a borderland whose cultural center was in Europe, is rapidly fading and being replaced by belief in a Canadian-centered culture.

Brazil's demographic history is quite different from Canada's. No homogeneous population, drawn from just one European nation, developed there. Nor was there in Brazil any long-lasting internal contention between conquered and conquering groups of Europeans, as there was in Canada. Other aspects of Europe's group-minded, hierarchical culture did, however, develop in the history of Brazil: slaves, both American Indians and Africans, for three and one-half centuries made up the bulk of the population of Brazil and were kept in that inferior social position by a much smaller group of wealthy masters and hereditary rulers descended from one European nation.

Despite the quite small population of Portugal among Europe's extra-continental imperialists—in 1500, 1.25 million; in 1700, two million—this small nation sent more emigrants (some 140 thousand) to Brazil during its first two centuries of history as a European colony than the much more populous nations of France and Britain together sent to Canada during its first two centuries of European settlement. The total emigration to Brazil between 1500 and 1700, however, was much larger than its European component. About three-quarters of a million persons entered Brazil during those centuries: the 140 thousand Europeans just mentioned and approximately 600 thousand Africans. This forced emigration from Africa was heaviest in the eighteenth century, as it also was in other places in the Americas. Portugal's small population and the Portuguese custom before the discovery of Brazil of trafficking in African slaves brought about this heavy importation of African slaves, who were used to build and work sugar plantations and mills and perform other heavy labor. Also, because of Portugal's small amount of manpower, significant numbers of American Indians were forced to labor in the Portuguese establishments in Brazil as slaves.

From all accounts of the formative centuries of Brazil's cultural history, miscegenation was an accepted and widely practiced cultural behavior from the beginning of Portuguese settlement and remained so even after Portuguese women began to arrive there. Thus, the demographic bases for Brazilian culture were more racially diverse and interfused than any other in the Americas. Elements from three continents became thoroughly mixed. The interfusion of African, American Indian, and European created a new racial identity—the Brazilian—and laid the essential foundation of Brazil's cultural sense of a singular nationhood, which is quite unlike the multinational culture of Spanish America.

Portugal could populate Brazil sufficiently through its already-established slave trade with Africa to assure profitability to the Portuguese crown without having to allow non-Portuguese Europeans to settle in Brazil. Consequently, most of the European element in the Brazilian population during its long colonial period—the formative centuries of Brazilian culture—was Roman Catholic Portuguese. No other religion was officially tolerated. But the Dutch and the French both established short-lived enclaves on the coast of Brazil at various times in its colonial history, and although these colonies were eventually expelled from Brazil by the Portuguese, some elements from their European populations remained behind in Brazil and were added to the Portuguese element. The Portuguese crown was never as active as the Spanish crown in enforcing its policy of excluding non-Portuguese and non–Roman Catholic Europeans. Jewish settlers were also, covertly, present early on in Brazil's post-1492 history and probably played a part in organizing the cultivation and refining of sugar cane, which was so important to making Brazil a wealth-producing Portuguese possession.

Mainland Spanish America's post-1492 population presents yet another demographically distinctive basis for culture. Between 1500 and 1700, Spain sent to Spanish America about 390 thousand carefully screened free emigrants of provable Roman Catholic orthodoxy and pure Spanish blood (*católicos viejos* and *sangre pura* were the terms used during the process of bureaucratic certification). Most of the estimated 300 thousand forced emigrants brought by the Spanish from Africa to the Americas went to the islands of Hispaniola and Cuba in the Caribbean rather than to the American mainland.

A firmly enforced imperial policy barred non-Spanish Europeans from Spain's American possessions. There was no need to populate these possessions because in 1500 they already had millions of people. Spain's imperial problem was not how to create a colonial population useful to its imperial purposes, but how to govern the populous civilized nations its soldiers had militarily and politically dominated. That conquest of populous civilized nations was the foundation of Spanish America's cultural formation.

Spain needed a ruling class of uniform Spanish blood and religion to administer in Spanish America the largest and most advanced population of American Indians anywhere in the American continents, a population that at the time of its conquest was immediately exploitable as taxpayers, consumers, laborers, farmers, miners, shepherds, artisans, and low-level administrative go-betweens because it was a population that had behind it a cultural tradition of civilization already thousands of years old. About three-quarters of a century after the Spanish conquest of Spanish America, that is, around 1600, approximately 200 thousand Spaniards and American-born descendants of Spaniards ("creoles") dominated a population of perhaps nine million civilized American Indians. This was more people than lived in Spain itself at that time.

Spain solved its problem of ruling millions of civilized Indians in the Americas through a combination of paternalistic laws emanating from the Spanish crown and the hierarchy of the church in Spain and the harsh local authority of the Spanish colonists in the Americas. An immigration policy that strictly excluded non-Spaniards and non–Roman Catholics was a basic part of that solution. Many of the Indians whom the Conquest brought under Spanish rule were taught to speak the Spanish language and to practice Roman Catholicism; all of them became subjects of the Spanish king.

The millions of civilized Indians and the Spanish-blooded subjects of the Spanish king in America were governed by viceroys in Mexico City and Lima who represented in their respective *reinos* (kingdoms) of New Spain and Peru the person of the Spanish king. They sat on their thrones as substitute kings for the European monarch who could not himself be present in America. According to this concept of their function, these symbolic kings lived in palaces on a truly regal scale and participated in elaborate court ceremonies. They were waited upon by households of liveried royal servants. Their lives were guarded by handsomely uniformed and splendidly equipped elite royal troops. The European cultural tradition of an authoritarian, armed ruling group constituted by the supposedly superior blood of conquerors, whose principal autocrat legitimized the division of spoils, was thus duplicated in Spanish America more thoroughly and more conservatively than anywhere else in the Americas.

England's immigration policy for its colonies in the Atlantic coastal plain of central North America was permissive in comparison to Spain's immigration policy for its American possessions not because England was less interested than Spain in imperial profit or ultimately less authoritarian as a European imperial power but because no large nations of civilized Indians existed in central North America to be politically, economically, and religiously integrated into the British body politic. England's permissive policy regarding immigration into its American colonies was dictated by the need to populate them as quickly as possible to make them imperially profitable. Between 1600 and 1775 England manned its colonies in central North America in the same way it manned its fleet during those centuries: (1) a core of English volunteers, (2) ready acceptance of all foreign volunteers, and (3) impressment—in this case slaves from Africa—to fill out the necessary complement of manpower. The policy worked for the British navy, with its strict martial law and day-to-day application of inescapable discipline, but it proved an unfortunate formula for long maintaining imperial allegiance among the burgeoning crew of mixed nationalities who went to America before 1776 and their American-born descendants.

From the time of the first permanent European settlement in central North America during the first decade of the seventeenth century, the United States acquired a population having a much larger proportion of European immigrants than Brazil or Spanish America had. And it was the only predominately European population anywhere in the Americas that had a mixture of nationalities and a variety of religions and that was growing rapidly, since Canada's entirely European population was quite small, stable, and singularly homogeneous in nationality and religion. (In the ten years of the 1630s, for instance, as many Europeans emigrated to one American colony, Massachusetts, as emigrated to Canada during the entire first 150 years of its history as a place of permanent European settlement.) England's imperial strategy for populating its American colonies as soon and as much as possible with self-selecting Europeans gave the emigrants to central North America a diversity that was radically different from the group uniformity of those Europeans who went to Canada, Spanish America, and Brazil.

During the colonial period of United States history (1607–1775), which was the period of the cultural formation of the United States, America received perhaps a million European immigrants of many nations and religious faiths, the majority of whom arrived before 1720. With few pauses or fluctuations, the number of Europeans choosing on their own to go to what would become the United States of America rose steadily from the early seventeenth through the late nineteenth centuries and into the twentieth century, as previous immigrants from Europe who had established themselves in America wrote back to Europe informing other Europeans of the advantages there and urging them to emigrate also—in a great many instances sending them the money to do so. Two out of every three of the estimated seventy million people who have emigrated from Europe during the last four centuries have gone to the United States of America.

SELF-SELECTING AND RESTRICTED EMIGRATION

America's singular, early proliferation of European nationalities and religions—which stands in fundamental contrast to the formative historical demographies of Canada, Brazil, and Spanish America—originated in Britain's imperial strategy.

The rulers of imperial Britain believed that its national power and wealth could be increased by allowing generally unrestricted emigration to its American possessions. This idea appealed to the British government because, unlike the European imperial masters of Canada, Brazil, and Spanish America in the seventeenth and eighteenth centuries (France, Portugal, and Spain), Britain had an internal displaced-persons problem. Even in the sixteenth century, changes in British agricultural practices in relation to increased weaving of wool had displaced many Britons from their homes. In the eighteenth century, British industrialization, which occurred notably earlier than in any other nation of Europe, led to an increase and also a displacement of population, leaving many inhabitants of Britain without employment or their customary living place. The British government addressed this problem by not restricting, and sometimes encouraging, emigration to America. To populate its American colonies quickly was regarded as especially beneficial because it would create growing markets for selling the increasing volume of goods that industrialization was producing, whose manufacture had in some ways improved living conditions in Britain and in other ways worsened them, while disrupting established patterns of employment and domicile. From the sixteenth century onward, governmental intolerance of nonconforming religious sects caused other social strains and conflicts in Britain which also made unselective emigration desirable. Therefore, from the time of the permanent settlement of central North America in the early seventeenth century, emigration had an appeal in Britain; and anyone willing to go to America to live was allowed to do so without being screened for any particular characteristics. Nor was any bar erected against foreigners adding to the increase of people in America, so long as they were loyal to the British crown.

Unlike what was established in Spanish America, in Brazil, and in French Canada, no governmental bureaucracy was established in the British possessions in central North America for screening those who wanted to go there from anywhere in Europe. Under this permissive policy to encourage rapid settlement—which had its origin in imperial motivations rather than in any political tradition radically different from that of the imperial govern ments of France, Spain, and Portugal—different kinds of colonizing enterprises were also allowed, resulting in a plurality of types of colonial governments in America to match its unique mixture of European nationalities and religions. At the beginning of settlement on the Atlantic coastal plain of central North America, some of the colonies were under the direct control of the king's government; some were governed by hereditary proprietary owners; some were directed by trading corporations. In Canada, Brazil, and Spanish America, on the other hand, only direct control by the French, the Portuguese, and the Spanish crowns was practiced, except for a brief experiment in proprietary rule in Brazil. But this difference, too, was merely a matter of the means by which profits were to be extracted for the imperial benefit of Britain rather than any difference between Britain, France, Spain, or Portugal regarding the ends of power and profit that extracontinental European empires were to serve.

During the seventeenth and eighteenth centuries, America received, in addition to Englishmen and communicants of the established state church of England, Scots, Welsh, Swiss, Dutch, Irish, French, Germans, Finns, Swedes, Portuguese, Danes, Flemings, Bohemians, Italians, Spanish, Poles, and other European nationalities who were in their religious practices Jews, Shakers, Methodists, Pietists, Presbyterians, Quakers, Congregationalists, and Roman Catholics, among others, and persons of no faith at all. The evidence of last names indicates that, by the end of the eighteenth century, probably no more than half of the population of the United States was of partly or wholly English stock. But it was by no means a certain indication of English blood to have an English name. There can be no doubt that in the first two formative centuries of American cultural history non-English immigrants in central North America sometimes took English surnames. Indeed, in the early records of Virginia there is even a reference to a "John Martin, the Persian."[4] During the first century of New York City's history, its inhabitants spoke eighteen European languages, though English—the language of government and commerce and of the first European settlements in central North America—progressively became the language chosen by the American-born descendants of European immigrants whose language of first use had not been English. The rate of population growth was so rapid in America from its exceptionally high level of natural increase and from increasing levels of immigration that, at the time Americans decided in 1776 to declare to the world that they were not in fact Europeans living in North America but an independent American nation, Philadelphia, the city where that declaration was made, which had been founded less than a century before in a primeval forest, was already the second largest English-speaking city in the world after London; yet, in the colony of which it was the capital, about one-third of the population appears to have been of German stock.

The rapid increase of native-born population in the Atlantic coastal plain of central North America, caused by a wide availability of inexpensive agricultural land, which encouraged early family formation, thereby prolonging the childbearing years of wives, and by a comparatively low infant mortality rate and high average longevity,[5] augmented by escalating immigration from Europe, soon created a European-descended population that far outnumbered the population of American Indians. In Canada, in Brazil, and especially in Spanish America, the situation was the reverse. The original populations of Indians in those places outnumbered for a long time the European populations they acquired. Furthermore, the sense of ascendancy among the European-descended settlers of central North America was not qualified by a more numerous population of Africans.

4. Marcus Lee Hansen, *The Atlantic Migration 1607–1860: A History of the Continuing Settlement of the United States* (Cambridge: Harvard University Press, 1941), p. 45.

5. Not until the 1890s did England achieve the high average longevity and low infant mortality rate that New England had in the 1600s. T. H. Hollingsworth, *Historical Demography* (Ithaca: Cornell University Press, 1969), p. 179.

Most of the forced African immigration to the Atlantic coastal plain of North America took place toward the end of the 1700s, after well over a century of rising European immigration and unusually high natural population growth. It was not until that time, the last decades of the eighteenth century, that the Brazilian plantation model, with its demand for large numbers of slaves, was introduced via the Caribbean into the American South and stimulated a considerable increase in forced African immigration. Reproduction rates among Africans were as high as among Europeans in central North America, and a great deal higher than they were among Africans in the English, French, and Dutch island colonies of the Caribbean (where a horrendous mortality rate was commonplace) or in Brazil. But they could not catch up with the reproductive headstart of the European immigrants in the 1600s, when nine such immigrants came to America for every forced immigrant brought from Africa, and the advantages nonslaves had in family formation. The cessation of the African slave trade in 1808, in combination with the increase of European immigration during the 1800s and the early 1900s, resulted in a steadily declining proportion of persons of African descent in the population of the United States. The proportion went from the peak of 19 percent in the first U.S. census of 1790 to 11 percent in the census of 1980 (though this long-term trend has in the last two national censuses shown signs of reversing).

Because France, Portugal, and Spain, for their own particular imperial reasons, pursued governmentally selective immigration policies in their American possessions, rather than the governmentally open policy that best suited the particular imperial needs of Britain, a different kind of European population came into being in Canada, Brazil, and Spanish America than developed in America. The self-selecting emigrants to America had a new social conformity. They themselves had individually made the decision, without any government screening and approval, to leave various societies in Europe and go to America. In doing so, they were constituting a new, non-European society in the sense that no society in European history had ever been constituted through the voluntary consent of persons acting individually on their own initiative. The European emigrants to Brazil, Canada, and Spanish America, on the other hand, in being screened by the governments of Portugal, France, and Spain for conformity to a single European nationality and the state religion of that nation, before they were allowed to take up residence in those places, reconstituted in the Americas the group consciousness they had been part of in Europe. The uniformity of nationality and religion among the European emigrants to Canada, Brazil, and Spanish America during the formative centuries of their post-1492 cultures had the effect of perpetuating and projecting European nationalism

in the New World and of preserving the hierarchical, group-minded, authoritarian culture of Europe; whereas in the United States, the promiscuous
multiplication and mingling of nationalities and religious practices, which
characterized life there, had the effect of replacing Europe's authoritarian,
group-minded, hierarchical culture with a mind-set comparatively free of
that outlook. Each of the other three major continental cultural areas of
the Americas had its own distinctive post-1492 population: an exclusively
uninational European population in Canada, an African base in Brazil, and
an American Indian base in Spanish America, and therefore each had its
own particular historical condition for a distinctive cultural formation. But
in all three, just one European group was replicated. French Canada was a
small extension of pre-Reformation France; Brazil and Spanish America
had more or less homogeneous, privileged groups of Portuguese and
Spanish descent who ruled large, subjugated groups of non-Europeans.
The comparative uniqueness of the population history of the United States
among the post-1492 continental cultures of the Americas was a fundamental condition for the comparatively rapid development of a cultural mind-
set that turned away from European domination much sooner in its history
than did the cultural mind-sets of Brazil, Canada, and Spanish America.

Because France prohibited self-selecting emigration to Canada, "New
France" (as Canada was then called) in the second decade after its founding
still had fewer than seventy inhabitants and no plowed land, only garden
patches. By 1640, some thirty years after its founding, its population stood
at a mere twenty-five hundred French Catholics. French Protestants, who
had good reason for wanting to leave France in the 1600s and who proved
excellent colonists in central North America, were prohibited by the French
government from living in Canada. Only French Catholics were permitted
to settle there. To keep this small, homogeneous colony viable, the French
king in the late seventeenth century sent to Canada at the crown's expense
a few thousand deliberately selected emigrants. The group included poor,
young, unmarried, Roman Catholic women of certified good character who
were to become wives of the Frenchmen living there and future mothers
of Frenchmen in Canada. Down to the time of the British conquest of
Canada, its population remained entirely French and entirely Roman Catholic and was, as a matter of policy, kept by the French imperial government
at the minimum level needed to maintain an effective military garrison.

In the 1600s and 1700s, Canada functioned with beautiful imperial
logic as a source for France of naturally produced organic materials that
needed little resident French manpower to collect or process (furs, fish,
timber) and as a strategic stronghold that required only a small civilian
population of farmers and artisans for its support. The almost-continuous

waterways of the St. Lawrence River, the Great Lakes, the Mississippi River, and their tributaries offered the only natural avenue of travel from the Atlantic Ocean into the faraway center of the North American continent, and the precipitous height at Quebec, which commanded the St. Lawrence, was the key to the entrance of that natural corridor. By fortifying and maintaining military control of the height overlooking the St. Lawrence at Quebec, France could, with a minimum investment of money and military power, control the North American interior, thus impeding Britain's imperial strength and making it more likely that France could continue its dominance in Europe. (One must really see from the south bank of the St. Lawrence at Quebec the extraordinary bluff that dominates the river there to understand how geographically sound this imperial logic was.) Unlike the millions of civilized Indians of Spanish America who became citizens of Spain, the tens of thousands of American Indian trappers who collected a wealth of rich fur pelts for France from the wilds of Stone Age Canada were never made French citizens because they did not have to be to profit from their labors in the wilderness. Similarly, exploitation of the teeming Atlantic fishing grounds off the mouth of the St. Lawrence did not require a large resident French population. From the early 1500s, and perhaps even before Columbus's voyage in 1492, these fantastically rich grounds were heavily fished by fleets from western European ports that returned home with their catches at the end of each season having had little contact with the North American mainland.

In part, the historic underpopulation of Canada by Europeans was the result of its harsh climate. As the first Frenchmen who wintered in the St. Lawrence Valley found out, to their dismay and near-fatal peril, Canadian winters have a protracted rigor unlike those of western Europe at the same latitude because the Gulf Stream passes too far to the east to warm Canada's Atlantic coast. But the underpopulation of French Canada was mostly policy—a matter of the most efficient use of the French empire's resources of money, material, and manpower in its imperial rivalry with Britain. Throughout Canada's exceptionally long history as a European colony, first under French rule and then under British rule, its population remained much smaller than its resources and climate would have supported.

The underpopulation of Canada did not appreciably change until Britain withdrew the last regiments of its imperial garrison from Canada in the 1870s. But in 1900, when British culture and political rule were still regnant in Canada, though perceptibly beginning to wane, Canada's population was still only one-fifteenth that of the United States. Today, however, at the close of Canada's century-long emancipation from European imperialism (1870–1980), the Canadian population has increased dramatically in relation to that of the United States. Now there is one Canadian for every nine Americans instead of one for every fifteen, as was the case some eighty-five years ago when Canada was still almost entirely under British domination. Like Brazil and several of the principal countries of Spanish America, not until the second part of the nineteenth century did Canada begin to have the kind of significantly large, mixed immigration that has distinguished the population increase of the United States from early in its history; and it was not until the 1960s that there was a big liberalization of Canadian immigration law. Today one out of eight Canadian residents is foreign-born.[6]

Emigration from Europe to Spanish America was controlled by an office of the Spanish government that was created three years before Columbus's death and that executed this function for the next three centuries. Nationality and religion were the main considerations in the government's selection process. Aside from a brief period in the early sixteenth century, when the king of Spain also ruled German subjects in Europe and allowed some of them into his possessions in North and South America, and another period in the late sixteenth and early seventeenth centuries, when Spanish kings ruled Portugal as well as Spain and allowed their Portuguese subjects entry into Spanish America, Europeans who were not of satisfactorily pure Spanish blood were kept out of this largest area of the Americas. In fact, except in rare cases, non-Spaniards were even prohibited from traveling to or temporarily residing in Spain's American possessions throughout most of their three-hundred-year-long history as overseas kingdoms of Spain. Furthermore, before an applicant could be considered eligible to emigrate, adherence to the Roman Catholic faith had to be proven by sworn affidavits satisfactory to the officials of the government bureau in charge of emigration. The purity of Spanish blood of an applicant for emigration also had to be officially documented before government permission to emigrate would be granted.

The importance of religious orthodoxy to this government-selected emigration is shown by the early institution in the Spanish territories of the Americas of a governmental inquisition to search out, prosecute, and punish (including by death), if guilt was established, all persons except Indians (whom the Spanish crown regarded with paternalistic indulgence) suspected of having departed from Roman Catholic orthodoxy of belief and practice. It is also noteworthy that, unlike British lords who dislocated tenants living on their estates both before and after British industrialization, Spanish grandees discouraged tenants who might be thinking of leaving

6. Andrew H. Malcolm, *The Canadians* (New York: Time Books, 1985), p. 65.

Spain for Spanish America by forbidding anyone on their estates, upon pain of losing their places, from buying the belongings of a person attempting to raise money to pay for their passage there.

Throughout Spanish America's long colonial history, the large number of functionaries who were needed to run Spain's political and ecclesiastical administration in the Americas often went to the New World with the idea of getting rich there and then returning to Spain to live out their days with the wealth they had acquired in "the Indies." (The same custom was also common among Portuguese emigrants to Brazil, who likewise often regarded Brazil as a place in which to make money without permanently settling there.) These bureaucrats and other intentionally temporary emigrants comprised a significant proportion of the carefully screened movement of persons who were allowed entry into Spanish America. They had a mentality akin to that of the conquistadors who conquered Mexico and Peru for themselves and the Spanish crown, about whom the Spanish author of a sixteenth-century history of the conquest of Peru remarked: "Many did not wish to settle in the country . . . but preferred to bring back what they had won at Cajamarca and Cuzco and enjoy it in Spain."[7] So numerous were the Spaniards who, during the centuries following the conquest of Spanish America, wanted to follow in the footsteps of the conquistadors and go to "the Indies" to get wealth to take home to Spain, that a term was created for such persons. They were called in Spanish *indianos.*

The plunder to be had following the conquest of Spanish America included many appointments to positions of official authority over millions of civilized Indians, appointments whose salaries might be modest but whose opportunities for moneymaking were famous. How lucrative these positions potentially were is seen in their having been customarily sold by the Spanish crown to the highest bidder. The king's patronage included the ecclesiastical hierarchy as well as the civil government in Spanish America.

After the conquest of the Indian civilizations in southern North America and western South America, the Spaniards who went there automatically became part of a ruling class. Regardless of their social status in Spain, these government-selected emigrants to the Americas felt themselves to be legitimate heirs to a legitimate military conquest and division of spoils, as members of a single, militarily superior, European group, which by right of conquest ought to dominate the groups it had subjugated. Their thinking

---

7. Agustin de Zarate, *The Discovery and Conquest of Peru,* trans. J. M. Cohen (Harmondsworth, England: Penguin, 1968), p. 141.

remained European. They were committed to a dominion founded on the mere fact of being born Spanish, without having to accomplish anything individually to prove their superiority—which had already, prior to their emigration from Spain, been officially proven by their certified consanguinity with the sixteenth-century conquerors of Mexico and Peru. Social and political distinctions in Spanish America were even made on the basis of whether a person was a Spaniard born in Spain or a person of pure Spanish blood born in the Americas.

So hierarchical in cultural mentality was the dominating European population of Spanish America that its one large area rich in uncultivated arable land, the Pampas of Argentina, remained only sparsely settled until the latter part of the nineteenth century because no civilized Indians lived in the Pampas to be ruled. Argentina's European population in 1850 (a generation after independence from Spain) was still only about twenty-two thousand. During the next ninety years, however, as the ideas of democracy first institutionalized in the United States spread in Spain and other parts of Europe, 6.6 million self-selecting European emigrants, three-fourths of them Italians and Spaniards, went to this large country and, behaving in the same way the population of the United States had been behaving for a long time, soon developed the Pampas throughout their extent. The late development of these marvelously rich agricultural plains, despite their being directly accessible from the Atlantic, contrasts with the following facts about the cultural behavior of Americans: in just the year 1787, one thousand flatboats transported eighteen thousand settlers westward on the Ohio River, along with twelve thousand head of their cattle; and by the time of the first national census of 1790, American traders and horse dealers had been in Texas for a decade and one hundred thousand Americans were living west of the Appalachian Mountains, beyond the Atlantic coastal plain. A generation later, in 1820, seven territories in the trans-Appalachian Stone Age wilderness had been sufficiently populated to be admitted into the union as states, and settlement was proceeding up the valley of the Missouri River, west of the Mississippi, at the rate of thirty to forty miles a year; and, another generation later, in 1850, nine more states were in the union, eight of them from the Stone Age wilderness beyond the Mississippi River.

This behavior cannot be attributed entirely to the transformable character of the Stone Age space-time continuum of central North America because the Pampas also presented such a wilderness (without the impediment of dense forestation) and were directly accessible to settlement from the Atlantic Ocean; and yet they lay comparatively lightly settled between 1500 and 1850. The different kinds of populations that historically developed in Spanish America and in the United States must also be considered when accounting for this difference. On the one hand, in Spanish America, an elite-and-peon population, a society of rulers and ruled, of the conquered and the conquerors, developed without much in the way of a middle strata; on the other hand, in the United States, a predominately European-descended population composed through self-selecting emigration formed a predominately middle-class society of workers who considered themselves to be of equal personal worth because of their equal necessity to work for a living and to prove their social worth through their productiveness. During the prolonged colonial histories of Spanish America and Brazil, to be of European descent was socially to belong to a comparatively small ruling group. To work with one's hands was to lower oneself socially. It was not so much to build anything by one's own sweat that Europeans emigrated to those places during the formative centuries of their cultures, but to benefit—as a European who had crossed the ocean and joined a ruling class—from the sweat of Indian peons or African slaves.

In comparison with Spain's strict control over emigration to its possessions in the Americas, Portugal's policy governing emigration to Brazil may be regarded as less severe. But it had the same basic features as Spanish policy: exclusion of all would-be non-Portuguese emigrants; conformity of belief within a national state church, which was enforced by a governmental inquisition in Brazil having extraordinary police and legal powers; and, institutionalized screening in Portugal of emigrants for purity of nationality and religion.

Canadian cultural beliefs and behavior have also been conditioned as much by the composition of its European-minded population as by its arctic and subarctic location. French-Canadian culture produced superb woodsmen, explorers, and frontier soldiers. But French Canadians thought and behaved as Frenchmen living on a transoceanic borderland of metropolitan France and carrying out a French imperial strategy, rather than as Canadians with an independent cultural purpose that might well have included moving west of the sea reach of the St. Lawrence Valley, but did not. Following the British conquest of Canada, the same European-centered, borderland mentality that had prevailed in Canadian culture under French rule continued to dominate cultural behavior in British-ruled Canada.

In the brief period between 1763 (the date of the peace treaty confirming the British conquest of Canada that was assured by the capture of the great fortress at Quebec in 1759) and 1775 (the onset of the first war between the United States and Britain), the British government had its hands too full in Canada, working out a policy for ruling its new, solidly French, solidly Roman Catholic subjects, to give much attention to anything else. The American victory in the American Revolution decided one thing, however, about British rule in Canada: no promiscuous immigration into Canada of the kind that had weakened the ability of Britain to maintain its rule over the multinational, self-selected American population would be allowed. Thus, the entirely French, entirely Roman Catholic population of post-1492 Canada was joined by a second group of purely British subjects. For a long time after the American Revolution, group loyalties and differentiated group rights continued to occupy the historical consciousness of Canada to such a degree that it remains a major focus of Canadian culture to this day.

After 1760 the tension that built up between the English-speaking, conquering "race," as it was and is called in Canada, and the French-speaking, conquered "race" reflected Europe's history of disunity, abiding hereditary antagonisms between groups, and national conflicts, as does also the quasi-nationalistic thinking of Canada's twentieth-century provinces. The idea of a non-European, Canadian culture has been slow to develop in Canada because the conflicts, policies, and imperial culture of Europe continued to dominate the historical consciousness of Canada's "racially" bipolar, postconquest population well down into the twentieth century. In 1914, for instance, Canada was still such an integral part of Britain that it was considered to be automatically at war with Germany, just as Scotland and Wales were, when Britain made its declaration of hostilities. And acceptance of that view was as general in English-speaking Canada as it was in Britain.

The great contribution of Britain to the distinctive cultural formation of the United States has not been a set of specific political rights or any heritage of law, such as freedom of speech or habeas corpus. Canada also manifests such influences; and yet American and Canadian cultures are notably dissimilar. Rather, it was the historical indifference on the part of the rulers of the British empire in the seventeenth and early eighteenth centuries about who lived in the Atlantic coastal plain of North America— as long as that population quickly increased for the benefit of the British empire. This permissiveness had little to do with political liberalism. It was merely the particular form of Britain's expedient strategy for imperially exploiting central North America. Britain entered and ruled central North America for exactly the same reason Spain entered and ruled southern North America and western South America. As became quite evident in the 1760s and 1770s, Britain's comparative indifference about how these colonies were populated and how they ordered their internal affairs was contingent upon their remaining loyal and subservient to the British crown and permitting their commerce to continue under the control and regulation of the imperial government in London.

The comparative freedom from close imperial supervision and emigrant screening, practices that had preserved in Brazil, Canada, and Spanish America a European group conformity, made it possible for the self-selecting emigrants to America and their American-born descendants to form a new sort of population by individual consent such as had never been seen in Europe, a population that responded far more readily and more rapidly to the peculiarities of their circumstances in America than would have been the case had the population been screened for uniformity and been subjected to closer government control from Europe. This European-descended population, because it lacked conformity to the group mentality of imperial Europe's hierarchical culture, developed non-European ways of thought and behavior from generation to generation more quickly and more completely than any other part of the Americas, as demonstrated in the comparative swiftness with which Americans separated themselves politically from Europe. The close supervision of internal affairs in Canada by the British crown—a policy stemming from Britain's experience of losing control of the American population—suggests what would have happened in America had the British government had the same policy of controlling emigration to America in the seventeenth and eighteenth centuries that it adopted in Canada after the American Revolution.

In contrast to the laxness of the imperial government of Britain toward emigration to central North America in the seventeenth and eighteenth centuries and toward control of the internal affairs of her colonies there, the Spanish crown by the end of the first one and one-half centuries of its rule in the Americas had issued four hundred thousand edicts to regulate the most trivial aspects of the lives of its subjects in the Americas. Many of these laws were naturally ignored by those distant subjects, whose conditions of life the Spanish crown could not entirely understand, despite its receipt of the bales of official reports generated by the Spanish colonial bureaucracy in the Americas. This plethora of royal edicts emanating from Madrid seems to have given the inhabitants of Spanish America a cultural skepticism about law in general; *obedezco pero no cumplo,* "I obey but do not comply," was a folk saying of the over-regulated colonials of Spanish America. Nevertheless, the sheer weight of the mountainous bureaucracy created to supervise affairs in Spanish America from Spain exerted a constant pressure to maintain a European orientation of thought and behavior. This pressure was strengthened by the Spanish crown's custom of always appointing Spaniards, rather than persons of Spanish descent born in the Americas, who might manifest an interest in an American point of view, to the most consequential political and ecclesiastical posts.

Part of the reason, of course, for the difference between the historical behavior of the Spanish and the British crowns toward their American possessions was that Spain ruled a territory that, at the time of its acquisition, already had a civilized population larger than Spain's and that was of immediate imperial value, while Britain had to attract as many colonists to its possessions as it could in as short a time as possible to give them imperial value. In addition, Britain could afford less centralized control of the coastal plain of central North America, a region not only much smaller than Mexico and Peru but also much closer to London than either Peru or Mexico is to Madrid. In fact, British rule was so permissive that no law was passed in London before 1740 to govern even the basic matter of naturalizing the many self-selected foreign immigrants in the British colonies in America. The matter was left to the various governments of the colonies themselves. Spain's empire in the Americas, on the other hand, became from the moment of its conquest the largest possession of the largest maritime empire in the world before the British empire of the late nineteenth century. From the start, simply governing it had been a highly lucrative business.

Each of the major continental cultures of the Americas had its own distinctive population base during the formative period of its culture. The United States did not have a population derived predominately from slaves, as Brazil did. It did not have a population made up mostly of subjugated, civilized American Indians, as Spanish America did. It did not have a small, stable population from a single European stock with a single religion, as Canada did. Rather, the United States of America, during its culturally formative centuries, despite its slave minority, was the only part of the Americas to have a rapidly increasing population predominately composed of or descended from self-selected immigrants from many different European nationalities and many different religions.

THE MENTALITY OF SELF-SELECTING EMIGRANTS

To understand that there were restrictions on the emigration of individual Europeans to Brazil, Canada, and Spanish America in the fifteenth through the eighteenth centuries but virtually no restrictions on free emigration to the United States from any part of Europe until early in the twentieth century, is to comprehend an essential condition of America's distinctive cultural formation. A certain kind of emigrant was motivated to take advantage of the freedom to go to America without being required by a European government to conform to a single European group identity.

Culture is created and perpetuated through behavior that enacts from generation to generation a set of simple ideas, and self-selecting emigration was a behavior unique to what became the United States. Therefore, the question has to be asked: What beliefs are manifested in the behavior of self-selecting emigration? The most credible comprehensive answer to this question is that the behavior of this type of emigrant manifests belief in self-responsibility. Self-selecting emigrants believed that by changing their place of residence to America on their own initiative they could get whatever it was that they thought they deserved to have but were failing to have in Europe.

Self-selecting emigrants did not blame themselves for their failure in Europe. They blamed conditions there. The mentality of the self-selecting emigrant was, in other words, basically the mentality of a self-respecting failure bent on success. To characterize such persons as self-respecting failures does not mean that all of them would necessarily have been judged failures by the standards of the nations of Europe they abandoned. What it does mean is that they were failures as judged by their own personal standards.

The sense that self-selecting emigrants had of their failure in Europe was not, however, the most important aspect of their mentality. Rather, it was their rejection of that self-judged failure, which their emigration to America manifests. They were driven to America not by despair, but by hope. They believed in themselves and believed also that in America they could fulfill their own concepts of success. They left Europe in pursuit of success, not to perpetuate their failure in Europe to have whatever it was that they desired. Through their behavior, they gave to their descendants a cultural model of belief in the rightness and necessity of everyone making an effort to fulfill their ambitions, rather than living according to the differentiated privileges and "stations" of duty defined by birth in a particular group, as in European culture.

In a rapidly growing population of such persons and their descendants, it proved impossible to perpetuate either subservience to Europe or the European cultural belief in a privileged ruling group of supposedly superior birth. There was no larger group of slaves or peons for these self-selecting emigrants and their descendants to rule. They themselves were the largest group. Despite their diversity of European ancestries and religious faiths (or lack of religious convictions), they had an equality of common purpose among themselves as self-selecting emigrants, namely their desire to go to America to find better opportunities than Europe afforded. Not through the design of an imperial European government but through their own self-selection, they constituted a population with a new kind of conformity, having a new cultural potential.

Because the self-selecting emigrants in going to America had each made the same kind of decision and faced the same chance-full ordeal, they naturally tended to regard themselves as being of equal worth and as having an equal opportunity to exert themselves in pursuit of whatever notion of personal success they had in mind. Self-selecting emigrants passed on to their descendants through their behavior their beliefs in the rightness of self-exertion, in improving the future of one's own life and the lives of others, and in the equality of liberty.

Patently, those Europeans who were satisfied with their lives in Europe or who hoped to succeed there were not among those who exposed themselves to the traumas of emigration. But, it must be emphasized, self-respect and dissatisfaction with conditions in Europe were not the only traits of self-selecting emigrants. Not every dissatisfied self-respecting European went to America. Courage and initiative were also necessary traits of self-selecting emigration. For it must be remembered that even in the extreme case of hunger as a motive for leaving Europe, only some of those who were hungry actually did emigrate. Only some impoverished Europeans found a way to get out of Europe to America. The absolutely cowed and despairing, the spiritually down-and-out of Europe were not candidates for self-selecting emigration, no matter how discontented they may have been with their condition or how distressing the pressures on them became. Those who were without hope, courage, and imagination never boarded the ships sailing to America.

The "push" of historical conditions in Europe and the "pull" of historical conditions in America do not, therefore, in themselves, satisfactorily explain the phenomenon of self-selecting emigration to America. Personal qualities determined who among all of those subject to these pushes and pulls would actually emigrate. Self-selecting emigrants were a type of person.

To be an American, wherever one has been born or may live, is to believe what Americans as a self-selected gathering of individuals into a people have believed, namely, that one's own personal aspirations are legitimate, that they can be pursued and be a source of good for all of society, that past failures can be overcome, that betterment is possible, that one human being has as much worth as any other human being. This is what makes an American, what has made the culture of America. There are Americans, in this sense, in every country and every race of the globe. For the culture of this nation expresses a love of liberty and a distrust of domineering institutionalized authority that is distributed among every nation of the earth. It is not even necessary to speak the language of America to be an American, for some of the staunchest citizens of the United States and the most valiant adherents to its culture, in every generation since the beginning, have spoken the language of America in a peculiar way or not at all. One thinks, for instance, of the German-speaking residents of the Mohawk Valley and of eastern Pennsylvania who fought in the American Revolution.

GOING TO AND LIVING IN AMERICA

The rich physical resources of central North America would never have been so highly developed into wealth and so widely distributed among the population of America except for the culture created by the energetic ambitions of millions of self-selected immigrants and their descendants, to whom the self-selected immigrants passed on their beliefs through their behavior. In just three centuries, a population of such persons did as much as had been done in Europe in six thousand years to civilize a Stone Age space nearly the size of Europe; and while doing so, created a single, unified nation. That historical feat cannot be explained merely in terms of the potential in the United States for wealth. A dynamic, egalitarian mind-set—a belief in equality of liberty and a behavior based on that belief—was also essential.

During the formative centuries of American culture and in the nineteenth century, the number of workers available in each American generation was never sufficient to the task of constructing a progressively improving civilization on a continental scale from a Stone Age past. North American Indian tribes of the seventeenth and eighteenth centuries were too different in their cultural beliefs and behaviors to become integral to a culture dominated by self-selected immigrants and their descendants. Consequently, they furnished few workers to help transform the Stone Age that existed in central North America, an imperative that was, in any case, culturally alien and abhorrent to them. Forced immigrants from Africa contributed their labor to the task as slaves. But from the beginning of America's permanent settlement by Europeans, the foremost, predominant labor source was self-selected European immigrants and their offspring.

Because the need for workers to develop land and to perform every other kind of work was always increasing in America, wages have historically been attractively higher in America than they have been in Europe, as much as three times higher.[8] At the same time, food has historically been abundant and of good quality and cheaper than in Europe. Likewise, arable land has also been attractively abundant, cheap, often excellently usable,

8. Fred Albert Shannon, *America's Economic Growth* (New York: Macmillan, 1940), pp. 73–74.

and more accessible in America than in Europe. In Brazil, Canada, and Spanish America, developable arable land was neither as abundant nor as important economically as it was in America. Until the nineteenth century, for instance, the profitable fur trade in Canada depended on maintaining wilderness as wilderness rather than transforming it into farms on the largest possible scale. And, mining for diamonds, gold, and silver was as attractive during the culturally formative centuries of Spanish American and Brazilian history as land development has historically been in America (by 1800, Brazil and Spanish America were producing most of the world's diamonds and 90 percent of its precious metals). Moreover, Brazil, Canada, and Spanish America lacked the burgeoning population that America had, which in itself contributed to an expansive economy with more and more need for human services and hence jobs. The rapidly increasing population, which required rapid economic expansion, has also been a fundamentally differentiating historical condition in the cultural formation of the United States. For all of these reasons, then, the ambitions of common European workers have had a more pervasive historical influence on the cultural formation of the United States than they have had on the cultural formations of Brazil, Canada, or Spanish America.

Labor was in such chronic short supply in America that as early as 1700 nearly every one of the colonies in the Atlantic coastal plain was using "some combination of advertising, grants of land, employment incentives, transportation payment, and guarantee of rights and freedoms to increase the flow of immigrants."[9] Ship owners and ship captains also promoted emigration, once they discovered early in the 1600s that many Europeans wanted to emigrate to America and that carrying them there could be profitable. The proprietors of colonies in the Atlantic coastal plain (most notably the proprietor of Pennsylvania) employed recruiting agents in Europe to populate their colonies so that the raw lands they owned would be bought and developed, thereby making their remaining, unsold land increase in value. The same interests moved corporate owners of colonies, such as the Virginia Company, to likewise recruit in Europe laborers and potential land developers. The custom continued for centuries. By the late 1800s, thirty-three states and territories of the United States were operating offices in Europe to encourage emigration to America.

It is safe to deduce from the behavior of those who took to heart the accounts of life in America and uprooted themselves from Europe to go there that self-selecting emigrants were persons willing to make a change,

9. Reed Ueda, "Naturalization and Citizenship," in *Immigration: Dimensions of Ethnicity,* ed. Stephan Thernstrom (Cambridge: Harvard University Press, 1982), p. 78.

to take a chance. In fact, they were often Europeans who were young, unmarried, and unattached to a secure job. The sums of money frequently sent back to Europe, in the self-justifying letters of immigrants who had taken the risk of going to America, persuaded more established Europeans who were interested in bettering their condition that life might indeed be better in America. One historian has put the matter this way, that "the greatest encouragers of emigration" were "people who had been emigrants themselves," noting that in just the year 1854 such persons sent back through brokers and bankers to just one nation in Europe (Britain) the sum of one and three-quarter million pounds sterling to pay the passages of friends and relatives wanting to go to America—and, astonishingly, even strangers. How much more money that year may have been sent directly to would-be emigrants themselves in that one nation of Europe is not a matter of record. How much has been sent to all of the nations of Europe during all of the years of the nearly four centuries of European emigration to America is likewise unknown. But another historian of the subject has estimated that "perhaps as much as one-third of all emigrant passages to the United States" were paid for by money sent to Europe by those who had previously emigrated. The comparative historical situation that drew a certain kind of European across the Atlantic to America and then led him to encourage others to follow him is indicated by the letter one such European wrote home calling America a "queer country" because in his conversations with working people there, during his journey from the Atlantic coast to Ohio, he had not talked with a single person who had not claimed to be eating at least three good meals a day; whereas, the letter writer reminded his European correspondent: "We have but two at home and they are scanty enough." A boy who had emigrated to New York put the matter more simply in a letter remitting money to his mother: "Provisions [here] are very cheap; plenty of work to be had. . . ." A European beggar who stowed away on a ship to America immediately found work on a railroad and wrote to his wife that he would soon be sending her enough money so that she could join him in what he called "the lands of promise"—apparently conceiving the states of the United States to be like the nations of Europe, each a separate land.[10]

The pattern of such immigrant testimonials about the character of life in America agrees with the assessment made by the French chargé d'affaires

10. R. A. Burchell and Eric Homberger, "The Immigrant Experience," in *Introduction to American Studies*, eds. Malcolm Bradbury and Howard Temperley (London and New York: Longman, 1981), p. 128; Terry Coleman, *Going to America* (Garden City, NY: Anchor/Doubleday, 1973), pp. 19, 12–13, 168, 221–22.

to America during the American Revolution. He reported that he had seen no paupers in the United States and had yet to meet what he called "a peasant" who was not well dressed and who did not have "a good wagon or at least a good horse." "The best of our kings was satisfied to wish that each peasant might have every Sunday a hen in his pot. Here, we have not entered a single dwelling in the morning without finding there a kettle in which was cooking a good fowl, or a piece of beef, or mutton with a piece of bacon; and a great abundance of vegetables; bread, cider, things from the dairy, and a profusion of firewood; clean furniture, a good bed, and often a newspaper."[11] The reference of the chargé to the newspapers he encountered in the homes of ordinary Americans indicates a diffusion of literacy in eighteenth-century America sufficient to impress an educated European observer. The evident achievement of a comparatively high level of general prosperity and education by a population of self-selected immigrants and their descendants, in less than two centuries from the time of the first permanent European settlements, engendered an unshakable feeling of superiority toward Europe that made continued political subservience to Europe intolerable to Americans.

The money so frequently sent back to Europe by self-selected immigrants proved that opportunities in America were real. To the wage earner, any place where the price of food is lower and wages are higher than where he works is always worth considering as a place to move to, even if he is doing well enough by the standards of his home place. The letters sent to Europe from America by immigrants were evidently full of such information about prices and wages and, frequently, sums of money earned in America.

Even so, not every European down on his luck or failing to get what he thought he deserved would respond to the evidence of letters from America or to the representations of the agents who were paid to recruit immigrants for America. There was, after all, an ocean to cross. The decision, whether to go to America or stay in Europe, was a contest between, on the one hand, the propulsive desire for a better way of life and the courage to face resettlement on another continent and, on the other hand, the inertia caused by the familiarity of known surroundings and fear of the unknown that binds every person to his native place and its customs, despite whatever problems and deprivations might be present. For a certain type of person, even misery and subservience are preferable to the unfamiliar step of embarking upon the terrors of the ocean for a faraway place.

11. "Letters of François, Marquis de Barbé-Marbors," quoted in John C. Miller, *The First Frontier: Life in Colonial America* (New York: Dell, 1966), pp. 9–10.

It was common knowledge in Europe that many who undertook the Atlantic passage to America in the seventeenth and eighteenth centuries, and even in the nineteenth century, died. In assessing the mentality of the self-selecting emigrants whose behavior and beliefs have had a determining effect on American culture, this fact must be appreciated: the journey there was known to be dangerous. During the centuries when the only way to cross the ocean was aboard a wooden sailing ship, an Atlantic passage with less than a 10 percent death rate was considered good.[12] Provisions of food for the passage—which in a sailing ship sometimes lasted for months—was provided by the passengers themselves or bought by them during the voyage from ship's stores; and if the winds proved light or contrary, and the voyage's duration was unduly prolonged, either the stores of food or the money to buy them could give out before land was reached. There was also the chance of the ship being sunk in a storm or by the deterioration of an aged hull whose seams became so loosened by the action of waves that the ship's pumps could not keep up with their leaking, even when all of the able-bodied passengers assisted the ship's sailors in manning the pumps. (A ship that did not leak was a rarity in the days of wooden sailing ships.) Piracy was also among the causes of ships disappearing in the Atlantic. Add to these risks of transoceanic travel in the seventeenth and eighteenth centuries the terror that the ocean can have for landsmen who have never spent days upon its heaving immensity beyond the sight of land, and one begins to appreciate that there is historical justification for the refrain in the verses of the national anthem of the United States that characterizes America as "the home of the brave." A self-selecting emigrant had to master his fears before he could embark on the voyage to America.

A small book published by an immigrant Englishwoman in 1848 called *A True Picture of Emigration*[13] presents a comprehensive idea of the experience of self-selecting emigration to America and the type of person that the self-selecting emigrant was. The author, Rebecca Burlend, emigrated from Barwick-in-Elmet near Leeds, England, to Illinois via New Orleans and the Mississippi River with her husband Edward and their five small children in 1831. She was thirty-eight years old and did not want to go to America, but her husband did after he had "travelled many miles" to read letters from America that had been received in their county in England.

12. Terry Coleman, *Going to America* (Garden City, NY: Anchor/Doubleday, 1973), chapters 6, 7, and 8, describes the dangers of the Atlantic passage.
13. Rebecca Burlend, *A True Picture of Emigration,* ed. Milo Milton Quaife (Secaucus, NJ: Citadel, 1968).

Yet at the point of the family's actual embarkation from Liverpool, Edward Burlend was overcome by fear and tearfully announced to his wife that he had changed his mind and wanted to go home. She reminded him of their true situation: they had sold all of their possessions to purchase the tickets to America; they had given up their place in Barwick-in-Elmet; and they, in fact, had no home to which they could return. She also reminded him that the conditions that had given him the idea of emigrating still remained true, that after fourteen years of farming leased land in England they had nothing to show for their efforts but a "gradual diminution of our little property."

During the two-and-one-half-month ocean voyage to New Orleans, the Burlends experienced "the much dreaded sea-sickness," anxiety about sinking in a great storm that hit their ship, a shipboard fire, and a scare from pirates, which caused the captain to get the vessel ready for combat. During the twelve-day voyage up the Mississippi on a river steamer to Illinois, a thief attempted to steal their money while they slept. Arriving in Illinois in November, they bought eighty acres of "improved land" for one hundred dollars (an amount less than the cost of their ocean passage). The improvements included four hundred maple-sugar trees and twelve acres cleared of trees. They paid an additional sixty dollars for the log cabin that had been built on the land and the winter wheat that had already been sown in three of the twelve cleared acres.

They regretted almost immediately having left England. Although they could buy venison for half a cent a pound, the lonesome Illinois forests seemed "interminable," and there were wolves in them. The bedclothes they had brought from England, which had been adequate there, did not allow them to sleep comfortably during the much colder winter nights of Illinois. Their personal clothing soon became ragged from rough usage, and they had to go into debt to buy food. In their ignorance of American fauna, they killed and cooked a vulture, thinking it was the famous wild turkey of America. A vision of "being cultivators of our own land" brought them to America, Mrs. Burlend recounted in her memoir. But she added, "Man's career in prospective is always brilliant; and it is providentially ordered that it should be so. Could we have foreseen our destiny [in Illinois], the prospect would have thrown us into despair. It would have . . . unfitted our minds for the difficulties with which we had to struggle." Self-selecting emigrants were persons moved by a hopeful imagination. Had they not been ignorant of the real conditions they would have to suffer in getting themselves established in America, they probably would not have had sufficient courage to board the ships bound for America.

During the Burlends' first spring in America, they learned how to make maple sugar from their trees and sold three hundred pounds of it; they cleared more of their land with the axe that the sale of the maple sugar allowed them to buy; and they planted a crop with hoes because they could not yet afford to buy a plow or oxen. The Illinois summer brought a rich store of wild plums, wild grapes, wild strawberries, and wild raspberries. They also had their first encounters with raccoons, whippoorwills, rattle-snakes, fireflies, mosquitoes, and hummingbirds. They discovered that a watch, which had cost less than a sovereign in England, could be exchanged in Illinois for eight acres of plowing because manufactured goods were still quite scarce. Much to their joy, they found that their land was "fat" without their having to manure it, as they had had to do in England. And they noticed that every man in America, without distinction, was addressed as "Mister" and that, as Mrs. Burlend put the matter, "The Americans are fond of the word liberty; it is indeed the burden of their song, their glory, their pride." To her way of thinking, there was too much liberty in America with regard to religion because, she reasoned as someone accustomed to the ascendancy of the Church of England, "no two conflicting creeds can both be right."

At the end of one full year of unremitting hard labor, the Burlends felt they were beginning to make some progress. Within two years, they owned six head of cattle and three pigs. (Since they had no barn at first to shelter their livestock, they let them forage outdoors all year round and kept them nearby and domesticated by regularly providing them with salt.) At the end of the third year on their land, they were able to trade a cow, a heifer, and seventy bushels of wheat for a parcel of fifteen more acres of improved land with a better house on it. After fifteen years' work of the kind Mrs. Burlend details in her account of her first years in America, she reported that they had a good house, a "superabundance of the essentials of housekeeping," furniture, an ample assortment of farming implements, "no lack of good food, such as beef, pork, butter, fowls, eggs, milk, flour, and fruits," pigs, sheep, much poultry, seven horses, and twenty horned cattle. Most importantly, they were the owners of 360 acres of farmland of "excellent quality and very productive," over half of it under cultivation by themselves and some of the rest leased to others at one dollar an acre per year. And during those fifteen years, the forests, which had at the beginning of their settlement surrounded them, had been considerably cleared, several little towns had been founded, and many other farms had been established.

Mrs. Burlend returned to England in 1846 for a visit. While there she dictated her story for publication and persuaded six families among her former neighbors to follow her back to America.

In the nearly sixty years between 1717 and 1775, as a way of relieving the labor shortage in America and also relieving Britain's crowded eighteenth-century prisons of some of their inmates, the British government shipped approximately twenty thousand convicts to America for seven years of contract labor. The number of these forced emigrants from Europe made up, however, only a tiny fraction (2 percent) of the total estimated emigration to America during the formative centuries of American culture, and after completing their penal labor, some of these forced emigrants chose to stay in America rather than to return to Britain, thus becoming self-selected immigrants.

Of far greater significance to understanding the influence of self-selecting emigration as a basic historical condition of the cultural formation of the United States was the practice among destitute Europeans of putting themselves into "indentured servitude" in order to get to America. Something between one-third and one-half of the one million self-selecting European emigrants who went to America during the 1600s and 1700s (between 330 and 500 thousand persons) wanted to go so badly and were so destitute of funds and possessions to pay for their ocean passage that they adopted this extreme expedient to get there.

A form of temporary, contractual slavery, indentured servitude was invented by the Virginia Company in the early 1600s, as a way of allowing impoverished Europeans to pay their passage to Virginia by selling the right to command their labor without wages for a period of time specified in a contract or indenture. The person who signed such an indenture agreed to work for whoever owned it. By this means, any able-bodied self-selecting emigrant, no matter how poor, could obtain passage across the Atlantic. Food, lodging, and clothing were provided the indentured servant by the owner of the contract. A skilled worker who entered into indentured servitude could insist that his or her contract exempt them from field work, and some non-English-speaking skilled workers made it a condition of their contracts that they were to be taught by their masters to read the English of the Bible.

The contract was signed in Europe with a ship's captain or an organizer of contract labor, such as the Virginia Company, who intended to sell it in America to someone who needed a worker. Impoverished European women as well as impoverished men used this method to get to America. At the end of the term of the indenture, which was usually from four to seven years, the indentured servant received his or her liberty and contracted "freedom dues." These parting gifts from the master of the indentured servant consisted always of some clothing and typically of some combination of money, food, seeds, arms, or tools as well, and occasionally, but not usually, a few acres of land. Because the contracts of female indentured servants could be bought by someone who wanted to marry them, women often did not serve out the full term of their indentures. Some indentured servants ran away from the holder of their indenture once they were in America.

Although protected in their right to go to law to defend themselves against personal abuse or breaches of the terms of their contracts, indentured servants were virtual slaves to whoever owned their contract. They could not leave the employ of their master, they could be severely punished for running away, and they could neither marry nor engage in any commercial activity without the consent of their master. Some masters fed their indentured servants little and worked them hard.

Since between one-third and one-half of the self-selecting emigrants during the seventeenth and eighteenth centuries went to America as indentured servants, and since a large proportion of them were later evidently able to send money back to Europe to pay for the passage of others to follow them, it is reasonable to conclude that indentured servants did in many cases find, after serving out their indentures, the better working conditions and the hoped-for opportunities to improve their lot in life they had sought in crossing the Atlantic. In the year 1727, perhaps as many as 90 percent of emigrants to America from Ireland were having their ocean passages paid for by money sent from America; in 1776, one out of every seven of the signers of the Declaration of Independence was a foreign-born immigrant; and it has been estimated that during the first 350 years of American history "perhaps as much as one-third of all emigrant passages to the United States" were paid for by previous emigrants.[14] Just how fundamental self-selecting emigration has been to America's distinctive cultural formation is clearly shown in the U.S. Constitution in those clauses that make citizenship for a period of seven years a requirement for election to the House of Representatives and nine years for election to the Senate (Article I, Sections 2 and 3). The Constitution requires only the president of the United States to be a "a natural born Citizen" (Article II, Section 1).

If America had not rather consistently satisfied the self-selecting European emigrants of the seventeenth, eighteenth, and nineteenth centuries, emigration to America would not have exhibited the rapidly increasing

14. Maldwyn Allen Jones, *American Immigration* (Chicago: University of Chicago Press, 1960), p. 24; Barbara Kaye Greenleaf, *America Fever: The Story of American Immigration* (New York: New American Library, 1970), p. 26; R. A. Burchell and Eric Homberger, "The Immigrant Experience," in *Introduction to American Studies,* eds. Malcolm Bradbury and Howard Temperley (London and New York: Longman, 1981), pp. 127–28.

volume observable in those centuries. For over three hundred years America was the most preferred destination, by far, of all overseas migration in the world. Only since the late nineteenth and the early twentieth centuries have Brazil, some of the countries of Spanish America, and Canada experienced the kind of immigration America had from early in its history.

The rapid development of a civilization from a continental expanse of Stone Age wilderness in central North America required sustained hard work from generation to generation. From this basic imperative of the history of America, it must be concluded that, for the most part, the self-selecting emigrants to America were willing and able to make sustained exertions. Because they were from the working class of Europeans, rather than from either the upper class or the down-and-outers, they considered work a normal part of life. They would not have expected a better way of life to be handed to them gratis; nor did they make their way across the Atlantic seeking the kind of patronage dispensed in Europe because they knew there was no ruling class of hereditary nobility living in America to dispense it. As an English magazine editor remarked in the nineteenth century about the history of settlement in America: no one should ever forget that with but few exceptions the founding of communities and the peopling of America had not been accomplished by Europe's "aristocracy" but rather by "miscellaneous individuals" who came from "the more humble, or, at all events, struggling classes of European society" and who "possessed the spirit to cross the Atlantic in quest of a fortune, rather than sink into pauperism at home."[15] It was the predominance of the spirit of such persons that produced the cultural formation of the United States.

The population history of America, as compared to the predominately slave and peon populations in Brazil and Spanish America, favored a cultural belief in the goodness of manual labor. Whereas "Everyone agreed America was no place to go unless you could work with your hands,"[16] in the post-1492 populations of Brazil and Spanish America, working with one's hands—especially the dirty work of farming—was mainly reserved for slaves and peons born to it. In the population that predominated in America, on the other hand, virtually everyone was a worker with his or her hands, and neither the idea of social superiority based on birth in an upper class nor the idea of social inferiority based on whether one per-

15. Terry Coleman, *Going to America* (Garden City, NY: Anchor/Doubleday, 1973), p. 16.
16. Terry Coleman, *Going to America* (Garden City, NY: Anchor/Doubleday, 1973), p. 14.

formed physical labor became a cultural belief. Successful work performance was what culturally conferred social distinction and respect in America.

Hordes of self-selected "commoners" from Europe and their descendants created in America a truly new kind of culture, the first modern society in the world, if by modern we mean a rejection of the ideas of hereditary merit and a fixed elite. It was a culture based on belief in equality of liberty and free association of individuals and on workers enjoying much more benefit from their exertions than they did in Europe. Society in Europe in the seventeenth and eighteenth centuries had never been structured by such cultural beliefs. But it was in America because of the dominant example of the behavior of self-selected immigrants and their descendants. Belief in equality of liberty was reinforced from generation to generation in the cultural formation of the United States by the arrival of more and more of the same type of person.

The cultural rightness for Americans of individual exertion, including physical labor, was not the result of what has been termed the "Protestant work ethic" because atheists, agnostics, Jews, and Roman Catholics also manifested the belief through their behavior in America. Rather, it resulted from the historical necessity for hard work in America and the uniqueness of a population created principally by self-selected immigrants, a type of person disposed to work hard to better his life and the future of his children. Labor had a dignity of opportunity in America and a rewarding respectability for individuals that it could not have in Europe's historically hierarchical, aristocratic, group-minded culture, or in the predominately slave and peon societies of Brazil and Spanish America, where labor was mainly performed by members of a permanent underclass and therefore had a kind of social stigma.

As the examples of the Burlends, detailed above, and many other self-selected immigrants indicate, life was hard for the Europeans who chose to go to America. It must have been especially hard for dependents who had had to follow a determined spouse or parent across the Atlantic without themselves having a desire to abandon Europe and its familiar scenes and customs. But homesickness in some degree probably afflicted even immigrants who had been highly motivated to leave Europe. In the unknown world of America, an ocean away from Europe, it was seldom that any city, building, river, slant of light, soil, forest, mountain, shoreline, work pattern, or climatic condition offered the comfort of familiarity to newly arrived Europeans. The adjustment to the new landscape and society that were to be one's new homeland required getting used to outlandish things and performing unfamiliar tasks, learning the terms of unprecedented decisions, and perhaps even acquiring a whole new language. These stresses produced an important secondary process of self-selection: those who were completely disheartened by the demands inescapably thrust upon them by the new way of life in the new kind of society America was becoming, who could not stand the strain of adjusting to new sights, new decisions, new responsibilities, and new customs, and who consequently suffered a breakdown of courage or hope, sometimes returned in defeat to the old, familiar, less individualistic demands of life in Europe. This return emigration, while small in comparison to the number of those who went to America as self-selecting emigrants and stayed on to struggle there, strengthened—by its further selection of the type of person best suited to life in America—the formation of a distinctive American character.

Each self-selecting emigrant who left Europe for America had his or her own reason for leaving. But whatever the particular personal motive, they and their descendants in America who imitated their parents' and their grandparents' behavior had in common underlying beliefs in self-responsibility, self-improvement, and equality of liberty. This configuration of belief and behavior, established by the same type of person selecting themselves for emigration to America from generation to generation—not the specific reasons for emigrating, which varied with each individual—is what has been historically effective in the formation of American culture. The beliefs of self-selecting emigrants in self-improvement, equality of liberty, and self-responsibility, when multiplied in the thinking and behavior of the one million such persons who arrived in America during the seventeenth and eighteenth centuries and the tens of millions who followed them in the nineteenth and twentieth centuries and the many more millions born in America who caught the vital cultural example of the thought and behavior of their immigrant ancestors, gave individualism and belief in progress an importance in the cultural formation of the United States that they did not have in European culture.

American individualism originated in the behavior of the self-respecting failures who left Europe for America in the 1600s and 1700s bent on their own success. What prevented such persons and their descendants from formulating an anarchistic culture in America was the discipline imposed on them by the great common enterprise of building a new civilization, which would make the realization of individual ambitions possible, and a desire to justify, through lasting achievements, the rightness of their emigration to themselves and to those whom they had left behind in Europe.

AMERICA VERSUS EUROPE

Americans have felt superior to Europe because their cultural ancestors all rejected Europe in favor of the belief that they could individually make a better way of life for themselves in America. The government-selected European emigrants to Brazil, Canada, and Spanish America during the formative centuries of the cultures that developed in those places after 1492 also aspired to self-betterment. But, because the radically different process of the government selection of these emigrants ensured conformity to a single European group, their mentality remained European and group oriented in a way that the mentality of America's burgeoning mixture of self-selecting emigrants from many European groups did not.

By the time central North America was settled during the first decade of the seventeenth century, Europe had already undergone a prolonged general development of civilized property, which had become concentrated in the hands of aristocratic classes, state churches, and religious orders. The availability of land in America to large numbers of aspiring individual property owners, however, and the actual acquisition of land by a large proportion of the society (more than 90 percent of Americans lived on farms at the time of the Revolution), prevented the duplication in America of Europe's division of society into those with land and those without it and the mentality of upper-class authority, responsibility, and privilege based on such a division. The manifest need in American society to develop and improve land from a condition of wilderness, in combination with a rapidly growing population of self-selected immigrants interested in pursuing their ambitions, generated the cultural expectation in America that as many people as possible should and would become property owners. The notion that each person in society should strive to create and improve property for his own benefit and the general good of society became a cultural behavior and a cultural belief.

Levels of property ownership in European history had become culturally identified with levels of birth—the nobility and peasantry that existed in European society prior to the early twentieth century. The whole force and nature of the historical experience of Americans, however, regarding property made European ideas of fixed social stratification irrelevant. The American expression "easy come, easy go" makes no sense in European history. But in America, as each person strove to improve his lot in life, a great deal of property was constantly changing hands, new properties were increasingly coming into existence to be further improved, and many people were going broke or getting rich all the time.

In America, both land ownership and manners were much less fixed than they were in Europe because in American history there was never any stratification of noblemen and peasants and little sense of a fixity of residence within the borders of a constricted space. The whole center of a continent much larger than Europe provided the American sense of a homeland. No borders barred freedom of movement within this space. On the European political map, there are no straight lines marking boundaries between nations because natural frontiers, such as rivers and mountains, delineating ancient defensive positions between antagonistic tribes, have determined borders between modern European nations. But in the United States, which lacks such a history, every state except Hawaii has at least one of its borders laid out in the straight-running lines of geographic units that had their origins in administrative reasoning and land development rather than in age-old antagonisms.

Furthermore, the curious European word *breeding,* which suggests a linking of one's birth to one's education in manners, has had little meaning in the cultural formation of America. In America every man was "Mister," and the pertinent expectation was that every man would improve his social status through personal achievement and make a contribution to society. American culture was committed to the idea that anyone could succeed if he made up his mind to it. The wisdom of social stratification is the wisdom of knowing one's place and staying in it, while carefully minding one's manners and being humbly grateful for whatever favors may be conferred by one's "betters" in a higher social "station." This European outlook did not fit the conditions in America. The wisdom of American culture centered on the individual who "got ahead." Social life in America was thought of as a contest to be won, rather than as a historically fixed stratification by birth to be perpetuated or endured—depending on whether one was born into an upper or a lower stratum. Rather than teaching a person to be properly subservient to his betters, according to his place in a long-established social hierarchy, American culture dispensed with the idea of the cultural rightness of an established hierarchy.

In the cultural beliefs and behavior of Americans, personal power was not as important as "making something" of one's life through personal improvement. American culture has historically upheld the behavioral model of striving instead of subservience. The idea of each man's equal right to strive after his own happiness in his own way, so long as he did not interfere with the equal liberty of others to do so, was a different idea altogether from the idea of "commoners" and "lords." A society in which "Mister" is indiscriminately applied as a title of respect, fundamentally diverges from a society in which it is believed that only some men deserve to be called "Mister," a few have the title "Sir" conferred on them, and a small handful are addressed with feigned or real reverence as "My Lord." The radically new element in the American conception of equality was not just that the lowborn are equal as human beings to the highborn but that the highborn are no better than the lowborn as human beings and that there is no inherent reason why the two might not change places after they began life, depending on a person's individual qualities and achievements. Given the idea of the reciprocal equality of all men, American manners were necessarily simpler than manners in Europe, and American culture never developed a belief in a fixed upper class where the power and responsibility of government were concentrated.

Historically, American culture has not only been preoccupied with improvement but also with each individual's equal responsibility for improving his own lot in life and his society. The two processes have been viewed by Americans as different aspects of the same thing. Americans have not seen any inherent contradiction between the needs of society and the needs of the individual because American society, in terms of its unique immigrant history, has always been made up of a collection of individuals. The idea of each person's equal responsibility for society does not seem to have been basic to the European conception of society or to the formative thinking of other cultures in the Americas.

Another European cultural idea that could not be transplanted to seventeenth-century America, though the Puritans of seventeenth-century New England attempted to transplant it, was the usual European connection between religious conformity and personal rights. Just as an abundance of developable land accessible to many individuals and a society taking its behavioral model from self-selected immigrants made the establishment of aristocratic privileges and differentiated manners unnatural to life in America, so also the multiplicity of religious practices in America produced by self-selecting emigration prevented any one church from considering itself superior to all others. This also had a freeing effect on the thinking of Americans.

At no time in the history of the United States has a state-supported church ever been a part of the national system of government. Even the idea of such a church cannot be taken seriously from an American cultural perspective because, in American culture, the form and content of religious belief are a matter of personal choice, not a matter of governmental decision. Even in New England, where a regional theocracy was established and perpetuated for two generations, the non-European nature of American society and the availability of land prevented the perpetuation of the ancient European cultural belief in and practice of a state religion. In Massachusetts in the seventeenth century, during the attempt to maintain a "one church–

one state" government that equated religious belief with political rights, laws were passed prohibiting church members from living beyond a specified distance from a place of regular worship and preaching. But such a law in America was impracticable. The Quakers of Pennsylvania also failed in their similar attempt to prevent their members from moving from one place to another without first obtaining permission from the elders of their meetings, as Quakers called their churches.

The first article in the Bill of Rights in the Constitution of the United States, prohibiting the establishment of a state religion, describes the historical reality of religious life in America, which was the absence of a national state church. The religious histories of Brazil, Canada, and Spanish America, however, resemble Europe, where an established connection between religious belief and government culturally existed and the religion of the king was historically the only religion tolerated or approved by the state. In French Canada, the archbishop of the state church was a member of the council of government, and during the period that Brazilian and Spanish American cultures were forming, penalties for failure to conform to the practices and religious beliefs of the church established by the state were enforced by government tribunals having simultaneous ecclesiastical and civil jurisdiction. Even in the twentieth century in the constitutions of some of the nations of Spanish America, only one religion has been tolerated.

The unique freedom of religion practiced in central North America was not an inheritance from England because no such freedom existed there at the time American culture was coming into being. England had Roman Catholicism as its state religion until 1534 and then established a new orthodoxy called the Church of England as the state religion. Failure to conform either before or after 1534 resulted in civil penalties.

European philosophers in the 1600s and 1700s wrote about the idea that human beings have equal worth by virtue of being born human beings. But during America's cultural formation in those centuries, belief in equality of birth was not enculturated behavior from generation to generation in Europe. And at the time of the first war between Britain and America (1775–83), social identities fixed by birth were as much in force in British culture as they were anywhere else in Europe, and hierarchical group privileges were as real as they were on the European mainland. Liberty and equality are, as European philosophers claimed, natural ideas for human beings to have because "commoners" and "peasants" in many nations of Europe who either "read very little" or "were unable to read"[17]—and therefore could

17. Terry Coleman, *Going to America* (Garden City, NY: Anchor/Doubleday, 1973), p. 18.

not have had their behavior influenced by reading philosophy—when given a chance to go to the one place in the Americas where no state church was established and where social distinctions were a matter of achievement rather than of birth, continuously left Europe on their own initiative for that place during the course of many generations, in the most massive migration to one destination in human history, despite the intimidating difficulties of getting there. Until the settlement of central North America in the early 1600s, there was no place in the world where middling and lower-class Europeans who believed in their equality with other human beings could form a new population and a new civilization based on that belief. One may well ask whether the idea of equality would ever have become credible and influential throughout the world, including the continent of Europe, if there had been no nation like America where, from generation to generation, unprecedented historical conditions allowed that idea to become enculturated through behavior among a large population.

The war fought in central North America between Britain and the disaffected European commoners and their descendants who populated that place does not deserve to be called a revolution. A revolution did, nonetheless, happen there. The real American revolution was the new cultural formation that took place in central North America between 1600 and 1750, which the war for independence from Europe expressed. Even brief reflection reveals how completely that cultural formation deserves to be termed a revolution. If, between 1775 and 1783 (the years of the military struggle called the American Revolution), there could have been in the British Isles a war that resulted in: (1) the permanent elimination of all royalty; (2) the severance of the connection between church and state; (3) the dissolution of the British House of Lords, where titled noblemen and prelates of the Church of England held seats for life; (4) the abolition of all titles of nobility (titles that were conferred until the nineteenth century in Brazil and Spanish America and down to the twentieth century in Canada); (5) the confiscation and dismemberment of the great estates of the lords temporal and the lords spiritual of the land, and the redistribution of this property to many small, independent farmers; (6) the widespread access by the poor of Britain to cheap, undeveloped, arable land; (7) the creation of conditions that brought about a cultural unity unprecedented in British history, which led Welsh speakers, Scotch speakers, and Irish speakers and their offspring to voluntarily give up their mother tongues and speak only English—would such a series of basic changes have represented a change in British thought and behavior sufficient to be written about in European history as a revolution? The question answers itself. Yet this was the set of changes and developments that characterized life in American society during the 150 years before the so-called American Revolution, though none of them took place violently or were mandated by any legislation.

The English nation was too deeply rooted in its European culture to tolerate for very long the so-called English Revolution in the 1600s, which attempted to abolish kingship; and after the passage of a few violent years of hereditary dictatorship by a military leader and his son who were not of legitimate royal blood, the son of the English monarch who had been beheaded was respectfully restored to his father's soiled throne. The only thing permanently changed by the execution of Charles I was the idea of the king's hereditary supremacy in his realms. The parliamentary representatives of the ecclesiastical establishment of England, the commercial interests, and the great landlords of the king's realms had group rights, it turned out, which were more important than the crown's, and were established in a bill of parliamentary supremacy in 1689. None of this changed English culture, however, which retained, until the early twentieth century, its cultural belief in and practice of the idea that the hereditary power of "lords" and adherence to a state-established church should confer political privileges. In America by the early part of the eighteenth century, the belief that men have an equal social worth regardless of who their parents were, the belief that individual achievement and competence should be the basis of social distinctions, and the belief that religion is a matter of individual conscience having no relation to government, had become enculturated through generations of behavior.

The American Revolution neither separated America from Britain nor marked the beginning of a new, non-European culture in America. Three thousand miles of ocean have always separated America from Europe, and by the time of the American Revolution in 1775, the behavior of five generations of self-respecting failures from many nations of Europe and their descendants born in America had already effected America's cultural separation from Europe. That so-called revolution—misnamed as all wars are that pretend in themselves to make a cultural difference—merely forced the government of Britain to recognize the reality of a revolutionary change of culture that had already occurred during the previous century and a half. It was the reality of America's already-existing cultural separation from Europe that determined the wording in the rebellious American declaration on July 4, 1776 that the "United Colonies *are,* and of Right ought to be *Free and Independent States*" (italics added).

It was not the philosophy of the constitutional monarchist John Locke, who earned his living as a functionary of the British aristocracy, that aroused Americans to join together to fight the British king's troops but a knowledge in their bones of belonging to a culture that was different from Europe's and that needed to be defended by force of arms. The bloodshed of the war against Britain made them and would-be emigrants from Europe more aware than they could have been before 1776 of the difference between American and European culture.

The opinion that the Constitution of the United States of America is merely a transatlantic variant of the British constitution is an Anglophilic fantasy. The idea of checks and balances in British constitutional history is not as culturally significant as what it has applied to: an elected "Commons," a monarchy, an aristocracy, and a state-established church whose bishops were appointed by the king as the head of both the state and the church. What was checked and balanced in the Constitution of the United States in the late eighteenth century was something altogether different.

As of 1790, America was a republic of voluntarily united states with a constitution written by a national convention elected for that purpose, a constitution that had also been debated and ratified in thirteen elected state constitutional conventions. Each branch of the national government under this written constitution was elected or, in the single instance of the Supreme Court, which was charged with upholding the Constitution (an institution that has never existed in Britain), chosen and empowered by the elected branches. No part of this government held office for life, though the nonelected justices of the Supreme Court served "during good behavior" (Article III, Section 1, U.S. Constitution). Britain, when the U.S. Constitution was written and ratified by fourteen bodies of elected delegates, was a country governed by an accumulation of statutes and political traditions that had been determined by historic conflicts over group rights among hereditary lords, hereditary kings, the "Lords Spiritual" of the hierarchy of a state church, and an elected but misnamed "House of Commons" (misnamed because in the eighteenth century a great many of its members, like the men who sat for life in the "House of Lords" without election, belonged to the hereditary aristocracy of Britain).

The thirteen British colonies of central North America took united action against Britain because they were linked by culture with each other in ways far more authentic and powerful than any link they had with Britain. Before the end of the 1600s, *American* was already in use as a term of self-reference by inhabitants of what was to become the United States. As George Washington and other American leaders came to realize in the 1770s: the power that lay with Americans in their conflict with the British empire was the power of a people already independent from Europe in their beliefs and behaviors.

Other cultures in the Americas have not had the conscious rivalry with

European culture that the United States has had. Outdoing Europe was how a society made up of self-selected immigrants and their descendants justified having turned their backs on Europe. Self-selecting emigrants went to America in expectation of opportunities to be grasped and with a determination to work hard to make the most of their opportunities. They dreamed of a personal future better than their past lives in Europe with its historical consciousness of the chronic oppressions of one group—a class, a nation—by another. Europe was rife with memories justifying vindictiveness and retribution; America, whose Stone Age starting point was a still-older historical consciousness than civilized Europe's, offered a sense of a new beginning free of that oppressive history. America was rife with the hopes generated by an equality of liberty because it had a new kind of population whose members had freely chosen to belong to it. The hopes of the self-selecting emigrants who populated America had been strong enough to compel them to give up their native cultural identities in pursuit of their hope for betterment. Once committed to that common pursuit by their embarkation from Europe, they and their cultural descendants in America were committed to justification through accomplishments.

Only by outproducing and generally outdoing Europe, by having more freedoms, more mobility, more opportunity, more food, more goods—by being more progressive—could they, together, as a culture deriving its beliefs and behavior from a population of middle- and lower-class seekers and strivers, prove the rightness of their ancestors' decisions to leave Europe for America. The desire to be progressive and to have tangible signs of success became a central concern of American culture. The idea of demonstrating to Europe the superiority of America by developing a general prosperity and making innovative improvements remained a piece of unfinished business in every generation of the cultural descendants of the self-selecting emigrants to America. No matter how good life might become in America, it could never be good enough for a culture whose ideas were shaped in fundamental ways by the hectic drive and restless dissatisfactions of a population descended mainly from disaffected Europeans, a culture committed to rapid, constant improvement of their new homeland. The very abundance of natural resources in central North America increased dissatisfaction by making it seem that realization of every individual's dream ought to be possible. The American expression "things could be better," though usually uttered with a sense of reasonable satisfaction with the way things are at the moment, is an index of the American cultural expectation of betterment. Having descended from ancestors who expected to improve their lives in America, Americans measure the present not by the past but by their culturally inherent feeling that things should be better.

The idea of society as made up of individuals who are responsible for both their own well-being and the general good of society is the demanding social model Americans have believed in from generation to generation, not a society made up of groups, some of which are theoretically supposed to know better than other groups what is good for society.

AMERICAN INDIVIDUALISM

Neither European culture nor European political models or traditions initiated the American cultural belief in the social importance of the individual. Nor did life in America make the millions of self-selecting emigrants who went to America individualists. The self-selecting emigrants who left Europe for America manifested their individualism by their emigration. When they got on the ships, they were already individualists. Before they ever sighted, from the rolling decks of their ships, the thin line of the low-lying coastal plain of central North America on the horizon, they were already individualists. The decision to go to America showed that these self-respecting failures placed a greater value on themselves and their own beliefs than they did on the cultural beliefs and native social bonds they abandoned in going to America.

The cultural ancestors of Americans were not Englishmen. They were self-selecting emigrants. They were people who rejected living in England or some other part of Europe in favor of participating in a new kind of society in America. Their individual acts of crossing the Atlantic cumulatively constituted a social revolution. The personal solution of the self-selecting emigrant to whatever discontent he felt in Europe was swifter than any attempt to reform European society could have been, more complete for him than any political revolution, and more dependable than pinning one's hopes of betterment on the benevolence of some ruling group or some patron. It was the lonely, personally revolutionary, individual solution of leaving one's ancestral homeland to seek a new kind of society and make a fresh start in life. The history of self-selecting emigration to America is the history of millions of individual revolutions against Europe. Collectively they produced a new kind of culture that has had an incalculable influence on the thinking and behavior of Europe and the rest of the world.

The greatest historical peculiarity of the American population and its most culturally significant feature is that it is the only large population in world history mainly descended from persons who individually chose to belong to it without having had to conform to some test of selection by blood or belief. That history of self-selection is the basis of American individualism. It would, therefore, be wrong to see the phenomenon called the American frontier as the origin of American individualism. A frontier requires self-reliance to be an already-developed or at least latent and readily developable trait in the character of those who move to it. Moreover, if one may judge from life in the wide-open spaces of Wyoming and Montana today—where to pass by a stranger in need is unthinkable—life in a thinly populated region fosters friendliness, cooperation, and mutual helpfulness as well as self-reliance. When a person has only a few neighbors, even if they live miles away, he is more likely to be aware of them and have a more solicitous feeling for their needs and welfare than is possible to have for most of one's fellow residents in a modern city, simply because it is beyond the capacity of human feeling to respond as a neighbor to the millions of persons one lives among in a big city.

In a densely populated place, tolerance of the individual quirks of those around one may be greater than in a place with a small population, but so is indifference to most of those one sees daily, unless something else than mere proximity creates a sense of responsibility toward them. In thinly populated settings, there are no permanent strangers. Proximity alone constitutes an obligation, a relationship, a mutual responsibility, a bond of community, no matter how seldom one actually sees one's neighbors. The rural, small-town distribution of population, which characterized America during the two formative centuries of its culture, promoted a sense of neighborly obligation, civic responsibility, and abhorrence of any behavior that deviated from these values. Although the conditions of the seventeenth and eighteenth centuries that gave rise to those cultural belief-behaviors have changed, cultural inertia (the principle that a culture once formed tends to persist in that form) has perpetuated those belief-behaviors to the present.

In recent decades, however, it sometimes seems that self-responsibility is no longer bonded with social responsibility in American culture. Indeed, in the late twentieth century, it sometimes seems that the idea of the general welfare, as represented by collective individual responsibility for society, has degenerated into single-minded special-interest groups that represent organized demands on government to deliver what is supposedly due from society to various groups. This is the old European idea of group privilege, without noblesse oblige. It even sometimes seems that the only source of social responsibility is the national government, which necessarily lacks the vital spirit of human welfare because it deals with statistical abstractions.

Worse than this abstraction of people into statistical, sociological categories is the simple fact that the more the national government is empowered to provide to people, the more it can take away from them; hence, the more it controls them, rather than the people controlling it.

The basic imperatives of life in America in the seventeenth, eighteenth, and nineteenth centuries kept the individualism of self-selected immigrants from becoming anarchistic. The effort to civilize and progressively improve upon the transformable Stone Age wilderness of central North America required effective teamwork and cooperation. Conditions in America then were fundamentally conducive to the recognition that voluntary group efforts to accomplish general social, economic, and political goals were of benefit to all individuals; and this idea became one of the belief-behaviors of American culture. Discontent in Europe (not the rigors of the American frontier) was the source of American individualism; America itself was the place where self-interest gave every member of society an equal and conscious sense of responsibility for the constitution of society and the general welfare. Given the lack of any hierarchically responsible ruling class in America, everyone became socially responsible. There could be no society to benefit anyone without each individual putting restraints to his personal behavior. The way the Constitution of the United States was written and ratified by elected representatives demonstrates the general recognition of this collective social responsibility. The Constitution has endured as the fundamental law of the United States because it was an act of self-interest for all Americans to "form a more perfect Union, establish Justice, insure domestic Tranquillity, provide for the common defence, promote the general Welfare, and secure the Blessings of Liberty" for themselves and their posterity. The government-selected European populations of Brazil, Canada, and Spanish America felt no personal responsibility for the kind of society they belonged to. As in Europe, government in these societies was decided by ruling groups who believed that only they had the interests and the background to qualify as rulers. Birth more often than not determined one's social status and obligations in those cultures; and a person's primary loyalties were not so much to oneself and to society as a whole—because "the authorities" were responsible for society—but to one's family or whatever other group within society one felt most attached to by birth.

In the great task of developing a civilization from the Stone Age of central North America that would rival and surpass the civilization of Europe, American individualism became highly energized by the congruence between the ambitions of individuals and the need to create a civilization. The matter of one's birth, the question of one's parentage, had little relevance in a society voluntarily constituted by individuals from many nations and religious faiths. What has mattered historically in America, and mattered a great deal, has not been where or of whom you were born, but what you could do. American society has been fluid in a way that European society and the more European-oriented societies of the Americas have never been because American society has historically been committed to satisfying the aspirations of individuals. The social rigidities that historically pertained in Brazil's predominantly slave society and in Spanish America's predominately peon society or between Canada's polarized French-speaking and English-speaking groups did not pertain in the cultural formation of the United States of America.

European culture arose from a history of fiercely competing groups and a continentwide stratification of ruling classes legitimized as levels of "noble" versus "common" birth. Because of these characteristics, social change in Europe has been either slow or convulsive. In American social history, however, change has been normative and rapid from the beginning. Radical change, a fresh start in life, was the whole purpose of the ancestral crossing of the Atlantic to live in America. And change became a cultural expectation, a statistically measurable annual result, in a burgeoning society of hard-working individualists who were seeking self-improvement in voluntary cooperation with each other. Whether a self-selecting emigrant to America happened to be a Greek shoemaker who emigrated in the 1930s, an unskilled Irishwoman in the 1850s, an indentured servant from Germany in the 1720s, or a farmer out of England in the 1630s, they had in common a belief in self-responsibility and the equality of liberty. It was this conformity—the result of a collective similarity of individual character, which manifested itself in their mutual rejection of Europe and attraction to America—that made them the progenitors of a new, non-European cultural formation.

Just as the memory of ancestral wandering in search of a new homeland provided a basis of cultural identity for Jews and for tribes whose migrations into and within Europe led to the configuration of nations that we see in Europe today, so, too, has the ancestral journey across the Atlantic been fundamental to American culture and the American sense of history. But, unlike the ancient migrations just mentioned, the ancestral migration that has been fundamental to America's distinctive cultural formation has been an individual, not a group, journey. This centuries-long migration of self-selecting individuals and their families to the United States has been the most massive continuous movement of human beings to one place in the history of mankind: somewhere between "well over 45 million people" and "close to 50 million."[18]

The group migration, group coherence, and group discipline that the history of seventeenth-century New England Puritanism manifests has had no decisive influence on the population and cultural formation of America. It was a regional phenomenon that disappeared as a cultural behavior in the third generation of the New England settlement. Other organized groups that occasionally emigrated to America as such likewise usually dissipated within a generation or two after their arrival in America in the general mélange of free-forming, voluntary associations and freewheeling mobility that the ever-expanding and opportunity-rich space of America fostered. Historically, conditions of life in America have required innovation and individual initiative rather than programmatic utopian ideologies and group mentalities. The rare immigrant group that has retained its identity unchanged over time in America, such as the Amish, has done so through self-imposed apartheid. Such groups have had no formative influence on American cultural behavior.

"The essential fact about immigrant groups in America is their instability," the historian of immigration John Higham has written. "They undergo attrition unless their cohesiveness is reinforced by powerful religious or racial peculiarities, as in the case of the Jews or the Chinese; and even then the difference in assimilation may be one of tempo or degree. In the typical process of ethnic development an increasing proportion of every generation after the first marries outside the group and ceases to be identified with it. A hard core, freshened by new immigration, can persist indefinitely. Yet the importance of the group as an ethnic minority declines sharply in the third generation and after."[19] No other country in the world's history has so freely attracted so many persons from so many different countries of the world and formed a population that senses itself to be one people. The unity of the American people and the enduring strength of American political institutions have historically derived from the mutual recognition by diverse individuals of their cultural status as believers in equal liberty, which their emigration to America or their ancestors' emigra-

18. Richard A. Easterlin, "Economic and Social Characteristics of the Immigrants," in *Immigration: Dimensions of Ethnicity,* ed. Stephan Thernstrom (Cambridge: Harvard University Press, 1982), p. 1; R. A. Burchell and Eric Homberger, "The Immigrant Experience," in *Introduction to American Studies,* eds. Malcom Bradbury and Howard Temperley (London and New York: Longman, 1981), p. 127.

19. John Higham, "Immigration," in *A Comparative Approach to American History,* ed. C. Vann Woodward (New York: Basic Books, 1968), p. 103.

tion conferred on them, and from their mutual willingness to cooperate freely with one another on that basis.

The many possibilities in America of changing places of residence and occupations—and in some ways the cultural imperative to do so in order to "get ahead"—comprise one of the principal causes of the usual breakdown of group allegiance in most of the few groups that have emigrated to America with the idea of retaining their group identity from generation to generation. The leaders of the Puritan church-state of seventeenth-century Massachusetts, as already mentioned, recognized very early the adverse effect of American conditions on their desire to maintain a theocracy in Massachusetts and passed laws restricting members of their society from living far from the authority of their ministers—all to no avail. The authoritarian Quakers also felt the need to require their members to remain under the influence of their leaders and mandated that any Quaker who wished to remain a Quaker had to obtain permission from his church to change his place of residence or to marry. And Quakerism steadily lost influence in Pennsylvania because such rules proved impossible to maintain, given their basic incompatibility with the natural freedom of movement and choice in America.

During the first three centuries of American cultural history, when the Atlantic Ocean was a barrier presenting many hazards, the passage to America was a test of one's fitness to be an American. Crossing the ocean barrier by choice was a shared heroic experience that provided an ancestral basis for American identity and unity apart from the question of the place of birth or the religion of one's European ancestors. It was a shared memory of a rite of ancestral initiation into American society. Regardless of where one's ancestors may have come from or the language they used or the religion they may have had, the decision to come to America bound them together and gave them something in common that transcended their particular origins and reasons for coming. The sense of that still continuing migration of individuals is ingrained in the American mind as a folk experience. It is the history that is known and shared by the American people despite any passage of time that may have obliterated factual information about the names and origins of one's self-selected immigrant ancestors. The knowledge that one must have had such ancestors is a known heritage for an overwhelming proportion of Americans. Those who have learned the names and places of origin of immigrants from whom they descend, particularly if from the first or second century of America's settlement, regardless of how humble those ancestors were, feel a particular pride in such knowledge. But such information really does not matter. The folk memory of having had self-selected immigrant ancestors is what matters and goes deeper than the heterogenous ethnic variety that has always existed and will always exist in American culture.

The self-selecting cultural ancestors of Americans were not interested in changing Europe. They wanted to change their own lives by leaving Europe. The frequent movements of their descendants within American space and their frequent changes of occupation represent a cultural behavior that continues to reflect the beliefs of the ancestors who wanted to start life over in a new place. The Atlantic crossing was described by one American writer in the early nineteenth century in these terms:

> The vast space of waters that separates the [eastern and western] hemispheres is like a blank page of existence. There is no gradual transition, by which, as in Europe, the features and population of one country blend almost imperceptibly with those of another. From the moment you lose sight of the land you have left, all is vacancy until you step on the opposite shore, and are launched at once into the bustle and novelties of another world.[20]

The ancestral self selecting emigrants, whose beliefs and behavior led to the formation of American culture, all had that once-in-a-lifetime, revolutionary experience of voyaging to another world.

---

20. Opening paragraph of Washington Irving, "The Voyage," *The Sketch Book of Geoffrey Crayon* (1819), ed. Haskell Springer (Boston: Twayne, 1978).

CHAPTER

3

THE FREEDOM OF "OTHER PERSONS"

America's cultural formation has resulted from a rapidly growing population of self-selected European immigrants and their descendants continuously transforming, unifying, and developing within self-imposed geographic limits, a continental-size Stone Age wilderness of fabulous potential richness during the seventeenth, eighteenth, nineteenth, and twentieth centuries. From the earliest times, however, American culture has also included the idea of "other persons." The term appears in the Constitution of the United States in reference to the most numerous of these historical groups whose origins and experiences have differed in significant ways from those of the great proportion of Americans.

None of these "other persons" has had a European immigrant ancestry. To them such historical beliefs of American culture as the equality of individual worth, openness of opportunity, free pursuit of happiness, self-responsibility, and undifferentiated personal rights have not applied. In some cases "other persons" have even been excluded from the right to receive wages for their labor and have been denied the right to move at will within American space. They have been regarded as belonging to perpetual classes constituted by birth because, in all cases, the mark of being "other persons" has been dark skin color, which is a matter of birth not of individual performance. In being regarded as members of a perpetual class constituted by birth, rather than in being judged as individuals on the basis of their performance, these Americans experienced the most oppressive feature of their lives: being treated as persons without a right to pursue happiness on terms of equal liberty with every other American.

The idea of "other persons" has had a prominence out of proportion to the number of such persons in American history, probably because the idea of "other persons" stands out as an exception to the primary beliefs of American culture and because so much of the social violence and conflict in America (most notably the Civil War) has stemmed from this one idea— something that is important to the writing of history because history seems often to be conceived of as a record of social violence and conflict. The idea of "other persons" has worked to the detriment of American culture by distorting the free, individual development of too many Americans from generation to generation. Without the distractions of human energy it has occasioned, the progressive development of central North America by Americans would have undoubtedly proceeded at an even more astonishing rate than it did, and the newness of American culture in comparison with the cultures of Europe, Brazil, Spanish America, and Canada would have been even more pronounced than it has been. But belief in the idea that the rights of any person should be those of all persons has been as vigorous in American culture as belief in the idea of "other persons." Exclusionary class thinking and granting special privileges according to categorical restrictions have been consistently opposed in American cultural history, and in this century fewer and fewer Americans have been regarded as "other persons." In the present generation American culture may be said to be on its way to finally eliminating the idea of "other persons" from its set of beliefs.

FROM MAJORITY TO MINORITY

Indian Americans are the only Americans having a cultural history in America apart from and earlier than the new culture that began forming in what is now the eastern United States in the 1600s. The formation of that new culture impaired belief among Indian Americans in the superiority of their cultures; and in its physical effects, the cultural formation of the United States separated Indian Americans from the continuum that had given them behavioral vitality as Indian Americans. Before the 1600s in Stone Age North America, many Indian American cultures were transmitted by the behavior of culturally confident peoples who occupied and could sovereignly defend their territories against each other. In the two centuries between the early 1600s and the early 1800s, the wilderness that had existed in the Atlantic coastal plain and the mountains of the eastern United States was progressively replaced by the civilized structures created by self-selecting European emigrants and their American-born descendants. During these centuries, with some allowance for exceptions, Indian American cultures in this region were drastically reduced, became incompletely practiced traditions rather than the cultural entities they had been, or vanished altogether. With the elimination of the Stone Age wilderness, the sustaining physical basis for the beliefs and behavior of Indian American cultures was removed.

Where the new cultural formation had contact with Indian cultures, the Indian cultures were diluted. The superior durability and utility of some even second-rate goods of European manufacture (though they had no superior aesthetic value) planted seeds of doubt in the minds of Indian Americans about the superiority of their cultures. Whenever they entered into trade for European firearms, European cloth, or European domestic implements in preference to the implements, clothing, and arms of their own Stone Age culture, Indian Americans compromised the integrity of their cultural independence, which in turn led to changes in their thinking about themselves. When European immigrants and their descendants attained military superiority, through their better military equipment, burgeoning population, and much greater unity, this was impressive to cultures in which achievement in battle was often considered a sign of superiority. The diseases that entered North America with European settlement created yet another, more powerful impression of European superiority because these new diseases seemed to discriminate against Indian survival by mysteriously devastating their numbers while leaving white populations comparatively intact. The greater activeness of white settlers, who were intent on transforming the wilderness on a large scale—in comparison to the behavior of Indian Americans, who were at home in the wilderness and felt no compulsion to alter it in any radical way—also conveyed a sense of change that increased the activity of the whites and made Indian Americans wonder about the power of men who could desecrate nature as God created it without bringing down on themselves divine punishments.

Once established, the process of transforming the Stone Age seemed to become irresistible. The destruction of forests, the drainage of wetlands, the plowing of prairies, the more and more heavily trafficked avenues of communication all made wild game less plentiful in the former hunting grounds of Indians adjacent to these activities. Wherever a scarcity of game occurred, the cultural independence of Indian Americans was compromised. Whenever Indian American tribes moved away from the white man's towns, farms, and roads in search of better supplies of the animals that had afforded basic materials to them, they left vacant or sparsely populated lands, which the white men then felt justified in occupying for that very reason, thus beginning a new cycle of transformation, scarcity of wild animals, and further retreat by Indian Americans who lived adjacent to the newly transformed lands. Where Indian American military resistance to transformation of the wilderness was attempted, the population pressure of the whites—which was constantly heightened by the arrival of more and more immigrants from Europe and an exceptionally high American birthrate—proved, in combination with the declining numbers of Indians, decisive.

It was, however, the power and the willingness of the self-selected immigrants and their American-born descendants to destroy the wilderness and replace it with something else that essentially brought on the decline of American Indian culture. Whether effected by the transformation of the wilderness or by military force, every retreat by Indian Americans was not only a tactical defeat, resulting in further loss of land control and sovereignty, but also a strategic cultural demoralization, resulting in a further lessening of the will to resist the advance of the new culture. That advance across the entire central part of the continent came to be seen as irresistible both by those making it and those wishing to halt it.

In little more than two hundred years after the first permanent European settlements along the Atlantic coastal plain of North America, only a few Indian Americans remained, in greatly reduced circumstances, east of the Mississippi River. They were usually tolerated on "reservations" of land so constricted that the practice of their ancient cultures was no longer possible. Most members of the eastern tribes had died in battle or succumbed to epidemics or fled westward of their own accord or been removed to "reservation" lands west of the Mississippi by military force. Few tribes remained where they had been and in their previous condition. The idea of Indian Americans as "other persons" had become so fixed in the expanding new culture by the early 1800s that even when one surviving eastern tribe, the Cherokee, manifested a definite aptitude for adopting basic features of American culture, including a constitution modeled on that of the United States and a written language in an alphabet imparted by their great cultural leader Sequoya (1766?–1843), for whom the giant trees of California are named, they and other civilized tribes were nonetheless forcibly removed from their ancestral lands to the trans-Mississippi West. The impetus of transformation of the Stone Age wilderness was so strong by the middle of the nineteenth century that not even the war between the states (1861–65) could interrupt it. By the beginning of the twentieth century, the initial transformation of the Stone Age throughout central North America was virtually complete, from ocean to ocean, and further developments were continuing at an accelerating rate. Outside of Alaska, the aboriginal behavior of most Indian cultures by 1900 was no longer practicable within the territory of the United States. Nor could its authenticity have been restored without returning America to the condition it had had at the time of the first European settlement.

The U.S. Supreme Court ruled in 1831 that title to North American lands the government of the United States had purchased from European powers was "independent of [the] will" of whatever Indian Americans might actually be occupying those lands. This judgment (*Cherokee Nation v. Georgia*) declared Indian American tribes to be "domestic dependent nations . . . so completely under the sovereignty and dominion of the United States" that any attempt on the part of any other nation to acquire lands from them or to "form a political connection with them" would be regarded by the United States as "an act of hostility." Being in this peculiar condition of "domestic dependent nations" without effective sovereignty made Indian Americans wards of the federal government, with no final responsibility for their own well-being or circumstances. Despite the fact that Indians were made citizens of the United States in 1924, wardship continues to this day to be, as it has been since 1831, the distinguishing characteristic of Indian Americans as "other persons"—insofar as they indeed remain in that status in the latter twentieth century.

In the 1980 U.S. Census, 1,361,869 Americans (six-tenths of 1 percent of the 1980 American population) identified themselves as Indian Americans. Another 56,276 identified themselves as Eskimos and Aleuts. Of these Americans, only a little more than half in 1981 were living on reservations, which comprise about 2 percent of the area of the United States.

Dependence on the federal government for payments of money, for distribution of goods (such as food, clothing, and tools), and for such basic services as education and health care is, and has been, the chief sign of the drastic alteration of Indian American culture and of the status of many Indian Americans as "other persons." More and more, however, Indian Americans seem willing to accept American culture and responsibility for themselves. But, as long as the unique status and special treatment of Indian Americans as members of "domestic dependent nations" continue, Indian American self-respect is unlikely to develop fully. As long as Indian Americans remain government wards, the lives of a significant proportion of them will remain comparatively depressed.

IMMIGRANTS FROM WITHIN

The terms *black Americans* and *American blacks* have different meanings. The latter term suggests that Americans who have black skins belong to some larger black-skinned culture. That is not the case. When an organization was founded during the second decade of the nineteenth century to resettle free black Americans in Africa, no enthusiasm developed on the part of the free black Americans for the help that was offered. From 1817, when the American Colonization Society was founded, to the beginning of the Civil War in 1861, only about twelve thousand persons accepted the Society's offer of resettlement in Africa, though as early as 1810 there were approximately one hundred thousand free black Americans in just the southern states of the United States. Neither was there any appreciable movement to Africa among black Americans in the latter half of the nineteenth century after the Civil War had made freemen of every enslaved descendant of Africans in America. In Brazil, on the other hand, where Africans had formed the predominate social class, and not, as in the United States, a small though significant proportion of the population, the situation was fundamentally different. Both black slaves and black freemen in Brazil maintained a close identity with African culture. Even before the final abolition of slavery there, many Brazilian slaves who became freemen sought and found ways to return to Africa, and for twenty years after slavery was abolished in 1888, the return of blacks to Africa from Brazil was so constant that a regular steamship line was profitably maintained between Bahia and West Africa to restore blacks to the continent of their ancestors and to bring back to Brazil food and other products of West Africa which were in great demand in Brazil.[1]

Several historical facts might be adduced to account for this difference. However, the primary reason African culture remained strong and cohesive in Brazil, but not in the United States, was because forced African emigrants and their descendants constituted the great proportion of the Brazilian population. It is estimated that, during the three hundred years of the Atlantic slave trade, 50 percent of the millions of forced African emigrants went to the Caribbean islands belonging to Spain, France, and Britain; 38 percent were landed in Brazil; and only 6 percent were sent to what is now the United States (the same proportion as went to the Caribbean islands belonging to Holland and Denmark). Not only did more Africans over an appreciably longer time go to Brazil, as well as to Spain's American empire, than went to the United States but those who went to Brazil were permitted to retain their African languages. In the United States, on the other hand, the forced emigrants from Africa were made to stop speaking their native languages and adopt English. But in Brazil the European population that constituted its ruling class was a minority population too small to prevent

---

1. Carl N. Degler, *Neither Black Nor White: Slavery and Race Relations in Brazil and the United States* (New York: Macmillan, 1971), p. 60.

the continuation of African languages in their midst. This fact of Portuguese minority in Brazil's demographic history has been basic to Brazil's cultural formation. It was a fact that necessitated greater tolerance of African culture and a generally different attitude toward slaves than the situation in the United States required. In the United States, European immigrants and their descendants historically outnumbered blacks by a great margin and even a small amount of African blood made one "black." In Brazil, with its great black population, the situation was opposite. There, a small amount of European blood made one "white."

Back-to-Africa appeals have also been made to black Americans in the twentieth century; and they also, like the appeals to go back to Africa in the nineteenth century, have had little effect in inducing black Americans to resettle in Africa. Evidently black Americans are affected by African culture in much the same way that white Americans are affected by European culture: they feel some curiosity and some admiration for it, but proportionately few have wanted to resettle in their ancestors' homelands. Black Americans are Americans who happen to be black. They belong to no other culture than that of their birth. They are Afro-Americans in a more generalized sense than some Americans are nostalgically Italian Americans, Polish Americans, or Irish Americans. Because forced African emigration to the United States virtually ceased around the year 1800, most black Americans in fact have had more of their ancestors born in the United States than most white Americans have.

The peculiar experience of Indian Americans has been to suffer cultural diminution in their homeland, but black Americans have suffered the most peculiar institution in American history: 250 years of slavery. (The term "other persons" is a euphemism for slaves in the U.S. Constitution.) Unlike Indian Americans, black Americans have been "other persons" within rather than apart from American society. They formed families and were workers inside American society from the time of the earliest settlements on the Atlantic coastal plain. But black Americans could not be inside American culture until they were freemen and free in their own minds, and until they became regarded in the minds of white Americans as having an inherently equal right to liberty with other Americans.

Black Americans have individually and collectively been making this psychological immigration to America since before the American Revolution. Five thousand black Americans served in that war as American soldiers, and those among them who were slaves earned their freedom from slavery by doing so. In the early 1800s, when slavery remained an institution in only the southern part of the United States, tens of thousands of black American slaves won their freedom by running away to the free states of the American North and to Canada. And during the years of slavery in the North as well as the South, tens of thousands more, against great odds, acquired skills that allowed them to keep for themselves a portion of the wages they earned for their masters as skilled workers, thereby making it possible to save money to buy themselves out of slavery. Once having purchased their own freedom, ex-slaves were then in a position to devote all of their skill, instead of just a portion of it, to earning money to gain the freedom of some person whom they loved who still suffered enslavement. Freedom and prosperity have thus been as strongly associated in the cultural thinking of the descendants of the men and women who were forced to come to the United States from Africa as they have been in the cultural thinking of the descendants of the immigrants from Europe who chose to come to America.

During the years of the American Civil War, there was no rising of black American slaves in the southern states of America, but two hundred thousand runaway black American slaves and black American freemen rebelled against slavery by joining the armies of the North to fight for the freedom of enslaved black Americans. Even during the nadir of disenfranchisement, abusive unfairness, terrorism, and pathological hatred of black Americans by some white Americans (perhaps for having "caused" the bloodshed of the Civil War)—a condition that lasted from the 1870s through the first decade of the twentieth century in many places and in every region of the United States and included three thousand lynchings of black men and women, often accompanied by atrocious torture, dismemberment, burning alive, and mob frenzies by white men and women—the psychological immigration of black Americans to the land of their birth nonetheless continued. Service in the two world wars of the present century and innumerable examples of personal achievement by ordinary black Americans have finally given the lie forever to the cultural idea of black Americans as "other persons." In the middle of the twentieth century, the self-respect of black Americans has begun to be matched by respect from their fellow white Americans.

The historical experience of black Americans has been similar to the experience of white Americans, but so different in degree as to give an appearance of being a different kind of experience. Nevertheless, basic similarities are evident. The voyage from Africa to America involved the same trauma of leaving one's familiar bearings behind that self-selecting European emigrants underwent in their Atlantic crossing but was an infinitely more shocking experience because the African emigrants did not will it in expectation of a better life. Without any personal motive whatever for making the journey, and confused or ignorant about the true purpose of the Atlantic crossing and the fate that lay at their journey's end on another continent, the fear of the unknown was infinitely greater among African emigrants to America's shores than it was for self-selecting European emigrants. The Atlantic passage itself involved the same sickness, squalor, and death for Africans that European emigrants faced in the seventeenth, eighteenth, and nineteenth centuries, but was infinitely worse in degree for the forced African emigrant who was crammed for weeks or months in a prone position in nearly suffocating, mournful, excremental darkness, weighed down by heavy irons that could chafe their way through bone as well as skin. Fed and kenneled on the journey to America the way an animal might be, by men of a different color and language whose brutalizing practices aboard the "floating coffins" they manned made them seem pale devils with no other purpose than to inflict pain and death on black men, the Africans landed in America after such a voyage in such a state of spiritual, mental, and bodily trauma that some of them were permanently dispirited and physically impaired. Their relief at leaving the sea and gaining land was followed by the trauma of realizing that, although the afflictions of their nightmare passage from Africa to America had ended, a lifetime of slavery was just beginning. It was at this point that the dream of freedom began among the strongest and bravest Africans to survive the Atlantic crossing.

This dream in the minds of slaves who refused to accept their enslavement as a permanent condition was the same kind of dream that motivated self-respecting failures to leave Europe for America. But instead of deciding to cross an oceanic barrier to a land of promise, the most daring spirits among the forced emigrants from Africa and their American-born descendants had to face the much more problematic decision to cross a barrier that existed in their own minds and the minds of white Americans, which the self-selecting emigrants from Europe and their descendants had never had to face.

These extraordinarily strong, extraordinarily self-respecting persons— these slaves who refused to accept their enslavement as a permanent condition—were often discouraged by their fellow slaves because their persistent efforts to attain the dignity of freedom and equality of opportunity invariably caused trouble. They were resented or feared by less strong-willed black Americans as well as by white Americans who believed in the cultural idea of "other persons." From generation to generation, however, the spiritual and mental resilience of such exceptional individuals among black Americans inspired more and more of their fellow sufferers in the condition of "other persons" to have faith in themselves, to dream of freedom and equality of opportunity, and to think and behave in terms of self-responsibility. In a performance-oriented culture that valued self-responsibility, only self-responsible performances could finally suffice, when practiced by enough black Americans over successive generations, to halt and reverse the cultural idea that black Americans were racially unfit for participation in American culture. It has been neither through the enactment of laws recognizing their equal right to liberty nor through the encouragement of some white Americans that more and more black Americans over the generations have won their birthright as Americans and overcome the idea of "other persons." Rather, it has been through their own faith in themselves and in the beliefs of American culture and through the manifestation of that faith and that belief in their behavior during a long period of adversity.

Movement is culturally associated with freedom in the minds of Americans who descend from the self-selecting European emigrants who crossed the Atlantic. So, too, have freedom and movement been associated in the minds of black Americans. The first self-determined movements by the first black Americans were naturally attempts to escape from slavery by running away. And during the closing campaigns of the Civil War, when the armies of the North invaded the deep South and freed slaves, hordes of these newly freed men and women took to wandering the roads of the region for no other reason than to prove whether they were indeed truly free and to taste at last the sweet reality of that most basic of American freedoms: the open road. During the next generation and a half (1865–1910), movement continued within the South where nine out of ten black Americans then lived. It consisted of poor black farm workers moving into southern urban areas. Fifty years after emancipation, the same proportions of southern black Americans lived in urban and rural areas as southern white Americans, whereas before emancipation southern blacks had been heavily concentrated in rural areas.

Though comparatively small, significant movements of black Americans out of the South to other regions of the United States also took place in the first decades after the Civil War. These also were movements mainly to cities, where opportunities for self-improvement were greater than they were in either the rural or the urban areas of the South. Like the newly arrived nineteenth-century immigrants from Europe, southern black Americans could expect to find in northern and western cities of the United States companionship and support in enclaves of persons like themselves who were making the cultural transition to a self-determined way of life. Sometimes, however, like native white Americans in their attitudes toward recent arrivals from Europe, the old, settled populations of black Americans in New York and Philadelphia (some of whose ancestors had been in those cities since before the Revolution) were hostile to the rural, uncouth black Americans who moved north in search of happiness. They resented the increased competition for jobs these newcomers posed, just as the descendants of these late-nineteenth century black American migrants would later, in the twentieth century, resent the competition of black, Spanish-speaking emigrants to America from the Caribbean, whom they stigmatized as "monkey-chasers" and "spics." As with self-selecting emigrants from Europe, most of the black Americans who constituted this interregional movement from the South to the North and the West after the Civil War were young and unmarried persons. Like their counterparts from Europe, these American-born migratory pursuers of freedom wrote letters home to the South describing the opportunities they had found by moving north and west and bragging of their successes. Also like the immigrants from Europe, they often sent job information and ticket money to friends and relatives still in the South, so that they, too, could improve their lives by migrating.

Not until four decades after the Civil War had ended, however, did a major interregional movement of black Americans begin. Then, in a single decade, 1910 to 1920, one million black Americans left the South: three-quarters of them for the North; one-quarter for the West. By 1950, nearly one out of every three black Americans was living in a state of the United States other than the one in which he or she had been born, and one-fifth of all black Americans were living outside the region of their birth. Since the end of World War II, an average of 5 percent of black Americans (as compared to 6 percent of white Americans) have migrated every year. Like white Americans, black Americans living in the north and north-central regions of the United States have recently begun to move to the South in large numbers; and between 1970 and 1975, for the first time, the number of black Americans moving into the South exceeded the number moving out of the South. As much as anything else, this phenomenon signifies that the idea of "other persons" no longer determines the cultural behavior of black Americans. Now these Americans freely occupy all of American space.[2]

The enslavement of Africans and their American-born descendants was peculiar in American culture because it was the only institution in American society based on the idea of a permanent class defined by birth. (Indian Americans were also, in a few instances, enslaved; and surprisingly, both black and Indian Americans, in some instances, became owners of black and Indian slaves.) It would be more accurate, however, to say that the

2. The information in this chapter on the historical movement of black Americans has been derived from Daniel M. Johnson and Rex R. Campbell, *Black Migration in America: A Social Demographic History* (Durham, NC: Duke University Press, 1981).

institution of slavery in American was founded on the *idea,* rather than on the reality, of differences in skin color because in much of America, well into the twentieth century, a person might be considered "black" if one of his or her ancestors to the third, fourth, or even the fifth generation were known to have been black—no matter how *actually white* that person's skin color might be. The European cultural idea that one's bloodlines defined one's social status and privileges thus followed the self-selecting emigrants across the Atlantic and took root in this limited, peculiar way in America, and it had a limited but pernicious, centuries-long duration as a cultural behavior within the non-European cultural formation that the behavior of self-selected immigrants established in central North America.

The idea of "other persons," consigned by birth to a permanent underling status, contradicted American cultural beliefs that individual performance determined one's social status and that no one should have privileges based on their parentage. The fact that the social status of "other persons" had no relation to their individual achievements was the special horror of their position in a culture whose beliefs put a high value on "getting ahead" and "doing the job right."

The psychological immigration of black Americans to America, led by the example of the behavior of strong-minded visionaries from generation to generation, has been accomplished by continuous efforts to overcome the heritage of passivity that eight generations of enslavement bequeathed. Every slave could see that his or her efforts primarily benefited someone else. Only slaves of extraordinary imagination, capacity for hope, and courage could see any reason to excel at their work and to take diligent advantage of the slight personal rewards that the slave system necessarily allowed to make it economically productive. Such persons were the first black Americans to stop being "other persons." The example of their behavior became more credible when the freeing of the four million slaves in America in the 1860s sent a wave of hopeful jubilation surging through the black population of America. But a cultural mentality eight generations old is not instantly overcome. Despite the emancipation of slaves between 1863 and 1865, the idea of "other persons" still applied to most black Americans for another two generations in the way they were regarded by most white Americans.

The idea of "other persons" had a vicious closedness that made it especially tenacious and difficult to remove from American culture: white Americans could not see black Americans as equals unless they performed like equals, and the mentality ingrained by slavery had not accustomed the majority of black Americans to believe in themselves as capable of competing with their fellow white Americans. In the mind-set of American culture in the late 1860s black Americans were "other persons" regardless of the Emancipation Proclamation or amendments to the Constitution of the United States, and two generations later, in the 1920s, black Americans were still "other persons" to most white Americans. But by then, the idea had been weakened by the respectable performances of black Americans in many walks of life.

For slaves, the decisions about the jobs they would perform, the amount and quality of their food, their clothing, their housing, their education (if any), their old-age retirement, and their health care were made by their owners. The condition of a slave is the condition of complete welfare dependency. Even after the abolition of slavery in the United States, the idea lingered on that a black American was not like other Americans because he must be taken care of by some responsible person with the resources to do so or by some special system. It has historically been this Old World, aristocratic paternalism from which black Americans have psychologically emigrated.

"OTHER PERSONS" BY CHOICE

Mexican Americans have a more mixed cultural history than that of any other American group. Like most Americans, their ancestors have been for the most part self-selecting emigrants to America. But Mexican Americans also have a few ancestors who did not emigrate to the United States because they were living in territories conquered by American armies. And Mexican Americans are the only Americans (except for French-Canadian Americans) who have ancestors who emigrated to the United States from a geographically contiguous culture having a different language than the United States. They have generally remained a self-conscious group concentrated in the southwestern region of the United States bordering the culture of Mexico. Furthermore, Mexican Americans have been the only large group of Americans who commonly retain from generation to generation in the United States the language of their non-English-speaking ancestors and commonly learn English as a second language. Though Mexican Americans, like Indian Americans and black Americans, have behaved as loyal citizens of the United States, some of them have not manifested the same desire of black Americans or of the self-selected European immigrants to embrace American culture completely. In each generation of Mexican Americans born in the United States, some have been "other persons" by preference.

Historically, many Mexican Americans have been neither primarily Mexican nor primarily American in culture. Rather, they have attempted to embrace both cultures simultaneously. That attempt has, of course, been unsuccessful not only because the ideas of American culture are especially antithetical to a class of "other persons" constituted by preference but also because the nature of culture—any culture—inherently opposes simultaneous acceptance of another culture. The attempt to do so has persisted, however, among Mexican Americans because at the beginning of their history as Americans in the nineteenth century, following America's war with Mexico, they believed that they had a right to be "other persons" in the United States if they chose to be, a belief that originated in the knowledge of Mexican Americans that persons of European descent from Mexico had settled in what is now New Mexico before New England was settled by persons of European descent and that other pioneers from Mexico had made permanent settlements in Arizona, Texas, and California (in that order) before the American Revolution.

In addition to having been "other persons" by choice, Mexican Americans, who often resemble Indians because of their Mexican descent, have also been "other persons" by birth. Thus, they have been more thoroughly "other" than black Americans who, although of another race and historical background than the great majority of Americans, have always lived in American society without perpetuating a non-American culture. In fact, there has been a tendency by black Americans to look down on Mexican Americans because of their willingness to embrace a non-American culture.

What might be thought of as a more thorough "otherness" of Mexican Americans (constituted by, in addition to a difference in appearance, a different historical background and different cultural behavior) has perhaps made them more variously vulnerable, including, in a few places, vulnerability to a kind of loss that black Americans have not suffered but American Indians have: loss of sovereignty. Some Mexican Americans who became American citizens as a result of the U.S. conquest and purchase of northern Mexico owned farming and grazing lands their ancestors had developed from Stone Age wilderness by exploiting Indian American laborers. Two years after America's war with Mexico ended in 1848, there were about sixty thousand Mexican Americans in New Mexico and ten thousand elsewhere in the Southwest and more than four times that number of Americans in the region (most of whom had arrived during the previous fifteen years). This drastic change, from being the dominant population in California and New Mexico and an important minority in Texas to being the subordinate group throughout the Southwest, happened in less than one generation. The change was too sudden to allow sufficient time to adjust to the new institutions of law, government, and finance that Americans introduced and sometimes used to their advantage.

Despite their problems, Mexican Americans have, until recently, not publicized or protested their condition or aroused sympathy and help as black Americans have. They have suffered in comparative silence, perhaps for three reasons.

First, the choice of maintaining a dual cultural allegiance has, in effect, made them unable to appeal to the sympathies of American culture the way black Americans have been able to do. They have maintained a stance of inarticulate aloofness for the simple reason that, in many instances, the primary language available for their protests, Spanish, could not be understood by most Americans.

Second, Mexican Americans have historically not made their plight known perhaps because, despite whatever sufferings they may have encountered as "other persons," life in the United States has been materially better for those who immigrated from Mexico and for their descendants in the United States than what Mexican culture materially afforded. Though living apart from Mexican culture, its standards continued to be a cultural awareness for many Mexican Americans in a way that no African or European culture could be for other Americans; and judged by those standards, any injustice that might have been suffered in the United States was much more sufferable than it would have been if judged by an exclusively American consciousness.

Third, deference to persons in authority by Mexican Americans has been an effect of their Mexican heritage that may also have contributed to their not making their sufferings widely known. Poor (as opposed to middle-class) Mexican emigrants to the United States were enculturated to the authority of the *patrón* and to peonage in Mexico; they found in the United States similar authority figures in American landowners and labor contractors and culturally deferred to them, accepting without complaint whatever was offered, which was usually more than they were accustomed to receiving at the hands of such persons in Mexico.

Since 1910, however, significant changes have begun to take place among Mexican Americans. That year marked the beginning of the first large-scale sustained emigration from Mexico to the United States. By 1930, 1.5 million persons born in Mexico were living in the United States, a rate of immigration exceeding that of even the largest sustained immigration to America from any single nation of Europe (i.e., between 1820 and 1970 Germany provided the largest number of immigrants from a single country, 6.8 million, but in less than one-seventh of that time, in the early decades of the twentieth century, nearly one-fourth that number of persons came from Mexico). Except for a lag during the Great Depression of the 1930s, large-scale immigration from Mexico has hardly slackened since it began in 1910 and, indeed, has increased immensely beyond the twenty thousand legal Mexican immigrants allowed each year under the 1976 American immigration law. The number of successful illegal entries of Mexicans into the United States was probably in the range of hundreds of thousands each year during the half decade between 1980 and 1985, but no one knows how many of these persons migrated with the hope of becoming permanent residents of the United States and how many planned—like so many Spanish emigrants to colonial Spanish America—to work for a time to get money and then return to their families in Mexico to enjoy their gains. It is certain, however, that the money sent by them to Mexico from the United States is a significant source of national income for Mexico. (Approximately three billion dollars was sent in 1979.[3]) The rapid, great increase to the Mexican American population of the Southwest has produced an increase in the sense of importance this population has in the region, which is still the preferred destination of most Mexican immigrants. Mexican Americans now comprise some 15 percent of the Southwest's total population. There were in 1980 five million Mexican Americans in the population of the United States as compared to twenty-three million black Americans.

The steep rise of immigration from Mexico beginning in 1910 coincided with the beginning of some dispersal of Mexican Americans from the Southwest into other parts of the United States. Perhaps as many as 10 percent of Mexican Americans now live in such places as Michigan and Illinois. This movement away from California, Arizona, New Mexico, and Texas suggests a new willingness on the part of Mexican Americans to immigrate psychologically to American culture—as also does an increasing rate of marriage with non–Mexican Americans, something quite uncommon until recent decades. Another indicator of a change in cultural attitudes has been the much larger movement of Mexican Americans from rural to urban areas within the Southwest.

The participation of Mexican Americans in the wars fought by the United States in this century has demonstrated a deep patriotism and fundamental commitment to American life on their part. In World War II, the rate of voluntary enlistments in New Mexico was so great that not enough young men remained to fill the state's quota for the draft. In the post–World War II period, many Mexican American veterans helped found organizations promoting patriotism and full participation in the American political process. The most significant indication of a new inclination away from dual cultural allegiance was revealed in 1969 when it was discovered that 90 percent of Mexican Americans were U.S. citizens and that, although

3. Aaron Segal, "The Half-Open Door," *Wilson Quarterly* (New Year's 1983), VII, No. 1, p. 126.

85 percent had learned Spanish as their first language, only 70 percent were actually using Spanish at home—in other words, 15 percent had chosen to make English their language of preference for themselves and their children. The recent stress among Mexican Americans on mastering English also represents a significant new emphasis on better preparation for participation in American culture and the opportunities of self-responsibility and economic improvement that America holds forth—opportunities not available to persons speaking only Spanish or having a poor secondary command of English.

In the ways already mentioned, Mexican Americans have made themselves in the last two generations more and more a part of American culture and have more and more claimed the rights and opportunities that could not be theirs as "other persons."[4]

4. From the middle of the nineteenth century to the present, the greater part of the participants in the comparatively small immigration from South America, the Caribbean, East Asia (China, Japan, Korea), the Pacific islands, southeastern and southern Asia, and the Middle East have been regarded by the majority of white Americans as "other persons" and have been treated accordingly, in the ways that the more numerous groups of "other persons" already discussed have been treated. The imprisonment during World War II of Japanese American citizens of the United States is only the most egregious instance. Each of these groups has its own distinctive and particular history in America. Their collective aspirations, however, have basically resembled those of other self-selecting emigrants to America. That is, they have wanted to achieve a new and better life in America and to overcome, through their individual performance and voluntary community organizations, barriers against their full participation in American society.

CHAPTER
4

A TRANSFORMABLE STONE AGE

On October 12, 1492, armed boat crews from three European ships stepped ashore on a small, low-lying island in the western Atlantic, two hundred miles southeast of Florida and one hundred miles from Cuba. They found on it people who wore no clothes and painted their bodies and who did not understand the properties of metal and cut their hands by grasping the blade of a drawn sword as though it were a stick. In sight of these Stone Age men and women, the voyagers from Europe unfurled their flag and formally proclaimed the island a possession of the crown of Spain.

In the next fourteen years during three more voyages, Columbus established the first European city in the Americas and discovered the mainlands of both of the American continents. (Unfortunately for him, he touched the coast of North America south of the Aztec civilization.) Not long after the death of Columbus, the Aztec and the Incan civilizations of North and South America were detected and conquered in military campaigns that lasted respectively from 1519 to 1521 and from 1531 to 1534. And by 1550 Spaniards had traveled throughout the length and breadth of the twenty-three-hundred-mile-long tapering isthmus that comprises southern North America, had traversed the Amazon Basin from the Andes to the Atlantic, and had explored the Florida peninsula, the north coast of the Gulf of Mexico, the Caribbean shores of South America, the coasts of western South America, the Andean uplands, Paraguay, northern Argentina to the estuary of La Plata, California, and central North America as far inland as northern Arizona, Kansas, and Tennessee. By 1565, Spain, in order to support and protect communication by sea through the Gulf of Mexico with its rich conquest in southern North America, had established a fortress on the Atlantic coast of the Florida peninsula. But it was not until 1607 that a permanent European colony was effected in central North America north of that necessary military establishment. In that year, a handful of Englishmen just barely managed to survive their miseries on a small tidewater peninsula in Virginia between the departure of the ship that left them there and the arrival of new supplies from England.

Why was there this hiatus of more than one hundred years between the founding of an enduring European settlement in the Americas by Columbus in 1493 during his second voyage of discovery and the founding of Jamestown, Virginia, in central North America in 1607?

The century-long hiatus is difficult to explain in terms of the capacities of western Europe's imperialistically ambitious maritime nations, several of which financed expeditions to cross the Atlantic and explore the coasts of central and northern North America hard on the heels of Columbus's discovery that continental landmasses could be reached after a comparatively brief sail westward. Certainly France, Holland, and England all possessed the technical skills, resources of money and ships, the seafaring knowledge, and the manpower to have permanently settled central and northern North America long before any of them in fact did. This omission on the part of all of Europe's maritime imperialists to establish any permanent settlement in central and northern North America for a century after they first explored these coasts is even more striking when one considers how much closer northern and central North America are to Europe than either Mexico or Peru. Neither a lack of opportunity nor a lack of means explains the 115-year gap between Columbus's first voyage to America and the first permanent European settlements north of the Florida peninsula, which took place within a year of each other in Virginia and Quebec during the first decade of the seventeenth century. Some other consideration in the 1500s besides opportunity or means determined this long delay. And that something was most probably the European perception of Stone Age central and northern North America.

Europeans permanently settled in Stone Age Brazil thirty-two years after the Portuguese discovered it in 1500 because its closeness to Africa made it useful as a strategic base for protecting and supporting the sea-lanes of the already-established and important Portuguese trade with Africa and the even more important Portuguese trade routes around Africa to the Far East. The eastward-thrusting bulge of Brazil is only a third as far from Africa as the North American mainland is from Europe, and the fact that a Portuguese mariner discovered Brazil by accident in 1500, when a storm blew him off the sea routes the Portuguese had pioneered around Africa to Asia, illustrates the strategic closeness of Brazil to Africa. The existence of a valuable wild-growing dyewood on the coasts of Brazil (which gave the country its name) was another inducement to the settlement of Brazil soon after its discovery by Europeans.

Spain had the will and found the means in the 1500s to immediately settle the Stone Age islands of the Caribbean because they were (mistakenly, of course, but nonetheless effectively) perceived as the uncivilized outposts of China and India, and therefore the keys to the riches of the Orient, which the Portuguese traveling eastward around Africa had already reached by sea. It was because of this perception of the Caribbean islands that Columbus, when he returned there on his second voyage, in 1493, commanded a strong fleet of seventeen ships and a small army of Spanish *hidalgos* and soldiers as well as skilled workmen to build settlements. The discovery of Mexico and Peru not long after Columbus's death proved that his bold westward venture had not reached the outskirts of the known Asian civilizations but rather had discovered the route to unknown continental civilizations. Despite the wrongness of Columbus's belief about his discoveries, his basic premise, that the shortest way to civilized riches for Europe's imperialistically minded maritime nations lay to the west, across the Atlantic, was eminently verified by the findings of Hernán Cortés in southern North America and Francisco Pizarro in western South America.

No civilized wealth existed in central and northern North America, however, and those places lacked the strategic value that Stone Age Brazil had. They made no cultural sense to the Europeans who followed up Columbus's discoveries by exploring the seaboard of central North America from Georgia to Nova Scotia and its interior as far inland as Tennessee, Kansas, and Arizona. Whereas the civilized empires of the Aztecs and the Incas made such immediate cultural sense to Europeans that they immediately undertook to conquer and dominate them, no European in the 1500s could perceive the Stone Age space-time continuum of central and northern North America as compellingly attractive. Instead, it was culturally repelling, a world so old and so unfamiliar to Europeans of the 1500s as to be more forbidding than the military power of the Aztec and Incan empires. Only gradually during the course of the sixteenth century did the perception form that the central and northern parts of North America might be worth a determined effort to colonize and civilize them.

AN OLD, TRANSFORMABLE WORLD

Everywhere that the Stone Age existed in the Americas in the sixteenth century—in South America outside the areas of the Inca and the Chibcha civilizations and in North America outside the elongated southern third of the continent where the Aztec, Maya, and other civilizations were encountered—Europeans had the same three choices: live in it as it was, transform it to make it amenable to their cultural beliefs and practices, or avoid it. The scorn of Europeans for life in a Stone Age space-time continuum is apparent in the report made by a Spanish captain sent to investigate the northern border region of the Aztec suzerainty in the early 1500s. He put the matter with a soldier's bluntness in saying he had found an uninhabited wilderness "except for some savages who eat roots and wear deerskins."[1] The Aztec emperor, who ruled from a great city built on a man-made island and who was attended by hundreds of noblemen dressed in beautifully woven robes whose various colors indicated their rank in his court, would certainly have agreed with this assessment of the region to the north of his imperium; and one does not have to read much of the history of the Incas written by a son of the first Spanish governor of that civilization's conquered capital city (Cuzco, Peru) and an Inca noblewoman to know the attitude of the Incas toward the uncivilized Indians on the borders of their empire.[2] Europeans were quick to conquer and quick to settle in the regions that had already been civilized by the Incas, Chibcha, Maya, Aztecs, and earlier peoples native to the Americas, and the fundamental historical condition in the cultural formation of Spanish America was the relation of European culture to these indigenous civilizations of the Americas. However, except for the special cases of the main Caribbean islands, Florida, and Brazil, Europeans made no successful effort, for a long time, to settle in the vast Stone Age regions of the Americas after their discovery of them, although they jealously maintained their claims to such regions, based on the idea prevalent among the maritime imperialists of Renaissance Europe that precedence of exploration conveyed a right to claim ownership of uncivilized regions.

Because of the forbidding conditions in the Amazon heartland of South America, transformation of Stone Age Brazil did not become a historically continuous, continental process. That process was limited to the areas adjacent to Brazil's long coast. The Europeans who finally settled Stone Age Canada, a century after Columbus's death, also faced geographical constraints that discouraged the transformation of that continental expanse

1. *The Conquistadors: First-Person Accounts of the Conquest of Mexico,* ed. Patricia de Fuentes (New York: Orion, 1963), p. 206.

2. Born in Cuzco six years after the conquest of the Incas, Garcilaso de la Vega "the Inca" published his book on his noble mother's people, which has been translated into English as *The Royal Commentaries of the Incas,* in Spain in 1609, 1616.

of the Stone Age space-time continuum. Even today, much of northern North America remains as it was in the year Columbus first sailed westward to the Americas. (Imagine a capacity crowd from some modern sports stadium spread out through New England, New York, New Jersey, Pennsylvania, Delaware, Maryland, Virginia, South Carolina, North Carolina, Georgia, Florida, Alabama, Mississippi, Tennessee, Kentucky, Illinois, Indiana, Ohio, Michigan, Wisconsin, Iowa, Missouri, Kansas, Arkansas, Louisiana, Oklahoma, and Texas, and you will have some idea of how sparsely populated the far north of Canada is today.) The same is true of large parts of the interior of Brazil. Its Stone Age heartland, the watery equatorial jungle known as the Amazon, has resisted change on a continental scale in the same way that the Stone Age heartland of Canada—the arctic and subarctic North—has. To this day, the population of Canada is heavily concentrated in the lowlands adjacent to the Atlantic sea reaches of the St. Lawrence River valley, and nowhere in Brazil is there yet a city as populous and as far inland from the Atlantic Ocean as Atlanta, Georgia. In North America, the only nomadic hunters still existing (albeit now equipped with modern hunting implements and canvas tents and rapidly losing their independent, hunting ways) live in Canada; while in the interior of Brazil, there are still small pockets of the pre-1492 Stone Age. A European explorer of Brazil's interior as late as the 1930s reported that there were immense tracts of land between the Araguaia and the Xingu rivers and between the Xingu and the Tapajós rivers that no white man had ever attempted to enter.[3] Even now, some 450 years after its discovery by Europeans, one can still fly for hours over the Amazon and see below an ocean of treetops with singularly few signs of human presence, and the primeval silence of the Amazon's seemingly endless rain forest can still intimidate men not acculturated to a Stone Age jungle, in the same way that it intimidated the nineteenth-century European plant collector who lived in it for years who wrote: "The few sounds of the birds are of that pensive or mysterious character which intensifies the feeling of solitude rather than imparts a sense of life and cheerfulness. Sometimes a sound is heard like the clang of an iron bar against a hard, hollow tree, or a piercing cry rends the air; these are not repeated, and the succeeding silence tends to heighten the unpleasant impression which they make on the mind."[4]

Perhaps the Amazon as a whole can never be civilized because its excessive rains so thoroughly leach the soil of minerals as to make it

3. Peter Fleming, *Brazilian Adventure* (New York: Charles Scribner, 1934), p. 18.
4. Henry Walter Bates, who lived in the Amazon from 1848 to 1859, quoted in Tom Sterling, *The Amazon* (Amsterdam: Time-Life, 1975), p. 134.

unsuitable for extensive agriculture without exorbitant expenditures for artificial fertilizer. The floodplains of the Amazon, where nutrient-rich soils do exist, are periodically under as many as thirty feet of water. (The floods of this incredible "river sea," as it is correctly called by the Brazilians, periodically inundate an area in the interior of Brazil larger than the Mediterranean Sea.) Climatic and topographical conditions in the Amazon, by limiting development of the interior of Brazil, are the principal reasons for the historically European orientation of Brazilian culture; but the highlands that stretch along the coast of Brazil south of the Amazon have also made large-scale movement inland difficult. These precipitous uplands are as high as the Appalachian Mountains of the eastern United States but much broader and much closer to the coast. They lie next to or near the Atlantic almost without interruption south of the protrusion of Brazil toward Africa that Brazilians call "the Northeast." The topography of much of Brazil south of the Amazon is as if the eastern United States had no coastal plain and the region between the Atlantic Ocean and the Mississippi River were nearly filled by the Appalachian Mountains. Unfortunately, Brazil's Northeast, where broad lowlands extend far inland from the coast, is a region of chronic, killing droughts.

Only in central North America, within the principal boundaries of what is now the United States of America, could the Stone Age space-time continuum that existed in most of the American continents at the time of Columbus's voyages be completely transformed on a continental scale. Because this part of the Americas offered the only continental-sized Stone Age area that could be transformed to make it habitable to large numbers of Europeans and their descendants, a different kind of culture, deriving in large measure from the behavior of transformation, arose in the United States than arose in Brazil or in Canada, which had Stone Age continental spaces that could not be completely transformed, or in mainland Spanish America, which already had large civilized areas at the time of its European discovery and did not, therefore, require complete transformation. Because Canada and Brazil lacked transformable interiors, these continent-sized nations developed essentially European-oriented cultures with populations heavily, and for a long time almost exclusively, concentrated near their Atlantic seaways. The region that became the United States of America, because it had a transformable Stone Age interior, attracted a larger population of European immigrants after it was finally settled than either Canada (which has a larger area than the United States) or Brazil (which approximates in area the forty-eight contiguous states of the United States). The inability of Brazilians and Canadians to move inland en masse to populate a continental interior and the lack of a continental heartland in Spanish

America needing complete transformation made Brazilians, Canadians, and Spanish Americans more mindful of the controlling European centers of their post-1492 cultures than was the population of the United States, which soon became aware of the transformable interior of central North America.

The comparatively non-European culture of the United States is, then, in large measure, the result of a unique historical condition: the presence of a forbiddingly old, Stone Age space-time continuum whose continent-size interior could be inhabited and transformed on a large scale. That condition was essentially an opportunity for changing oldness into new-ness. It did not present the opportunity to conquer an already-formed civilization, such as existed for Europeans in Spanish America, but rather the opportunity to start civilization over again on a continental scale, to make an expansive new world as quickly and as thoroughly as possible. And, of course, given the scale and the haste of the process and the uniqueness of the opportunity, it was not possible to repeat the history of European civilization in central North America; nor was the duplication of European history in central North America desirable to those who engaged in the process of making this new civilization—as has been discussed in chapter 2.

The perception of an opportunity to transform oldness into newness has been fundamental to the cultural formation of the United States and has to be comprehended imaginatively if it is to be comprehended at all. The process involved something more difficult than the mere perception of a Stone Age presence and an absence of civilization. It required the ability to envision in that which was present that which could be: "to see" the still-to-be civilization that was not yet present. The difficulties of such perception must be fully appreciated to understand the cultural formation of the United States.

In the decades immediately following Columbus's discovery, the ex-plorers commissioned by England and France to scout the coast of central North America north of the Florida Straits were looking for exactly what Columbus had been looking for: evidence of a passage to India and China. They found none. What they found instead was a continuous condition so primeval to the historical sense of a Renaissance European as to require the whole of the sixteenth century before it could be accepted as a place for permanent European habitation, despite its considerably greater close-ness to the imperialistically ambitious maritime nations of western Europe in comparison to southern North America and western South America.

Europeans who explored the Atlantic coast of central North America and its far interior in the early 1500s remarked on the quick intelligence of the native inhabitants, their healthy handsomeness, the straightforwardness of their manners, their comparatively unspecialized occupations, and their nakedness. Nowhere in North America north of Mexico did they see what was seen there and in western South America: large cities built of dressed stone, adobe brick, hewn wood, plaster, and tile; monumental stone sculptures; great forts and temples; palaces and formal gardens; social stratifications of nobles, merchants, and peons; systems of paved roads; large-scale intensive agriculture, including beautifully engineered irrigation works; great and extensive population densities; shepherds tending herds of domesticated, state-owned animals; exquisite gold and silver smithing; bronze implements; state schools for training administrators and professional soldiers (both the Aztec and Incan empires had such schools in their capitals); or women whose fashion of dressing could be compared with that of European women.

Instead, what the Coronado expedition of 1540–42 into the interior of central North America saw on the high plains of Kansas were nomadic Stone Age hunters following herds of buffalo across uninhabited grasslands hundreds of miles in extent, with their tents and gear transported by "packs of dogs harnessed with little pads, pack-saddles, and girths."

> When these Indians kill a cow [i.e., a buffalo] they clean a large intestine and fill it with blood and put it around their necks to drink when they are thirsty. After they cut open the belly of the cow they squeeze out the chewed grass and drink the juice, which remains on top, saying that it contains the substance of the stomach. They cut open the cow at the back and pull off the skin at the joints, using a flint the size of a finger, tied to a small stick, doing this as handily as if they used a fine large tool. They sharpen the flints on their own teeth. It is remarkable to see how quickly they do it.[5]

Another European, who was shipwrecked on the coast of Texas in 1528 and wandered with three companions for nine years as a slave and medicine man among the Stone Age tribes of the interior of the western regions of central North America, wrote of one tribe with whom he lived that its members acted on the dreams they had during sleep to the point of "destroying even their male children on account of dreams." They also "cast away their daughters at birth; the dogs eat them":

> They say they do this because all the nations of the region are their enemies, with whom they war ceaselessly; and that if they were to

5. *Narratives of the Coronado Expedition 1540–1542*, eds. George P. Hammond and Agapito Rey (Albuquerque: University of New Mexico Press, 1940), p. 262.

marry off their daughters, the daughters would multiply their enemies until the latter overcame and enslaved the Mariames, who thus preferred to annihilate all daughters than risk their reproduction of a single enemy. We asked why they did not themselves marry these girls. They said that marrying relatives would be a disgusting thing; it was far better to kill them than give them to either kin or foe. This is also the practice of their neighbors, the Yguaces, but of no other people of that region. To marry, men buy wives from their enemies, the price of a wife being the best bow that can be got, together with two arrows or, should the suitor happen to have no bow, a net a fathom square.[6]

A European explorer of the coast of northern North America in 1534 wrote that it was a land of "stones and wild crags . . . a place fit for wild beasts":

To be short, I believe that this was the land that God allotted to Cain. There are men of an indifferent good stature and bigness, but wild and unruly: they wear their hair tied on the top like a wreath of hay, and put a wooden pin within it, or any other such thing instead of a nail. . . . They are clothed with beasts skins as well the men as women, but that the women go somewhat straiter and closer in their garments than the men do, with their waists girded; they paint themselves with certain roan colors; their boats are made of the bark of birch trees, with the which they fish and take great store of seals, and as far as we could understand since our coming thither, that is not their habitation, but they come from the main land out of hotter countries, to catch the said seals and other necessaries for their living.[7]

In 1620, the coast of Massachusetts made the same impression on the first Europeans to settle there:

. . . what could they see but a hideous and desolate wilderness, full of wild beasts and wild men? . . . for which way soever they turned their eyes (save upward to the heavens) they could have little solace or content in respect of any outward objects. For summer being done, all things stand upon them with a weatherbeaten face; and the whole country, full of woods and thickets, represented a wild and savage hue. If they looked behind them, there was the

6. *Cabeza de Vaca's Adventures in the Unknown Interior of America,* trans. Cyclone Covey (New York: Collier, 1961), beginning of chapter 30.

7. "The First Relation of Jacques Cartier of St. Malo, 1534," in *Early English and French Voyages Chiefly from Hakluyt 1534–1608,* ed. Henry Sweeter Burrage (New York: Charles Scribner, 1932), p. 10; spelling modernized.

mighty ocean which they had passed, and was now as a main bar and gulf to separate them from all the civil parts of the world.[8]

Central North America during the sixteenth century was a continuous continental expanse of Stone Age space and time that Europeans had difficulty envisioning as an attractive habitation for themselves.

Nature had been altered by mankind in central North America by the time Europeans saw it, but not profoundly or broadly. The face of the land was, for the most part, as the undirected forces of nature had made it. Wild animals and birds, wild marshes and swamps, and wild prairies and forests constituted its fundamental aspects. The human beings within it lived mostly in bands of seasonally roving hunters-gatherers-fishermen or in bands of unspecialized farmers-hunters-gatherers-fishermen in more or less permanent villages or clusters of dome-shaped dwellings of bark, brush, pole, skin, grass, or wattle, a few of which were enclosed by palisades of logs. The lower Mississippi Valley and the southeast regions were the most agriculturally advanced and populous. In the extreme southwest of this part of North America—the northernmost reach of Mexican influence— were a few permanent agricultural towns constructed of stone, sometimes in the shelter of massive south-facing cliff overhangs. Here and there in the Mississippi Valley and the Southeast were abandoned groups of man-made mounds. One of these groups (the Cahokia Mounds) near the confluence of the Mississippi River with its two principal tributaries and a third large river, within sight of present-day St. Louis, had probably once had a resident population of forty thousand people and was the only urban center yet known to have existed in central North America before its settlement by Europeans. But all of these places had been abandoned by the peoples who had built them for such a long time before the advent of Europeans that no oral tradition existed to identify their builders. Central North America was in this sense in a cultural relapse when first seen by European eyes.

A high Stone Age reality prevailed there in the 1500s, as it still did a century later, when the first permanent settlements were made by Europeans north of Florida. A silence that was audible pervaded its desolate tidelands, prairies, mountains, forests, and deserts—a hush accented by the calls of wild birds and animals, the sounds of waves and surf lapping and crashing on great stretches of lonely lake and sea shores, and the almost deafening screech and whir of swarms of summer insects; or the sound of ice-sheathed trees clacking together in winter forests, the roar of

8.   William Bradford, *Of Plymouth Plantation,* ed. Harvey Wish (New York: Capricorn, 1962), p. 60; spelling modernized.

the great blizzards and tornadoes that swept the plains, and the steady drone of falls and river rapids; or the rushing, rumbling crash of mountain avalanches and the crackling roar of wildfires burning wildernesses of grass and trees until checked by some natural barrier or soaked down by rain. (Fire was also a tool used by the Stone Age hunters and agriculturists of central North America in shaping the land to their purposes.) The pungent smell of the immense forests of conifers that then grew on the primeval coastal plain of central North America could be smelled one hundred miles to sea by European mariners approaching those shores in the summertime when the sun-warmed sap in the giant pines and cedars flowed profusely. Great flocks of wild water birds of every description migrated back and forth over the estuaries, swamps, bays, marshes, ponds, streams, rivers, and lakes of the land. Sky-darkening concentrations of woodland pigeons also migrated north and south with the seasons, eating the mast of the forest and the seeds of the grassland. Clamorous roosts of wild parakeets and wild turkeys agitated the unbroken crown of the southern stretches of the ancient forest, which had begun growing at the end of the last Ice Age ten thousand years before. Tidal and fresh waters yielded abundant succulent shellfish, as well as saltwater and freshwater turtles. Heavy-bodied gamefish annually clogged bays, rivers, and streams with their spawning runs. Many different kinds of nut-bearing trees provided seasonal harvests. Wild honey, wild grapes, wild plums, and wild berries of many kinds could likewise be gathered. Food was abundant through foraging, hunting, and fishing, but much of it was only a seasonal plenty, with periods of scarcity between seasons of plenty; and in some places food was chronically scarce—as Álvar Núñez Cabeza de Vaca, during his nine-year sojourn in the trans-Mississippi region in the early 1500s, and the Lewis and Clark expedition, across the western part of central North America in the first years of the 1800s, both observed.

The Stone Age Indians of California, however, did no farming and made no pots for food storage to get them through seasons of scarcity, not because they were ignorant of these techniques (neighboring tribes to the east of them did farm and make pots) but because the waters and lands of California afforded a reliable daily sufficiency of food from fishing, hunting, and gathering in every season of the year without the need for farming or food storage. And this region had a population apparently as numerous and healthy at the time of the earliest written records of it as any place in central North America where agriculture had begun to be practiced to supplement hunting and fishing and the gathering of naturally growing food.

Some species of large game animals probably existed in the 1500s and the 1600s in every region of what is now the United States, as indicated in the reportedly wide distribution of wolves and cougars, predators that live off such game. All but the most sterile wildernesses had some species of deer, and elk were common where the climate was cool. Small game could be found nearly everywhere. Moose, musk-ox, and great herds of caribou ranged in the northern woodlands and the arctic tundra; and the wild sheep and wild goats that are native to central and northern North America, and that now exist only in remote mountain fastnesses, were then herd animals living on the grassy plains of Alaska, western Canada, the western drainage of the Mississippi, and the intermontane basins of central North America. Antelope were also common in the western parts of central North America. And horizon-filling dark herds of buffalo moved through the river bottoms and plains west of the Mississippi, while lesser concentrations of these big animals inhabited the woodlands and grasslands that then existed east of the Mississippi. In addition, there were large mammals—whales, porpoises, manatees—in the coastal waters; rookeries of sea lions, seals, and walrus along the seashores; and islands covered with the egg-ladened nests of seabirds. Black bears were everywhere. And in the western parts of the continent lived many of those great, fearless bears that Americans call grizzlies because of their white-tipped fur; while in the subarctic and arctic north lived monstrous brown bears and the entirely white, aquatic bears that stalk men as prey. No varied and widely distributed large fauna such as this existed in southern North America or anywhere in South America.

In the century following Columbus's initial voyage, North America north of the Florida Straits and the Gulf of Mexico was a continent in which ideas of empire were as culturally strange (perhaps one should say unnecessary) as they were familiar in Asia, Europe, parts of Africa, western South America, and southern North America. In the 1500s, central and northern North America were still rich Stone Age hunting, fishing, and gathering grounds, and they remained so until Europeans and their American-born descendants in the 1600s inaugurated a rapid transformation of central North America and replaced that space-time continuum during the next three hundred years with a civilized continuum.

Nowhere in North America north of Mexico did the first European explorers find extensive and numerous agricultural plantations like those Cortés and his men saw in Mexico in 1519, and its population in the 1500s appears to have been much smaller than the populations of the Aztec and Inca empires and the Maya and Chibcha civilizations, which occupied large regions between Mexico and Peru. Central and northern North America in the sixteenth century apparently had a comparatively small, but vigorous and healthy, population which lived within natural means of nourishment, was not yet essentially or generally dependent on domesticated plants, and had no domesticated fowl or animals except the dog. Unlike the civilizations to the south, agriculture in central North America was still in the process of evolution and establishment, and city building had not yet begun to have a continuous history there because enough food was still obtainable through a combination of migratory gathering, fishing, and hunting without the practice of settled, large-scale cultivation of domesticated plants or basic dependence on domesticated poultry and animals. Spiritual and material satisfaction in the Stone Age space-time continuum of central and northern North America in the 1500s was just as possible for those acculturated to it as such satisfaction was in civilized Asia, Europe, Africa, western South America, or southern North America.

The culture of the human beings who were native to Stone Age North America was in harmony with the continent's physical reality and a part of that reality. There, in the century following Columbus's discoveries, human beings still had a pervasive and vital relationship with wilderness. The relationship was the material and spiritual basis of culture. Any appreciable change in that physical reality of wilderness on which the culture of the human beings living in it depended would directly and immediately affect their existence because a fundamental change in any culture's physical basis (climate, topography, resources used) affects cultural behavior. The civilized American Indians living in western South America and southern North America could continue their cultures to some extent after being conquered by Europeans because these civilized American Indians shared with their European conquerors certain basic cultural outlooks: belief in a strict social hierarchy, in a state religion, in loyalty to hereditary lords and emperors, in paying tribute, in specialization of work, in dependence on agriculture, and in the benefits of settled life and urban centers. But in central and northern North America, no such basis of integration pertained. European civilization in the 1500s was as culturally wrong and senseless to the Stone Age tribesmen of central and northern North America as the way they lived and the space-time continuum they inhabited were culturally wrong to the sixteenth-century Europeans who first saw it and to those Europeans who, a century later, became the first permanent settlers in the Stone Age wilderness of central and northern North America. Neither way made cultural sense to the other.

What existed in central North America in the 1500s made it forbidding to Europeans. It was a space-time continuum that had not existed in Europe for some six thousand years: approximately the number of years one would have had to go back in European history to find the kind of pervasive, high Stone Age condition that existed then in central North America. Europeans who entered western South America and southern North America in the 1500s, however, felt no such disjunction from what they considered a normal space-time continuum (though of course there was some, particularly in regard to religious practices). The letters and reports of the Europeans who conquered Mexico and Peru favorably compare those places to their European homeland. No such comparisons occur in accounts of central North America in the 1500s, which was seen as a howling wilderness and as a land fit for the punishment of the biblical Cain.

The sense of a Stone Age presence and the absence of civilization, which was the perception of central North America by Europeans in the 1500s and which led to their choosing not to live in it during that century, cannot be grasped without a concrete sense of why Europeans felt an immediate affinity for the civilized presences in Mexico and Peru.

CONQUERABLE CIVILIZED WORLDS

When Europeans first saw the imperial state called by its Inca rulers the "Land of the Four Quarters," it extended from southern Colombia to central Chile and from the arid west coast of South America inland across the stream-laced valleys and shining snow peaks of Ecuador, Peru, and Bolivia, and down the eastern slopes of the Andes, the longest column of great mountains in the world—large parts of which have a tropical latitude that gives their middle elevations a temperate climate—to the tropical rain forest of the Amazon and the "green hell" of the Mato Grosso: an area equivalent in size to all of western Europe. In the high valleys where the Inca civilization was centered, snow seldom falls because the season of precipitation coincides with the warm months of the year. Cultivation in the sun-warmed rarified air of these immense mountain valleys is almost year-round, with the harvesting of some crops overlapping the planting of others.

Well-built military roads unified this extensive empire. One Spaniard who traveled the twelve-hundred-mile-long northern road from the capital city of Cuzco to Quito, the principal city of the Inca empire in the north—a road mostly paved with stone, and sometimes with a locally available bituminous material—noted that it exceeded in length the main road that had run from Rome to the principal western cities of the Roman empire in Spain. Another Spaniard who saw the Cuzco-Quito road in the sixteenth century, when it was still being maintained under the authority of the Incas, said that the construction of such a road was beyond the engineering skill the king of Spain had at his command.

The main road south from the Inca capital of Cuzco was longer by one thousand miles than the northern road. And it was just as well maintained as the main road to Quito and just as heavily trafficked by uniformed messengers, troops of soldiers, porters, imperial administrators, caravans of pack animals carrying goods and produce, shepherds conducting state-owned flocks of domesticated wool-and-meat-producing animals to new pastures or shearing stations, whole populations from newly conquered borderlands being moved under guard to interior regions of the empire, and peoples already pacified and loyal to the Incas being escorted from the interior of the empire to settle on the newly conquered lands.[9] Trunk roads, representing more thousands of miles of construction, ran along the coast of the Land of the Four Quarters, paralleling the north-south roads in the highlands, and were connected with the highland system at key points by lateral arteries. Wherever an Inca road had to traverse boggy ground, it was raised (one twenty-foot-wide section near Cuzco was raised eight feet for a distance of eight miles), and where it had to cross running water, either a culvert or a bridge was built. Pontoon and corbel were the most common types of bridge construction, but in the gorges of the Andes, some forty suspension bridges were also erected, each capable of bearing the weight of many men or animals and having clear spans of from two to five hundred feet. Where roads traversed deserts, substantial high walls were erected along their sides to keep out drifting sand. Nothing like this integrated system of roads existed in Europe in the 1500s.

Among other engineering marvels of this Indian civilization were tremendous irrigation projects, which included catchment dams as wide as one-half mile, straightened and stone-embanked river channels, stone-lined and earthen ditches, underground conduits, and elevated aqueducts. These systems transported water hundreds of miles (the longest continuous channel is five hundred miles) and distributed it over immense regions of otherwise unproductive land. Gradients in earthen ditches were exactly engineered so that the water flowing in them would be fast enough to prevent any buildup of silt and weeds, which would have blocked the ditches, yet slow enough to avoid erosion of the ditches' earthen sides. Inns, baths, tombs, temples, barracks, warehouse complexes for the bulk storage of weapons, footgear, cloth, and dehydrated food, great stone citadels, and thousands of miles of agricultural terraces that sometimes encompassed huge mountainsides (many of which are still being farmed)

9. Russian czars began the practice of population exchanges in their empire about a century after the Incas, and in eastern Poland and eastern Germany following World War II, the imperialist government of the Soviet Union forced the largest population exchange in human history.

were also part of the impressive engineering projects of the Inca empire and earlier civilized American Indians, whose accomplishments the Incas had appropriated and added to. One of the warehouse complexes maintained by the Inca state had 497 buildings of cut stone for storage and thirty more stone buildings for receiving and processing the materials brought to it and housing the keepers of the stores, the workers they supervised, and their administrative records. The most imposing bastion in the empire, large enough to accommodate the entire population of the city of Cuzco, had stocks of food and water to withstand a long siege and was built of stone blocks weighing up to sixty tons. The joints of these mammoth blocks of worked stone were exquisitely fitted; even to this day, despite the frequent earthquakes of the Andean highlands, a sheet of paper cannot be inserted between them, so perfect is their jointure. It is a high aesthetic pleasure to see and to touch the precise, fine line of the joints cut by the ancient Andean stonemasons. At times, their use of their materials seems to have been unnecessarily complicated, almost as if skillfully and intricately joining together massive stone blocks had been a challenge.

The most wonderful buildings in the Inca empire were those of the Temple of the Sun in the capital city, which was the center of power of the Inca civilization and expressed the cultural idea that legitimized the authority of the Incas as a noble class of rulers: the belief that they were Children of the Sun. The six principal buildings of this imperial center enclosed a huge court paved with stone called the Field of the Sun, in which a fountain made of gold (the bright metal of the sun) flowed never-endingly from a hidden source. The great hall of the temple was a kind of mortuary throne room. There, the mummies of all the Inca emperors were enthroned in state and revered alongside life-size effigies of them in gold. Sheets of silver (the pale metal of the sun's consort, the moon) and gold paneled interior surfaces of the main buildings. Tapestries up to seventeen feet in width, woven from the silklike wool of the vicuña, also adorned the walls. In a marvelous garden of the enclosure, agriculture and herding were celebrated in full-size replicas of plants and trees growing from a turf of golden earth, with birds and insects in gold placed here and there on their delicately molded golden branches and leaves. In the midst of these marvels of Andean metal sculpting were twenty equally marvelous life-size statues of llamas and their young, attended by life-size shepherds dressed in their native costumes and equipped with slings and crooks, all in gleaming gold.

The Incas thoroughly exploited the peoples their armies conquered, integrated into the empire, and, in some cases, civilized. To this end, inventories and censuses were necessary and were constantly being taken, and the information thus gathered was reported up the chain of bureaucratic control to Cuzco. The large herds of domesticated animals belonging to the Inca state as well as the human inhabitants of every district in the empire were regularly counted. Even the wild animals and birds in every district were inventoried periodically. And every person in the empire was classified in one of twelve administrative categories determined according to various combinations of age, sex, health, and skill; and everyone, including children, was made to do work at some task appropriate to his or her category. Other resources—such as a district's available water, pasturage, farmland, crops, stored food, bowstrings, pottery, woven cloth, minerals, and so on—were likewise recorded and the resulting information sent to the capital. These comprehensive imperial inventories and censuses were kept on clusters of cords of different colors and lengths, called *quipus,* by tying different kinds of knots on the cords in different places and by joining them together in various meaningful relationships. How to encode and read these knotted, colored, spatial messages was taught in a special school in Cuzco, and masters of this indispensable administrative skill were stationed everywhere in the empire.

The civilization of the Inca empire was the product of no less than twenty centuries of cultural development in the Andes and along the adjacent coasts of western South America. Many of the engineering marvels of the Inca empire had been put in place by those earlier civilizations. More important than the fabulous booty of gold and silver artwork and the rich mines of precious metals that the conquest of this cumulative civilization yielded to one of Europe's extracontinental imperial powers in the early sixteenth century, its conquest conferred control over more valuable, because sustainable, resources of imperial wealth and power, specifically a long-established system of tribute paying, millions of imperially disciplined workers (many of them highly competent weavers of beautiful woolen and cotton goods), and productive agricultural establishments. The Inca empire was a pastoral, farming, mining, fabricating, city-building, early Bronze Age civilization. (Luckily for the Europeans who wished to conquer it, no deposits of iron ore occur in the territories of the Inca empire.) Growing cotton in the warm coastlands adjacent to the Andes, as shown by Andean funeral clothes, predates the development of that agriculture in ancient Egypt. The same sort of evidence also indicates that Andean weaving, long before the establishment of the Inca empire, had achieved a density of weft that European weavers did not achieve until the last two centuries. Remains in ancient tombs in the Andes likewise reveal that pre-Incan surgeons used hard bronze scalpels and chisels to perform successful skull surgery, amputations, and bone transplants, and had at their disposal an effective pharmacology of anesthetic and medicinal drugs.

Throughout their empire, the Incas manifested a passion for bureaucratic control and uniformity not yet equaled even by twentieth-century imperialists. They imposed one law, one language (called by them "manmouth"), and one completely centralized administration. When the Spaniards conquered this empire, there may have been as many as one imperial official for every ten inhabitants. The hierarchy of authority, which ultimately was concentrated in the person of an absolute king who was also a god, was the principal source of the great power exercised by the tribe that made itself lord of the central Andes through military conquests, whose members came to be called Incas, a word meaning "lords" in their language. But the Incas' extreme centralization of absolute authority in the person of a god-emperor proved a great weakness with the appearance off the coasts of their early Bronze Age civilization of white-skinned strangers encased in steel, whose culture did not include belief in god-kings, and who, after they landed, proceeded to capture and then to kill the thirteenth Inca emperor to rule the Land of the Four Quarters.

The Spaniards' execution of the emperor decapitated the huge body of the Inca bureaucracy and was a death blow to the Inca state. This disaster happened to occur soon after a decimating epidemic disease had crossed into the empire, after slowly spreading southward from the Caribbean following the first appearance in those waters of European ships, and after a bloody, unprecedented, fratricidal war had also weakened the Land of the Four Quarters. The steel head and body armor that protected the vitals of these European invaders had much to do with their overthrow of a military caste who commanded resources of manpower on an imperial scale because it gave them near immunity to disabling wounds, thus immensely increasing their confidence in combat against Inca troops and multiplying their killing efficiency by a factor of hundreds. Nonmetallic shields and hard-quilted cotton armor were the standard protection for Inca armies. The Europeans' terrifying war-horses, slow-loading but deadly firearms, and heavy-bodied, trained-to-kill, spike-collared war-dogs were also instrumental in the conquest because the Inca generals had no tactics to counteract such unprecedented means of waging war. The immunity of Europeans to the devastating novel diseases that their mere presence in the Americas naturally introduced into the Land of the Four Quarters also had a demoralizing effect on the Incas because the sickening and dying of so many Indians in conjunction with the appearance of the Europeans seemed to them to fulfill the prophecies of Inca soothsayers that a race of white-skinned foreigners would one day supplant them as lords of the Andes. Perhaps the most important single factor in the conquest of this empire, however, was the astuteness of the Europeans in immediately perceiving, and deftly exploiting, the cultural beliefs that structured the power of the centralized Inca civilization.

The Europeans who invaded the Inca empire found it familiar in the same way that any early Bronze Age civilization of the eastern Mediterranean would have been familiar to them had they been put down in its midst. And it may be said that in certain aspects of medicine, surgery, mathematics, textile manufacturing, road building, irrigation engineering, gold and silver smithing, calendar making, and astronomy, the Indian civilizations of the Americas that existed at the time of Columbus's epochal voyage equaled or surpassed the achievements of European civilization in 1492 in those fields of human endeavor.

The genuineness of the respect that Europeans evinced for the civil accomplishments they also discovered in Mexico is unmistakable. As the Spanish military probe moved inland from the Gulf of Mexico in 1519, it encountered a city that appeared to one of the Spanish chroniclers who saw it "more beautiful than the cities of Spain, because it is very level, and contains many towers"; another "very pretty" urban center, which they likened to the ancient Castilian city of Valladolid; and others that were comparable in their minds to the cities of Segovia and Granada in their European homeland, as well as a fort protected by "walls, and barbicans, and moats," which the Spanish commander deemed superior to half of the fortifications he had seen in Spain. Moreover, they passed through intensely cultivated districts where "not a palm of land" went untilled and "good order and politeness" prevailed. In the lesser American Indian cities of Mexico, as the Spaniards approached the great Aztec capital Tenochtitlán (the city that has become Mexico City), they observed another quite familiar sight of civilized life: "many poor who beg among the rich in the streets, and at the market places, just as the poor do in Spain, and other civilized countries."[10]

The night before arriving in the capital city of the Aztecs, the Europeans slept in a smaller city than Tenochtitlán, having "some twelve or fifteen thousand households," whose best dwellings they declared to be "as good as the best in Spain" in size, workmanship, and the quality of their building

10. *Letters of Cortes; The Five Letters of Relation from Fernando Cortes to the Emperor Charles V,* 2 vols., ed. Francis Augustus MacNutt (London: G. P. Putnam, 1908), I, pp. 197, 220, 221; *The Conquistadors: First-Person Accounts of the Conquest of Mexico,* ed. Patricia de Fuentes (New York: Orion, 1963), p. 176.

materials, as well as in their arrangements for domestic comfort. The Spanish commander reported that his lodgings that night had both an upper and a lower story and "very refreshing gardens, with many trees and sweet scented flowers, and bathing places of fresh water, well constructed, with steps leading down to the bottom." Within the splendid garden of this noble house was "a great pool of fresh water, very well built with sides of handsome masonry," containing "many fish, and water fowl, such as ducks, cranes, and other kinds of water birds," and enclosing the gardens were "well laid tile pavements" wide enough for four persons to walk abreast and making a square "four hundred paces" long on each of its four sides; and bordering this magnificent tiled promenade was "a lattice work of canes" behind which were "arbours planted with fragrant shrubs."[11] Another Spaniard stayed in an equally noble mansion that night, which he described as: "very spacious and well built, of magnificent stone, cedar wood, and the wood of other sweet-smelling trees, with great rooms and courts, which were a wonderful sight, and all covered with awnings of woven cotton." The walls of this palace were "shining with lime and decorated with different kinds of stonework and paintings," and its garden was "choked with roses and other flowers."[12]

One twentieth-century historian has characterized the Aztec capital Europeans first saw in the autumn of 1519 as "one of the great cities of the world" in the sixteenth century, with a density of population in its environs "substantially higher than that of the Iberian peninsula then or now."[13] The Aztec metropolis that Cortés and his men entered over a long stone causeway was a very populous, strongly fortified city built on landfill a couple of miles out from the nearest shore in the larger of the two big lakes that then existed in the central valley of Mexico, but which have since been almost entirely filled in. Besides the traffic between this water-surrounded city and the lakeshore over its three stone causeways, each of which was defended by a series of guardhouses and drawbridges, an estimated fifty or sixty thousand canoes also serviced the city each day, ferrying provisions and other goods from twenty other cities and the farming districts around the lake. Potable water was conducted into the city from copious springs on the mainland through a huge aqueduct of cut stone. The palace in which

11. *Letters of Cortés: The Five Letters of Relation from Fernando Cortés to the Emperor Charles V,* 2 vols., ed. Francis Augustus MacNutt (London: G. P. Putnam, 1908), I, p. 231.

12. Bernal Diaz del Castillo, *The Conquest of New Spain,* trans. J. M. Cohen (London: The Folio Society, 1974), p. 215.

13. Charles Gibson, *The Aztecs Under Spanish Rule: A History of the Indians of the Valley of Mexico 1519–1810* (Stanford: Stanford University Press, 1964), p. 5.

the Aztec emperor housed his European guests had "canopied beds with mattresses made of large mantles, and pillows of leather and tree fiber; good quilts, and admirable white fur robes" and "very well made wooden seats, and fine matting."[14] Seventy-eight large buildings occupied the center of the city, one of them a polychromatic temple-pyramid two hundred feet high.

Among the most impressive sights of Tenochtitlán for the Europeans who first saw it was its central market, the murmur of whose throngs could be heard several miles off. This awesome marketplace had its own tribunal and police force to maintain order and to ensure fair measure and honest dealings. Its scale of business surpassed the annual regional fairs of the Spanish homeland in the sixteenth century; yet it was held every day of the year. One could hire such amenities as baths and haircuts in the daily central market of Tenochtitlán in 1519 and buy cakes made from eggs, savory stews, pies, spiced corn porridge, bread stuffed with meat and beans, and tamales; fresh, salted, and dried fish, small dogs for eating, frogs, venison, rabbits, hares, and armadillos; finely worked gold and silver and jewelry of precious and semiprecious stones; bolls of raw cotton and bolts of finely or coarsely woven cloth, in either a natural or a dyed finish; mirrors, soaps, and combs; transparent goose quills charged with gold particles, which were used in balancing accounts; axes of copper and bronze, and copper bells; hewn planks, boards, beams, tiles, adobe brick, and both rough and dressed building stones; timber, firewood, charcoal, and bulk fertilizer; carpeting, stoves, benches, chairs, stools, cradles, beds, mantles, and cushions; caged birds of prey, partridges, pigeons, doves, and domesticated ducks and turkeys; shirts, sandals, cloaks, and gorgeous capes of iridescent feathers; paper and ink; corn syrup, chocolate, and honey in various forms, and a kind of caviar from the eggs of a species of water insect that lived in the lake that surrounded the city; rope, resinous torches, flints, pipes, and smoking tobacco; various kinds of sculptures; razor-sharp obsidian knives; calabashes; amaranth, peppers, many kinds of dried beans, various fresh fruits, sweet potatoes, oil seeds, cornmeal, bulk dry corn kernels, fresh corn, different kinds of leafy fresh vegetables, the eggs of several kinds of birds, salt, spices, and herbs; poultices, charms, and medicines; a seemingly infinite variety of plain, decorated, and glazed vases made from an unusually fine clay; much exceedingly good everyday earthenware; brightly painted wooden dishes; tanning compounds and the raw and tanned skins of wolves, jaguars, otters, pumas, and other animals;

14. *The Conquistadors: First Person Accounts of the Conquest of Mexico,* ed. Patricia de Fuentes (New York: Orion, 1963), p. 147.

thread, needles, and awls; as well as other goods, produce, and—the Europeans reported—slaves.

Equally impressive were the Aztec emperor's zoological and botanical gardens. They contained every species of animal, reptile, bird, freshwater fish, and amphibian in his realm, as well as a collection of deformed human beings, dwarfs, and albinos. Three hundred keepers did nothing but look after the caged birds. Other keepers who worked in this zoo did nothing but tend to sick specimens.

Mexico in 1519 was indeed a new world but one that was familiar to Europeans, and, in many of its most fundamental aspects, it was comparable to life in their own homeland. On the basis of what he observed, the Spanish commander Cortés reported to his sovereign in Europe, the Holy Roman Emperor, Charles V, king of Spain, that he had encountered in America a civilization whose "fashion of living" was "almost the same as in Spain, with just as much harmony and order," adding that, "considering that these people were barbarous, and so cut off from the knowledge of God, and other civilized peoples, it is admirable to see what they attained in every respect."[15] The phrase "other civilized peoples" is crucial. It explains the subsequent merger of certain aspects of European civilization with the Indian civilizations in southern North America and western South America that were conquered by Spain in the second, third, and fourth decades of the sixteenth century.

Fundamentally, the marked difference between the European refusal for more than a century following Columbus's voyage, to settle in central and northern North America and the immediate desire of Europeans to live in Mexico and Peru was a matter of perceptions. Europeans knew at once what to do with the familiar worlds of the Aztec and the Inca civilizations: conquer and rule them. Armed groups had been doing that to each other in Europe for centuries. And so European lords replaced the Indian lords of these American civilizations.

The continental expanses of central and northern North America and central, eastern, and southern South America, however, offered no already-formed civilized worlds that were perceived to be of immediate worth. In these places where the three huge countries of the United States, Canada, and Brazil developed, there could be no conquest and dominance of extant indigenous civilizations. There could only be, as far as Europeans were concerned—and it took a long time for them to perceive this in North

15. *Letters of Cortés: The Five Letters of Relation from Fernando Cortés to the Emperor Charles V*, 2 vols., ed. Francis Augustus MacNutt (London: G. P. Putnam, 1908), I, p. 263.

America—a transformation of an old, old world into a new civilization. But only the continental expanse of central North America, where the United States was to develop, could be transformed throughout the whole extent of its Stone Age space-time continuum. Central North America had a quality of malleability radically different from Brazil, Canada, Spanish America, or Europe in the seventeenth and eighteenth centuries, the centuries when the set of cultural beliefs and behavior of the people of the United States of America were formed.

THE AMERICAN CULTURAL BELIEF IN CONTINUOUS IMPROVEMENT

In the history of Europe, the transition from the Stone Age to civilization took place piecemeal during a six-thousand-year-long period of time. In the United States, which has an extent of land nearly equal to that of Europe, that change occurred in three centuries. This difference is profound. In Spanish America, the change from a Stone Age to a civilized space-time continuum was accomplished before the arrival of Europeans; in Brazil and Canada it could not be accomplished everywhere. In central North America a continental-size transformation was possible and resulted in a cultural expectation of continual improvement that did not develop in Spanish America, Canada, or Brazil. Because of cultural inertia, this expectation, once it developed, persisted beyond the initial radical change from a Stone Age to a civilized space-time continuum.

During the middle and late 1600s and the 1700s, the skies over the Atlantic coastal plain of central North America were often hazy from the burning of the cutdown trees of its Stone Age wilderness. In the 1800s, west of that coastal plain, the process of destroying the Stone Age and replacing it with something radically new continued with ever-gathering momentum, first in the region between the Appalachian Mountains and the Mississippi River and then in the regions beyond the Mississippi. James Fenimore Cooper correctly remarked in the middle of the nineteenth century on the rapidness of this accelerating and continuous transformation: "Five-and-twenty years have been as ages with most things connected with America."[16]

The difference between the historical experience of Americans with the Stone Age and the much different experience of the other post-1492 peoples of the Americas can best be illustrated with reference to the culture

16. Final page, "Author's Introduction," dated March 29, 1849, James Fenimore Cooper, *The Spy: A Tale of the Neutral Ground* (New York: Dodd, Mead, 1946), a historical novel first published in 1821.

that most closely resembles that of the United States in this matter: Brazil. Like Americans, Brazilians soon manifested in their history a desire to go into the heartland of the continent whose shores they began to occupy in the first part of the sixteenth century. And the first constitution Brazilians wrote after gaining their independence from Portugal in the early nineteenth century stipulated the building of a new capital city away from the seaboard to encourage settlement inland. But that removal of the capital from the coast did not happen until 1960.

In the United States, on the other hand, a president of Yale University named Timothy Dwight stated before his death in 1817—before the first Brazilian constitution was written—that the already well advanced rapid developments he had observed during his lifetime in the remotest parts of New England and New York made it certain in his mind that "the people of the United States will in their progress fill almost the whole continent of North America, populate in the end all the extensive regions which are north of Mexico, and station themselves within half a century on the shores of the Pacific Ocean."[17] In other words, before 1817, Dwight had observed a transformational behavior that was already so encultured as to seem to him, as an American, inevitable in its continuance. His "forecast," as he called his prediction that Americans would populate and transform the entire space of central North America, from the flat Virginia Capes to the steep headlands of California and Oregon, was correct—except that he was too conservative in his estimate of how long it would take: Americans stationed themselves on the shores of the Pacific Ocean within a quarter of a century, rather than the half-century he predicted they would need.

Noah Webster expressed the same cultural belief on the last page of his Preface to his great *American Dictionary of the English Language* (1828), which he published when the population of the United States stood at fewer than twelve million. He announced there that he had performed his monumental feat of scholarship, which had taken him twenty years of single-minded research and compilation in nineteen languages to accomplish, in order to benefit the three hundred million Americans who would, he predicted, eventually inhabit the United States and speak the American language. Noah Webster's vision of the growth of the American population has proven to be accurate. And the series of dictionaries that have been based on his lifetime of labor have indeed been of great benefit to every generation of Americans since he published the first of them in 1828.

17. Timothy Dwight, *Travels in New England and New York,* 4 vols., ed. Barbara Miller Solomon (Cambridge: Harvard University Press, 1969), IV, p. 368.

The three centuries during which Americans had the unique experi-ence of transforming the whole of central North America from coast to coast induced in them as a people a cultural belief that whatever was old (according to the accelerated sense of history that developed in American culture) had to be continually made new and improved upon. In their unique historical experience of accomplishing in three centuries what had taken sixty centuries to accomplish in Europe, Americans came to believe culturally that there was no limit to what they could do as a people if they put their mind to it. The transition from the Stone Age to civilization became a precedent for a cultural belief in constant improvement. Americans are future oriented in the sense that they are improvement oriented. The future in American culture is merely the locus for improvement.

Progress for Americans has no fixed or finally perfect end. From the American experience of starting history over again "from scratch"—which was the experience of making a new beginning of civilization—came a belief in the rightness of newness. Generation after generation, Americans have acted on the cultural idea that newness is good and oldness is not because the initial ancestral act of changing the ancient Stone Age of central North America to a civilized continuum was perceived by the cultural ancestors of Americans as an unequivocal good.

No "new world" was discovered by the cultural ancestors of Americans in central North America. Instead, it was an incredibly old world—so old as to defy immediate perception as a habitable space. It had to be seen as having a potential for transformation into something new before it could be lived in. This world could have no value unless, and until, it was transformed. For this reason, as well as others, change (i.e., improvement) came to be regarded in America as culturally normal.

Since the origin of civilization for Americans in their history as a people has had a conscious starting point in the Stone Age, and since this origin had been lost to the European consciousness of history by the sixteenth century, the process of progressively making an old world into a new world, on a continentwide scale, launched the descendants of the Europeans who settled central North America into a non-European consciousness of history. In the United States, the opportunity existed for a non-European cultural behavior of continually transforming and improving a continental contin-uum. Canada and Brazil, however, persisted in being primarily outposts of European civilization in the Americas in large part because they lacked such an opportunity, even though the cultural ancestors of Canadians and Brazilians confronted a partly tranformable Stone Age. Spanish America remained even more locked into the European consciousness of history because Europeans found there an opportunity culturally familiar and congenial to them: the opportunity to conquer and rule other civilized groups.

The attempts in central North America to continue Europe's cultural mentality and behavior—such as those by the New England Puritans and the Lord Proprietors of the Carolinas, who dictated through their secretary John Locke an incredibly complicated set of statutes for government in the Carolinas, in a vain attempt to institute feudal hierarchies of titled privilege—all failed because they did not satisfy the American cultural belief in making things new. Canadians, Brazilians, and Spanish Americans experienced the making of a new world from an old world only in a limited scope and did not, therefore, develop the same cultural beliefs and behavior that Americans were already manifesting by the early 1700s. The self-awareness of those three post-1492 populations remained, as the self-awareness of Americans did not, that of Europeans living in the Americas. The Brazilian *bandeirantes*, for instance, who followed the flag of a leader into the Stone Age interior of Brazil in the seventeenth century, did not make their heroic journeys to live in and transform the Stone Age but rather to make raids upon it and extract from it its most valuable material essences (gold and diamonds) to carry back to the coast and ship to Europe and to capture Indians to sell as slaves to the sugar plantations on the coast. The seventeenth-century French Canadian *coureurs de bois* likewise operated in Canada's Stone Age heartland to the same purpose: prolonged forays into the interior to collect portable distillations of its wealth (furs in this case) to take back to the coast to send to Europe. While such expeditions into the continental expanses of Stone Age Canada and Stone Age Brazil were being made in the seventeenth and the eighteenth centuries, clouds of hot smoke in ever-increasing volumes billowed skyward from the burning of the Stone Age on the coastal plain that would become the eastern United States, until that many-thousands-of-years-old forest was entirely gone.

The analysis that American cultural beliefs and behavior had one of their prime sources in an absence of civilization (the Stone Age space-time continuum) which, after a long delay, was finally "seen" as having a potential for becoming a new, continental civilization, means that Americans as a people developed a cultural belief in acting on what is visible only to the eye of faith. In the early twentieth century, the American writer F. Scott Fitzgerald seems to have had in mind this cultural trait of being able to foresee a new reality in remarking that to be an American is to have a certain "willingness of the heart." And in the early nineteenth century, James Fenimore Cooper was comically portraying this trait when he had a male character in chapter sixteen of his novel *The Pioneers* (1823) invite a young kinswoman to accompany him on a brief inspection of the "improvements," as he calls them, that he has made since her last visit to the settlement. When she inquires where these improvements are—because she can see no particular change in the landscape he shows her—he exclaims impatiently: " 'Where? Why everywhere. Here I have laid out some new streets; and when they are opened, and the trees are felled, and they are all built up, will they not make a fine town?' " A self-selected immigrant to America, the Norwegian-American novelist O. E. Rölvaag, makes the same point in *Giants in the Earth,* his novel about immigrant pioneers on the Dakota plains in the late nineteenth century: "Now and then Tonseten would turn their conversation toward the future; he was more interested in visualizing how things were going to turn out than in making a bare statement of how they actually were. . . ." The visionary capacity was, in Rölvaag's mind, crucial to becoming a self-selecting emigrant. The principal character in *Giants in the Earth* exclaims about Europeans, " 'There are some people, I know now, who never should emigrate, because, you see, they can't take pleasure in what is to come—they simply can't see it!' "[18] A cultural faith in visions of future improvements also appears in Timothy Dwight's meditation on his observation of the transformation of the New England and New York hinterlands in the late eighteenth century, which led him to see a reality yet to be:

> Let me bring to your recollection the rapid progress of our population, the progressive state in which most of the articles which I have recited actually exist at the present time, and the promise which they give of superior advancement. With these objects in contemplation, a traveler passing through the countries which I have described, surveying the scenes which they everywhere present to his eye, and remembering within how short a period and amid how many difficulties they have been raised up in a howling wilderness, will think it no extravagance of imagination to believe that throughout this vast empire, villages innumerable will everywhere speedily adorn its surface with the same beauty and cheerfulness which he beholds around him. To these he will add the flourishing towns and splendid cities which not only the shore of the ocean, but the numerous lakes and rivers, will in the interior see rising on their borders, the seats of various useful manufactures and of an inland commerce resembling and excelling that of the Chinese empire. Everywhere he will foresee neat schoolhouses stationed at little distances, diffusing each over

18. O. E. Rölvaag, *Giants in the Earth,* trans. O. E. Rölvaag and Lincoln Colcord (New York: Perennial Library, Harper & Row, 1955), pp. 348, 375.

its proper circle the education necessary to every human being, and contributing to create a new national character by elevating the minds of those of whom the great body of every nation is formed. To these his fancy will add, at distances somewhat greater, the vast collection of superior schools communicating more extensive information to a multitude, less indeed, but still very great. Within every twenty thousand square miles, his mind will easily station a college, where literature and science will shed their light upon a number of votaries sufficiently great to perform all the kinds of human business which demand extensive information. Nor will he hesitate, since he sees the work already begun, to fix here and there seats of professional science, in which shall be taught whatever is known by man concerning medicine, law, policy, and religion: or to superadd those national institutions designed not so much to teach as to advance the knowledge of man.[19]

What is culturally significant about this statement by an eighteenth-century American is that his vision became reality. The vast trans-Appalachian and the trans-Mississippian regions of Stone Age wilderness in central North America were in fact transformed by generations of visionaries like himself into a new and progressive civilization having a widely distributed system of public education at every level of knowledge, all the way to the Pacific Ocean. American culture, because it had its origin in the Stone Age, had to be a culture of visionaries.

The liberty for many persons to envision something new and magnificent for themselves and their fellow Americans, as well as for future generations of Americans, and the freedom to work freely with others to realize their visions were among the benefits bestowed by the presence of a transformable Stone Age in central North America. Americans have been and remain a people united by a belief in the necessity of transforming what is into what the visionary eye can see. Because the compelling visions of Americans had to operate on a harsh and demanding reality, the creation of the envisioned new improvements called forth the highest possible development and discipline of varied human talents and energies, from dictionary writers to canal engineers.

As the long passage quoted above from Timothy Dwight's *Travels* shows, the liberty to think of making oldness into newness—which started with the perception by common people that the Stone Age space-time continuum of central North America was continentally transformable—increased in cultural appeal and coherence with each successful comple-

19. Timothy Dwight, *Travels in New England and New York,* 4 vols., ed. Barbara Miller Solomon (Cambridge: Harvard University Press, 1969), IV, pp. 370–71.

tion of the initial stage of transformation and with every subsequent improvement that was made upon that initial transformation. The awareness of the possibility of making that which is old and perhaps good enough into something new and even better has constituted the historical consciousness of American culture in a way not possible for other parts of the Americas or Europe, with its density of conflicting groups, each of them ambitious to dominate some other group or anxious to protect itself from domination. In the United States, the authority of European culture has, therefore, not made as much sense as it has in other parts of the Americas and has had comparatively less influence on cultural behavior. The unique American encounter with a transformable continental space presented a kind of prehistory on which to project new visions rather than a continuation of the old wisdom of European culture. And a rich panoply of materials and a rich variety of human skills and interests for the enactment of new realities came into conjunction in central North America through self-selecting emigration.

To Americans, the past is not dead and offensive because the American past was the Stone Age and that has been transformed into something vital and ever-promising. The past has become for Americans whatever is ready at hand awaiting further improvement. The history of America has been millions of common people finding the freedom to fashion their ideas into reality. The historical consciousness that such behavior from generation to generation has given rise to is the belief that nothing is impossible for a person, or a nation, given enough hard work and a visionary perception of reality. Americans have acted on this cultural belief from generation to generation and continue to do so today. It is the famous "innocence" and "naiveté" of Americans so often remarked on by Europeans. Yet the belief of Americans that anything is possible, given enough hard work and a visionary perception of reality, has a valid foundation in the actual historical experience of Americans. It is simply not a sense of history that has any meaning for persons on the continent of Europe, where rulers, not visionaries, have been the most esteemed historical figures.

CHAPTER

5

AMERICAN SPACE AS FREEDOM

To human beings, a space is defined not only by its physical characteristics but by what human beings do in it over time. This is its cultural dimension. The dynamic of American culture has been freedom of physical space enhancing and being enhanced by freedom of thought and behavior.

In the central part of North America, the Stone Age as a continental space-time continuum began to end in 1600. By 1900 it had ceased to exist in what is now the contiguous forty-eight states of the United States. Such a radical change to such a large area in such a short time was unprecedented in human history. Because the Stone Age continuum had no recognizable value for the self-selected immigrants and their cultural descendants who worked that change, they felt an extraordinary sense of freedom in replacing and developing it to suit their own ideas of what it ought to be. Thus, American space came to be culturally defined as freedom of action.

The potential of this continental space for producing wealth through its progressive transformation, in conjunction with the absence within its continuum of any forbidding climate or topography, or any formidable and persistent military threat on its borders, made it the ideal building material for the self-selected immigrants who came to it from Europe. Such a space attracted workers having a daring, self-motivating mentality; and once enough people with this type of character had accumulated in America, their behavior made American space more convincingly attractive to others like themselves who were still in Europe and who also had a daring belief in their ability to better themselves and society by acting on their equality

118

of liberty with other like-minded persons. The self-selected immigrant's belief in his right to determine his own happiness, on his own terms, through his own efforts, found an extraordinary physical freedom for expressing itself in behavior from generation to generation in central North America.

The idea of a collection of strangers voluntarily and consciously endeavoring to work together—without any unifying discipline imposed on them from above by an authoritarian ruling class—to build something new for themselves and their posterity on a vast scale, which would satisfy their individual and social longings, has never been a part of the historical consciousness of Europe. Nor has it played a part in the cultural formations of Brazil and Canada, where the Stone Age proved unmalleable on a continental scale, or in the cultural formation of Spanish America, where extensive civilizations comparable to the early stages of European civilization were already in place in the early sixteenth century, thereby making European-style conquest and dominion, rather than transformation, the fundamental cultural behavior in Spanish America.

During the transformation of the Stone Age continuum of central North America, the creation of wealth and unifying communications became the principal human activity. Each success in that process heightened the confidence of the self-selected European immigrants and their American-born descendants. This, in turn, led to other new cultural beliefs (such as the belief that success is in the nature of things) and to radically non-European concepts of history, space, and time.

A DESTINY OF LIMITED, SELF-DETERMINED GROWTH

Except for minor adjustments effected by Brazilians after their independence from Portugal, Portugal and Spain—with some initial help from the papacy—determined Brazil's boundaries during its colonial history; and Spain, during its dominion on the American continents, determined the extent of Spanish America, except for the loss of the northern part of Mexico to the United States following that nation's independence from Spain. The actions of France and then Britain, during the seventeenth, eighteenth, and nineteenth centuries, determined Canada's boundaries. The United States is, therefore, the only one of the four major continental cultures of the Americas that has decided its own boundaries. This is another fundamental cultural difference between the United States and the other continental cultures of the Americas.

The way in which Americans determined their own boundaries is also distinctive: title to four-fifths of the increase of territory beyond the original territory of the United States (2,182,000 square miles out of an increase of 2,724,000 square miles) took place through diplomacy and purchase rather than through war. No other large nation in the world's history has acquired title to so much of its territory in this way.

So frequently did events on the international scene seem to favor America's peaceful acquisition of title to new territory that Americans in the early nineteenth century came to believe that God's providence ordained the growth of their nation. Furthermore, the expansion of American space prevented the crowding that should have accompanied the kind of sustained population growth that took place in the United States. In the eighty years from 1790 to 1870 following the establishment of government under the Constitution, the population of the United States increased tenfold, but density of population increased only two and one-half times (from 4.5 to 11 persons per square mile) because the extent of U.S. territory during that time quadrupled. In the next eighty-year segment of American history, 1870 to 1950, population nearly quadrupled, going from 40 million to 150 million persons, while density of population increased four and one-half times from eleven to fifty persons per square mile. But even this small excess in the rate of increase of population density over the rate of increase of population size can hardly be viewed as an adverse crowding of American space. During the formative centuries of American culture, growth without penalty seemed to be the manifest destiny of America.

A diplomatic victory far greater than the success of American arms against Britain between 1775 and 1783 obtained America's original territory of nine hundred thousand square miles. The area won in the treaty that ended the American Revolution exceeded by far the area Americans had actually settled as of that date. The evidently already-enculturated American idea of a continental transformation of the Stone Age wilderness in central North America seems to have given American diplomats in 1783 a supreme confidence at the bargaining table. Britain, for instance, could have claimed all of the Great Lakes Basin as pertaining naturally to Canada, but the southern half of this basin went to the Americans in the treaty of 1783. From it, five large states (Ohio, Indiana, Illinois, Michigan, and Wisconsin) and part of another (Minnesota) were eventually formed. The boundaries negotiated by American diplomats with Britain after the Revolution gave America the whole eastern drainage of the Mississippi. This original national territory—the Atlantic coastal plain between Maine and the Florida peninsula and the then-untransformed trans-Appalachian lands to the Mississippi—comprise one-fourth of the 3.6 million square miles of the national territory of the United States today.

Twenty years later, the United States acquired through purchase from

France title to almost all of the western drainage of the Mississippi River: an area about equal in size to the original 889 thousand square miles of the national territory east of the Mississippi. The failure of the army sent by Napoleon from Europe to reverse the successful revolt by African slaves in Haiti, a French colony considered by him to be a crucial strategic base for the creation and protection of a projected French empire in the center of North America, led directly to the acquisition of these lands between the Mississippi River and the Rocky Mountains. The United States government paid the French government fifteen million dollars for title to "Louisiana" as it was called, a purchase that included the eighty-five-year-old town of New Orleans controlling entrance to the Mississippi River. Five whole states (Arkansas, Missouri, Iowa, Nebraska, and South Dakota) and large parts of eight more (Louisiana, Oklahoma, Kansas, Colorado, Wyoming, Montana, North Dakota, and Minnesota) were formed from this accession to the national territory, which in 1803 approximately doubled the size of the United States.

Fifteen years after the Louisiana Purchase, American diplomats negotiated a small cession of territory from Britain at two widely separated points on the U.S. border with Canada, from which were formed the northern tip of Maine and parts of Minnesota and North Dakota. The next year, 1819, America acquired through a treaty with Spain that country's territories east of the Mississippi: "West Florida" (the area that is today the Gulf coasts of Alabama and Mississippi, the southeast corner of the state of Louisiana, and the Florida panhandle) and "East Florida" (the Florida peninsula), which added seventy thousand square miles of territory to the United States, or about 2 percent of the final national total. Britain's two decades of military occupation of East Florida and the settlement there between 1763 and 1783 of British loyalists from America had impaired Spanish control of the Florida peninsula, just as the American purchase of Louisiana and the rapid settlement by Americans of the inland parts of what is now Alabama and Mississippi and the area around the eastward curve of the Mississippi River near New Orleans had impaired Spanish control over West Florida. This negotiated purchase was concluded during the rebellions in Spain's larger-than-Europe kingdoms in South and North America, events that made Spain willing to sell off border areas it no longer had firm control over. The price for East and West Florida was the assumption by the American government of five million dollars in liabilities against the Spanish government.

The diplomatic compromise negotiated in 1846 with Britain regarding the disputed territory to the north and east of the American settlements in Oregon (present-day Washington and Idaho and part of Montana) and the purchase in 1853 for ten million dollars of what is now southern Arizona and a small part of New Mexico brought more than three hundred thousand additional square miles within America's borders through peaceful means. The American government's hesitant approval in 1867 of the treaty pressed on it by the imperial Russian government for the purchase of the Alaskan peninsula and the adjacent coasts and islands, which Russian fur traders had settled at the time of the American Revolution—a thinly populated overseas territory imperial Russia considered vulnerable to British naval domination and possible seizure from British-ruled Canada—added another six hundred thousand square miles to American territory. The price in this case was 7.2 million dollars.

Cumulatively, the area gained in acquiring East and West Florida from Spain, the disputed areas of "Oregon" from Britain, the Gadsden Purchase from Mexico, and "Seward's Folly" (as the purchase of Alaska from Russia was called at the time) closely approximated the size of the Louisiana Purchase and completed the unprecedented purchases and negotiations of title to national land by American diplomats. Another diplomatic accession of territory, but without purchase, was the absorption of a large sovereign nation into the American union in 1845 after years of effort by it to obtain such admission. Texas was not the only or the first independent nation in the Americas to petition for admission to the United States of America; but the envoy that El Salvador sent to Washington in 1822, with instructions to ask for admission as a state in the United States, could not be officially received because a Mexican army's takeover of his nation abrogated his diplomatic credentials.

The Republic of Texas had been a vast region in the Mexican state of Coahuila. Americans had settled there with the encouragement and permission of, first, the Spanish government and, then, the Mexican government, in such numbers that by 1830 American Mexicans outnumbered those of Mexican descent four to one. When the government of Mexico and the liberal constitution of 1824 were overthrown by Mexican conservatives in 1835, the American Mexicans of the state of Coahuila joined with Zacatecas and other states of Mexico in rebelling against the new regime in Mexico City, which insisted on strong central control from the national capital as opposed to the states' rights policies of the previous government and its constitution, under which Americans had emigrated to Texas. The petition of the Texans to become a Mexican state apart from Coahuila but still within the Mexican nation having been denied and the Mexican army sent to put down their rebellion having been defeated, the American Mexicans in Texas wrote their own constitution and declared themselves a separate, sovereign republic. Immediately Britain, France, and other European countries recognized the Republic of Texas as an accomplished fact; finally, in 1837, so did the United States. The Republic of Texas had diplomatic relations with many countries, a national debt, and other essential features of nationhood when it successfully defended its sovereignty for a second time, between 1842 and 1844, against an invading Mexican army sent to try again to force its reunification with Mexico. In 1845, the year after this second successful defense of its national territory by the Republic of Texas, the efforts of Texas to gain admittance to the union of American states likewise met with success.

The territory claimed by the Republic of Texas when it was admitted to the United States embraced four hundred thousand square miles of land. Included in that territory, besides the present state of Texas, were the eastern part of New Mexico and portions of Colorado, Wyoming, Kansas, and Oklahoma—all of which the state of Texas sold to the United States for ten million dollars in 1850.

The refusal of the government of Mexico, even after its defeat in 1844 in its second war with the Republic of Texas, to recognize the established sovereignty of Texas and the right of the Republic of Texas, therefore, to negotiate its admission into the American union of states; the natural desire of the United States to acquire by purchase title to the territory between the Pacific coast of central North America and the lands that the accession of the Republic of Texas had incorporated into the United States; and the equally natural desire of Mexico to retain that land, even though it also was rapidly being settled by Americans, especially California and Utah, led to America's only war of conquest against a neighboring nation to gain territory for new states. The war began in 1846 and developed into a four-pronged American attack on Mexico: an overland invasion of California, which was also invaded by sea and attacked by an uprising of its American settlers; an overland invasion of New Mexico; an overland invasion of the northern states of Mexico; and a seaborne invasion of central Mexico by an expeditionary force that fought its way inland from the Gulf of Mexico to Mexico City. European military analysts sent to observe the performance of American forces in this war generally agreed that they could not win it, operating as they were in the center of the Mexican population at great distances from their own centers of population and supply. But, in 1848, after a year and a half of campaigning, the war terminated with the American capture of Mexico City. A major factor in the American victory in this war was the almost chaotic instability of the Mexican government during the thirty-five years following independence from Spain, a period that saw a short-lived Mexican monarchy, three successive constitutions, and more than twenty presidents come and go. Santa Anna, the leader who conducted most of the fighting against the United States, was president six times and less formally the country's leader on five other occasions during the tumultuous three and one-half decades of Mexican history between 1820 and 1855.

America's conquest of Mexico is unique not only in American history, as the only U.S. border war for territorial conquest, but also in the history of such wars in the world because at the conclusion of hostilities the United States, the conquering nation, paid Mexico, the conquered nation, for territory it already held militarily. Furthermore, the United States withdrew its armies from other territory that they had likewise conquered and were militarily occupying. This war was a forced purchase. The part of northern Mexico that the Americans conquered and also paid for was the same part of Mexico they had offered to buy from Mexico before the war, and the amount the United States paid for this already-conquered territory was the same as the United States had paid Napoleon for the much larger territory of Louisiana: fifteen million dollars. Under the terms of the Treaty of Guadalupe Hidalgo (1848), which terminated the Mexican-American War and specified the terms of this purchase, the American government also assumed 3.25 million dollars in claims against the Mexican government, making the total purchase 18.25 million dollars. This unprecedented payment of reparations to a completely vanquished nation by a completely victorious nation may have astonished European observers even more than America's successful logistical support of its armies, its uninterrupted series of victories, and its withdrawal of U.S. military forces from control over the world-famous gold and silver mines of Mexico, payment for conquered lands being unheard-of in European history. From the territory the United States forced Mexico to sell were organized the states of California, Nevada, and Utah, half of New Mexico, most of Arizona, part of Wyoming, and part of Colorado: about 15 percent of the present national territory of the United States.

The island state of Hawaii, representing .002 percent of the national area, became a territory of the United States in 1900. Acquisition followed the rebellion against the Hawaiian monarchy in 1893 that was led by American residents of Hawaii.

A natural limit to size seems to exist among the large nations of the world, except for the 8.6 million square miles of the domestic empire of nations called the Union of Soviet Socialist Republics, which is in a class by itself and covers more than one-seventh of the world's land surface. America's self-determination of its 3.6 million square miles of territory put it close to the 3.5-million-square-mile average for the large nations of the world (apart from the Soviet Union): Canada, 3.8 million square miles; China, 3.7; the U.S., 3.6; Brazil, 3.3; and Australia, 3.0. In 1848, following the war with Mexico, America had an area the size of Australia, about three million square miles, and stopped trying to acquire further national territory. Without the purchase of Alaska from the imperial government of Russia, after years of Russian diplomatic efforts to conclude the sale, the United States today would have the same size as the only large nation of the world whose borders are entirely determined by oceans: the continent-nation of Australia.

Had all of Mexico been retained by the United States in 1848, following its conquest by American naval and land forces, and had some of the one-million-strong, combat-trained U.S. Army been ordered north at the end of the American Civil War to take Canada—as the British government and many Canadians expected would happen because of British aid to the rebelling southern states during that war—nothing could have prevented the huge, already-mobilized land and sea forces of the United States from also taking over the small North American nations to the south of Mexico, all of the main islands in the Caribbean, and the Danish territory of Greenland, thus giving the United States the entire 9.4 million square miles of the continent of North America and making it the largest country the world has ever known, exceeding in area even the present aggregate of nations in the USSR. But none of that happened in the twenty years between 1845 and 1865. The United States did not become during those two decades, as it might well have done from a military point of view, the United States of North America. Its not having done so is culturally significant behavior when one thinks of the history of Europe.

What did happen between 1845 and 1865 was the withdrawal, in 1848, of the completely victorious American armies from southern Mexico and the payment to Mexico of a great deal of bullion for the already-conquered northern territories. And in 1865, rather than mount an invasion to take Canada, the United States merely sent some of its huge army of combat veterans to the U.S.–Mexican border and issued a stern warning to France to evacuate its troops from Mexico, where, with the diplomatic collusion and military support of Britain, in bold defiance of the Monroe Doctrine of the United States, France had installed a European archduke as emperor of Mexico while the United States was preoccupied with its civil war. Then, America demobilized the largest army the continent of North America had ever seen and sent the soldiers home—just as it was to do after World War II, when for a crucial period from 1945 to 1949, it had a monopoly on the most intimidating weapon ever devised, the atomic bomb, and the means to deliver it anywhere in the world, as well as an already-tooled war-production industry of immense capacity and the only completely un-scathed large economic base in the world. When the army of the United

States triumphed over the revolting southern states in the spring of 1865, it numbered one million soldiers; by the end of 1866, it consisted of twenty-five thousand men and remained at that level until 1898 even though America's population during those years increased by some thirty-five million people.

Americans have believed that their culture would be progressively imitated in the world; they have seen themselves as destined to transform the central part of North America between the Great Lakes and the Gulf of Mexico westward to the Pacific. That self-limited vision was the height of their ambition as a people: to be a large and prosperous and self-determining nation. The American cultural idea of self-determination has been evidenced as much in the history of what Americans as a people could have done in North America but refrained from doing as it has been in what they have uniquely done in determining the boundaries of their nation. No other modern nation in the world has been in the military position to expand its territory to 9.4 million square miles, as America was in the period from 1845 to 1865, and chosen not to do so. Samuel Eliot Morison has succinctly stated the military self-restraint of Americans in North America in 1865, in the following terms: "It was assumed in Europe that President [Andrew] Johnson, with a big army at his disposal, would grab Canada as 'compensation' for war losses, or invade Mexico to oust Maximilian. But, beyond sending an army of observation to the Mexican border to give moral support to [Mexican president] Juárez, he did nothing in either quarter; and a few years later, Congress refused to buy a naval base in the West Indies, indicating that 'manifest destiny' had come to a full stop."[1] In short, the distinctive freedom of American space has been *not* to use military force when its use to attain territory could not have been resisted by those against whom it would have been applied.

THE FREEDOM OF A LARGE, UNIFIED SPACE

The geographies of Brazil, Canada, and Spanish America presented greater obstacles to unity of communication than did the geography of the United States of America. In Spanish America, the difficulties consist of soaring mountain ranges and great distances. (The Andes have many peaks over twenty thousand feet high, and from the southernmost part of Argentina to the northernmost point of Colombia on the South American continent and from there to the extreme northwest of Mexico is close to eight

1. Samuel Eliot Morison, *The Oxford History of the American People,* 3 vols. (New York: New American Library, 1972), II, chapter 24, paragraph 4.

thousand miles.) In Canada, water that is usually in the form of ice has been a great obstacle to communication. All of Canada was under thousands of feet of ice eleven thousand years ago, and the melting of that continental ice cap left it with an inland sea and innumerable marshes, bogs, rivers, streams, great lakes, and ponds to an extent that Canada seems almost to consist as much of water as of dry land. When not frozen, these waters in the seventeenth, eighteenth, and nineteenth centuries facilitated canoe travel across northern North America to the Arctic and the Pacific oceans; but the wide band of watery wilderness that runs from south-central Canada northwest to Alaska, Canada's subarctic and arctic climates, and the granitic Canadian Shield have all posed problems for the construction of modern all-weather roads and railroads across Canada. In Brazil, the awesome continual flooding and other peculiarities in the basin of the Amazon rain forest and the steep terrain of much of the broad highlands south of that basin have hindered communications. The combined effect of these features of Brazilian geography has been to keep most of its population crowded into a comparatively narrow band of settlement not far inland from the South Atlantic. The difficulties of communication by land and water within Brazil's national space have had much to do with the significant contributions of Brazilians to the development of air transportation.

In comparison to the other peoples of the major continental cultures of the Americas, Americans have been blessed by a homeland whose geography and climate have presented fewer impediments to its unification by land and water, none of them insurmountable even with the technologies of the eighteenth and nineteenth centuries. From the beginning, the original territory of the United States between the Atlantic Ocean and the Mississippi River could be unified by roads and waterways that were usable most of the year. As the boundaries of America expanded, Americans rapidly integrated the additional territories into existing systems of communication.

The Mississippi and Missouri rivers, once most or all of their drainages had been included within America's borders, provided, along with the Ohio River, a natural system in the American heartland of north-south and east-west transportation by water. Communication from the east into this expansive interior network of large rivers was not long in being established. By 1825, a 350-mile-long barge canal having a vertical rise of 568 feet (the rise of the Panama Canal is eighty-five feet) had been dug across the length of New York State to connect the Atlantic Ocean with the four continuously navigable lakes of the Great Lakes above Niagara Falls and (via these freshwater seas) the far-distant interior farmlands of the continent. Less than a decade later 260 miles of canal in two segments and 140 miles of connecting railroad across southern Pennsylvania were lifting barges of freight and passengers 2,334 feet over the ridges of the Appalachian Mountains and making possible direct communication from the Atlantic seaport of Philadelphia to the upper Ohio River and the Mississippi system of natural waterways. Before 1830, north-south communications in the East were improved by digging a canal between the Delaware and Chesapeake bays, which shortened waterway communications between Philadelphia and Baltimore by three hundred miles, and another between the Hudson and the Delaware rivers, which shortened water transportation between Philadelphia and New York by 450 miles. By 1860, four long-distance, north-south canals connected the Great Lakes with the Mississippi and Ohio rivers; and a fifth canal connected the Erie Canal in New York with the canal-railroad system across Pennsylvania.

The earliest east-west land communication was the "road" established in 1775 by Daniel Boone through a great gap near the middle of the Appalachian Mountains at the place where the present states of Virginia, Kentucky, and Tennessee meet: a point more than half the distance from the Atlantic seaboard to the Mississippi River. By 1792 Boone's horse trail had been improved to a wagon road that, after traversing the length of Virginia in a southwesterly direction, passed through the Cumberland Gap in the mountains and continued across Kentucky to the western reaches of the Ohio River. This east-west Wilderness Road, as it was called, through the center of America's original national territory, remained the principal route of communication by land between the Atlantic coastal plain and the trans-Appalachian west until the federal government built a wagon road from the Potomac River through the mountains to the Ohio River west of Pittsburgh, which was called the National Road. This federal highway was paved with crushed stone and was completed in 1818; by 1833 it had been extended through the states of Ohio, Indiana, and Illinois to the confluence of the Missouri and Mississippi rivers at St. Louis, Missouri. A 780-mile wagon route from Missouri to the upper Rio Grande (the Santa Fe Trail) and a two-thousand-mile wagon route from Missouri across the high plains and the Rocky Mountains to Oregon and California (the Oregon Trail) were in use by 1822 and 1832, respectively. *Overland communications across central North America were, therefore, continuous, from the Atlantic to the Pacific, within fifty years of the end of the American Revolution.*

The building of canals and railroads in the United States kept pace with each other until 1840. In use that year were more than three thousand miles of railroad and more than thirty-three hundred miles of canal. In the decade 1840–50, however, the faster, more easily built, and more versatile of these two kinds of freight and passenger communications became the primary system, as six thousand additional miles of railroad tracks were laid, but only three hundred miles of additional canals were constructed. And just twenty-two years after the first locomotive engine ran on rail tracks in the United States, a railroad was in operation west of the Mississippi. A railroad bridge across the Mississippi linked the American East by rail with the trans-Mississippi American West in 1855. By 1900, America had 186 thousand miles of railroad. This was seventy-six thousand miles more than the combined trackage of Germany, Russia, India, France, and Britain—the other principal railroad-building countries in the nineteenth century.

America today has many railroads and domestic aviation routes, over three million miles of paved roads, and the world's largest telephone system. Inland waterways still carry about one-sixth of the freight transported within the United States (in huge "tows" of steel barges pushed by tugboats), but the only canals now in active commercial use are the more than eighty that shorten the loops of the Ohio and Mississippi and thus speed up water transportation on those rivers. In other words, the space of no other large nation in the world has been so effectively unified as that of the United States by so many different, heavily used communication systems for freight, people, and information. This unification of a large space is a primary characteristic of the cultural behavior of the American people. American geography allowed unifying systems of communication to be built, but the ideation of American culture mandated that they should be built. Such systems have given Americans an extraordinary freedom of space.

America's opportunities for expansion and development in combination with the ideas of American culture have led to the large, free, unified, self-determined space that is "American space." As a people composed like no other in the Americas predominately of rapidly increasing numbers of self-selected immigrants and their descendants, Americans in comparison to the other modern peoples of the Americas have had cultural beliefs suited to the behavior of movement. The will to move that brought, at considerable risk to themselves, the progenitors of American culture across more than three thousand miles of ocean also sent, at considerable risk to themselves, masses of migrants across three thousand miles of the North American continent. Brazilians and Spanish Americans did not have such a migrating population. Their cultures were predicated on the idea of a minority of one race ruling a majority composed of another race. Fixity of residence was, therefore, more desirable in Brazil and Spanish America. The majority in those cultures remained in one place either as slaves or as peons. The idea of one group ruling another also became part of Canada's cultural formation after the Conquest, as it is called in Canadian history, of the French "race" by the British "race." (These references to race were in use in the eighteenth century in Canada and remain in use now in Canadian social, political, and historical discourse.) The mentality of free movement within a rapidly expanding and highly unified continental space has not historically characterized Brazilian, Canadian, and Spanish American cultures, or any other culture in the world.

The Canadian Constitution Act of 1982 established a Charter of Rights and Freedoms (equivalent to the United States Constitution's Bill of Rights) that specifies and protects the rights of individuals in Canada for the first time; and, surprisingly, among the rights it guarantees is that of every Canadian "to move to and take up residence in any province and to pursue the gaining of a livelihood in any province." This provision of free movement speaks to the historically almost nationalistic separatism of Canada's provinces: "Section 6 [of the Charter of Rights and Freedoms] represents a new addition to the traditional list of human freedoms, in that mobility rights are explicitly recognized for the first time in Canada. At the insistence of the federal government, mobility rights were included in an attempt to prevent the 'balkanization' of the polity, so that the [Canadian] provinces could not continue to pass legislation designed to hinder interprovincial migration."[2] Britain, having seen what happened in the Atlantic coastal plain of North America in the eighteenth century, kept its colonies in Canada separated from each other until 1867. Then, at the instigation of Canadians, a semblance of national government was permitted, under the authority of an act of Parliament written in London by Canadians and Britons, which structured a greater degree of separation among the Canadian provinces than ever existed among the American states under the Constitution. This act of 1867 remains the foundation of the Canadian constitution.

In America, a national government under a constitution entirely written and ratified by Americans presided over America's self-determination of its borders and the organization and admission of new states into the union on an equal political footing with already-existing states. There was no such enlargement of national territory in Brazil or in Spanish America after their independence; and in Canada, the organization of new provinces in the West, which did not begin until the late nineteenth century, was stimulated by a separatist feeling and actual rebellions in those parts of Canada; and each of the new western provinces, under the provisions of the Canadian constitution, still had its own lieutenant governor, separately appointed by the British crown through its governor in Canada. The slow but steady

2. Ronald G. Landes, *The Canadian Polity: A Comparative Introduction* (Scarborough, Ontario: Prentice-Hall Canada, 1983), p. 388.

tendency of Canadian cultural history in the latter twentieth century, however, has been in the direction of an all-Canadian government, with authority centered in Canada, a greater unity of national space, and greater freedom of movement within that space.

Another distinctive trait of American space has been unity of language. This also has fostered the comparatively much greater unity and individual freedom of movement that distinguishes American space. Brazilians also have enjoyed unity of language; but only in a restricted area of their space, as the inviolable heartland of Stone Age Brazil long remained largely outside the effectively available national space. In Spanish America one language prevails, but the languages of the peoples whom the Spaniards conquered in the sixteenth century have persisted underneath the Spanish language. There are, for instance, still seven million speakers of Quechua (the language of the Inca empire) in Peru, Bolivia, Ecuador, Colombia, Argentina, and Chile, many of whom know no Spanish; and in the vastness of the jungle that covers more than one-half of the third-largest nation in Spanish America (Peru), there are still one hundred thousand Stone Age tribesmen whom neither the Spanish nor the Incas ever conquered. The same situation, involving other hundreds of thousands of Stone Age Indians, is true of the jungles of Ecuador, Colombia, Bolivia, and Brazil; and in Chile, between 300 and 350 thousand Mapuche Indians use their own language, although some know the primary language of the country. In Mexico—the largest Spanish-speaking community in the world—an estimated one-quarter of the population speaks languages belonging to thirty-one Indian language groups, including the languages of the Aztecs (Nahuatl) and Maya, Zapotec, Otomi, and Mixtec. After years of diligent educational efforts by the federal government of Mexico, a majority of Mexican citizens can now speak Spanish in addition to whatever first-use languages they may speak. In Guatemala, where about 40 percent of the populace is Indian, Spanish is the official and the commercial language, but twenty-one dialects of five Indian languages are the first-use and preferred languages of this large proportion of the Guatemalan population. In Paraguay, 90 percent of the population speaks Guarani as their language of primary use because 95 percent of the population is descended from Guarani Indians—although three-fourths of all Paraguayans can also speak Spanish. In Peru, where about 45 percent of the populace is Indian, there have been since 1975 two official languages: Quechua and Spanish. Prior to that year, the Quechuan language had been outlawed for nearly two hundred years because of the revolt of Quechua speakers in 1780, which was led by a descendant of the Inca Tupac Amarú—José Gabriel Condorcanqui—whom the Spanish authorities had unsuccessfully tried to enculturate by conferring on him the title and privileges of a Spanish marquis. Eighty thousand Spaniards and Indians were killed during that bloody cultural uprising, a number exceeding the battle deaths of the Confederate States in the Civil War.

The linguistic situation in Spanish America, that of many tribal languages, still bears some resemblance to what existed everywhere in the Americas before 1500, except in the Inca empire. In North America alone, for instance, it is estimated that there were five hundred languages. But, although many language communities still exist in Spanish America, cumulatively having millions of speakers, only one language, that of the Spanish conquerors, is known by a large proportion of the whole population of this area of continental culture. It is that fact that gives Spanish its importance. Even Quechua speakers constitute a language community that is less than 5 percent of the whole population of Spanish America.

Another dual-language culture in the Americas besides Peru—in which all but a few persons speak mainly one of two languages—is Canada. (In a bilingual culture, most persons would know both of the society's two main languages; in a dual-language culture, a great many persons know only one of the two languages mainly in use.) In 1971, one person in four in Canada spoke French as his language of first use and preference, and an overwhelming majority of these speakers were concentrated in the largest province of the country, Quebec, which embraces nearly one-sixth of Canada's area. The same survey revealed that about two of every three *Quebecois* spoke only French without knowing English, which in 1971 was the language of first use and preference of 67 percent of Canadians. Besides the 67 percent whose first language was English and the 25 percent whose first language was French, 8 percent of Canadians in 1971 used some other language. In the western provinces of Canada there are large groups of non-English and non-French speakers whose right to maintain and perpetuate their own languages, like the right of the French Canadians to do so, is recognized, protected, and supported financially by national law. This perpetuation of European linguistic separatism and divisiveness is valued in Canada as a sign of local freedom; whereas in the United States, unilingualism has conferred freedom within a national space.

The linguistic experience of Europeans has been that of Canadians and Spanish Americans: knowledge of more than one language because of the close proximity of multiple enclaves of language groups. But if Europeans could travel from one end to another of a continental space, as Americans can, without using more than one language, not many of them would become multilingual.

America's culture has been formed by self-selected immigrants who were generally willing to use one language, or to have their children do so, in order to be able to cooperate with each other in improving an expansive national space. Freedom of communication, including unilingual communication, has been a priority of American cultural behavior. American culture has been unilingual because voluntary unilingualism over a continental-size national space has conferred on Americans greater opportunity of movement, job selection, and social equality than can be the case in a multilingual culture.

The self-selected immigrants and their descendants who constituted the overwhelming majority of the American people were culturally resolved that their lives in America would be different and better than the lives Europeans led. The shared willingness of this type of person to sacrifice their European pasts to their mutual hope of making a better life together more often than not included a willingness to give up—or at least to have their children give up—the language of their native place when it differed from the language spoken by the initial group of settlers in what is now the United States. The task of transforming the Stone Age required unilingualism if it was to be accomplished rapidly on a continental scale. The past that the self-selecting emigrants to America left behind them in Europe was the measure of the newness they wished to inaugurate in America. And Europe's history of many disunified language groups was one of the most important measures of the new life of social unity in America. Unilingualism was a cultural behavior in the United States because such unity was fundamental to the desire for greater mobility and choice of occupation that motivated self-selecting emigrants to leave Europe.

The phenomenon of many European languages voluntarily merging into one language of preference did not happen anywhere else in the Americas and is culturally a quite different matter from having to learn another language to deal with intractable autonomous language groups within one's culture. In American culture, unilingualism has served to unify a continental space by giving every American the ability to communicate with every other American. For a European to have the kind of continental freedom of communication that Americans have enjoyed through their unilingualism would require the mastery of a score of languages.

THE FREEDOM OF RICHES

The Stone Age space that became American space was uniquely accessible for transformation; and its transformation promised immense potentials of food and other kinds of physical goods. What became America had abundant plowable soils, great expanses of grazing land, large tracts of timber and nut trees, plentiful supplies of good water above and below ground, seemingly inexhaustible amounts of ocean and freshwater foods, hydropower, quarries of sand, gravel, clay, and building stones, rich mines of many useful minerals, and great quantities of wild animals and birds yielding fur, down, hides, and meat. Exploitation of these riches began as soon as the Stone Age came to be viewed as transformable; and their exploitation naturally accelerated and extended the process of transformation. More, and more varied, material resources for food and civilized wealth existed in conjunction and became accessible to more people in America than has thus far been the case in any comparable continental space on earth.

The unprecedented scale of the potential riches of America, the rapidly increasing population of America, and the mind-set of the self-selected immigrant type precluded the possibility that America's wealth could be largely appropriated by any single, self-perpetuating group. The development of wealth from Stone Age central North America required the sustained, general initiatives that only a widespread hope of individual rewards can produce. That is why a Stone Age space comparable in size to Europe could be transformed into a civilized space in three instead of sixty centuries.

Both wealth and poverty have taken on new meanings in American culture. To be poor in the United States was, and is, to be rich by the standards common to most other cultures. Poverty in America has historically not meant fear of starvation. A majority of Americans has never been socially immobilized by an apprehension of not being able to satisfy minimal physical needs. In addition to food, other material goods of many kinds have been abundantly available at affordable prices. Historically, poverty in America has meant feeling deprived of one's fair share of the general wealth, not absolute deprivation. This feeling derives from the expectation of satisfaction that distinguishes the thinking of self-selected immigrants. No matter how good things may be in America in comparison to other cultures, they have never been good enough in a culture that has rejected belief in the rightness of fixed social status and fixed limits to individual happiness.

American levels of production and consumption have not, then, resulted merely from the vast resources of raw materials that have historically existed within the borders of the United States. These resources have been available. But it has been the beliefs of American culture that have caused American resources to be fully and rapidly developed and widely distributed. To put on the market an increasing variety of services and well-made goods of up-to-date design has been a persistent aim of American productivity, and concern for standards of excellence in production manifested itself early in American history. The drive of the American people to produce and to have a greater variety of food and other material goods of standardized excellence does not derive from the resources that have historically been abundant within the borders of the United States. Other areas of the Americas have also been blessed with abundant resources without manifesting such cultural behavior. Again, it has been geography in combination with cultural beliefs that has made American space what it is: the richest and most unified large space ever known.

Americans have worked hard during their history to make themselves prosperous as a people from the resources available to them within their own continental-size nation and to make goods available to as many workers as possible because such aims formed part of the mentality of the cultural ancestors of Americans. The ideas of self-discipline and voluntary cooperation and the legitimacy of higher and higher expectations of mass consumption have been as crucial to the production of American wealth as the cornucopian richness of America's soils, waters, and minerals. Americans did not themselves invent all of the technology of the automobile and its manufacture, but they were the first to want to develop the mass production of affordable automobiles; and they rapidly put into place in the United States extensive systems of paved roads and systems for the sale and maintenance of automobiles that made the freedom of individual transportation much more widely available in the United States than in Europe. The freedom-oriented, individual-centered culture of America and the cultural unity of American space meshed perfectly with the idea of mass-produced, affordable automobiles that would allow as many people as possible the widest possible freedom of individual movement.

Stoicism has never played much part in the national pride of Americans. In terms of the culture of the United States, suffering is not regarded as a normal, unavoidable condition. Therefore, Americans have not, as Europeans have tended to do, considered the ability to endure privation as a sign of national or individual strength of character. Americans have tended to brag about their production and distribution of goods. Those are the signs of great national character to the descendants of four centuries of self-selected immigration. In other words, Americans, like Europeans, have bragged about their kind of success.

American pride in production and distribution had its source in the thinking of ordinary people who, without being put through any government-imposed screening process, crossed the Atlantic to America. No theory of economics—no seventeenth-century Protestant theology (the so-called Protestant work ethic)—produced that deeply seated American cultural belief that whatever systematically serves to increase the possibilities of individual choice, physical comfort, and mobility for masses of people is good. Americans culturally descend not from Protestants or capitalists but from individualists, many of whom were peasants, all of whom wanted to be more comfortable and freer in America than they had been in the places they left behind. The American sense of what makes a culture superior has been defined in terms that any self-respecting peasant in the hinterlands of Europe at any time in the last four hundred years would have understood: eating meat, owning land or a house, paying lower taxes and lower prices, receiving higher wages, having quality goods; also, freedom to change residence and to seek better employment and freedom from being fined, imprisoned, or killed because of religious or political beliefs. What an intellectual or an aristocrat might consider culturally superior or worthy of respect has played little or no part in the cultural formation of the United States. Belief in the necessity and rightness of work in order to have these advantages—a necessity and a rightness that, again, any peasant would consider normal—has also distinguished American culture.

In European culture, what has been considered excellent has been defined at the top by the received, traditional tastes of the ruling class, which is usually what Europeans mean by "culture." Excellence in America has been determined by the sense and the approval of the majority. No widespread deference has been paid to the authority of tradition or to the ideas of intellectuals about culture or to the supposedly superior tastes of the rich and powerful. In American culture, work, newness, transformation, and distribution of goods have been the focuses of belief and behavior rather than power or the authority of "cultivated" tastes.

For Americans, there is a cultural satisfaction in statistics of production and distribution: in knowing that the 1980 national census revealed that two-thirds of the existing housing structures in America were free-standing, single-family homes; that nearly a million new single-family dwellings were completed in 1980 (82 percent of them with more than one bathroom); that between 1970 and 1980 American housing units that did not have complete plumbing facilities for the exclusive use of their occupants declined from 6.9 to 2.7 percent; that in 1980 more than four out of five housing units had two or more separate bedrooms; that 92 percent of American homes had at least one telephone; and that in 1980 there was a privately owned motor vehicle for every 1.5 of America's 226.5 million men, women, and children.

American interest in systematic improvements in comfort is a cultural behavior that European intellectuals and Europeanized Americans scorn as materialism. But such improvements are all of a piece with American culture's commitment to improved systems of communication and education: all are designed to enhance the range of choice and the personal satisfaction of as many individuals as possible. The implication of the European criticism that Americans are materialistic seems to be that Europeans have never attained the widespread consumption of material goods that Americans have because, as Europeans, they have considered it beneath their cultural dignity. This is the voice of a culture that has historically been orchestrated from the top down by a small, hereditary ruling class that was inordinately wealthy in comparison with other classes and that has kept political power remarkably concentrated in itself. In America in the decades before the American Revolution, because property qualifications for voting were easy to fulfill in a society in which they were relatively low and property was widely distributed, "about three-fourths of adult white males could vote";[3] whereas as late in the nineteenth century as 1830 in the British Isles, including Ireland, less than 2 percent of the population—only some 435 thousand out of the estimated population of twenty-four million—had the right to vote.[4]

From the perspective of some of the keepers of the flame of European culture, Americans supposedly inhabit a painless Eden of mindless cheerfulness. Seen from this perspective, as educated Europeans have been known to say, "America has no culture": widespread materialism has thwarted its development. Having simply lucked into a landscape of fantastic natural resources, and having been protected by oceans on either side of them from the truths of "history" and "realpolitik," such European-oriented critics hold, Americans have become "naive" and "innocent." They lack, according to this point of view, "a sense of the past"—never mind the many grass roots roadside museums in America; or America's numerous privately and publicly supported professional museums dedicated to history in large and middle-size cities; or its great system of public and private libraries that collectively consitute the largest, best organized, and most accessible single library system in the world.

The charge by European-oriented intellectuals that Americans are materialistic is an old one, going back as far as the post–Revolutionary War writers of Britain, which was then by far the wealthiest nation of Europe. In 1900, the South American writer José Enrique Rodó, a Uruguayan intel-

---

3. Alfred H. Kelly, Winfred A. Harbison, and Herman Belz, *The American Constitution: Its Origins and Development,* sixth edition (New York: W. W. Norton, 1983), p. 36.
4. "Reform Bills," *The New Columbia Encyclopedia,* eds. William H. Harris and Judith S. Levey (New York and London: Columbia University Press, 1975).

lectual, gave the accusation that the people of the United States are materialists classic form in his book *Ariel*. America, for its own part, has yet to produce a generally respected class of people who feel pride in being taken seriously as "intellectuals."

CHAPTER

6

AMERICAN CULTURE IN THE TWENTIETH CENTURY

The beliefs of a comparatively unique population in combination with comparatively unique geographical opportunities formed in what is now the United States a distinctively non-European culture before the organization of a national government in the eighth and ninth decades of the eighteenth century. And because any culture tends to persist, once its set of belief-behaviors is formed (the axiom of cultural inertia), the culture that was created in central North America in the seventeenth and eighteenth centuries has persisted in the nineteenth and twentieth centuries.

During the twentieth century, severe challenges to American culture have arisen. But none has been as dire as that in the nineteenth century when almost one-third of the states then in the United States (eleven out of thirty-six) seceded from the Union. The terrible crisis of that civil war threatened to destroy the coherence of American culture, because a secessionist victory would have eliminated from the culture's set of belief-behaviors both the idea of a self-determined, unified, continental space and the idea of equality of liberty (the belief that human beings are equal in their right to liberty, an idea not acted on with regard to black Americans at the time the nation was organized but nonetheless fundamental to American culture). The preservation of the American union and the abolition of negro slavery, which the victory of the Union armies in the 1860s made possible, gave American culture its validity in the eyes of the world. Thus, by the time the United States entered the twentieth century, the political institutions that President Washington had characterized in his farewell to the nation as an "experiment" were no longer in doubt. As the twentieth century began, a little more than a generation after the end of the Civil War, America was a fledgling world power, having become one of the largest nations in size of territory, with a population fifteen times larger than it had had in 1800, an increasingly competitive economic production, and a historically justified confidence in its revolutionarily new cultural formation. Events in the twentieth century, however, continued to test American culture.

TWENTIETH-CENTURY CHALLENGES

The United States began the twentieth century having just behaved somewhat as the great powers of Europe had been behaving for centuries. In a war lasting less than four months in 1898, American battleships and land forces seized and occupied far-flung insular remnants of Spain's once-mighty empire. This un-American behavior, however, was accompanied by the distinctly un-European behavior of making a large postwar payment (twenty million dollars) to Spain for the territories militarily occupied. Article III in the "Treaty of Peace with Spain Concluded at Paris December 10, 1898" stipulated this payment without explanation of its purpose or need.[1] Similarly, in 1922, *nineteen years* after having engineered Panama's separation from Colombia so that political arrangements satisfactory to the United States could be made to build an interocean canal across the Panamanian isthmus, the United States gave Colombia twenty-five million dollars to remove " 'all misunderstandings growing out of the political events in Panama in November 1903.' "[2]

The war with Spain was in part a European-style, imperialistic land-grab of one nation's colonies by another nation. But it was also, and primarily, an intervention in the war the Cuban people had been waging for three years to gain their independence from Spain, an especially vicious war in which concentration camps were used to subdue the civilian population. (The Cuban people had been unsuccessful in a ten-year war for independence earlier in the century.) After overseeing the writing of a constitution modeled on that of the United States and after building roads, improving sanitation, and negotiating a treaty with the newly independent Cuba that permitted the United States to intervene again in the island should

1. Henry Steele Commager, ed., *Documents of American History,* ninth edition, 2 vols. (Englewood Cliffs, NJ: Prentice-Hall, 1973), II, p. 7.
2. Quoted in Henry Steele Commager, ed., *Documents of American History,* ninth edition, 2 vols. (Englewood Cliffs, NJ: Prentice-Hall, 1973), II, p. 30.

any internal or external threats appear likely to reverse these improvements, the American forces that were occupying Cuba withdrew in 1903.

American military intervention in Cuba between 1898 and 1903 was a new development of the doctrine President James Monroe had laid down in 1823 as the cornerstone of American foreign policy. The two-part doctrine bearing his name held that, while the United States would not attempt to free any existing European colony in North or South America, it would respond to any attempt by a European imperial power to reimpose European rule over a former colony that had succeeded in gaining its independence. In intervening at the end of the nineteenth century in the second Cuban rebellion against Spain, the United States modified the first part of the Monroe Doctrine by directly engaging in helping an American colony of a European imperial power to make itself independent. But in thus more actively applying in relation to Cuba the doctrine that the United States has a permanent interest in the increase of self-government in the world, America itself also acted as an imperial power by seizing the Spanish colonies of Guam (two hundred square miles), Puerto Rico (three thousand square miles), and the Philippines (116 thousand square miles), none of which (unlike Cuba) was allowed self-government after being freed from Spanish rule.

The territory the United States gained control over in 1898 through military action and subsequent payment was a comparatively small "empire." Even if Cuba (forty-four thousand square miles) were to be considered part of it—on the grounds that the 1903 treaty between the United States and Cuba, which permitted America to intervene to preserve Cuban independence and to protect "life, property, and individual liberty" inside the country,[3] was virtually imposed on Cuba without the consent of its people—this empire was smaller than present-day Iraq (169 thousand square miles). Besides being extremely small by European imperial standards, this empire's existence was notably brief. The U.S. Congress acted in 1934 to grant the Philippines independence and to cancel the Cuban-American treaty, thus indicating, just thirty-six years after militarily occupying it, the desire of the United States to relinquish 98 percent of the territory involved in the Spanish-American War. As to the remaining 2 percent—Puerto Rico and Guam—Congress in 1917 gave U.S. citizenship to Puerto Ricans without the right to vote in federal elections or the obligation to pay federal taxes, and by 1948 every office of government in the island had been returned to the Puerto

3. See headnote to and text of "Treaty with Cuba Embodying the Platt Amendment May 22, 1903" in Henry Steele Commager, ed., *Documents of American History,* ninth edition, 2 vols., (Englewood Cliffs, NJ: Prentice-Hall, 1973), II, pp. 28–29.

Rican people, who, in 1967, in a national referendum, overwhelmingly voted to continue their qualified U.S. citizenship and their status as a "self-governing Commonwealth" "associated" with the United States. The inhabitants of Guam were given the same qualified U.S. citizenship in 1950 and elected their first governor in 1970. America remains, by the consent of the people of Guam and Puerto Rico, responsible for the external security of these islands, whose 1980 populations totaled 3.3 million and whose area altogether is smaller than Yellowstone National Park.

America's deviation into the behavior of European imperialism did not last long enough to be a threat to American culture because to be enculturated a belief-behavior must continue for more than one generation. However, Congress's authorization in 1898 of military intervention in Cuba to make it "free and independent" of Spain[4] was the beginning of a behavior that did continue beyond one generation. Ever since the Spanish-American War, the United States has intervened on the international scene beyond the Americas to protect its interest in the spread of government by consent of the governed and to curtail government by autocratic rulers in the world—the principle laid down with regard only to the Americas by the Monroe Doctrine. Some of the most severe challenges to American culture in the twentieth century have resulted from the application of the Monroe Doctrine beyond the American continents.

Four times in the twentieth century the United States has fought as a major combatant in wars between other nations outside of North America: twice in Europe and twice on peninsulas of the East Asian mainland. (Only once in the twentieth century, in the archipelagoes and seas of the Pacific Ocean, has it fought in response to an attack on its own territory.) America has expended immense amounts of irreplaceable national treasure in these wars. Minnesota's hundreds of square miles of open-pit mines of high-grade hematite iron ore, for instance, which began to be worked in the last decade of the nineteenth century, along with the immense Texas oil fields, which began pumping in the first years of the twentieth century, are now nearly exhausted, to the great detriment of America's economic well-being. These irreplaceable natural resources were too prodigious to have been used up so rapidly had it not been for their hyperdepletion in America's four twentieth-century wars of intervention and in the decades-long intervention by the United States to contain Soviet imperialism. Of America's one and three-quarters million casualties in its twentieth-century wars, four out of five of the casualties have been suffered in the interventions by the

4. Henry Steele Comager, ed., *Documents of American History,* ninth edition, 2 vols. (Englewood Cliffs, NJ: Prentice-Hall, 1973), II, p. 5.

United States in other nations' wars, on the side that was either losing or stalemated at the time America intervened. (Although Nazi Germany declared war first on America, four days after the December 7, 1941 attack on Hawaii by its Asian ally, Japan, the United States had for a year before that date been materially intervening in the war between Germany and other European countries by "lending" vital war supplies to Britain and—after its change of sides—the Soviet Union.[5])

The most remarkable cultural feature of American behavior in the twentieth century in repeatedly deploying huge armies and other military forces on far-distant continents and seas and in transferring colossal quantities of war supplies to distant allies has been that the United States has gained no territory as a consequence of its sacrifices of material and men in Europe in 1917–18, in Europe in 1942–45, in Korea in 1950–52, in Vietnam in the 1960s, and in the Cold War that has waxed and waned in many places since 1947. This was true also of the conflict in which America was not intervening in someone else's war but defending its own territory from attack: no reparations or transfers of territories were exacted by the United States from Japan after its unconditional surrender in 1945.

Declarations by the presidents who led America in the first and in the most recent of its twentieth-century interventions in Europe and Asia show a definite consistency. President Woodrow Wilson, addressing the U.S. Senate on January 22, 1917, defined "the doctrine of President Monroe" as belief in "government by the consent of the governed" and declared that the Monroe Doctrine expressed the essence of America's position toward the war in Europe which was then in its third year. Three months later, on April 2, in asking Congress to declare war on Germany, President Wilson said America sought "no conquest, no dominion" and desired "no indemnities for ourselves, no material compensation for the sacrifices we shall freely make," as "one of the champions of the rights of mankind":

> To such a task we can dedicate our lives and our fortunes,
> everything that we are and everything that we have, with the pride

5. The only country to fight on both sides during World War II, the Soviet Union was allied with Nazi Germany for two full years (from mid-1939 to mid-1941) and as a result of the alliance militarily occupied, with the cooperation and agreement of Nazi Germany, half of prewar Poland, all of Latvia, Lithuania, and Estonia, and most of Bessarabia, all of which territory was incorporated within the boundaries of the USSR. The German invasion of the Soviet Union in June 1941 broke the alliance and forced the USSR onto the eventual winning side of the war, thus making it possible for the Soviet government to retain what it had taken during its pact with Nazi Germany and to claim after the war a "sphere of influence" in what Europeans had always called Central Europe, where it soon forced into orbit a series of satellite governments.

of those who know that the day has come when America is privileged to spend her blood and her might for the principles that gave her birth and happiness and the peace which she has treasured. God helping her, she can do no other.

The basic principle of the Fourteen Points Wilson later proposed for making peace in Europe when the war ended was, he said, the belief that all peoples have a "right to live on equal terms of liberty."[6] John F. Kennedy, who was born the year Woodrow Wilson led the United States into World War I in Europe, expressed himself in these terms at his inauguration on January 20, 1961, when he spoke for the first time as president of the United States:

> the same revolutionary beliefs for which our forebears fought are still at issue around the globe—the belief that the rights of man come not from the generosity of the state but from the hand of God.
>   We dare not forget today that we are the heirs of that first revolution. Let the word go forth from this time and place, to friend and foe alike, that the torch has been passed to a new generation of Americans—born in this century, tempered by war, disciplined by a hard and bitter peace, proud of our ancient heritage—and unwilling to witness or permit the slow undoing of those human rights to which this nation has always been committed, and to which we are committed today at home and around the world.
>   Let every nation know, whether it wishes us well or ill, that we shall pay any price, bear any burden, meet any hardship, support any friend, oppose any foe to assure the survival and the success of liberty. . . . In the long history of the world only a few generations have been granted the role of defending freedom in its hour of maximum danger. I do not shrink from this responsibility—I welcome it.[7]

Thus spoke the forty-four-year-old American president who during his tragically brief term in office made the first military commitments of American men and material in the war that had been going on for years in Vietnam between communist and non-communist forces.

6. Henry Steele Comager, ed., *Documents of American History,* ninth edition, 2 vols. (Englewood Cliffs, NJ: Prentice-Hall, 1973), II, pp. 127, 131–32, 139.
7. Henry Steele Comager, ed., *Documents of American History,* ninth edition, 2 vols. (Englewood Cliffs, NJ: Prentice-Hall, 1973), II, pp. 654–56.

Harry Truman, the president who led America at the beginning of its many years of "Cold War" against Soviet imperialism, likewise invoked the principle of self-government that lay behind the Monroe Doctrine in his message of March 12, 1947 asking Congress to commit America's resources to thwart the aggressions of "totalitarian regimes." The choice "nearly every nation" faced in 1947, this president told the Congress—thirty years after President Wilson had requested congressional authorization to intervene in Europe for the first time against "autocratic governments backed by organized force which is controlled wholly by their will, not the will of their people"[8]—was between a way of life "based upon the will of the minority forcibly imposed upon the majority" that required "terror and oppression, a controlled press and radio, fixed elections, and the suppression of personal freedoms" for its continuance and, on the other hand, a way of life based on "the will of the majority and distinguished by free institutions, representative government, free elections, guarantees of individual liberty, freedom of speech and religion, and freedom from political oppression." Because the United States in 1947 was, President Truman pointed out, the only major democracy in the world not damaged by the devastations of World War II, it was the only country able "to support free peoples who are resisting attempted subjugation by armed minorities or by outside pressures"—such as had prompted the government of Greece to make an urgent appeal to him for assistance. President Truman summarized the essential American interest at the end of his message applying the Monroe Doctrine to the post–World War II scene in the simple truth that "the free people of the world look to us for support in maintaining their freedoms."[9]

Two months after President Truman's message calling upon Congress to give aid to Greece, he instructed his secretary of state to propose massive economic assistance to all of the devastated countries of Europe, including the Soviet Union and the nations it controlled, so that economic and social conditions could be reestablished "in which free institutions can exist."[10] And in 1949, 1950, and 1951, the United States annually gave more than 10 percent of its national budget to the Marshall Plan, as it came to be called,

8. Henry Steele Comager, ed., *Documents of American History*, ninth edition, 2 vols. (Englewood Cliffs, NJ: Prentice-Hall, 1973), II, p. 130.

9. Henry Steele Comager, ed., *Documents of American History*, ninth edition, 2 vols. (Englewood Cliffs, NJ: Prentice-Hall, 1973), II, pp. 526–28.

10. "Remarks by the Honorable George C. Marshall, Secretary of State, at Harvard University on June 5, 1947," Henry Steele Comager, ed., *Documents of American History*, ninth edition, 2 vols. (Englewood Cliffs, NJ: Prentice-Hall, 1973), II, p. 533.

in which fourteen nations of Europe participated.[11] The Soviet Union refused to participate in the Marshall Plan or to permit the participation of any
of the countries in the Balkans and Central Europe that it had dominated. In
December 1951, the head of the international organization that administered this unprecedented giveaway by the American people of their national
wealth reported that it had had an unprecedented success. In just three
years, the Marshall Plan had provided the peoples of the participating
countries the means for them to raise their economic output to 15 percent
above the prewar level of production.[12]

In contrast, at the end of World War II in Soviet-occupied parts of
Central Europe (including Poland, the country that fought Nazi Germany
from the outset of the war and that suffered the most for its resistance,
as well as the eastern part of Germany), the Red Army gathered up all
transportable goods and took them inside the Soviet Union. This behavior,
because it included Poland, exceeded the scope of the demands made by
the Soviet dictator on the leaders of Britain and the United States a few
months before the war ended. At the Yalta conference in 1945, Stalin had
insisted that Germany pay reparations from its existing stocks of manufactured products, heavy equipment, machine tools, ships, and rolling stock
and from its existing financial assets, with annual deliveries from German
industrial and agricultural production and "use of German labor" to continue until the value of twenty billion dollars had been obtained, and that
half of these reparations, or *ten billion dollars,* were to go to his country.[13]
Through the Marshall Plan, the United States gave *twelve billion dollars* to
European countries, including that part of Germany not under Soviet
control.

Similarly, under the terms of trade agreements that have been written
since the end of World War II between the Soviet Union and countries in

11. Under this program the people of the United States through their Congress gave
Europeans the money to buy whatever they themselves decided they needed to rebuild
their countries, much of which was purchased from the United States, the sole major
producer in the world in the late 1940s capable of supplying goods on such a scale; so that,
in effect, it was not so much their money but their manufactured goods and food that
Americans were giving away on a monumental scale never before witnessed in history.

12. "European Recovery Program December 30, 1951," Henry Steele Comager, ed.,
Documents of American History, ninth edition, 2 vols. (Englewood Cliffs, NJ: Prentice-
Hall, 1973), II. p. 570.

13. "Yalta (Crimea) Conference February, 1945," Henry Steele Comager, ed., *Documents of American History,* ninth edition, 2 vols. (Englewood Cliffs, NJ: Prentice-Hall,
1973), II, p. 490.

the Balkans and Central Europe over which it had acquired dominion, as a result of that war, without incorporating them into the USSR, the Soviet Union has been able to buy goods from these captive nations in rubles, a currency not negotiable outside the Soviet empire, at prices kept artificially low because of the high rate of exchange for the ruble within the empire, as set by the Kremlin. For their part, these countries are required to make their purchases from the Soviet Union in internationally negotiable currencies, such as Swiss or French francs, U.S. dollars, West German marks, and British pounds. And the goods the Soviet Union thus obtains for rubles at systematically low prices, it often sells for hard currencies at their much higher, true market value to countries outside the Soviet empire.[14]

The worst elements of the autocracy and imperialism that the rest of Europe has gradually abandoned during the nineteenth and twentieth centuries and some of the worst horrors of the one-party rule that Nazism represented have appeared in the history of the Soviet Union. Marxism-Leninism is a holdover from Europe's past. It has proven itself to be a successful blueprint for centralizing economic and political power in a self-perpetuating ruling class and also a wonderful theory for justifying conspiratorial, one-party dictatorship through the promise of an eventual conclusion of "the class struggle" in "public, communist self-government."[15] It has, thus far, failed to demonstrate any capacity for governing with the consent of the governed or providing up-to-date economic progress for those living under its absolutist government. The justification of "revolutionary" government put forth by this political theory has been that modernization of the backward Russian empire could only be accomplished under Marxism-Leninism. Consider, however, the report by a Soviet official in 1988, following seven decades of Marxist-Leninist government, that half of

14. Two elected officials of the Polish workers union *Solidarność* (Solidarity), Jerzy Nowacki, then a member of the presidium of the Posnan district commission, and Lech Dymarski, a representative to the National Coordinating Commission, told me during an interview at the union's headquarters in Posnan, Poland, in August 1981, that the main cause of Solidarity's formation and the reason it received such instant massive support in its 1980 general strike was the systematic exploitation of Polish labor by the Soviet Union. "We are tired," Mr. Dymarski said, "of working for the Kremlin instead of ourselves."

15. Preamble to the present Constitution of the USSR, ratified October 1977. All quotations of this document are from the John N. Hazard translation in volume 17 of *Constitutions of the Countries of the World,* eds. A. Blaustein and G. Flanz (Dobbs Ferry, NY: Oceana Publications, 1978).

the public schools of the Soviet Union still do not have any running water or sewerage system.[16] Because the coup d'etat by Lenin in October 1917 aborted the short-lived experiment in parliamentary government that had replaced the authority of the Russian czar in February 1917, it can now never be known how modern or how backward the domestic empire of captive nations that once made up the Russian state and that now make up the Soviet state would have been without that coup and all that followed from it. It remains to be seen whether the talk in the late 1980s of political and economic reform within the Soviet Union represents a change without a difference or will produce a nonimperialistic economic system and a popular government.

All that is certain so far in Soviet history is that the one-party dictatorship that constructed the Soviet state ordered the creation of a famine in the Ukraine in 1932–33 to terrorize the Ukrainian peasantry into collectivizing their farmlands, and that, during that state-sponsored famine—whose details have been kept well hidden and whose reality has been denied by all party leaders, including those currently in power—*as many human beings were deliberately starved to death as were later killed in the concentration camps the Nazi party constructed for its genocide.*[17] And what is just as certain is that when *five* of the fifteen hundred members of the Supreme Soviet of the USSR dared to vote against a proposal put forth by the leaders of this same party on December 2, 1988, and another *twenty-seven* abstained from the vote, their courageous minuscule protest made international news.

America's Cold War with Soviet autocracy has been a prolonged intervention in defense of the headway democracy made in Europe during the nineteenth and twentieth centuries. Without Lenin's coup against parliamentary government, democracy might now be in place in every nation of Europe. Instead, Marxism-Leninism has instituted, in the nations of the Soviet Union and in some countries in the Balkans and Central Europe, what it calls and praises as "true democracy"—a clear illustration of the theoretical redefinition of words that the Polish-Lithuanian poet-in-exile and Nobel Laureate, Czeslaw Milosz, has identified as crucial to "the growth

16. G. A. Yagodin, chairman of the state committee on public education in the Soviet Union, speaking at the communist party conference of June 1988; quoted in Robert G. Kaiser, "The U.S.S.R. in Decline," *Foreign Affairs,* LXIX (Winter 1988/89), p. 100.

17. See Robert Conquest, *The Harvest of Sorrow: Soviet Collectivization and the Terror-Famine* (New York and Oxford: Oxford University Press, 1986), the first full-scale scholarly study of this concealed atrocity against humanity, which Ukrainian exiles have long sought to make known to the world.

of the totalitarian state."[18] But far from being the true democracy that it calls itself, the Soviet system of elections has required citizens to agree with every choice made for them by the only party that Marxist-Leninist revolutionary theory allows to have power, which is to say that ever since Lenin displaced the parliamentary government that existed in Russia in 1917, Soviet voters have normally found when they arrived at the polls just one party-approved candidate on every ballot. By order of the party's present leaders, this "electiveness," as the Soviet Constitution terms it, is to be replaced by what is being called "competitiveness": from now on, two party-approved candidates will appear on each ballot.

In the Marxist-Leninist reversal of the meaning of words through revolutionary theory, imperialism becomes liberation and one-party dictatorship becomes true democracy. The "democracy" of the Marxist-Leninist system controls Soviet citizens not only by the "fixed elections" that Harry Truman referred to in 1947 but also by stipulating constitutionally that citizens' "exercise of their rights and freedoms is inseparable from the performance of their duties and obligations" (Soviet Constitution, Article 59). (This concept of conditional human rights was what President Kennedy opposed in his inaugural address in emphasizing that "the rights of man come not from the generosity of the state but from the hand of God.") Freedom of speech, freedom of the press, and freedom of assembly are all guaranteed by the Soviet Constitution, but only on the condition that these freedoms be used "to strengthen and develop the socialist system" (Article 50); the document likewise guarantees freedom of association, for the purpose of "building communism" (Article 51); and "freedom of scientific, technical, and artistic work" is also guaranteed, provided that such work contributes to "building communism" (Article 47). The only unconditional inherent rights apparent in the socialist system of the Soviet Union are those of the Soviet state. The rights of Soviet citizens depend on their performance of their duties and obligations to the state.

America's prolonged intervention in the late twentieth century to contain Marxist-Leninist "liberation" and "democracy" has required for the first time in American history maintaining tremendous military forces during a long period of undeclared war and also giving away vast amounts of America's national wealth to countries attempting to maintain at minimum their independence from Soviet imperialism, whether or not they had a democratic form of government. The effect of all of this on American culture has not been salutary. Besides the much swifter depletion of irreplaceable natural resources within the United States than would have otherwise

18. Czeslaw Milosz, *Nobel Lecture* (New York: Farrar Straus Giroux, 1980), p. 13.

occurred and the consequent decrease of American economic self-suffi-
ciency, it has led to an ever-bigger federal budget and to unprecedented
concentrations of power in the federal government, with an accompanying
blurring of the constitutional separations and balances of governmental
powers that have been fundamental to American democracy. The attempt
to contain the spread of Marxist-Leninist government and to preserve the
nineteenth- and twentieth-century gains of democratic government has
necessarily enlarged the province of the federal government in foreign
affairs, but this enlargement has carried over into the domestic scene. The
idea of the federal government providing for the welfare of various "interest
groups" within the United States—on the compelling analogy that if the
federal government is going to give away millions of dollars to meet the
needs of people in foreign lands, it can do the same for groups of its own
citizens—was becoming so chronic by the 1960s that President Kennedy
urged in concluding his inaugural address: "My fellow Americans: ask not
what your country can do for you—ask what you can do for your country.
My fellow citizens of the world: ask not what America will do for you, but
what together we can do for the freedom of man."

THE CHALLENGE TO THE NATURAL LAW

As pointed out in the preliminaries to this study, no culture has a set
of beliefs that is altogether unique. There are always beliefs in any cultural
formation that appear in some other culture—the axiom of cultural overlapping—and American culture belongs to the cluster of overlapping cultural
formations that has been called Christian or Western culture. This includes
all of the countries of Europe (the European parts of the USSR not, by
any means, excepted) and the countries of the American continents. An
increasing strain on one of the beliefs of this larger cultural formation,
brought about by the rise in authority of scientific thinking in the West
during the nineteenth and twentieth centuries, has produced a challenge
to American culture as part of Christian or Western culture. Though not as
readily evident in its effects perhaps, this challenge is at least as important
as the strains imposed in the twentieth century by America's repeated
interventions in Europe and Asia.

The growing influence of science during the last two centuries has
produced a pressure to redefine the nature of man. It has led to a shift
away from the idea of man as a creature having an irreducible spiritual
element that somehow transcends the material reality and toward the idea
of man as nothing but an animal, wholly determined, like all animals, by

heredity and environment. This transvaluation of man's nature is a tendency that has affected Western man's perception of himself, with, at times in the twentieth century, quite horrifying consequences. The ruthlessness, for instance, of the Nazi policy of attempting to "exterminate" whole races of mankind as unfit or "antisocial" has an undoubted connection with the view that man is merely and entirely an animal to be judged and treated like any other for its genetic qualities or utility, as perceived in this instance by an absolutist political party. Likewise, the materialistic determinism on which Marxism-Leninism is based permitted the political decision in the vast domestic empire of nations that is the Soviet Union to "liquidate" tens of millions of "class enemies" and "antisocial elements," in accordance with its allegedly "scientific" view of man and man's history. This scale of death testifies to what happens when the power of a single group usurps the whole moral authority of a culture and science becomes the only measure of man.

When regarded as animals, human beings have nothing transcendent to appeal to to defend their humanity from assaults by the power of the state; when the rights of man are seen as being the same as those pertaining to animals, man has no rights as man and is merely another animal.

The importance to American culture of a transcendent, spiritual reality to which man has some connection is highly visible in the references to "the Laws of Nature and of Nature's God" in the declaration that was made to justify the American Revolution (first paragraph in "The unanimous Declaration of the thirteen united States of America," July 4, 1776); in the protection of the freedom to worship from any abridgment by government in the first amendment that was made to the Constitution of the United States (ratified December 15, 1791); and in George Washington's designation of "religion and morality" as "indispensable supports" of American government in his "Farewell Address" (published September 17, 1796), as well as in references to God in presidential addresses down through the twentieth century. But not every American has, of course, believed in God, and such belief is not necessarily to be considered essential to the set of belief-behaviors that is American culture. What has been essential is the belief that a natural law, or an innate moral principle of right and wrong for man, exists in the universe. And this belief has, of course, more often than not, been powerfully associated with the Christian belief in God as the Creator of the universe that a majority of Americans in each generation has held. The thirty-three-year-old Thomas Jefferson was certainly invoking this principle in writing that the Laws of Nature and of Nature's God entitled the United States of America to self-government and that human beings are equally "endowed by their Creator" with the right to liberty, the right to life, and the right to pursue happiness—rights governments must regard as "unalienable."

And five decades before Jefferson expressed these American cultural beliefs in July 1776, Benjamin Franklin—that multifarious genius born in Massachusetts in 1706 to a self-selected English immigrant father and an American mother—had realized, as a young man in his mid twenties, as he would later record in his autobiography, that "*Truth, Sincerity & Integrity* in Dealings between Man & Man, were of utmost Importance to the Felicity of Life." Franklin in writing his autobiography recalled, regarding the subject of happiness, that in the 1720s, when he had been a young man, he observed in himself and in the behavior of his fellow man that certain actions were harmful while other actions were beneficial, "in their own Natures, all the Circumstances of things considered."[19] That is why, he then concluded, the Bible forbids some actions and commands others, though he gave no particular credence to the Bible's status as revealed truth. The revelation for Franklin was in nature, which he believed required a certain moral conduct of a man if he was to find happiness.

Two hundred thirty years later, in the mid-twentieth century, the American Nobel Laureate William Faulkner expressed the same kind of belief in the natural law, in referring to courage, honor, pride, compassion, and pity as "verities of the human heart" that must in the nature of things be heeded. A person, Faulkner observed,

> must be honest not because it's virtuous but because that's the only way to get along. That if people lied constantly to one another you would never know where you were, you would never know what was going on. That if people didn't practice compassion there would be nothing to defend the weak until they got enough strength to stand for themselves. If one didn't practice something of pride, one would have nothing to be proud about, to have said, I did well, I did nothing that I was ashamed of, I can lie down with myself and sleep. That is, they are the verities to be practiced not because they are virtue but because that's the best way to live in peace with yourself and your fellows.[20]

This kind of belief in the natural law has been part and parcel of American culture because no other Christian or Western people has had a historical

19. Benjamin Franklin, *The Autobiography of Benjamin Franklin* (New York: Library of America, 1987), pp. 1359–60.

20. Frederick L. Gwynn and Joseph L. Blotner, eds., *Faulkner in the University* (Charlottesville: University of Virginia Press, 1959), pp. 133–34.

experience that emphasized so strongly each human being's equality of liberty. Belief in the equality of liberty required belief in the existence of something that would prevent American individualism from degenerating into licentiousness and selfishness. That something was belief in an innate moral law in the universe. For these reasons, the shift away from the idea of man as a creature having a connection to a transcendent spiritual reality has put a particularly great strain on American culture.

Starting a new society "from scratch" in a Stone Age wilderness gave the self-selecting emigrants to America and their descendants a sense of returning to the beginning of God's natural order and beginning history anew. Everything was to be done over again, in accordance with the natural law. America was, at the beginning of its history, and has remained, a kind of Eden in the sense that its inhabitants were bound to obey an unwritten, unchanging fiat of naturally right behavior if they were to remain in possession of "God's country," as Americans have sometimes fondly referred to their country. Americans were free, as individuals, to obey or disobey this natural law, just as the first man and the first woman in the Judeo-Christian story of man's origin had been created free to live in happy obedience to God's injunction or in suffering defiance of it.

The pursuit of happiness—Franklin's "Felicity of Life"—has historically been a cultural goal for Americans because their culture has made the individual, not the group, the primary unit of social and political thought. Only individuals can aspire to happiness—groups cannot—because happiness is an individual emotion, which no society, no group of experts, no political party, no law can confer. In Europe, where a belief once prevailed culturally that the majority of human beings would pursue ends destructive to social order unless constrained by the power of some supposedly superior group, responsibility for the welfare of society and the preservation of social order was, in the past, generally considered to be the prerogative and the duty of such groups. But in America, human beings have culturally been seen as equal in the right to liberty and equally responsible for social order; and social order has been linked with each individual's free obedience to the natural law—something that William Faulkner recognized in the 1950s no less than Benjamin Franklin did during the 1720s.

The self-respecting failures who left Europe for America in the seventeenth and eighteenth centuries and became the progenitors of a distinctive new culture did not believe in the primacy of the environment of their native places. They believed in the primacy of themselves, as persons who had individually chosen, free of any governmental constraints on their decision, to immigrate to America. There, they found not an environment that dominated them but the freedom to make a new environment. They believed they could do that by working in free association with like-minded people. In the twentieth century, this belief seems to have been reversed in the minds of some Americans, who have come to believe that if slums are torn down and replaced by high-rise, government-subsidized apartment buildings, the behavior of the people taken out of the slums and installed in this new environment will be changed for the better by virtue of that change of physical environment. What often happens, however, is that the new apartment buildings soon become high-rise slums. If human nature is believed to be entirely indistinguishable from animal nature, if man is believed to have no transcendent spirit and is seen to be the creation of his environment in all that he thinks and does, then of course the material environment would be all-determinant. But American history does not support this view of man. Rather than demonstrating that the material environment determines what people think about themselves and how they should act, American history demonstrates that what people believe about themselves and how they should act determines their environment.

The belief in American culture that individual men and women are responsible for their physical environment, according to the natural law and their equality of liberty, has been challenged in the twentieth century by a belief in genetic inheritance, social conditioning, "history," and "the system" as the sole determinants of human behavior. Proponents of genetics and social engineering as the means to social betterment claim that these considerations are all-important, not the free choices of individuals guided in their decisions by a knowledge that some actions are good and some are bad, as Franklin discovered, "in their own Natures, all the Circumstances of things considered." Therefore, according to this view, scientific experts ought to assume responsibility for designing a social and economic system to improve human behavior. This thinking is a variation on the now passé European cultural belief in self-constituted and self-perpetuating ruling groups who believe they have in their own rulership the most competent answer to the question of what is best for society.

Freedom of choice, on the other hand, is not, in America's cultural formation, an ultimate good in itself. It is only the necessary precondition for seeking what is good in the nature of things. If the ultimate good were freedom itself, then whatever was chosen would be good, and considerations of justice would be irrelevant. It is, however, self-evident that equality of liberty apart from the natural law can produce licentious behavior and worse. The separation of equality of liberty from natural law has led a small number of twentieth-century advocates of freedom as an ultimate good in itself to claim that " 'sexual liberation' " should not be restricted to adults (anthropologist Richard Currier); that " 'the rights of children to control their own bodies' " are being denied to them (David Thorstad, pedophilia advocate); and that " 'It causes a lot of problems not to practice incest' " (Valida Davila, speaking as a member of Childhood Sensuality Circle).[21] The same mistaken claim for freedom as an ultimate good in itself, apart from any other consideration, is evident in the thinking of proabortion advocates, who would even justify as "the right to choose" and "the right to control one's own body" a decision by a financially well off, married couple to kill a deliberately procreated, healthy, developing human being if they discovered that the sex of the child in embryo was not the sex they wanted.

Whatever difficulties there are in knowing what is right, it is certain that goodness does not necessarily consist of whatever one may choose to do simply because that particular action accords with one's own personal feelings at the moment. Nothing could be more pernicious to American culture than acceptance of the belief that morality is a private affair, that morality is nothing more than freedom of choice being equally exercised by all human beings, that one "lifestyle" is as good as another, regardless of whether it is self-evidently destructive of life or not. (If the freedom to choose one's "lifestyle" were the main issue, then whatever a strong or clever person might feel entitled to do to a weak or foolish person would always be just on the grounds that it could be part of his "lifestyle.") The idea of morality as a private matter—in which all choices are equally good because allegedly no one can say what is good or bad, or because freedom of choice has been freely exercised, or (worst of all) because there is no such thing as "good" or "bad" and "everything is relative"—is contrary to justice, something which is inherently social, not private.

As the fundamental social effect of morality, justice has always to do with one person's behavior affecting another, rather than with the right of any one person to his "lifestyle." Should it ever come to pass that a majority of Americans practiced "a private morality," justice would be as impossible as communication would be if every person spoke his own "private language." Without the natural law, the individualism that is so pervasive in American culture would make social life impossible in America. Furthermore, should a majority of Americans ever come to see the behavior of individuals as determined only by their social, economic, and physical environments and their biological inheritance, the same result would per-

21. Quoted by John Leo in "Cradle-to-Grave Intimacy," *Time Magazine,* September 7, 1981, p. 69. Incest, like cannibalism, is not an issue for animals, but because of the natural law, it is for human beings.

tain: social life would become impossible because then the individual's freedom of choice would have been separated from his responsibility for social order. Everything would then be seen as the result of the impersonal influences of environment, "the system," and biology, and no one would ever be either liable to blame or subject to esteem as a person.

Willingness to cooperate with others to overcome challenges, courage to live with uncertainties without succumbing to the temptation of despair, and a determination to assume freely individual responsibility for social order, according to the natural law, in large measure define what it means to be an American. The stresses of American life in the twentieth century have at times appeared to be more severe than they ever were in the past. But that is only an appearance. Now, as surely as in every period of America's history, the continuance of American culture is by its very nature a challenge.

INDEX

INDEX

Amazon Basin: forbidding character of, and Brazilian behavior, 93–94

America, American: as names, xiii. *See also* United States

American culture: at beginning of 20th century, 139–40; equality of liberty in, linked to equal social responsibility, 58–59, 67; European condemnations of, 136–38; focus of, on satisfaction of individuals, 10; generated by majority, not upper class, 136; immigration policy during colonial period chief British influence on, 40–41; origin of belief in consent of governed in, 9, 12, 41, 63, 67; primacy of persons, not physical environment, to beliefs of, 153–54; validity of, confirmed by Union victory in Civil War, 139

—Indian and European civilizations in 1500: shared characteristics of, 101–2

—Indian population: in Canada at time of European settlement, 25; in 1492, widely divergent estimates of the size of, 23–24; massive die-off in, in 1500s, 24; state of culture and distribution of, before 1492, 24–25, 28, 32

—individualism: conditions preventing anarchism of, 67, 152–53; derived from self-selecting emigration, not frontier, 65–66

—life in 20th century: no more challenging than in earlier centuries, 156

—Revolution: as expressing existing cultural difference, 61–63

—sense of history: derived from accomplishing in 3 centuries 60 centuries of European development, 113–14; nature of, 119; radically different from European sense, 117

—sense of space: concept of a, 118–19; determined by culture, 129–30; distinguished by freedom of acquiring property within, 57–58, 133–35; early unity of, reflected in rapid development of integrated canal, rail, river, and road communications, 127–29;

Born and raised in Parker's Landing, Pennsylvania, John Harmon McElroy has served in the U.S. Navy and holds degrees from Princeton (A.B., 1956) and Duke (Ph.D., 1966). He has taught in the South (Clemson University) and in the Midwest (The University of Wisconsin) and has been a Fulbright Lecturer in Spain and in Brazil. He is presently a professor at the University of Arizona. Besides American cultural history, his main interest is American literature. His text of Washington Irving's *Life and Voyages of Christopher Columbus* was published in 1981. He and his wife, Dr. Onyria Herrera McElroy, have four children.

THE ATTENDING PHYSICIAN

A JOAN KAHN BOOK

The
Attending
Physician

by

R.B. DOMINIC

HARPER & ROW, PUBLISHERS
New York, Hagerstown, San Francisco, London

FIRST EDITION

Designer: Eve Kirch

Copyeditor: Paul Hirschman

Library of Congress Cataloging in Publication Data
Dominic, R. B.
   The attending physician.
   "A Joan Kahn book."
   I. Title.
PZ4.D673At   1979 [PS3554.0463]   813'.5'4   79–1702
ISBN 0–06–011084–8

---

80 81 82 83 84 10 9 8 7 6 5 4 3 2 1

— I —

In Washington, D.C., most of the local disasters are man-made. This does nothing to lessen their danger. After all, volcanoes can smolder harmlessly for a long time, but elections take place every other year. And, to add insult to injury, there are special prosecutors, ethics committees and the *Washington Post*.

As a result, politicians who become fixtures are politicians with survival skills. While new restaurants, new press secretaries and new policies attract all the attention, old Washington hands lean back, watching them come and go.

Congressmen Benton Safford (D., Ohio) had won enough elections to qualify as a veteran, particularly in the current House of Representatives, where he was unmistakably on the balding side of the generation gap. But, as luck would have it, he served on a subcommittee that was a veritable bouquet of hardy perennials.

Congressman Eugene Valingham Oakes (R., S. Dak.) had represented his hard-working, teetotaling, God-fearing constituents since time immemorial. "Yes, I believe I could use a little topping up, Ben," he said, studying the bourbon level in his glass. "Nothing like drafting a report to give a man a thirst."

His fellow Republican, Elsie Hollenbach of California, was made of sterner stuff. She accepted her second martini with a gracious nod, but stuck to the subject at hand. "I think we are submitting a fair survey of Medicaid abuse. Hearings in four cities—"

Congressman Anthony Martinelli, who came from Providence, Rhode Island, groaned aloud. "Passaic, Cedar Rapids, Scranton and Bangor! God, I hate these road shows." He did not wait for Safford to offer hospitality, but applied himself to the bottle at his elbow.

"Congressional committee hearings outside of Washington are an invaluable aid in bringing government closer to the people," said Mrs. Hollenbach, who had sailed around the circuit without visible wear or tear. "Although I was glad to get back to Washington yesterday."

She then dispelled this suggestion of weakness by continuing: "I want to keep an eye on what's happening over at Treasury. I don't like the way things are developing at all."

"What do you mean, Elsie? There hasn't been time for things to develop, at Treasury or anywhere else," said Ben, dutifully defending his party.

Six months earlier the American public had put a new man in the White House and, by extension, in every corner of the Executive branch. There were Democratic rookies everywhere you looked.

Martinelli, too, suspected partisan sniping. "Tell the truth, Elsie," he said with friendly malice. "Passaic, Cedar Rapids, Scranton and Bangor got to you, too, didn't they?"

"Certainly not," she replied. "I found our investigations very rewarding."

Val Oakes chose to take issue. "Rewarding? We knew before we started that half the doctors in the country are getting rich

2

off Medicaid. What's rewarding about traipsing from state to state hearing them deny it?"

Mrs. Hollenbach ignored him to address Ben. "And I am not discussing Treasury proposals, although I don't like what I hear about them. No, it's Sumner Fenton. I understand he may have to resign because of conflicts of interest."

"So soon?" Ben commented unwisely.

Oakes was with him in spirit. "This resignation business is getting out of hand," he declared. "People used to stick to their guns through thick and thin. Now, every little thing—and they roll over and play dead."

As always, there was salty wisdom in what he said. But Tony Martinelli had his own political savvy. "What little thing has Fenton been caught at?" he inquired.

Mrs. Hollenbach, sometimes described as the Conscience of the House, said: "There are allegations of improprieties in a bank he owns. Or I should say what appear to be improprieties."

This stung Congressman Martinelli. "Dammit," he exploded, "Republicans are supposed to own banks, not Democrats!"

"Times are changing, Tony," Ben told him.

"Not in South Dakota," said Val Oakes. "The only Democratic banker I ever heard of was run out of town forty years ago. Of course, back then we didn't call it impropriety. We called it robbing the cash box. And there wasn't any hogwash about appearances, either."

Again he had voiced the sense of the meeting. Even a moralist like Mrs. Hollenbach blanched at recent demands for nonstop displays of virtue. Not that she had anything to fear. Elsie was the embodiment of public and private rectitude, from her disciplined gray hair to her well-shod feet.

Martinelli hailed from a different political tradition. Removing an infinitesimal speck of lint from his Italian silk sleeve, he

3

said: "It's bad enough we've got priests in Congress. Now they want saints!"

If so, Benton Safford was out of luck. He was no saint. He was not even a campaign manager's dream. Still, he suited Ohio's Fiftieth Congressional District, possibly because he was reassuringly human—rumpled clothes, thickening waistline and all.

Val Oakes, on the other hand, was an unabashed sinner. "This, too, shall pass," he declared sonorously.

Elsie did not care to go that far. "Naturally, I support stricter requirements for public office—including complete financial disclosure."

"Sure, sure," said Martinelli.

She eyed him. "The public should have access to the income-tax returns of every candidate. There is no legitimate reason they should not."

"I can think of a few."

Sparring between Martinelli and Mrs. Hollenbach was an old story. It was more a product of their mutual respect and affection than of their profound political differences.

"Besides, why pick on politicians?" Tony continued. "Why not doctors, for example? We could recommend that doctors with Medicaid patients have to publish *their* income-tax returns, huh, Elsie?"

Given the subcommittee's recent trek from Passaic to Bangor, this was a timely if unscrupulous thrust. Mrs. Hollenbach was taking a deep breath when Ben Safford stepped into the breach.

"I guess we'd better start work," he said.

He drew fire from all sides.

"On what?" asked Tony, while Val Oakes shook his head ponderously.

Mrs. Hollenbach abandoned Martinelli to quash Ben Safford. "You haven't forgotten that we are simply submitting the testimony with a letter of transmittal, have you? We all

4

agreed—" she shot a look at Tony—"that recommendations would be premature."

"One hundred percent correct, Elsie," he said with a flashing smile.

"Best thing for you to do, Ben, is fill 'em up again," said Val, easing into his real message. "Blessed are the peacemakers when they know what they're doing. Otherwise they get blown out of the water."

Grinning, Ben complied with the suggestion. "Yes, Elsie. I remember it's a letter of transmittal—period."

Reform of the Medicaid system of assistance to the poor and the elderly was long overdue. But the strategy in Congress was to approach new legislation cautiously and to begin with the accumulation of data proving widespread abuse. The recent subcommittee hearings had been so much spade work, necessary but uninspiring.

"Let's look on the bright side," said Martinelli jauntily. "We send this damn thing off and we're finished with Medicaid and touring circuses—at least for the time being."

No sooner had he spoken than L. Lamar Flecker (D., Ala.), the subcommittee chairman, bustled into Ben's office. As always, he looked too harried for his own good.

"Sit down and take a load off your feet, Lou," said Val Oakes expansively.

Flecker sat and accepted a drink. But he lacked Val's genius for relaxation. "I've just come from the Speaker," he announced after a gulp.

"How's he settling in?" Ben inquired.

The House was undergoing changes, too. The new Speaker was not, of course, an unknown quantity. For over thirty years he had represented Cook County, Illinois, with bibulous charm and unswerving party loyalty.

"He enjoys being Speaker," said Flecker after giving the question due thought.

A vestigial sniff from Mrs. Hollenbach made him add: "And

5

I think he's going to do a real fine job."

The loyal opposition struck back. "Don't tell *us*, Lou," said Oakes. "Tell the White House."

Flecker was too preoccupied to notice this mild jibe. His kind, worried eyes rested on Ben Safford. "The leadership just told me about a change in plans," he said, apologetically enough to produce an uneasy silence. Into it, his next words fell like millstones. "They want us to hold one more set of hearings out of town—before we submit our report."

Ben Safford did not join the chorus of dismay. Instinct told him that Flecker was holding something back, and instinct was right. Finally, when Elsie's measured cadences trailed off, when Martinelli stopped boiling over, when Val finished quoting Ecclesiastes, Ben seized his opening.

"Lou, where are these new hearings going to be?"

Flecker could not face him. "In Newburg, Ben."

"Newburg—Ohio?" Ben asked hollowly.

There was no way to soften the blow. On Tuesday the subcommittee was scheduled to hold hearings on Medicaid abuse in Newburg, Ohio—the Fiftieth Congressional District, which Benton Safford had the honor and privilege of representing in the Congress of the United States.

"Why?" he was still demanding an hour later. "Why dump this on me? I've cooperated with the leadership! I've done my committee work! Hell, I even backed the rebate!"

Madge Anderson, Ben's highly competent and knowledgeable secretary, treated his questions literally. "I think it's just bad luck," she said.

He stopped pacing up and down before her desk, transfixed by the inadequacy of her response. "Bad luck?" he repeated. "Good God, Madge, do you realize what a can of worms they're handing me? Dear old Dr. Whatsit—in my own backyard."

"It's going to be tricky for you," she said with a small frown.

"Thanks for that much sympathy," he said grumpily.

Madge was unmoved. A slim, attractive young woman, she was spiritual kin in Washington to Ben's sister Janet back in Newburg. Her attachment to Ben's interests was wholehearted, quasi-maternal and more astringent than indulgent.

"By bad luck, I simply meant the coincidence of the timing."

"What coincidence?" he demanded.

Genuinely surprised, she said: "Didn't Congressman Flecker tell you?"

"No, he had to rush off to Ways and Means."

"And you haven't read the newspapers?"

Ben was getting tired of admitting his own inadequacy. "Look, Madge, I just got back from the wilds of Maine."

"Well, you'd better read them now," she said, indicating the display of Ohio newspapers adorning the table by the window.

On the whole, the Cincinnati *Inquirer* put it as pithily as anyone else.

NEW MEDICAID REVELATIONS BY HEW
7 Newburg MD's Paid $1,000,000

7

2

In Newburg, Ohio, the Department of Health, Education and Welfare occupied two floors of the Federal Building. When Congressman Flecker and the rest of his subcommittee descended two days later, the regional director there was almost too cooperative. Quentin Trumbull was deeply shamed by the corruption over which he found himself presiding. Yet, at the same time, he could not help taking perverse pride in its magnitude.

"Now, this one you won't believe," he predicted, brandishing another file.

Val Oakes corrected him. "After Scranton, we'll believe anything."

Tony Martinelli concurred. "They've got crooks there like nothing you've ever seen."

"Just take a look," Trumbull pleaded. "I don't say Newburg doctors are the biggest crooks in the world, but they've got to be the sloppiest."

By now the subcommittee knew more about Medicaid swindling then they wanted to. Even hometown pride could not make Ben Safford interested in further squalid detail. Only Mrs. Hollenbach remained indefatigable. She glanced through the folder, then frowned. "This is a vasectomy billing by a Dr. Yarborough," she commented. "As I recall, there is no Dr. Yarborough on the published list."

"He's not one of the Newburg Seven because he died ten months ago," Quentin Trumbull explained. "He'd practiced here for forty-five years, and for a while they wanted to name the new wing of the hospital after him. I seem to remember hearing you talk at the kick-off dinner, Congressman Safford."

Ben cast his mind back over the worthy causes that had called on him to eat a bad dinner and make a worse speech. "What did I say?" he asked warily.

Trumbull was enjoying his own private joke. "Among other things, that we'd never forget how Ned Yarborough gave of himself to the poor. His sons told everybody they were particularly touched by that remark."

Ben was resigned. "And I suppose he was in this swindle up to his ears?"

"He sure was. Yarborough may have spent time with poor patients, but that was to get their Medicaid numbers. They're the one essential for this racket. But what really makes me laugh is that it was the sons who let the cat out of the bag."

Martinelli was beginning to wonder if a childhood on the back streets of East Providence had left him too innocent for the world of modern medicine.

"You mean they fingered their old man?" he asked hoarsely.

Trumbull was able to reassure him. It had all been an accident. "And no one regrets it more than the Yarboroughs," he reported. "But they got into some squabble over the old man's estate, and the younger brother went to court to demand an accounting. So a lot of stuff became a matter of public record, including Yarborough's final year of Medicaid billings. It was the first time that anybody added them all up, and they came to over a hundred thousand dollars. Well, that made HEW think."

"Good," said Elsie militantly.

"Particularly," said Trumbull, sweeping on zestfully, "par-

9

ticularly when I remembered that Yarborough took six months off that year—to visit Tahiti and Hong Kong. I decided we'd better take a closer look."

"That's when you hired some computer time?" Ben asked.

"Not right away," said Trumbull. "We've got something better than a computer. Her name is Charlene Gregorian. She works downstairs in Social Security, and she's been there for years. The computer is okay for numbers, but Charlene knows all about the people involved—you know, everybody on old-age pensions, everybody who's blind or disabled. So I asked her to glance through the Yarborough file. When she pulled out that vasectomy billing, Mrs. Hollenbach, I thought she'd die laughing."

This daunted everybody but Mrs. Hollenbach. "Why is it so funny? Naturally, I'm assuming that Yarborough never performed the operation—"

With a happy yip, Trumbull interrupted. "He'd have had a hard time trying. The patient, Sidney Kincaid, is a forty-eight-year-old welfare mother."

Congressman Oakes was the first to recover. "You mean the doctors you keep around here don't even check on *that?*"

"I told you they were sloppy," Trumbull boasted. "They've got their little black book of Medicaid numbers. Whenever they need extra cash, they dash off a billing—for the first thing that enters their heads. They can't be bothered to simply pad their bills."

"But why not reduce the odds?" Tony Martinelli persisted. "Make it an appendix? At least everybody qualifies for that."

Trumbull shrugged. "For all I know, they like a little variety. Anyway, Charlene had a field day with Yarborough's records. Patients who were dead when he claimed he was treating them, people who'd moved to Florida. She found enough to justify our requesting computer print-outs on every doctor in town. And you know what came out of the woodwork."

"We sure do," said Ben Safford ruefully. "You found seven doctors in town who made over a hundred thousand each from

10

Medicaid last year—and you gave their names to the papers."

Val Oakes reverted to an earlier point. "Could be I was wrong. Newburg may be worse than Scranton. Then again, it may be that Scranton just doesn't have a Charlene Gregorian handy. I'd like to meet that little lady."

"You're going to," Trumbull promised, consulting his watch. "I told her we'd drop by this afternoon. She'll give you a real eye-opener about what goes on around Newburg."

"Cheer up, Ben," said Val as they trooped out into the hall. "All this will come in handy for you—someday."

But in the reception area of the Social Security office, the first eye-opener to come their way was the welfare system as it works at street level. The whole room was filled with people, all gesticulating, all shouting. At first glance, Ben spotted a clergyman, two students in Ohio State sweatshirts and a middle-aged woman sitting slightly apart, fanning herself with a magazine. A sudden rift in the tangle of activity revealed the eye of the storm, an elderly woman who was alternately sobbing and drumming the arms of her chair with her hands. The moment that the visitors saw her, she saw them. Levering herself to her feet, she pointed a gnarled finger at Congressman Martinelli and burst into a shrill foreign language.

"Hey!" Tony protested, backing away in alarm.

Supporters rallied around the principals. The clergyman bent over the crone with nervous reassurance. Mrs. Hollenbach courageously moved in front of Tony. The middle-aged woman froze in mid-sweep, and Quentin Trumbull settled back on his heels and bawled: "Charlene! Charlene, are you there?"

A flapping hand appeared from the turmoil. "Take them into my office, Quen. They're just making things worse."

Val Oakes led the retreat.

"It's always a madhouse down here," Trumbull apologized when they had reached safety. "I should have called first to make sure the coast was clear."

11

Mrs. Hollenbach was not used to treatment like this. "Things have come to a pretty pass when Congressmen need convoys to get through Federal offices."

"That was Italian she was shouting, wasn't it, Tony?" Ben asked. "What was the old lady saying?"

Martinelli was reluctant to interpret. "She confused me with someone else," he hedged. "But I'll tell you one thing—that woman was raised in the gutter."

Charlene Gregorian breezed in ten minutes later, treating the whole incident as part of a day's work. "We've got Mrs. Bertilucci squared away," she announced. "Sorry about her yelling at you. She thought you worked here."

"Tell her we're from Congress," Tony suggested.

"That would make it worse," Mrs. Gregorian said cheerfully, clicking her way around the desk.

She was a roly-poly woman, about fifty-five years old, who radiated bouncy practicality. Her hair had been so artfully streaked that the faded blond, the gray and the chemical frosting all blended into a silver-gilt aureole framing her round face with its slightly protuberant blue eyes. Neat little feet teetered precariously atop high heels transforming her natural four-foot-eleven into a statuesque five-foot-two. She was totally unimpressed by the arrival of a Washington delegation in her tiny office.

"Charlene," said Trumbull by way of introduction, "knows more than anybody in Newburg about Social Security."

"And a fine mess it is," she said stoutly.

The rest of the subcommittee could take a detached view of her comment. But Ben Safford got elected by the people flowing through Charlene's hands.

"What exactly was Mrs. Bertilucci's problem?" he asked.

"Oh, the usual thing. She's over sixty-five, but she doesn't have a birth certificate to prove it. In the old days, we'd scramble around and dig up her immigration papers or her marriage license. But these days . . ."

Lou Flecker thought he heard an accusation. "Now, Mrs. Gregorian, I know a lot of people don't like the new Social Security regulations we've passed. But how have they made it harder for Mrs. . . . Mrs. Bertilucci to prove she's eligible?"

"Oh, it's not you," she said promptly. "It's the others—the ministers, the students, the volunteers. Helping senior citizens has become very trendy. That's fine, I suppose, but it's also trendy to wage war on bureaucrats. Fifteen years ago Mrs. Bertilucci would have come in here with her daughter and we would have settled everything in no time."

Flecker conscientiously followed every word. He still did not see the problem. "Why can't she do that now?"

"Because she can't even get out of her own house without attracting a—a—" Charlene's plump little paws fluttered graphically—"a swarm of do-gooders. Everyone is ready to champion her when we try to grind her under our heel. By the time the whole gang gets here, the daughter's lost control— that was her, fanning herself—the old lady's hysterical and nobody will listen to a word we say."

Mrs. Hollenbach was less shaken by this vision of unbridled emotion than her male colleagues. "It's regrettable," she said, "but it makes no real difference, does it? Mrs. Bertilucci ends up with her Social Security checks."

Charlene was a good-humored woman. "It doesn't make any difference to Mrs. Bertilucci," she agreed. "And I suppose you could say that all the wasted time doesn't cost us more than three GS-10 salaries a year."

Having scored her point, she contemplated her visitors genially. "But why complain? What we're losing is peanuts— compared to the way Medicaid is being ripped off. Quen, did you tell them about the nursing homes . . . ?"

By the time Ben Safford reached home that evening he was a troubled man. His brother-in-law took one look and sympathetically handed him a glass without asking any questions. His

13

sister Janet, however, had hospitality on her mind.

"I'm sorry we're not getting to see the others until tomorrow," she said, bustling in with a tray. "We could have arranged dinner tonight."

"It's just as well," Ben said. "After what we learned about Medicaid in this town, nobody was in any mood for a party."

Janet was ruffled. The Safford seat in Congress was very much a family affair. Ben not only continued to maintain bachelor quarters in the big old house that he and Janet had inherited, he also relied on his sister, his brother-in-law and his tribe of nieces and nephews to mend fences, hit the campaign trail and provide political intelligence. Anything happening in Newburg that escaped the attention of one Lundgren or another was a rarity.

"Well, what did you expect?" she demanded with asperity. "You just spent a month looking into Medicaid abuse everyplace else. Did you think Newburg would be different?"

Ben hated to admit it, but that was exactly what he had thought. "I knew there'd be hell to pay once the Cincinnati papers started running stories naming the Newburg Seven. But it isn't just Medicaid, Janet. You wouldn't believe what goes on at the Social Security office."

"Oh, wouldn't I?"

Belatedly, Ben recalled the network of activities that took Janet into hospitals, schools, churches—and, presumably, welfare offices.

"All right. But you can't say that I don't do a lot with Social Security. Whenever I get a complaint, I do something, don't I?"

She sniffed. "You mean Madge calls somebody at headquarters. Forget about the Washington end, Ben. It's high time you saw what goes on at the Newburg level."

"Oh, let the man enjoy his drink," urged Fred Lundgren, a large, peace-loving man. "Like it or not, Ben's going to be seeing plenty of the seamy side of Newburg life."

"That's what that woman at Social Security kept saying," Ben told them without enthusiasm.

"Charlene?" said Janet. "I work with her quite often. She's got a lot of sense, Ben."

"I was afraid of that," he said with a groan. "I suppose you know all these damn doctors, too. Seems to me you spend half your time lining up medical attention for people, or finding nursing homes."

His relatives stared at him, then laughed aloud.

"You really do lead a protected life in Washington, don't you?" Janet finally said. "Doctors don't do things like that anymore. It's all social workers now."

Fred flourished his glass. "You don't see a doctor these days until you're lying there waiting for him to start cutting. Or," he added in the interest of greater accuracy, "unless you're selling something they want."

Ben had recently accumulated some information of his own about the medical profession. "I thought they all drive Cadillacs."

Fred Lundgren owned the Ford agency in Newburg, the largest dealership in southern Ohio.

"Sooner or later, plenty of them switch to Lincolns," he said comfortably. "And the younger ones give me a lot of business in four-wheel drives. Yes, I bet I've met every single doctor in Newburg."

"Including the Newburg Seven?" Ben asked provocatively.

"See them all the time. Hell, they've got to spend that money somewhere, don't they?"

Ben did not argue. "Have you seen them since they hit the headlines, Fred?"

After thinking about it for a moment, Fred said, "Only in passing. Now that you mention it, they've been making themselves scarce. I suppose they don't want to do much talking about this mess."

15

The oven bell brought Janet to her feet. But she paused at the door for a final observation:

"They don't want to discuss it with outsiders. But I'm sure they're doing a lot of talking among themselves, aren't you? I wonder what they're saying."

3

While the Newburg Seven might not be talking to the outside world, they were making sure to be seen by it. The next evening, the head of the local AMA showed the flag by accompanying two of the elect, and their wives, to a symphony performance in Cincinnati. Two other doctors hauled their wives out to the Trianon, Newburg's fanciest restaurant, for an extended meal designed to prove that they had nothing to be ashamed of. The remaining three were on display in the dining room of the Newburg Country Club. They were placed at a table for five because Dr. James Rojak was one of Newburg's swinging singles.

Except in giant cities, doctors are almost forced to socialize together. Who else can afford the price tag of their amusements, who else can arrange to play golf regularly at noon on Wednesdays, who else can close down an office for a week's medical convention, a two-week jaunt to Hong Kong, a four-month vacation in South America? They learn to live with each other in spite of different tastes. Howard and Connie White, in their late forties, were tanned enthusiasts of the

17

beach life, from Cape Cod to the Bahamas to Acapulco. Arnold Deachman, while only a few years older, gave the impression of belonging to another world and another generation. White was lean, but Deachman was thin to the point of emaciation. White was wearing a navy-blue blazer and a white turtleneck; Deachman's three hundred dollars' worth of tailoring was formal enough for a funeral. Both men projected an aura of success, but White normally exhibited an innocent satisfaction in this state of affairs, while Deachman was always alert for imperfections in his universe. He had found one that very afternoon.

"That lawyer of mine claims we have no case against these newspapers," he reported angrily. "Well, I certainly am not taking his word for it. I'll get another opinion, and if he thinks I'm going to pay some fat bill for that kind of help, he's in for a surprise."

His old friend had some advice for him. "You'll be wasting your time, Arnie. I went to mine yesterday and he said the same thing." White was pleased to have a new nugget of information. "It seems that reporters have the right to print government statistics."

"They don't have the right to defame me," Deachman retorted roundly. "There must be some way to stop them."

Neither Deachman nor White was pleased to discover that the third doctor was grinning sardonically. "Why don't you both wise up? The damage is done now. We know that we're simply beating the establishment at its own game. But newspapers don't raise their circulation by being realistic. They've got to pretend to be on a moral crusade. So there's no point in whipping yourself up about it. They're just doing their thing."

This authentic voice of the seventies had been a familiar instructor in modern values for over a year now. The Deachmans and the Whites had been spending most of their spare time together for two decades. Jim Rojak, fifteen years their junior, was a comparative newcomer to the group.

Connie White was always telling her husband that Rojak helped keep them abreast of the times. But today she had her own reasons for thinking that he had gone too far.

18

"It's all very well to be so detached, Jim," she protested, "but people are beginning to pay attention to these stories. Quite intelligent people, too. Do you realize that the Sierra Club is hesitating about reappointing me to the education committee?"

Rojak laughed outright. "Use your head, Connie," he urged, "and your clout, too. Why do you think you got on that committee in the first place? Just tell them you're reconsidering your annual donation and they'll get back into line fast enough."

Connie half admired, half deplored this frankness. Her husband rose above it. "This is more important than Sierra Club committees, Jim. And you can't fool me that you enjoy being painted as some sort of crook any more than we do."

"It will die down." Rojak shrugged indifferently. "In the meantime I can live with it."

"That's right," Nesta Deachman said coolly. "This is just a cheap publicity gimmick. As soon as the next sensation comes along, the papers will forget all about us. Everybody knows that."

Connie stiffened. Like many a middle-aged woman before her, she welcomed guidance about the brave new world from an attractive younger man. The same tuition from a younger woman raised her hackles. When Arnold Deachman, two years earlier, had divorced his wife to marry his beautiful nurse, he had disrupted Connie's life almost as badly as Margaret Deachman's. From the day he led Nesta to the altar, Connie was doomed to sit across tables listening to Nesta dismiss housewives, their children, their recipes. When the talk turned to fee scales or prepayments, Nesta did not withdraw into the PTA. Oh, no, she was right in there, a professional among professionals. Then in the powder room, while Connie vigorously brushed her sun-bleached crop, Nesta would comb a luxuriant cloud of black hair and provocatively moisten a finger to smooth the dark eyebrows that arched over astonishingly blue eyes.

And, to top it all, Connie had to watch Nesta coax displays of uxoriousness from Arnold that Howard White would never

19

match in a million years. Luckily, on this occasion Nesta had rubbed her husband the wrong way.

"You forget, Nesta, that, unlike Jim here, I have a family to consider. They're just starting out in the world and they're being exposed to all this filth, they're reading these innuendoes." Deachman paused to make the strongest possible effect. "I not only have to think about my children, I have to think about my grandson."

Nesta was careful about some children. "If little Trigger is reading any innuendoes, he's making headlines himself," she said indulgently.

This sally elicited reluctant smiles, even from Connie White. Arnold Deachman Taggert had been born only six months ago, but he had already achieved a hammerlock on his grandfather's affections.

"That's beside the point," Deachman said with the fretful authority that was second nature to him. "I can tolerate passing discomfort as well as anyone. This may have permanent consequences."

"You're right on the button, Arnie." White's forehead was creased by an unaccustomed frown. "We've worked hard to establish our reputations and we've been looked up to in this community. If you ask me, it's a crying shame to have all that go down the drain because some reporter wants a front-page byline."

In many ways Jim Rojak was the most straightforward person there. As long as he could keep his license to steal, he did not insist on public acclaim.

"Who cares what the bastards in Newburg think?" he demanded. "They're probably all ripping off something on the side themselves. What gives them the right to be so superior?"

"Nobody has suggested this is a question of moral superiority," Deachman snapped.

Rojak nodded approvingly. "That's just it. This is a question of power. We're the doctors and we've got the power to run our practices any way we want. All the talking in the world isn't going to change that. We run the hospitals, we run the whole damn health-care system. People may not like our meth-

20

ods, but if they want any treatment, they've got to come to us. It's that simple."

Deachman could not disagree, so he cast around for some other target. "All this worry is playing hell with my stomach, and I don't even have my pills," he complained, fussing through the contents of his pockets. "Nesta, you know I shouldn't leave the house without them. Why in God's name didn't you remind me?"

"Because you resent being reminded almost as much as not having them. So *I* brought them." With a flourish she produced a small container from her evening bag. "I may not be able to stop the pressure, dear, but I can see that you take proper care of yourself."

This display of wifely solicitude mollified Deachman. "Tit for tat," he said with creaking playfulness. "You remembered to bring my tablets and I remembered to deposit the money for your coat."

"Oh, Arnie!"

But even as Nesta rhapsodized, her eyes slid sideways to Connie White and her lips folded in a secretive smile of satisfaction. Connie bit down hard. When Nesta's mink coat had first been mentioned, Connie had instinctively reminded everyone of her commitment to the preservation of wildlife. She forgot what she had managed to produce in honor of the diamond bracelet and the Mercedes convertible, but even to her own ears these protestations were beginning to sound like sour grapes.

"Aren't you lucky, Nesta?" she said, forcing herself into feminine enthusiasm. "I can hardly wait to see it."

But now that Howard White had begun his career as a worrier, he was finding material in unlikely corners. "For heaven's sake, I hope you're going to be tactful, Nesta. This isn't the best time to flaunt thousands of dollars' worth of fur in Newburg."

Rojak was amused. "That's good, coming from you, Howard. Whose boat was on the front page this morning? And how much did that yacht set you back, anyway?"

"Dammit, that picture is over a year old. There wasn't anything I could do about it. And it's not a yacht, it's just a sailboat."

"Try explaining that to some of the clowns who've got to make do with a Sunfish." Rojak leaned forward persuasively. "Christ, Howard, I don't have anything against your boat. They may dig up an old picture of me with my plane any day. That's why I say it's no use sucking up to every would-be critic that comes crawling along. We're rich, everybody knows it, and instead of trying to hide it, we should be using it like a hammer. I'll tell you one thing: there isn't a merchant in this town who doesn't know that, long after the stories have stopped, we're still going to be big customers."

Howard White chose to think that yacht brokers warmed to him personally. He wouldn't believe that his money had anything to do with their cordiality.

"You're leaving a lot out, Jim," he said quietly. "There are plenty of people who aren't trying to sell us something. Like those Congressmen who are investigating us. You can afford to relax. You're third down their list of witnesses, and plenty can happen before they get to you. But I'm the one who has to testify tomorrow."

Deachman, who was second on the roster, naturally sympathized. "It's disgraceful that we should be pilloried in public this way. I told Perrin that it was the AMA's job to stop these hearings. But you know him—he has the backbone of a rubber band. He said it wasn't his job to get involved."

"He was absolutely right."

The four outraged gasps that greeted Rojak's statement brought an involuntary grimace to his lips. "Look, whose side do you think I'm on?"

"I sometimes think you forget when you're trying for an effect," Deachman said tartly.

Rojak shook his head. "You're not facing this sensibly. There's been a big story with headlines screaming corruption.

22

Nothing in God's name could choke these pols off from their grandstand play. They've got to make themselves look good at our expense. Perrin would just be wasting leverage trying to stop the subcommittee."

"That's wonderful," White said sarcastically. "So you're saying I go on the stand tomorrow morning and it shouldn't bother me because nothing can stop it from happening. Even though anything I say may be wrong and there's everything at stake."

"Like what?"

White stared.

Rojak repeated his challenge. "Like what? Oh, I admit it may be embarrassing at the time. I don't expect you to enjoy it, and I won't either when my turn comes. But it's all a bunch of hot air. What do you think they can do to us? Take away our license to practice medicine?"

From the uproar, he might have suggested the House of Representatives could have them drawn and quartered.

"For Chrissake, Jim," exclaimed White, "what are you talking about?"

Connie was just as shaken. "They can't do anything like that."

"I should think not," Deachman said. "Laymen have no call to interfere with professional standards."

Nesta alone did not bite. "Oh, for heaven's sake, don't let Jim get you going. Congressmen don't have any jurisdiction to yank medical licenses."

But nobody was listening to her, and Rojak went on enjoying the tumult he had created. "No, I haven't lost my marbles. I'm simply reminding you that this subcommittee can't stop us practicing. So what's the next thing bugging you?"

They were now on delicate ground and Howard White had difficulty choosing the right words.

"Of course I was never worried about practicing as such. But I don't want any interference either." For a moment he stalled, unable to get over the hump. "The thing is, we've all worked out the routines under which we do our best work. I don't say there isn't an occasional clerical error. But what's that compared to the cures we effect? My office is set up for a certain flow and I don't want anybody tampering with it."

Jim grinned understandingly. He had no trouble following his colleague's thoughts. "You mean you don't want HEW claiming we can't submit any more Medicaid billings? Well, that's the point at which Perrin comes into his own. That's when he does his work. Medicaid and Medicare give the patient the right to choose his own doctor. That hands the AMA all the ammunition they need if any dummy in Washington thinks he can blacklist us. They can scream their heads off about not depriving the patient of his rights. Perrin will like it because he doesn't have to sound as if he's covering for us, and every MD in Newburg will back him. Give these bozos the right to select doctors and we might as well have socialized medicine and be done with it."

Part of the gloom oppressing White and Deachman had been the sense of isolation from their fellows. At this prediction of professional solidarity, they both brightened.

"I suppose HEW might try to recover some of the past billings." Deachman was quasi-judicious now, all signs of temper dissipated.

"Don't you believe it!" Rojak snorted. "Why do you think they published those totals? First, it's all they've got. There aren't any breakdowns they can use. Second, they can't lay a finger on us and they know it. So they try and embarrass us into being good little boys. Well, they need more than that, as far as I'm concerned."

Nesta was right in step with him. "All it takes is enough guts to outface them. They're used to dealing with people who run if you say boo. Well, that's not us, is it, Arnie?"

While her husband accorded only tempered enthusiasm to this view, Howard White was more responsive.

"Here, boy!" he called. "Get me the wine waiter. We're going to have some champagne to this."

The sommelier was living proof of Rojak's thesis about merchants and customers. The wine waiter was almost reverential as he sold White the most expensive magnum in the cellar.

When it came, White could hardly wait for it to be chilled. "You've been right all along, Jim," he said with heartfelt relief. "That damned subcommittee can't touch us at all."

Rojak was watching the bubbles rise in his glass with dreamy content. "It's better than that, baby. Nobody in the whole world can touch us."

4

Champagne produces a glow, not a roaring fire. Jim Rojak was coaxing the last drops out of the bottle when Arnold Deachman pushed back his chair.

"Time for us to be going, Nesta," he announced. "Jim, Howard—I'm glad we had a chance to talk this thing through."

"Calling it a night already?" Rojak protested. But he obediently jammed the bottle down into the ice bucket and rose to assist Nesta.

"Arnie and I are real early birds, Jim," she murmured. "Howard, the champagne was just lovely. Thank you so much."

This reminded Deachman of a nicety. "Howard," he said, "good luck with the subcommittee tomorrow. Remember, you've got a lot of friends rooting for you. Coming, Nesta?"

Rojak was about to follow the Deachmans when he saw that neither Howard White nor Connie had budged.

"We're staying on for a couple of dances," explained White.

For a moment Rojak suspected champagne-inspired bravado. But Connie, who had a harder head than her husband, was determinedly cheerful, too.

"You're absolutely right, Jim," she said. "About not letting them embarrass us. Howard and I love to dance, and that's what we're going to do any time we please—including right now!"

"Enjoy yourselves," said Rojak, indifferent to the gesture and to dancing at the sedate Newburg Country Club. "Give me a call tomorrow, Howard, and let me know how it goes."

"Absolutely," White said, tapping his foot to the energetic rhythms that the three-man combo was striking up.

Connie jumped to her feet and tugged at him. "Come on, Howard—or Jim! How about you?"

"No, I'd better be moving," he said, with a hasty farewell salute.

The Whites danced extremely well, especially with each other. They executed intricate maneuvers with flawless timing and swirled smoothly around the dance floor while others shuffled through two-steps. Their performance was more athletic than graceful, but it was skilled.

However, they were always having trouble with duffers. A dazzling twirl at the finale of "Galveston" cannoned them into another couple steering a more modest course.

"Oops—sorry!" said White, breathing heavily from his exertions. "Fred Lundgren! What brings *you* here?"

Fred Lundgren had belonged to the Newburg Country Club for years, but he didn't find it necessary to say so. He greeted Fred Astaire and Ginger Rogers civilly and waited for them to twinkle away.

Unfortunately, Connie White had to demonstrate how unembarrassed she was. Brightly she said: "Janet! I've been meaning to call you for weeks! Margie Flannery told me that you're organizing the WNCH Telethon—"

Fred interrupted to introduce his partner. "Mrs. Hollenbach, may I present Mrs. White—and Dr. White."

Elsie placed Howard White instantly. Medicaid bills of one

hundred seventy-three thousand dollars. She nodded courteously but silently.

Connie's contrition was exaggerated. "Oh, dear! My awful memory for faces. You know, I blame it on Howard having so many patients. It's hard to keep everybody straight!"

"Well, it's good seeing you here, Fred," said Dr. White with meaningless geniality. "Nice to have met you, Mrs. Hollenborn—"

There were limits to Fred's good nature. "Congresswoman *Hollenbach* is here in Newburg for the subcommittee hearings," he said firmly enough to break up this unfortunate encounter.

Mrs. Hollenbach was ready to second him. "It's been a pleasure," she said, preparing to yield the dance floor.

The Whites, however, could not leave well enough alone. In rapid succession they passed from surprise to consternation.

"Congresswoman Hollenbach! Of course," said Dr. White with chagrin. "I beg your pardon."

"Not at all, Doctor," said Elsie, moving faster.

But Mrs. White trailed after them. "That's right, your brother-in-law's on the subcommittee, too, isn't he, Mr. Lundgren? I suppose you know that Howard will be testifying tomorrow morning, don't you, Mrs. Hollenbach?"

Talking compulsively, she dogged Elsie, leaving Fred with no alternative but to bring up the rear with Dr. White. The whole caravan arrived at the table where Janet, Ben and Val Oakes were enjoying their after-dinner coffee as only nondancers can.

"Mrs. Lundgren!" Connie cried. "Can you imagine! I mistook Mrs. Hollenbach for you when we bumped into her—literally bumped into her, didn't we, Howard?"

"Yes, we certainly did," said Dr. White with a hearty smile that didn't reach his eyes.

For once, Janet's composure was not equal to the occasion.

28

She stared blankly at the Whites, then at her husband. Fred, who had an unpredictable sense of humor, said, "You can never tell who you'll meet when you're dancing. Want to try this one with me, Janet?"

The situation was getting out of hand when Elsie Hollenbach intervened. "Ben," she said with a sympathetic look at Janet, "I don't know if you know the Whites . . . ?"

This broke the trance. Janet pulled herself together, introductions were performed and somehow the Whites were sitting down. Fortunately, Mrs. White's nervous vivacity seemed to have subsided, so they were spared relentless small talk. Dr. White, in fact, opted for a certain openness.

"I expected to see your committee down at the Federal Building tomorrow morning, Mr. Safford—not here at the club tonight. If I'd known you were all going to be here, I'd have brought my lawyer along."

"We're off duty right now," Safford replied briefly. He did not want to disconcert Dr. White, but he was not encouraging familiarity either.

"Besides, we're not all here," said Val Oakes with deceptive easiness. "You're safe for the time being, Doctor."

With a stickler's precision Mrs. Hollenbach enlightened White. "As you perhaps know, there are two other members of our subcommittee. But they were not able to accept Fred and Janet's hospitality tonight."

"Oh," said White. Then, with an effort: "Well, I wish I looked forward to meeting them. I suppose I shouldn't say that. Tomorrow isn't going to be too bad, is it?"

He struck only one responsive chord. "For heaven's sakes, of course not," said Connie White vigorously. "You don't have anything to hide, so what is there to be afraid of?"

Val Oakes, of all people, took pity on Dr. White. While everybody else pretended not to hear Connie White's challenge, he tackled it head on: "Nothing I admire more than a wife

29

who sticks up for her husband. The Angel in the House—isn't that what the Poet calls her? Her price is above rubies, isn't it, Ben?"

This magniloquence naturally flabbergasted Mrs. White. Satisfied that there would be no more trouble from her, Val contemplated the doctor.

"And your good wife is right. All we're going to do tomorrow morning is ask you a few questions. You'll get the opportunity to tell the truth and shame the devil."

Unexpectedly, White responded to the substance, not the flourishes. "I know you're going to have questions," he said, "but I'm planning a prepared statement that I want to read."

Ben was willing to encourage a pedestrian discussion of procedure. "You can read a statement, or you can just submit it for the record."

White was stubborn. "I want to present it myself."

"I'm sure the chairman will consider it," said Ben cautiously.

White wanted to argue further, but thought better of it. "Well, we'll be going over all this tomorrow, won't we?"

"We sure will," said Val Oakes largely.

White acknowledged him ruefully. "I repeat, I wish I could say I was looking forward to it. Connie . . . ?"

The Whites' departure left a silence waiting to be filled. Fred Lundgren obliged. "He's not the brightest guy in the world. But White's got more on the ball than you might think."

Connie White knew this better than anyone else. Unlike his patients and his fellow doctors, she alone heard the true Howard White. Tonight his monotone filled the car all the way home.

". . . sometimes Jim Rojak is too damned smart for his own good, but this time he's right, Connie. I can handle them. I can handle them with no problem at all."

For some reason, this made her nervous all over again.

5

The Subcommittee on Medicaid Abuse assembled at nine o'clock the following morning and summoned its first witness thirty minutes later. Dr. Howard White requested and received Lou Flecker's permission to read a statement, and did so with relish. The script had been prepared by the lawyer at his elbow, but White enjoyed reviewing his qualifications, his experience, his dedication. In the audience, Mrs. White clasped her hands in her lap and watched him worshipfully.

". . . doctor-patient relationship. This calls for long and arduous training on the part of the physician, and trust and confidence from the patient. . . ."

By now the subcommittee had heard such self-serving outpourings from Bangor to Passaic. A fog of boredom descended as White turned page after page, lifting only when he finally shuffled his papers into a neat rectangle. Wearily, Lou Flecker said: "Thank you, Doctor. We're happy to hear your introductory remarks. Now, since it's getting on toward noon, we'll take a luncheon recess and begin our questions to you about specific billings at two o'clock."

As the gavel fell, a nondescript man in gray strode to the witness table and thrust a folded paper at Dr. White. White, who had been frowning at Flecker, glanced at it distractedly. Then he turned to his lawyer.

"Stayman," he said, too bewildered to lower his voice, "does this mean somebody's suing me?"

That roused Stayman. Jerking a warning thumb at the committee table, where Elsie Hollenbach, at least, was showing an interest, he began propelling White down the aisle. He could not keep his client quiet.

"Malpractice? What do they mean, malpractice? Stayman—"

The man in gray had stepped aside to let them pass. When the pneumatic door-closer cut Dr. White off in mid-sentence, he approached the subcommittee table.

"Are you a process server?" Flecker demanded severely.

"Not exactly. I'm the attorney for the plaintiff. Theodore Karras is my name and I think I may owe you an apology, Mr. Chairman."

Ben, standing to get the stiffness out, decided that there was some justice in Janet's claim that Congressmen lead protected lives. It was years since he had seen a lawyer like Karras. In Washington they all wore expensive clothes, carried attaché cases and flourished Philippe Patek watches. Attorney Karras' hard, shiny suit could have come from a discount store. A battered red accordion envelope held his papers.

Testily, Flecker said: "You could have served your summons someplace besides this hearing room."

Karras was unawed. "It's not easy to catch Dr. White in Ohio. For all I know, he's heading to Cape Cod as soon as he's testified. But that's not why I want to apologize."

"Oh?" said Flecker.

"You see, White's usefulness to you as a witness may be limited," Karras continued serenely, "now that he's the subject of judicial proceedings. And I'm going to need some HEW records that you may have planned to use. I don't like to wreck your timetable, but naturally my client's interests come first."

Congressmen have grown leery of a reporter's duty to his

32

sources and an attorney's duty to his clients. Lou Flecker swallowed hard. But Val Oakes was less inhibited.

"It's a convenient time for your client's rights to surface," he observed. "Maybe you ought to apologize to Dr. White's lawyer. *He's* going to have to face the jury."

"Stayman? Oh, he doesn't have to worry. He'll be out of this. And, for that matter, a jury may be, too." Karras picked up his envelope with a half-smile. "I won't keep you from lunch. I just wanted to make sure you knew the score."

Then, with a gesture that was more benediction than farewell, he drifted toward the hall, where he was lost in the shuffling throng.

Tony Martinelli waited until the coast was clear. "Does that joker think we're dumb? Tell us the score? Hell, we still don't know the half of it."

Mrs. Hollenbach shook herself briskly as she rose. "Don't worry about it, Tony," she advised. "I have a strong feeling that people will be falling over themselves explaining this situation to us."

There were, as she predicted, explanations on all levels for several days.

One of the first came from the director of Newburg's HEW.

"I'm sorry to ask you down on such short notice. I hope I'm not disrupting your schedule," Quentin Trumbull began.

"What schedule?" Martinelli asked realistically. "Once Dr. White was back in the witness chair yesterday, his lawyer socked us with the need for a week's recess—"

"I got a subpoena, too," Trumbull said in agitation. "For documents in the HEW files. And Theo Karras is going to be dropping by any minute now to pick them up."

Lou Flecker scented danger. "Trumbull, if you've asked us to come down here to help figure out how HEW and this plaintiff can stick a knife into Howard White, you can think again. We have other fish to fry."

There was a stranger sitting by Trumbull and at this he intervened. "No, no, Mr. Congressman, I don't work for HEW."

Belatedly, Quentin Trumbull performed introductions. Lawrence Fournier was a vice-president of Great Lakes Insurance Company. And, as Fournier himself amplified grimly, Great Lakes carried Dr. Howard White's malpractice insurance, and most of the malpractice insurance in Newburg County.

"So Larry' here will be representing Dr. White's interests, and Karras of course is acting for the patient," said Trumbull to allay any suspicions on that score. "But that's not what worries me. It's this subpoena by Karras. He knows exactly what to ask for—the dates of billings, the amounts, our own file and document numbers. I don't see how he can have all that information unless he's actually been in our files."

The sanctity of files rarely worries outsiders. "Just what are these billings that Mr. Karras is using against Dr. White?" Mrs. Hollenbach demanded, brushing aside the lawyer's source of information.

Over Fournier's objection, Trumbull said: "Dr. White billed HEW on three separate occasions for performing a complete hysterectomy on Mrs. Wanda Soczewinski. Then, this year he billed us for an abortion on her."

Val Oakes turned to Lawrence Fournier. "And Great Lakes is handling White's defense?"

Stiffly, Fournier concurred.

"It should be a lulu," said Val jovially.

Fournier remained unsmiling. "There isn't going to be any defense if HEW hands those documents over. I'm here to ask Trumbull to demand a hearing."

Genuinely curious, Ben Safford asked: "On what grounds?"

"The confidentiality of medical records," said Lawrence Fournier.

"But Mrs. Wanda Soczewinski *is* the patient," Trumbull protested. "Anyway, this isn't HEW's fight. The court has ordered us to hand over the records, so that's what we're doing."

Their wrangle might have continued, but Trumbull's secretary entered, ushering in Theodore Karras. He lost no time. Leaning over the desk, he painstakingly checked items on his list. There was a liberal residue of cigarette ash on his jacket, and his eyeglasses were ancient steel-framed spectacles. But being the shabbiest man present did not impair his spirits.

"Fine," he said at last. "Everything I need is here. Thanks, Trumbull."

Fournier could not restrain himself. "You're putting the screws on White and on Great Lakes even though you know he never went near your client. That's a great touch."

"And new, I think," said Karras mockingly. "But you never can tell—it may catch on."

"Like hell it will!" Fournier shot back. "You're not going to make a career of suing these—" Abruptly, he decided on a new tack. "Now look, Karras. Think of the hardship this is going to cause a lot of innocent bystanders. The committee here can't hold its hearings. HEW is going to get raked over the coals about security. Great Lakes is going to be bled. Dr. White—"

"Crap!" Karras interrupted harshly. "You don't know what you're talking about. Sure, the committee and HEW will have to make some adjustments. And Great Lakes will cover its losses by raising rates. But if you want to know what hardship is, you ought to see what Mrs. Soczewinski has to put up with."

"Save your eloquence for a jury," Fournier said sourly.

But Karras' emotion had subsided. "If Great Lakes is as smart as it's cracked up to be, there won't be any jury, Fournier."

"We'll see about that."

Fournier's defiance lasted long enough for Karras to make an offhand farewell and depart.

"He's right," Fournier grunted. "We can't take this thing to court."

Lou Flecker, meanwhile, was putting two and two together.

"And you think Karras managed to buy his way into HEW files?" he said to the unhappy Trumbull, who shrugged helplessly. "You know, I'm getting curious about him. Ben, this is your hometown. Is he some kind of crook?"

"I never heard of him," said Safford, shaking his head. "I'm going to ask around. But, Lou, if he's a crook, he's a pretty smart one—no matter how he got his hands on HEW files. He's got White and Great Lakes over a barrel, doesn't he?"

Congressman Martinelli was appreciative. "It's beautiful," he said, disregarding the feelings of others. "White bilks Medicaid for operations he never performed. But those fake records for hysterectomies, then an abortion, let the patient claim that the doctor bungled the hysterectomy. White can't come out and say he was just ripping off HEW. So the patient gets the judgment. And unless the patient's a real dog, Fournier, Karras is going to take you for a bundle."

His ebullience infected Quentin Trumbull. "I called Charlene Gregorian to find out about the patient," he said, grinning as he named his authority. "Wanda Soczewinski was a nice, hard-working girl who married her high-school sweetheart, who was a nice, hard-working boy. They had two children and they were a credit to the community." The grin faded. "Then the husband got multiple sclerosis. He's back home, slowly wasting away, while Wanda supports the family with a welfare check. Karras wasn't far wrong when he said we didn't know what hardship is."

Fournier responded defensively. "What am I supposed to say? Sure, Karras has a dream client. And I'll go further: he's got a dream case. No, as much as I hate to admit it, Karras is right. There won't be any trial."

Insurance companies may deserve sympathy, but they rarely get it.

"Karras was right about something else, too," said Tony Martinelli robustly. "You'll pass your loss along by raising rates—and that will be the end of it."

Suddenly, Lawrence Fournier went on the attack. "There's where you're wrong, Mr. Congressman. It won't be the end by a long shot, except for Dr. White. Because Great Lakes will yank his malpractice coverage. And I personally will see to it that no other company touches him with a ten-foot pole. Believe me, it won't be hard."

— 6 —

Dr. Howard White's lawyer was trying to deliver the same message.

"But, Stayman, that's why I've been shelling out a fortune for malpractice insurance, isn't it? To protect myself against shakedowns like this."

Morton Stayman studied his client. He was still not altogether sure where the boundary between deception and self-delusion lay. "It's a little more complicated than that, Howard," he said slowly. "Just let me take it from the top. Great Lakes will certainly settle this Soczewinski suit out of court—no, let me finish—because you don't have any defense. Are you with me so far?"

Fright made Howard White shy at this sticking point again. Blustering, he said: "But I've paid through the nose—"

Stayman held up a hand. "And," he said implacably, "Great Lakes will decide that because of your fraud—"

"They're crooks! Her and that lousy lawyer!"

Patiently, Morton Stayman waited. "If you say so, Howard,

but let's stick with fraud. Now, Great Lakes may or may not try to recover from you."

They were, at last, pushing onto new ground. From Howard White's sudden stillness, Stayman guessed that he was only now facing the full implications of the disaster.

"Time will tell," Stayman continued briskly, "but I advise you to prepare yourself. And, Howard, you'd better brace yourself for something else: no matter what they decide about recovering, Great Lakes is almost certainly going to cancel your malpractice insurance."

All of White's attention was fixed on the immediate financial threat. "Then I'll have to go to some other company," he muttered absently.

"If Great Lakes cancels, no one else will give you malpractice insurance—ever." Stayman underscored each word, using his pencil as metronome.

A full minute passed. Then, almost petulantly, White said: "But then I couldn't practice medicine."

"That's right."

Other Newburg lawyers were dealing with their clients. Dr. Arnold Deachman was doing the talking to one of them.

". . . no, I am *not* ready to testify before the committee— and you can tell them so. Look, you tell the committee to go jump in the lake. I've got more important . . . Yes, I'll be in your office at ten. . . . Right. . . . You're damned right it's an emergency."

Nesta Deachman, still in a peignoir, was drifting past the phone. Of all the luxuries Deachman had presented to her, leaving the breakfast dishes on the table for somebody else was one she never stopped enjoying. So, nine times out of ten, she was perfectly willing to play the adoring little woman.

But Nesta had been Arnold Deachman's nurse for four years before she married him. She knew far more about him and his affairs than Margaret ever had. And she knew, none better, the close connection between those affairs and the good things of

39

life she was learning to enjoy so much.

"Arnie," she said when he hung up, "wouldn't it be better to have it over and done with, like Jim said?"

With tight self-control he said, "The situation has changed radically, Nesta."

Suddenly alert, she stood stock still. "Radically? But the subcommittee still can't do anything, can they?"

He looked at her dully and shook his head.

"What is it?" she demanded, her voice edged by alarm.

Suddenly Deachman's feelings overcame him. Forgetting his dignity, his position, his caution, he found himself talking and talking. Everything bottled up inside came spilling out—Theodore Karras, the HEW files, Great Lakes' threats.

Nesta stared at him, aghast. Even during the bitterly fought divorce she had never seen him like this, not even when he had realized how much the property settlement was going to cost him if he wanted Nesta.

"I'm sorry, Nesta," he mumbled, mopping his brow. "But you might as well know what we're up against. Testifying to the committee—well, that's nothing. But this suit against Howard is a time bomb for us all."

She was light-years ahead of him as he continued, "If Karras can get his hands on HEW files whenever he wants to, he's got a malpractice suit against me as well as Howard. He could blackmail every single one of us. And, Nesta, if that happens, I could face what Howard's facing." Breaking off, he averted his eyes. "I could lose everything."

Neither of them noticed that it was *I*, not *we*.

Nesta, in fact, was not listening at all. She was struggling with a sudden, overpowering dismay. With an effort, she pulled herself together. What Arnold needed now was support. She reached out to touch his arm. "It won't happen, Arnie. Don't torture yourself! It won't happen. It can't!"

Dr. James Rojak knew that it could happen. So he did not want explanations, he wanted preventive action.

"You're my Congressman, aren't you?" he said with a quirk of his lips. "Well, I want some protection. I'm not going to sit still and be a patsy—"

"Whoa," said Benton Safford. "Why don't we both sit down and talk it over?"

This response to a heated constituent was automatic. In his office, in Washington or out on Plainfield Road, it was reasonably effective. It did not work so well in the lobby of the Federal Building in Newburg, which Ben had just entered.

"Look," Rojak told him, "I've been upstairs talking to that creep Trumbull—"

"Why don't you tell me who you are and what this is all about?" Safford said bluntly. He had a deep-seated dislike of bullies.

The scowling young man facing him was taken aback. "Dr. Rojak," he snapped arrogantly. "Dr. James Rojak."

"Oh, yes," said a new voice. "One of our witnesses."

The arrival of Elsie Hollenbach defused the confrontation only superficially. Glancing from one to the other, Rojak said: "Yes, one of your witnesses. But *not* one of your sitting ducks."

"Precisely what does that mean?" asked Mrs. Hollenbach with glacial dignity.

Ben Safford answered for Rojak. "I think the doctor is worried about a possible malpractice suit, in light of what happened to Dr. White. Right, Rojak?"

Rojak did not conceal his hostility. "The doctor wants to know how some cheap lawyer got hold of confidential HEW information. Aren't you supposed to guard citizens' rights? Or do you and that guy Trumbull think you can play God?"

"Mr. Trumbull assures me that he does not know how HEW information reached Mr. Karras," said Elsie. "He is investigating."

41

"Oh, sure!" said Rojak with a contemptuous laugh. "Well, if you think I'm going to stand still, you've got another think coming."

With that, he stormed out, leaving Elsie and Ben free to continue upstairs.

"We may not be getting through to these doctors, but this guy Karras sure as hell is," said Tony Martinelli when Dr. Rojak's outburst was described. He stared out before him with lackluster eyes. There were lawyers pleading extenuating circumstances, requesting delays, protesting procedure. "Not a doctor in sight. They're scared to death. None of them mind robbing the Federal government blind, but mention a malpractice suit and you've got them where they live."

"Look on the bright side, Tony," Val Oakes told him. "Ben's friend Karras may have found a rough-and-ready way to reform medicine in Newburg. God knows it's more than Congress has been able to do."

Ben felt constrained to repeat that Theodore Karras was not a friend. "But here's to him anyway. I can hardly wait to hear the next installment—although I can do without more of Dr. Rojak."

As he was to learn within twenty-four hours, they came in the same package. The morning news carried the story into breakfast all over Newburg.

"... attorney Theodore Karras. According to authorities, Karras was shot in his office on River Street. The body was discovered early this morning by Dr. James Rojak, a prominent allergist. The police are still investigating at the scene of the crime. . . ."

7

"Maybe you'd go over your story again for the stenographer,
Dr. Rojak," Lieutenant Doyle suggested.

Rojak pinched the bridge of his nose with thumb and fore-
finger. "Why not?" he said with exaggerated weariness. "I've
told it to everyone else."

"Thank you," said Lieutenant Doyle, unmoved, as he continued to inspect his witness.

Of medium height, Dr. Rojak conveyed an impression of
driving strength. He was a blocky man with solidly set shoulders, a square head, a square face and even square hands. A
quick check at Police Headquarters had already told the Lieutenant about the customized Porsche (three speeding viola-
tions), the six-seater Cessna at the airport (one citation for failing to file a flight plan) and the impressive collection of guns
(all duly licensed).

At the moment, however, nobody would have envied Rojak.

"There isn't much to tell," he began. "I had an appointment
with Karras. When I got here, I found him dead."

Doyle held up a hand. "Let's take it a little slower. This appointment of yours was for eight o'clock this morning? Isn't that pretty early to see a lawyer?"

"Not if you have hospital rounds to make. I can see you don't know much about doctors."

"I'm willing to learn," Doyle said mildly.

For an instant Rojak frowned. "When I got here, the maintenance man told me that Karras was in Room 201," he continued. "So I came up the stairs and walked in. You know what I found."

"Tell me anyway."

"Karras must have lived for several minutes after he was shot. At least, that's how it looked to me. I'd guess that he was hemorrhaging badly right from the beginning. Anyway, there was blood all over the place—the desk, the floor, the chair. I crossed into the room just far enough to make absolutely sure he was dead, but that was a formality, believe me. Then I ran downstairs and phoned you people from the drugstore next door."

Lieutenant Doyle was nodding like a mandarin as he consulted his notebook. "And Headquarters logged in your call at eight-oh-seven. So that accounts for your time, all right. And we appreciate it when public-spirited citizens get us on the scene as soon as possible—instead of just high-tailing it." He paused and smiled blandly. "But then you didn't have much choice, did you? The maintenance man saw you arrive."

Rojak took up the challenge immediately. "What difference does it make who saw me? It didn't need a medical degree to see that Karras had been dead for hours before I showed up. I don't know what kind of games you're trying to play, Doyle, but as soon as they do the autopsy, your own men will tell you that I couldn't have had anything to do with Karras' murder."

This was scarcely news to Doyle. The police doctor had already delivered the unofficial opinion that Theodore Karras had been shot during the previous evening. But innocent witnesses are usually unnerved by a corpse. Not this one, however. It was Jim Rojak's unnatural assurance that was holding Doyle's interest.

"There's one thing that puzzles me," he continued, "and

that's the phone on Karras' desk. You couldn't have helped seeing it. So why go out to the drugstore?"

"For Christ's sake! Sure I saw the phone, but there was blood congealed all around and Karras' hand was brushing up against it. I knew the static I'd get from you people if I disturbed all that. It seemed safer to use another phone."

"Most people don't manage to keep their heads like that in an emergency."

The remark could have been congratulation or condemnation, but Rojak simply brushed it aside.

"Hell, it would have been different if the guy had a spark of life left. Then I suppose I would have just yanked the phone up and yelled for an ambulance. But with him already dead, a couple of minutes more didn't make that much difference."

"Probably not. As you say, he'd been shot hours earlier. By the way, Doctor, I see that you have a permit to carry a handgun in Newburg."

Rojak did not let him go any further. "Me and every other doctor in town. You know what that parking lot at the hospital is like at night. And it gets worse every year."

Doyle knew that doctors had a high rate of gun permits. This was not entirely due to police negligence, however. By and large, doctors were wealthy men with a predilection for cash. They lived in homes stuffed with jewels and furs. They operated out of offices stocked with drugs. And occasionally they were called to the hospital at night. They were prime targets.

No hint of these thoughts showed on Doyle's face. "Got the gun on you?"

"No, it's where it always is. In the glove compartment of my car."

"Mind if we take a look?"

Rojak reached into his pocket and produced a key ring, which he tossed over to the Lieutenant. "Be my guest," he said sarcastically. "It's the Porsche parked by the corner."

After that performance Doyle knew that the gun would be clean. It was with genuine pleasure that he pressed forward into an area where Rojak might be more vulnerable.

"While we're waiting, Doctor, let's talk about something else. You've explained why your appointment was so early and what you did when you got here. But you haven't told me what business you had with Karras in the first place. Or is that covered by the attorney-client privilege?"

Jim Rojak snorted. "Listen, when I need law work, I go to a reputable attorney, not some shyster. And let's not kid each other. I'll bet you know all about Karras' suit against Howard White."

"I've heard it mentioned," Doyle admitted.

He could scarcely have helped it. When Theodore Karras had served his summons inside the Federal Building, he had alerted the entire Courthouse fraternity of Newburg. Within minutes lawyers, judges' clerks, bailbondsmen and court reporters were buzzing. Doyle had known all about *Soczewinski* v. *White* before Great Lakes or even Dr. James Rojak.

"Then you know he was pulling a fast one," said Rojak flatly. "It was no accident that the suit was filed after the Cincinnati papers did a job on us."

"I didn't think it was."

"Hell, that's why all seven of us had a meeting yesterday afternoon. We figured we were all in the line of fire. And that's why I wasn't surprised when Karras called me after dinner last night."

Doyle leaned forward intently. "Just out of the blue?"

"We'd never met, if that's what you mean. But, as I said, I was half expecting him to try and shake me down."

"Now, wait a minute. Is that what he said?"

"Of course not." Rojak was impatient. "He said he thought it was advisable for us to have a meeting to discuss something that had come up. So I said I'd see him at eight this morning."

Doyle expelled his breath in a long sigh. "So you're not sure what he had in mind?"

"Come off it! You only have to look at this dump." Rojak gestured expansively at the battered file cabinets, the old-fashioned paneling, the worn carpet. "What kind of lawyer practices out of an office like this? And everybody knows Karras greased some file clerk at HEW. He *had* to be pulling a fast one."

Lieutenant Doyle bit down hard as he recalled Dr. Rojak's billing methods. That was somebody else's problem.

"All right. We can't prove it, but let's assume that was what Karras had in mind. What were you going to do about it?"

Rojak stared back defiantly. "It depended how cheap he came. If he could be bought off with a couple of thousand bucks, I was going to pay him. But if he had big ideas, I wasn't. You know, I can pull up stakes and go practice someplace else. I don't say I want to. But I'd do it before I let myself be bled— and certainly before I shot somebody!"

Doyle doubted if the options were that simple, but he deferred the point in favor of a new idea. "Still, the mere possibility that Karras might file a malpractice suit was enough of a danger to bring you here pronto."

"It wasn't a danger, it was an inconvenience."

"Okay." Doyle accepted the correction amiably. "Call it an inconvenience. But then it would be an even bigger inconvenience if he already had filed suit."

Rojak narrowed his eyes instantly. "I don't know anything about that," he said.

Doyle's next witness did not see the implications quite so swiftly.

"It was a case of harassment, pure and simple harassment," Dr. White said firmly.

Jim Rojak carried his confidence with him wherever he went, but Howard White preferred to answer police questions in the reassuring atmosphere of his own office. When Rojak had voiced his opinion of Theodore Karras' quarters, Doyle had not felt its full force. From the viewpoint of Newburg's dilapidated police station, Karras had not seemed underprivileged. But from the viewpoint of this downtown professional building, nothing could be more tawdry than a grimy venetian blind.

Dr. White had his own interpretation of poverty.

"And I fail to see why you are taking up my time because of some crime in another part of the city," he concluded.

"I haven't singled you out, Doctor. I'm talking to all seven of you."

"But why are you bothering us when you should be investigating Karras' associates? A man like that could have been up to *anything*. He probably had Mafia clients. They're the ones you should be talking to."

Lieutenant Doyle sounded like a kindergarten teacher explaining the alphabet. "If Karras had been into the Mafia, he would have been a lot richer. Their lawyers aren't on the other side of town, they're right in this building."

"Then he was involved with low-level criminals," White insisted. "My point is that he didn't have anything to do with people like us."

"I don't see how you can say that. Karras had already filed suit against you. The others were afraid they might be next in line, afraid enough to join you in a general meeting yesterday afternoon. You must have been plenty bothered by him."

"We certainly were!" Dr. White agreed. "The whole situation is an outrage. We were being persecuted and the authorities were standing by, doing absolutely nothing. I was going to demand that the medical association take a very strong position."

Lieutenant Doyle stared across the desk. To his certain knowledge, Howard White was under subpoena by a Congressional committee, he was about to be hauled into a court of law by Wanda Soczewinski and he was being questioned by the police about a murder case. God only knew what other hot water he was in. And still he thought that the only authority that counted was the American Medical Association.

48

"I don't see what the medical association could do about Theodore Karras."

White blundered on. "Good God, it wasn't Karras we wanted them to pressure, it was Great Lakes." Belatedly, caution reared its head. "You wouldn't understand these technicalities, Lieutenant, but I can tell you it concerns the cost of malpractice insurance. If the company were to raise its rates, then the already high cost of medical care in Newburg would soar. And we all want to avoid that."

"As you say, Doctor, I wouldn't understand about technicalities like that," Doyle said smoothly. "So let's come to something I do understand. Can you tell me where you were yesterday evening from nine until midnight?"

"I suppose that kind of question is typical of our police force," White retorted. "As a matter of fact, I was right here. My accountant will corroborate that I was going to spend the evening assembling my records. For some reason, he wants even more material for this tax audit. Naturally, you're wondering why a doctor of medicine has to spend nights doing clerical work."

"No," said Doyle, rising. "No, that isn't what I was wondering."

It was the end of a long, hard day when Lieutenant Doyle reported to Chief Owen Jones.

"Well, I've seen all seven of them and, no matter how you slice it, they're a weird bunch," he summarized.

The Chief had swiveled sideways so that he was parallel to the desk, with his feet in a drawer, his head tilted to observe the ceiling and his hands cradling a cardboard cup of coffee.

"All doctors are like that," he growled.

"Maybe so. But some of them, somewhere, must have an alibi for last night."

"You mean none of yours do? I know you said Rojak was

alone in his apartment and White was alone in his office. But, Jesus Christ, weren't any of them home with their wives?"

"So they say." Doyle shook his head dubiously. "But it doesn't work out that way from where I sit. Dr. Costello was home, all right, but from ten to eleven he was walking the family dog."

The Chief's eyebrows shot up. "It was pouring last night and he claims he walked the dog for a solid hour?"

Doyle spoke in a voice of doom. "Curryville just passed a leash law."

These cryptic words explained the whole situation to Jones. When Newburg's leash law had gone into effect, it had taken weeks for life to return to normal.

"And the others?"

"I had high hopes of Deachman. He went out to a dinner party with his wife. But he got called to the hospital around nine and didn't bother to go back. So the next thing we know about him is that his wife found him at home when she came in around eleven thirty. Then there's the guy who claims he never stirred from his house. Unfortunately, his wife had some kind of ladies' meeting, so he went down to his workshop and wasn't seen from eight to eleven."

"What the hell?" said Jones on a wave of fellow feeling. "That's what *I* do when Marge has the girls over."

"I'm not saying it couldn't be true. I'm just saying that none of them have alibis and they all have guns—nice, clean guns, fully loaded and freshly oiled."

"Ballistics any help?"

Doyle was disgusted. "Not on your life. The bullet passed through Karras' head and into the air-conditioner on the windowsill. The unit was on and the bullet got chewed up. All the lab boys will say is that it was a small caliber."

For a few moments the Chief of Police considered this information. Then, as if reaching a decision, he swung his feet to the ground and turned foursquare to the desk. "I admit the way this murder was timed, the doctors stand out like sore thumbs. But you don't want to lose sight of other possibilities, George. We don't know much about Karras. He could have had wife trouble, he could have been a chaser, he could have been into the loan sharks."

"Sure," Doyle agreed. "I've got a couple of men working on the background. But it doesn't look like it's going to give us much, Owen. Karras was sixty-five and a solid family man until his wife died a year and a half ago. Since then he's been working nights a lot, but otherwise his habits haven't changed. Every couple of weeks he goes to Cincinnati on business and he always stays with his married daughter. During school vacations she brings the grandchildren to Newburg for five or six days. On Sundays, regular as clockwork, he has dinner at his sister's. She and her husband own the Roadcoach Restaurant on Route 25."

"Oh, I didn't realize Karras was Nick Andreades' brother-in-law."

"He was, and Nick says there was no chasing. Just the opposite. The last month or so Karras has been squiring around some Greek widows. He wanted to remarry and have a home life again."

Jones sighed, but accepted the obvious. It was difficult to connect a crime of passion to a sixty-five-year-old widower in search of a congenial widow.

"What about money?" he continued.

"That's a washout, too. Karras' income is fully justified by his practice and he was living well within it. He never moved out of the old neighborhood and he was putting a little something by for the grandchildren."

"Maybe that explains the shakedown," Jones reasoned. "Maybe he wanted something bigger for the grandchildren."

Doyle grinned. "If you talked that way to Karras' secretary, you'd get your eyes scratched out. She says Karras never had any HEW documents until Mrs. Soczewinski brought hers in,

51

and that he was pure as the driven snow. Of course, she's worked for him fifteen years, thinks he was a wonderful man and was crying buckets while I was there."

Owen Jones dismissed character references by devoted secretaries with a wave of the hand. "No reason why he should let her know what he was up to, anyway. But did she say anything about his appointments, either for last night or for eight o'clock this morning?"

"No, and the diary didn't list any, either. But she says Karras was casual about logging appointments he made himself. He figured he'd remember them unless they were two weeks in the future."

"So we just have Rojak's word for his appointment—or the whole shakedown story, for that matter."

Lieutenant Doyle was determined to be fair-minded, even about witnesses he disliked. "You have to be reasonable. If Patrick Costello, for instance, went to a meeting last night that ended in his blowing someone's brains out, he sure as hell isn't going to tell us all about it."

"That applies to Rojak, too," Jones pointed out. "He could have gone back this morning because he thought it looked better, or because he left something behind."

"Or because someone else did." Doyle hesitated before continuing his speculation. "I'll tell you something I noticed about Rojak. He thinks the police are beneath him, and he didn't give a damn whether I liked most of his answers. But he went out of his way to justify using that drugstore phone. It's fishy as hell. He would have used the secretary's phone if he'd been willing to take a chance on being overheard. He wanted a nice, soundproof booth. And once he was there, I know he called us. But I'd give a lot to know who else he called."

Owen Jones plucked his lower lip thoughtfully. "We seem to have gotten right back to your doctors," he complained.

"You can't stay away from them. Look, when I said they were a weird bunch, I meant it. Any doctor in Newburg can make eighty thousand a year on the up-and-up. And plenty of them are satisfied with that. I expected to find these seven were extra greedy. But it's deeper than that. I also expected to find that they were embarrassed at being caught. Not on your life! They weren't embarrassed by the publicity, they were mad as hell. And that's before there was any real threat. Every single one of them is convinced he's got a God-given right to anything he wants and nobody should even ask questions." Doyle paused to order his thoughts. He was very serious. "After White let the cat out of the bag, I checked with Great Lakes. With Karras, it wasn't simply going to be a question of a mortifying cross-examination. He could put these bums out of business. And when bone-deep arrogance meets an obstacle like that . . ."

Jones supplied the conclusion for himself as Doyle's voice trailed into silence. "Then you expect bullets to start flying?"

Doyle screwed up his empty coffee cup and dropped it into the wastebasket as punctuation for his final observation.

"Well, it wouldn't surprise the pants off me."

8

While the police quietly moved around Newburg in civilian clothes and unmarked cars, the Cincinnati papers were not so discreet. Ever since naming the Newburg Seven, the *Inquirer* had followed every twist and turn in the scandal. Quentin Trumbull had been harried for one statement after another, the doctors had been photographed plunging in and out of cars, the subcommittee had been interviewed and Dr. White's testimony had received full coverage. Under these circumstances the murder of Theodore Karras became instant journalistic property. Within twenty-four hours everyone in southern Ohio knew that Karras had been shot down after starting a malpractice suit against Dr. Howard White.

The results of this paper onslaught were immediate. The HEW switchboard was jammed, the White household was in a state of siege, the subcommittee had adjourned for forty-eight hours and the Mayor of Newburg was yelling for his Congressman.

"I told him you'd be there first thing this morning," Janet said as she poured coffee.

A half-hour later Ben discovered that Mayor Wilford Wilhelm, normally a man who loved his work, was seriously perturbed.

"Ha! Congressman Safford," he barked.

Since they had been on first-name terms for years, Ben instinctively looked around. There was not a reporter—or a voter—in sight.

"We had a nice, peaceful town until you and that gang of yours stirred up the wild animals," said the Mayor sternly. At eighty plus, he was slowing down a little, but his voice was still in fine shape.

"What about the strike out at Frawley's?" Ben countered.

"Nobody got killed," said the Mayor, peering over his glasses at Ben.

"No," Ben conceded, without adding anything about rock-throwing, truck-burning or fistfights.

"Nice and peaceful," said Wilhelm firmly. This point established, he unbent. "Just had the Chief on the line. He says they're investigating a lot of leads. Pfa! Owen watches too much TV, that's the trouble."

Civic pride wanted an immediate arrest. But was there one in the works?

"That's why I told Janet to send you down, Ben," said Mayor Wilhelm craftily. "The Chief wants a crack at the dirt your staff has dug up on those doctors."

Under Wilhelm's wise old eyes, Ben was not going to pontificate on the relationship between Congress and local law-enforcement agencies. "All right. I'll give Owen a ring and we'll get together this afternoon."

Suddenly harsh, Wilhelm continued: "And I told him I wouldn't stand for any horsing around. You know how the police pussyfoot with doctors."

Ben did. In towns the size of Newburg, doctors seem to miss all the speeding tickets, even with liquor on their breath.

"I laid it on the line. Told him he can do whatever he pleases when he catches one of them in the Reservoir Motel with a high-school kid—but murder's different."

There is an old morality, as well as a new morality. Having expressed it, the Mayor relaxed. "Glad to get that settled. You shoot us whatever you can. The sooner we clean this up, the better. Hell, I've got a new incinerator to worry about."

Ben still had private doubts. There was almost too much information about the doctors available. What was lacking was information about Theodore Karras.

"Did you know him, Will?" Ben asked.

"Never met him in my life," said the Mayor, echoing Janet Lundgren and Fred. "Heard his name a couple of times."

"How come?" Murder apart, Ben was getting curious about his dead constituent. How many Newburg lawyers had practiced as long as Karras with such a low profile?

"He had some clients who sued the city," said Wilhelm. "A couple of them got pretty good settlements, too."

This gave Ben a clue. Karras had been active, all right, but in different circles. It occurred to him that the man who knew about those circles was within walking distance. For many reasons, Ed Daly, chairman of the Newburg Democratic Organization, had offices close to the Courthouse, City Hall and the Federal Building.

Daly was reading the *Newburg News* when Ben strolled in.

"Henry wants to go to war to keep the Panama Canal," he said by way of greeting. Henry Hurd was the rock-ribbed Republican editor of the *News*. "It's all your fault, Ben."

Safford didn't see why until Daly spelled it out for him. Armed intervention in Panama was Henry's way of distracting public opinion from domestic events.

"So Henry's waving the flag," he concluded. "He's going to

start pushing for us to annex Canada next. How are you, Ben? Stirred up a real mess this time, didn't you?"

Since Daly sounded amused, Ben inferred that the eruption of murder into the Medicaid hearings raised no problems at the polls that Daly could foresee.

"No, the police will eventually get whoever shot poor Theo, and that's that," said Daly. "As for going after local doctors—hell, everybody in Newburg is cheering you on. Except Henry Hurd of course. The only millionaires I advise you to watch your step with are basketball players."

Ben met realism with realism. "I'll try to avoid tangling with any rock singers."

Daly thought about it. "As long as they don't lower the voting age to twelve, you'd be safe. Speaking of teenagers, this employment bill . . ."

Ten minutes of shop talk ensued before Ben got around to asking his question.

"Sure, I knew Karras," said Daly. "And so did you."

A memory for names and faces was part of Congressman Safford's stock in trade. Without hesitation, he contradicted Daly. "Nope. First time I ever saw him was when he served that subpoena under Lou Flecker's nose."

"You sure, Ben?" Daly asked. "Theo was a poll-watcher down in the Third for years."

"What!" Ben was startled. True, his tour of the precincts on election day was a blurred montage. But if Theo Karras had been one of the party faithful . . .

"No," Daly reassured him. "Karras was the International Justice Party. Been big with them for years. I don't think he ever ran himself, but he was secretary, treasurer—you name it. Theo's the one who finally got them on the ballot. You remember that fight—ten, twelve years ago."

While Daly spoke, Ben tried fitting this piece into the picture. A small, one-man office in a rundown part of town, the

International Justice crowd—a dwindling band of aging ideologues who had brought their lost causes with them when they arrived from the old country.

"Not the kind of guy you'd expect to try blackmail," Ben observed.

From his perch in Courthouse Square, Ed Daly had seen just about everything. "There's always Robin Hood."

"Robin Hood with a malpractice suit?" Ben wondered. Any quixotic romance in Theo Karras had been well hidden. "Speaking of robbing the rich to give to the poor, are you getting any feedback on the Curry River Flood Control Project?"

"Jobs," said Ed Daly, packing a lot into one word.

Ben left with plenty to ponder. Any politician worth his salt is a juggler, and even the best jugglers miss a trick now and then. The Curry River Flood Control Project was too big to fumble.

Lost in thought, Ben found that force of habit had led him to drop in at Phil's Coffee Shop. Phil was leaning over the counter, studying the *Newburg News*. For a customer he would have straightened. For Ben he stayed comfortable. "Hi, Ben. I see you got a big treat in store for you."

Ed Daly's appreciation of "Pound Panama!" had let him skimp another front-page feature: "PERRIN TO TESTIFY."

"What's this?" said Ben, unceremoniously appropriating the paper.

"Too cheap to spend a quarter, huh?" said Phil equably.

Ignoring him, Ben brought himself up to date. Chairman L. Lamar Flecker (D., Ala.), bowing to demands of the Newburg Medical Association, was allowing its president to read a statement to the Medicaid subcommittee when it resumed hearings.

Phil craned his neck. There were no customers within earshot.

"Perrin's a horse's ass," he said cheerfully.

"He has to be if he's going to stand up in public and defend Medicaid swindling," said Ben.

58

"You know these doctors. They think they've got a right to—"

Phil broke off in midsentence as two customers entered and headed for a booth. Summoning the smile of a host, he waited until they were settled before offering two menus.

"Morning, ladies. We've got some of the cinnamon coffee cake you like today."

The older, a woman around fifty almost obscured by a mound of shopping parcels, settled for this suggestion. Her companion, a pretty girl in her twenties, wanted blueberry cheesecake with her coffee. After they had been served, Phil returned to Ben and identified them.

"The first Mrs. Deachman," he said in a whisper that spoke volumes, "and the daughter."

Ben's eyebrows rose. "I suppose that means there's a second Mrs. Deachman."

Phil's hands sawed an hourglass from the surrounding air. "A real dish," he murmured. "Poor old Deachman never had a chance once Nesta Malone decided being a doctor's wife beat working."

Mulling over this exchange when he was back in his car, Ben wondered if the doctors yet realized the full consequences of being in the public spotlight. Arnold Deachman no doubt thought he had lived down his divorce. But today Phil could not see his ex-wife without remembering the circumstances— and passing them on. Ben was willing to bet that all over Newburg similar memories were reviving. If any of the White children had ever been busted in a drug raid, today's *Inquirer* would bring back the details for some people. If any of the doctors had a wife who had been dried out in a sanitarium or a son whose forged checks had been covered, it would all be part of dinner-table conversation tonight.

Except, of course, where there were more important things to worry about, like the Hackett farm, into which Ben pulled at the end of forty minutes.

59

Elroy Hackett shooed Alma and her hospitality away. "We've got business," he said sternly, leading Ben into his office.

Out near Murren there were farms with hex signs on the barns and colonial plows over the mantel. Elroy ran a real farm. He had a minicomputer on his desk and facts at his fingertips. He was also state chairman of the Farm Bureau.

". . . reducing the soil-conservation allotments. But hell, Ben, they shove this dam down our throats and we're losing ten thousand acres. And God knows what those damned fools will do to the water table."

Only Elsie Hollenbach had a lower opinion of the Army Corps of Engineers.

Ben listened. With Elroy, he didn't have to explain about pressure from Columbus, from Washington, from Newburg. Neither did he have to say he would do his damnedest. Acres and farmers were important to him, too.

"So you cogitate about it," said Hackett, his austere old face crinkling into a smile. "Now let's go see what that woman's up to."

Alma was ready for them in the kitchen with lunch and a little gentle gossip.

". . . Loomis' oldest boy—you remember him, Ben—he's getting married. And the Archibald farm is up for sale."

Both the lunch and information from an old friend were appreciated. Ben knew how to reciprocate.

"I suppose you've been reading all about the doctors," he said.

"Never would have believed it," she said. "And murdering this lawyer, too."

"Well, they're not sure they've gone as far as that," said Ben.

"From what it says in the paper, it sure sounds that way to me," she retorted.

"Now, Alma, you know you can't believe what you read in the paper," said Elroy weightily.

On this familiar theme Ben took his departure, gathering one more straw in the wind as Elroy accompanied him to the car.

"No, we haven't had a doctor out this way for twenty years. So, if I'm going to travel, I'm not going to settle for second best. Went up to Mayo for my gallbladder."

By two o'clock Ben was back in Newburg, satisfied that his morning had been well spent. He was not the only one who had been busy.

"I've packed your things, Arnie. Do you want to take some books with you?" Nesta Deachman closed the overnight case and looked at her husband, who was striding restlessly around their bedroom.

"Don't bother," he said absently. "Anything I need, Friend or one of the nurses can run out and get."

A shadow touched Nesta's lovely eyes. It was wonderful to see Arnie so collected. But there was such a thing as being too collected. "That's true. But, Arnie, you're supposed to be going into the nursing home for complete rest and relaxation, don't forget. It wouldn't look right for you to be asking the staff to run a lot of little errands for you."

"You think of everything, don't you, Nesta?"

"I'm sure Graham Friend will tell you the same thing," she persisted. "After all, our story is that this is an emergency. You're on the verge of collapse. . . ."

Seeing that he was not going to respond, she went on, "So I'll just put in something for you to read. Of course, I'll be coming by every day—"

"If Graham Friend thinks I should have visitors," he interrupted sardonically. Graham Friend would do exactly what Dr. Deachman told him, as they both knew.

This levity took her aback. "Oh, Arnie, don't," she said reproachfully.

"Just a joke," he said without apology.

61

"Well, this is no time for joking!"

Still pacing back and forth, he said over his shoulder: "Nesta, this would be easier on both of us if you'd stop fussing."

There was a moment's silence. Then, as if their last exchange had not taken place, Nesta said: "Once you're in Riverside, nobody will be able to bother you until the whole situation calms down."

He looked at her keenly. "Maybe *you* should be checking into Riverside instead of me."

This made her whirl away from the suitcase. "Will you please stop talking like that? You're the one the police have been questioning, aren't you?"

"Don't I know it," he retorted. "I've gone through it once and I don't intend to do it twice. We both agree that Riverside is the best idea, under the circumstances. But there's not much point in discussing it endlessly, is there? I think it's about time for us to get going."

In many ways, Nesta decided, it would be a relief to have him out of the house.

"I'm not driving you down," she said. "I thought it would be wiser if we had the ambulance. They'll be here any minute. I'm going along, of course, but I'm going to follow in my car. Then I'll give the subcommittee the good news."

"And be sure you make it good and strong," he ordered.

Before she had time to reply, the front doorbell buzzed a summons. "That's the ambulance," she said, drawing a deep breath. "Come on, Arnie. I'll help you down the stairs."

At the door, the burly ambulance attendant took one look and said what he always said: "Don't worry, ma'am. We'll take good care of him."

"I know you will," she said brightly, nipping Deachman's arm tightly to remind him of his role.

"And you'll be a lot more comfortable in a little while," the driver continued, helping Deachman into the ambulance.

"Yes," said Dr. Arnold Deachman weakly. "Yes, I hope so."

Downtown, meanwhile, Ben Safford was just mounting the steps of the Federal Building when he spied a familiar back.

"Owen!" he called. "I'm right here, and I'm sorry if I'm late."

The Chief of Police explained that he was deliberately early. "I couldn't stand it down at Headquarters anymore, Ben. You can't move without stepping on a reporter. Those Cincinnati papers act as if they don't have any scandals in their own town."

Ben offered the fruit of his own experience. "People are interested in doctors these days. And when you throw in grand larceny and murder, you've got a story that everybody's following."

"The way I look at it, Ben, the murder is my baby and the larceny is yours. I figured maybe we could help each other out."

Prudently Ben delayed his reply as they passed through the usual crowd in the lobby. Not until they were alone in the elevator did he say:

"Don't get your hopes up, Owen. The larceny isn't really my baby in the sense you mean. Sure, HEW has been cranking out some grand totals for us. But our mission is to find out how badly the system is working, not to zero in on particular abuses. I told Wilhelm you were welcome to what we've got. I didn't tell him I think it's useless."

Jones grinned as they emerged from the elevator and started the trek down the corridor. "It would have been a waste of time," he agreed. "When Wilhelm is in one of his moods, there's no point talking sense to him. But maybe I can pick up something from your files just by looking at them from a different point of view."

"Good luck to you," said Ben, leading the way into the temporary quarters of the subcommittee. At first sight they looked deserted, but the rumble of voices from the inner office told him that Lou Flecker had not forgotten his promise to be on hand. "Over here, Owen," he said, forging ahead and then stopping short on the threshold. Flecker and Tony Martinelli were in conference with an unfamiliar woman.

"Come in! Come in!" Flecker sounded suspiciously happy to be interrupted. "Mrs. Deachman, I don't think you've met Congressman Safford."

At first glance Ben was disappointed. Mrs. Deachman was certainly an attractive woman, but she didn't live up to her billing at Phil's Coffee Shop. Then, as he took in more detail, he realized that she was deliberately underplaying her charms. A severe gray suit with a black handbag was enlivened only by a touch of white at the throat. Her long, dark hair was drawn back into a low knot and she wore almost no make-up.

"I have been explaining to these gentlemen that my husband won't be able to testify," she said to Ben in tones barely above a whisper. "This morning he became very seriously ill."

"I see," Ben replied, committing himself to nothing.

"It seemed right that you should know as soon as possible."

The funereal tempo afforded Ben a sudden insight. Mrs. Deachman had decked herself out in half-mourning so that the subcommittee would recognize the gravity of the situation.

Lou had pushed his chair back from the desk. "I'm glad you dropped by. And we'll certainly take Dr. Deachman's condition into consideration when we prepare our schedule of witnesses."

She paid no attention to the farewell note in his voice. "My husband is not a well man at the best of times. Of course, he's been overworking himself for years. But he simply has no reserves to fight an illness. I can only hope that with rest and care he'll make a good recovery."

"Come now, Mrs. Deachman," Ben said hearteningly. "Try to look on the bright side. I'm sure your husband's physician doesn't take such a dark view."

Flecker's voice was completely expressionless. "Apparently Dr. Deachman doesn't *have* a physician. He's making his own diagnosis."

Nesta lowered her eyes. "I can only thank God my husband

is a doctor," she said, as if she were agreeing with Flecker. "He recognized the symptoms immediately, so we knew exactly what to do."

The implication was that the Deachmans had rushed to the nearest hospital. Tony Martinelli did not want to see Ben under any false impression, so he said helpfully, "Dr. Deachman thought that the best place for him to take these symptoms was some kind of nursing home."

Mrs. Deachman nodded. "We both know how good the care is."

Lou Flecker had decided that finesse was futile. Rising, he padded across the room and held the door open.

"I know you want to get back to your husband's bedside, so we won't keep you now. But we'll be in touch—about rearranging his appearance."

"I'm afraid that can't be for some time," she said gently, as if denying a request with great reluctance.

Flecker was more than a match for her. "That's too bad," he said with unimpaired amiability, "but at least you can be sure Dr. Deachman will be getting the best attention available. If he doesn't make good progress, we won't hesitate to send in our own doctors."

Nesta ignored the iron fist. "We'll all just have to pray for the best, won't we?" she said, departing with a sad, brave smile.

In stupefied silence, the four men listened to the retreat of her clicking heels, then the latching of the door. The Chief of Police, whose existence Nesta had steadfastly ignored, was the first to recover.

"And which nursing home would that be?" he asked.

Flecker consulted his notes. "Riverside Manor," he reported.

"Stands to reason. Deachman owns seventy-five percent of it. They'll say whatever he tells them to."

Ben was racking his memory trying to separate the seven doctors. "Let me get this straight. Was Deachman next in line to testify?"

65

"Sure thing." The whole scenario was clear as a bell to Flecker. "He probably wasn't crazy about the idea to begin with. But then look what happens. White testifies, White gets socked with a lawsuit. So Deachman decides he wants out. This morning he ducks into this tame nursing home and tells them to lock the gates. His wife's part is to do a snow job on us about overwork and heart attacks."

Tony Martinelli shook his head in disgust. "Well, he sure picked the right dame. That one expects the whole world to dance to her tune." He turned to the Chief of Police. "Say, Trumbull told us none of the doctors had an alibi. How come Mrs. Deachman didn't swear she was by hubby's side every minute? It would be just her style."

"She would have if she could have gotten away with it," Jones agreed. "But Deachman was called to the hospital from a dinner party. So the best she could do is claim that by the time she got home he was already there. Not that all the other wives aren't the same. White's wife started to tell my boys he was in all evening before she realized that the maid had seen him leave. And I hear one of the others tried persuading her bridge group to alibi the husband."

"Do you realize what you're saying?" Tony groaned. "If they do everything alike, then all seven of them will bolt into quarantine and we'll be stuck in this two-bit town for weeks." As his words floated on the air, as Lou Flecker stared at him reproachfully, he realized the famous Martinelli tact had slipped. "Sorry about that, Ben," he muttered.

While Ben flapped a forgiving hand, Flecker did some constructive thinking. "You know, we could turn this to our advantage. I don't much like holding these hearings in the middle of a police investigation, particularly when we can't count on a smooth schedule. If Elsie and Val are willing to go along, I say let's go back to Washington and let these doctors stew in their sickbeds for a week or two."

"Yeah. We can always boot them out when we want them."

Martinelli's eyes gleamed with enthusiasm, at the prospect either of escape or of cracking the whip.

Owen Jones decided that his remarks had been misconstrued. "Now look, don't get me wrong. What I meant is that all doctors—and their wives—think there are special rules for MD's. But they're different types and they react differently. Deachman, in case you haven't guessed, is the kind who thinks that if he pretends a problem doesn't exist, it will simply go away. Now, Rojak, he's the tough one. He'll give you a stand-up fight because he's convinced that, with the AMA and enough money on his side, he can tell the world to shove it."

"Well, that would certainly make a change from Howard White," said Flecker skeptically. "All *he* told us was that doctors should be rich and happy, and any legislation on the subject is un-American."

Jones shrugged. "I guess White reacts to pressure by taking it out on someone smaller than he is. The boys tell me he tried to raise hell with Wanda Soczewinski for daring to sue him."

"I thought she was just a pawn." Ben was genuinely puzzled. "Did White think she might be Karras' partner in the shakedown?"

"Hell, no! She's not much more than a kid. White just wanted to hit out at somebody who wouldn't hit back."

The Chief of Police continued, but he had lost some of his audience. Ben Safford was suddenly aware of his own remissness. Too much attention had been lavished on HEW, on the Newburg Seven, on Theodore Karras, while one participant had been overlooked. In the meantime Wanda Soczewinski had been brow-beaten by her doctor, interrogated by the police and left without a lawyer.

Under the circumstances, she might welcome a call from her Congressman.

— 9 —

It had been in the back of his mind for some time, but never insistently enough to surface into action. He only knew that Wanda had two small children and a husband with multiple sclerosis.

Janet always claimed that Ben was a coward about this sort of thing, and, on the whole, she was right. Human suffering never left him untouched. That was the reason he had gone into politics. He was willing to work day and night to make the country everything it should be, to see there was enough food and work and decency for everyone.

Where he fell down was on the personal level. Easy sympathy did not flow naturally from Ben. At best, he was tongue-tied. At worst, he wanted to haul off and punch someone, which was not always the best way to convey compassion.

But if he was a coward, he was also a man of conscience. Squaring his shoulders, he set out for South Newburg, where Mrs. Soczewinski lived.

It was one of the bungalows on Marengo Avenue, a long street narrowed to one lane by cars parked on both sides. Ben, looking for 1432, pulled up behind a large green station wagon blocking progress. There was a passenger in the car but no driver. On the sidewalk, a stout woman stood talking to a young girl. Sighting Ben's car, the matron pantomimed her intention to move on, said a final word to the girl and bustled back to the driver's seat.

"Take your time," Ben bawled out the window.

The station wagon proceeded, and Ben followed, noting out of the corner of his eye that the girl was waving vigorously. When he walked back from his parking place, she was just opening the door of 1432.

"Yes? I'm Mrs. Soczewinski," she said.

Ben introduced himself and started to explain his mission when she broke in.

"I know you! I voted for you—and so did Tommy. Oh he'll be so mad he missed you!"

"You don't look old enough to vote," said Ben truthfully.

"Come on in," she said with a glowing smile. "The place is a mess. . . ."

There was a crib in one corner of the minute living room. In another, there was a wheelchair. It was clean as a whistle.

"Maybe if you don't mind the kitchen," she suggested with a look over her shoulder. "The kids are in the backyard."

In the kitchen there was a rack of drying dishes on the sink, some potted plants on the windowsill and crumbs on the table, which Wanda Soczewinski whisked away.

"Mrs. Soczewinski," Ben began

"That's Tommy's mother," she said with a pert smile. "Why don't you call me Wanda? And can I get you a cup of coffee, Mr. Safford? There's some left. Oh, I can't get over it. A Congressman—right here! Wait until I tell Tommy."

While she spoke, Ben revised his preconceived notions. Wanda Soczewinski was a tiny thing, barely five feet tall. And she was so thin that her face was all eyes. But despite the boyish cap of blond hair, she was not the little girl Ben had taken her for on the sidewalk.

"Oh, was that you?" she exclaimed. "That was Mrs. Williams from the Ladies' Guild. They take Tommy out once a week."

With a sudden wary look at him, she asked, "You know . . . my husband˜. . . ?"

Not trusting himself with words, Ben nodded and she seemed to breathe a sigh of relief. "You see, we don't have a car. And it's hard on Tommy, never getting out. So Mrs. Williams or one of the others takes him around to different places like the zoo or the arboretum. Tommy really appreciates it."

She could have been defying him to see any poignancy in the situation. Ben, better with facts than emotions, said, "I didn't know whether Tommy was able—to go out, I mean."

Putting down a cup of coffee for him, she settled herself opposite and told him about multiple sclerosis, the cruel wasting disease that afflicts young adults. In the process, she told him a lot about herself. Wanda Soczewinski had learned the terrible part about *no known cause* and *no known cure* by rote. But she was not a lecturer; her eloquence sprang from the heart.

". . . important to understand that his mind's the same as it always was," she said earnestly. "And Tommy's brilliant. So it means a whole lot for him to get out of the house—"

A sudden uproar outside made her jump to her feet. Barks, children shouting . . . and Wanda was gone. Ben went over to the window to look out. There was a pandemonium of activity, all swirling around an aged beagle.

When Wanda reappeared, she had a pint-sized replica tucked under an arm.

"This is Robin," she said, flopping Robin onto her lap like a rag doll.

Robin, sex unknown to Ben, stared at him unnervingly, tears forgotten at the fearsome sight. Ben smiled tentatively.

"Robin won't leave doggie alone," said Wanda.

The little face crumpled slightly, and, fearing the worst, Ben burst into speech. "Have you ever heard about Wheels for Shut-Ins?" he asked.

Wanda shook her head and Robin stared.

"Maybe they could help you out," Ben continued, trying to re-

70

call the details of one of Janet's many good works. "Zoos and arboretums are okay, but I know Wheels organizes outings to baseball games and things like that. Of course, I don't know if Tommy likes—"

"That would be wonderful," she broke in, unconsciously hugging Robin. "Tommy's nuts about sports."

"I'll tell my sister to get in touch with you," Ben said, withdrawing his pocket diary to jot a reminder. Looking up, he caught Wanda and Robin watching him with fascination. Robin was transfixed by the pencil.

"That would be wonderful," Wanda said again.

Ben kept on writing. He didn't always say the right thing, but sometimes he avoided the wrong one. He knew better than to ask when Wanda ever got out. It would turn out that she didn't like to leave Robin and Robin's brother with strangers. Or that Tommy needed her. Or something else.

"The reason I dropped by was this trouble with Dr. White," he began, only to be silenced by a warning look.

"Do you think you can play with Bully without pulling his tail?" she said, rising to place Robin on her chubby legs.

Robin gave assurances of some sort, cast a last longing look at Ben's pencil, then let Wanda lead her to the kitchen door.

"Now you be a good girl!" her mother yelled before turning back to Ben. "They pick up more than you think," she said solemnly.

It was not the murder of Theo Karras that was unfit for Robin's ears.

". . . couldn't make head or tail of it when it came in the mail. But there was a note explaining that all this stuff showed what Dr. White was telling the government," she said, color mounting in her cheeks.

Dr. White had charged three hysterectomies and one abortion to the Medicaid account of Mrs. Wanda Soczewinski.

"It made me see red," she confided.

"I don't blame you," Ben replied.

"It wasn't as if—" Whatever she was going to say, she thought better of. "Anyway, the note explained it all. Because, you see, the only thing wrong with me when I went to Dr. White was anemia. That was all. So the note said I should take everything to Mr. Karras. Tommy and I, we talked it over for a couple of days. I wasn't sure, but Tommy was so mad . . ."

Everything Wanda said was straightforward. Out of the blue, a packet of Medicaid documents had arrived at 1432 Marengo with a typed note explaining Dr. White's money-making scheme and directing the Soczewinskis to Attorney Karras.

"Did you know Karras before all this?" Ben asked.

"No," she said, quickly defensive. "That's what the police keep asking. But I never met him before in my life." Misinterpreting his silence, she cried, "My father-in-law knew him, but we didn't."

"I didn't mean to upset you," Ben apologized. "I was just wondering if Karras himself sent you—"

Half exasperated, half alarmed, she interrupted: "I know! That's what Lieutenant Doyle said too. But I told him how Mr. Karras was real surprised when I turned up. I could tell. Then, when he started reading the stuff I brought, he began talking to himself. You know, the way people do when they don't believe what they're seeing? Then he began figuring out how much money Dr. White made—and started swearing."

Anxiously, she studied him. "You think we're in on it together," she said flatly. "Just like Dr. White."

"What?" Ben exclaimed.

Dr. Howard White had not hesitated to accuse Wanda of every crime in the book. There were jails for people like her, he had told her in a tirade that included recriminations, threats and, apparently, obscene language.

Ben was shaken, and when he recovered he found he had been speaking his thoughts aloud.

Wanda was not shocked. "That's what Tommy said, too. Anyway, I had a few things to say to Dr. White myself. But he wasn't the least bit ashamed of what he'd done—in fact, he claimed it was none of my business. That's when I stopped hesitating about going on with the suit. That—" here she smiled—"that and the money. Mr. Karras said we might collect one hundred thousand dollars."

For the first time her voice trembled. In this family, what would a sum like that mean?

Gently, Ben asked.

"We'd get off welfare," she said simply. Then, hurriedly: "Oh, I don't want you think I'm not grateful. . . ."

This was the point at which Ben Safford wanted to start swinging, preferably at Dr. Howard White, his tanned wife or his tanned children.

She was going on. "We'd get ourselves a car. They have them with special equipment for Tommy. That would make a big difference. Then, well, you know how expensive kids are."

"Yes," said Ben harshly.

It was not as inadequate as it sounded. Wanda was emboldened to air a private worry.

"Do you think . . . I mean, now that Mr. Karras is dead . . .?"

There was nothing wrong with Ben Safford's ears. "Don't worry about it. Your suit goes on, Karras or no Karras. And you're going to get a whopping big settlement, too. I'll get hold of a good lawyer for you. And if that doesn't work out, I'll represent you myself. I've got a law degree I've never used."

She laughed aloud at his vehemence, but sobered immediately. "That's terrible, isn't it, after what happened to Mr. Karras. He was awfully nice to me. You know, he came here to the house to talk things over with Tommy."

She was no child, as Ben had already discovered. "You know the doctors claim that Karras was blackmailing them," he said.

"That's not true," she said with calm certainty. "Not Mr. Karras."

Again, this told Ben something about Theo Karras, and more about Wanda. She was midway between what she had been and what she had to be. Once Tommy had been a tower of strength for her. Once she had been overawed by policemen, by lawyers, by Dr. Whites. Now this was a luxury she could no longer afford. For the life she faced, Wanda had to rely on her own hands and heart and brain.

"I'm willing to bet you're right about Karras," said Ben slowly.

"Excuse me, I'd better check Robin," she said, jumping up and darting to the door.

Ben rebuked himself. There were too many problems in this house to leave Wanda much margin for outside puzzles.

"Behaving like an angel," she said, on returning.

It would be heartless to ask if there was anything he could do to help her. "I've got to get back," said Ben, rising. "I'm sorry I missed Tommy. If it's convenient for you, I'll drop in tonight after dinner. I'd like to talk things over with him."

She looked at him as if he were a sleeping baby Soczewinski.

"Also, these rules and regulations can be pretty confusing. I want to be certain you're taking advantage of all the assistance you're entitled to. I'm going to ask—"

"Oh, thank you," she said. "But down at Social Security they've been just wonderful. Mrs. Gregorian spent hours with the books. Would you believe we get forty dollars extra every two months because Robin has an allergy? Mrs. Gregorian says we're entitled to every penny we can get. And, boy, do we need it!"

"Right!" said Ben.

She grinned up at him. "You know, there are a whole lot of good people in this world."

Congressman Safford made himself say it. "There sure are."

— 10 —

Forty hours later Theodore Karras was laid to rest next to his late wife. The attendance—consisting mainly of family, local residents from South Newburg and members of the International Justice Party from a tri-state area—did not suggest that the funeral had any significance over at the other end of town. Nonetheless it was a signal for movement on several fronts. Six doctors cautiously emerged from their houses, while the seventh testily told his nurse to take that bed table away and put his tray on the balcony. A whole clutch of reporters checked out of the Sunset Motel and began the drive back to Cincinnati. Val Oakes, Elsie Hollenbach and Tony Martinelli caught the breakfast flight to Washington. Even Lou Flecker, held up by administrative detail, was able to make the eleven o'clock plane.

"Thanks for the lift, Ben," he said in parting. "I know you'll keep an eye on the situation here."

Ben promised that if anything happened Lou would be the first to know. "Not that I expect any developments over the weekend. And I'll be at the House on Tuesday."

As he strolled back through the terminal, he realized that others were returning to normal as well. A cheerful party was marching toward the corridor which led to the private-aircraft area. There was not much doubt about their destination, as the roly-poly man in the group was encased in a raccoon coat and carrying an Ohio State pennant. But what caught Ben's attention was Nesta Deachman prancing along on the arm of a familiar young man. Today her black hair was flying loose over her shoulders and she was wearing a white fisherman's sweater with tan suede jeans tucked into glossy boots. There was red on her lips, blue on her eyelids and long gold earrings glittering as she turned her head in vivacious chatter. Ben grinned to himself. He had a strong suspicion that this was the real Mrs. Deachman, as opposed to the subdued creature in the Federal Building, bowed down by premature widowhood.

"So much for sitting at a hospital bedside," he muttered under his breath.

Even Nesta felt some explanation was required.

"I still don't think it looks right," she said, leaning across Jim Rojak to address the Whites. "But Arnie's feeling so much better that he's taking charge again. He says we've got to start living life normally. So here I am."

"Great," they said perfunctorily.

Rojak, on the other hand, looked at her oddly. Nesta was a strange combination of conventionality and extravagance. He could see that she was ready to have a wonderful time. But simultaneously she was worried about appearances. He had absolutely no doubt that she had balked at coming until Deachman insisted.

They were setting off on one of Jim Rojak's famous parties. In the middle of the summer, long before his world started coming apart at the seams, he had marked the date on which Ohio State (his own alma mater) played Notre Dame, which Howard White had attended. It seemed like the ideal occasion for airborne hospitality, but the closer the day came, the less likely it appeared that the outing would materialize. With flashbulbs popping wherever he went, even Howard White re-

76

alized that he should be seen on errands of mercy, not pleasure jaunts. But then, within forty-eight hours, the stormclouds had begun rolling away. The police were at a standstill, Wanda Soczewinski's lawsuit was becalmed and, as an additional fillip, the subcommittee had folded its tents and returned to Washington.

Rojak, who was a gambler by nature, knew that it was now or never. Gone were thoughts of a modest afternoon expedition. It was going to be a tailgate party at the airport, seats on the fifty-yard line, then on to a suite in Chicago and a night on the town.

Rojak had planned a show of strength. But he had found himself saddled with an embarrassment. What had thrown a crimp into his plans was the guest list. Originally, it had included the Deachmans as well as Dr. and Mrs. White and Rojak's companion of the moment. When Deachman went into hiding, Rojak had begun thinking about alterations. But then Deachman phoned from Riverside Manor and talked and talked and talked. As a result, Rojak found himself squiring Nesta while the Costellos filled the rest of the six-seat Cessna.

So Rojak was not expecting to have a marvelous time. Still, there was enough festivity in the air to pass muster. Nesta was reveling in a young escort and the prospect of her first college football game. She was providing almost as much satisfaction for Connie White, who intended to store up all of Nesta's gaucheries and relay them to Margaret Deachman. Howard White, temporarily liberated from the cares of Newburg, could almost forget they existed. The Costellos, long envious of the good times provided by Jim Rojak, were in seventh heaven. Patrick Costello had spotted the straw basket from the Curryville Petit Gourmet the minute he entered the plane. Round-eyed, he ticked off smoked salmon, caviar, goose-liver pâté. This, he decided, was the way to live. The discovery that her high heels and fur stole were all wrong had not noticeably dampened Ethel Costello's spirits. The real test was still ahead and she had every confidence that the suitcase at her feet contained the perfect outfit for dinner and dancing.

As for Rojak himself, he knew perfectly well that his trou-

77

bles had not evaporated, but he had always believed in seizing the moment. The ritual of take-off with its emphasis on his commanding position, the open admiration of the Costellos, Howard White's fatuous comparison between air and marine navigation all acted on him like a tonic.

"Next stop, South Bend!" he sang out as they leveled off and began cruising.

If anything further was needed to make spirits soar, the tailgate hour provided it. The weather in South Bend was well-nigh perfect, with a few fluffy clouds impelled across a clear blue sky by a spanking breeze. The Petit Gourmet had excelled itself, ably assisted by the Newburg Liquor Mart. And, best of all, they were in full view of every other private aircraft debouching passengers for the big game.

"Boy, will you take a look at that," marveled Costello as a sleek jet began to unload ten or twelve couples.

He was soon set right.

"It's just some corporation entertaining customers," sniffed Howard White. "When you get right down to it, everyone there works for someone else."

He was just slightly off target, as they learned when one of the new arrivals hailed Rojak as a classmate. A Cleveland bank was hosting some local businessmen. Any doubts about the superiority of the Newburg contingent's position were laid to rest by the deference which greeted Rojak's lordly offer of caviar sandwiches and Bloody Marys.

In rapid succession there arrived a retail chain rewarding its most successful managers, an embryo sports syndicate wooing participants and a manufacturing company from Akron with a full load of purchasing agents. Not until Connie and Ethel were packing up the debris did another single-engine plane arrive.

"Hi, Jim," said the pilot as he strolled past.

"Hi, Pete!"

They were two sovereigns.

Rojak's explanation came as no surprise to his guests. "Pete's an orthodontist in Toledo. I didn't know him at school, but we run into each other a lot these days."

Inside the stadium they had sacred rituals to help them prove what a good time they were having. Pat Costello and Connie White produced a mock-fierce rivalry requiring agonized groans or ecstatic yells at every movement of the ball.

"Call that passing?" scoffed Connie as the ball sailed into the hands of a receiver surrounded by the entire Notre Dame defense.

Then, arriving from nowhere, two Ohio State giants cleared a hole in the forest, and the receiver, with an agile swivel, evaded a pair of clutching hands and began to snake-dance toward freedom.

"C'mon, twinkletoes!" Costello roared.

When Ohio State scored on the next rush, he exploded into an orgy of pennant-waving, back-thumping and exultant screaming.

Rojak and White were less partisan. Busy exchanging courtesies with nearby spectators, greetings with passing classmates and college reminiscences with each other, they only occasionally rose to their feet for an obligatory war cry. Ethel Costello, profoundly grateful not to be chilled to the bone, broiled to a crisp or soaked by a downpour, assumed the Mona Lisa smile she reserved for sports events and refreshed herself too frequently from the flask Jim Rojak had provided.

Nesta Deachman needed no stimulants. She was drinking in the whole spectacle—the gyrations of the cheerleaders, the marching bands at half-time, the students unfurling signs in front of the television cameras. She enjoyed eating hot dogs, recognizing the Governor of Ohio and mastering the intricacies of point-spread betting.

"Then if Notre Dame makes this touchdown," she said toward the end of the final quarter, "you owe me seventy-five dollars, Pat."

Ethel Costello had a bookkeeper's mind. "That's in addition to the fifty you'll get from Jim," she pointed out, more in a spirit of accuracy than reproach.

Nesta was hunched forward, her chin cupped in a hand, her

gaze intent on the field. Her tongue flicked out to remove a dab of mustard before she replied. "I can use it all," she said dreamily.

Two minutes later both Notre Dame and Nesta had won. As the same goal was putting money into Howard's pocket, even Connie White was pleased.

Only one event marred the afternoon. As they were making their way to the exit, a classmate of Rojak, with more brandy than sense in him, yelled a greeting over intervening heads and struggled toward them.

"Jim, old buddy! How're ya doing? I see you're getting your name spread all over the papers."

Evasion was impossible. They were hemmed in as effectively as if they had police guards.

"Say, Jim, we've got a room for the class of '65 and we're going to have a ball. Bring your friends and tell us all the dirt about Newburg."

There was a glint in Rojak's eye. "Sorry, Gene, we'd like to stop by your little get-together, but we've got a suite at the Ritz waiting for us. And I don't do my drinking until after I've finished flying my plane." He paused to flick a playful fist at Gene's shoulder. "Good to run into you, though. I hope they're treating you all right at that high school where you teach."

After that, Gene was only too glad to let them escape to the exit and, ultimately, to Chicago. At the Ritz there was no need to fear tactless references to events in Ohio. This was partly due to the high standards of the hotel, partly to their palatial accommodations and mostly to the fact that nobody cared. They were all used to being big frogs in a small pond and normally they resented the anonymity of large cities. Today, however, they reveled in it.

In the cocktail lounge they were conscious of being one of the most attractive groups present. Even Pat Costello, shorn of football regalia, was revealed as a portly figure of distinction. In the most expensive restaurant on Michigan Boulevard, they all emerged as knowledgeable gourmets, with Jim Rojak and Howard White more than upholding the honor of Newburg in their wine selections. And the discotheque which climaxed the evening was an unalloyed triumph. They could switch partners often enough to avoid boredom.

"Nesta certainly seems to appreciate the good time you're showing us, Jim," purred Connie White.

Rojak was amused. Several rounds earlier Nesta, in a burst of enthusiasm, had lightly clasped his knee, and way out on the dance floor Connie's eyelids had blinked open and closed like a camera shutter. And like a camera she had recorded the moment for all time.

"I'll tell her you said so," he promised.

Whatever he passed on to Nesta, her reaction was enough to draw Pat Costello's attention.

"Jim doesn't seem to have the magic touch," he observed to Howard White as they made their way back to the table. "Nesta looks mad as fire."

White was not surprised that Rojak's gently shaking head should induce Nesta to lift her chin in defiance. "Well, he's saying no, and pretty ladies don't like that."

He could have added that they don't sit still for it.

"I wonder where Nesta and Howard have gone off to," Ethel Costello said idly later in the evening. "I haven't seen them in ages."

Rojak had no doubt that they were innocently occupied somewhere, but that Nesta would delay any return until Connie had noticed their absence. "They may have found another room," he said vaguely. "This one is getting pretty crowded."

Ethel was placidity itself. "That must be it."

In a wave of approval Rojak urged food, drink or another dance on her. Already regretting his mischief-making, he was finding it restful to spend some time with a woman oblivious to the undercurrents between the other two.

Fortunately, Connie and Pat had barely seated themselves when Nesta returned, leading Howard by the hand.

"It's so stuffy down here that we went upstairs for some air, and the time flew by," she twinkled. "I simply had to drag Howard back. I hope we haven't held you up."

But Connie was far too old a hand to show displeasure. Like a veteran tennis player, she might not be as fast on her feet as the youngsters, but she had mastered tactics that Nesta was still developing.

"What a good idea!" she said warmly.

On this happy note they returned to the Ritz, capped the weekend with a leisurely Sunday brunch, then finally piled into the Cessna for the trip home.

Like every weekend, this one had its period of anticlimax when thoughts began to leapfrog to the week ahead. But there was a geographic dimension to the process as well. Every sweep of the minute hand brought the plane's passengers closer not only to Monday but also to Newburg, where their problems lay in wait. What would have been unthinkable on Saturday morning was brute reality by Sunday evening: they had been granted a breathing space, not a permanent remission.

Nesta Deachman didn't see it that way.

"What are you all so down in the dumps for?" she demanded, breaking the silence that had prevailed since Rojak announced they were in radio contact with Newburg Airport. "It isn't as if we have anything to worry about."

"Are you crazy?" White's voice was so high it threatened to crack. "I sometimes think we're just as badly off as we were at the beginning of this mess."

Nesta inspected him in the deepening gloom of the plane's interior. Doing the hustle with him was fun, but Nesta cherished no illusions about Dr. Howard White, or any of the Newburg Seven.

"Howard," she said impatiently, "that woman doesn't have a lawyer for her suit anymore, the subcommittee has left town and nobody's stealing files from HEW. How can you say that things are just as bad as ever?"

Pat Costello's ebullience had been deflating for over an hour. "God knows what the police have been up to while we've been out of town," he said dolefully. "And the subcommittee has simply adjourned, Nesta. They may come back any day."

She found it impossible to take him seriously. "Well, they may come back," she said mockingly, "but they're not going to trouble Arnie. *He's* still sick."

The triumph in her voice grated on Rojak. "That's just fine.

82

Do you expect *me* to stand up and cheer? Remember, I'm the one who'll get called in Arnie's place."

"But, Jim," she protested, "you yourself have been saying that the subcommittee is no reason to get uptight."

He sighed with exaggerated patience. "That was before we were all part of a murder case, Nesta baby. Now there's plenty to worry about."

Anger began roughening her style. "Then why the hell don't you do something about it? The trouble with all of you—and I'll include Arnie, too—is that you spend too much time talking and not enough doing. No wonder these creeps think they can kick us around."

It would have been wiser to leave her unanswered, but White couldn't let the subject rest.

"Exactly what do you suggest?"

She had plenty to suggest. "For openers, isn't there some way to get to Safford? You're doctors, you know other doctors. Maybe he's had a nervous breakdown, like the one who ran with McGovern. Or—he's a bachelor, isn't he? Can't you find out if he's gay?"

This ruthlessness left White speechless. Jim Rojak took over. "Look, Nesta, this isn't TV and we're not private eyes. Besides, just forget about Safford and the subcommittee. Our real problem is malpractice insurance. Great Lakes is running scared because of this lawsuit against Howard—"

"Good God, that suit's over and done with!" she cut in.

"Wake up!" he replied harshly. "Somebody got rid of Karras, but they didn't get rid of every lawyer in Newburg. Sooner or later, one of them is bound to pick up this Soczewinski woman. I'm sorry for Howard, but Great Lakes has already half-swallowed one suit. If there's a second, Larry Fournier will go up in smoke."

"Then get to Fournier some way," she said fiercely.

"You mean, prove *he's* gay, too? So that Great Lakes will roll over and play dead out of sheer embarrassment? Listen,

I'm worried about the same thing Fournier is. I'm afraid there's somebody out there trying to get us."

"Well, why don't you try to find out who it is?" she asked with perfumed venom.

"My, my!" said Connie White with a silvery laugh. "You two could be married to each other, the way you argue."

"Bitch!" said Nesta lightly under her breath.

But Connie had performed a useful function in diverting Nesta long enough to let Rojak lower the temperature of the discussion. "I know it looks as if you're taking all the lumps, Howard," he said. "But if there's only one lawsuit, and if we all stand together, I'm sure we can make Great Lakes play it our way."

"That's one hundred percent right," Costello chimed in loyally. "Hell, they've been making a mint out of us for years and this is the first time they've had to shell out."

Nesta, meanwhile, had begun assembling her possessions as the lights of Newburg Airport appeared ahead.

Connie White thought she saw an opportunity to score a point. "They're right, you know. If we all stick together, everything will come out all right in the end."

For the first time in memory, Nesta spoke to her as one woman to another. "*We?* Who are you trying to kid, Connie? You've got your problems and I've got mine. And you can run right back to dear Margaret and tell her that from me!"

But by the following morning all the Deachmans had something else to occupy them. Jim Rojak's worst forebodings came true with a vengeance. A second malpractice suit was filed.

This time the defendant was Dr. Arnold Deachman.

— II —

It was just as well for her peace of mind that Nesta was not present during the electrifying half-hour after the arrival of the summons at Riverside Manor Nursing Home. Arnold Deachman outdid himself in an emotional spectacular that began with shock, escalated rapidly into rage at the entire world, then distilled itself into wild threats against his adversaries. What he wanted was someone to join him in these sentiments with perfect, unfeigned sincerity. With the best will in the world, Nesta would have had a hard time playing this role.

But, fortunately, sitting at his bedside was just the woman to fill the bill. Penelope Deachman Taggert was twenty-four years old, a wife, mother and chatelaine of a substantial household, but she was still the little girl who had been raised by a mother saying: "Your father is a wonderful man, dear." Even after the great apostasy Margaret Deachman had merely shifted to: "Your father was simply putty in that woman's hands." To Penny, Arnold Deachman was an indulgent father, a doting grandfather, a bounteous provider, whose furies—never directed at her—were the natural response to a world that was just too unfair.

At first her uncritical sympathy poured over Deachman's wounds like balm.

"The nerve of it! Imagine a malpractice suit—against you, of all people!" she exclaimed as indignantly as he could wish.

"They'll pay for this," he stormed. "I've taken care of troublemakers before. They won't get away with it."

"I should think not!"

The wild glare in his eye began to fade as he modulated into self-pity. "I don't even remember who this Atkins is."

"That just shows," she chimed in as if making a tremendous debating point.

"Whoever he is, he has big ideas. He's asking for three hundred thousand dollars."

Penny gasped. She lived a life in which houses, cars and charge accounts simply appeared, and would have been stupefied if anybody had ever calculated the total expenditures of the Taggert family. In all honesty, she was convinced they led a simple life. Why, she even had to go to Daddy when they decided to park Trigger with his grandmother and spend their vacation in Greece.

But numbers had never been able to claim her attention long. "And to do this when you're sick! They think you won't be able to fight back."

"He's probably a welfare patient," Deachman grunted.

"Well, doesn't he have any consideration?"

Unhappily, the more Deachman returned to rationality, the less useful his daughter was. Partisanship she could provide, but not campaign strategy.

"Of course, in my weakened condition I can't be expected to cope with this," he began significantly. "I could never answer for the consequences."

"You mustn't even think of it." Penny was all eager action. "I'll call your lawyer right now. We can give him the summons and he'll take care of everything."

"You will not!" Deachman came upright in a hurry. "I'm not going to be saddled with the bills for this ridiculous suit.

This is the insurance company's problem. That's what they're paid for."

His daughter was willing but bewildered. "Then do you want me to call *them?*"

"God, no! That will just bring them down on me. This has to be handled carefully, and Nesta's the one to do it. God knows I've taken care of her well enough—"

"You certainly have," Penny said too quickly. The news of the forthcoming mink coat had already been relayed by Connie White.

The smooth rhythm of Deachman's fault-finding was interrupted. Normally, he would have gone on to an examination of Nesta's flaws, but he was reminded that this was one issue upon which he and his daughter were not as one.

"Nesta is a very competent woman," he said, giving credit where credit was due. "She kept that subcommittee out of my hair, and now she'll make Great Lakes understand that I refuse to be involved. So *she's* the one for you to get hold of."

"If I can," Penny retorted. "Maybe she's not back from her big weekend. If you ask me, it's a bit much, traipsing off to a football game while you're in the hospital."

"Nobody *has* asked you, young lady. That was my idea, in case you're interested. Nesta wasn't really enthusiastic." His lips twisted maliciously. "And, for that matter, neither was Jim Rojak. He probably didn't like not being able to take one of those stewardesses of his, thought it cramped his style having my wife along. But I wasn't having that bunch think we have any more to hide than they do. And why should Rojak have fun and games right now? He's in this just as much as we are. Does he think he's entitled to a free ride while Howard and I take all the knocks? It's high time he pulled some of the weight. He's great on talk, but when it comes to action all he does is . . ."

"All he does is what?" Penny pressed when her father showed signs of running down.

But Deachman preferred not to go into detail during his appeals for sympathy. He leaned back and pulled the blankets around him. "Get Nesta," he repeated. "She'll take care of this. I'm far too unwell to be disturbed."

"Oh, I know, Daddy. You must feel simply terrible."

At Great Lakes they felt even worse when they heard the news.

"Do you realize how much these jokers in Newburg can cost my division?" Larry Fournier stormed at his staff.

The division accountant made the mistake of answering. "They could put us in the red."

"I thought they shot the guy who was in back of this," someone else said hastily.

"Well, they didn't do a good enough job."

The news flashed through the medical circles of Newburg within hours.

"Naturally, I think it's terrible, but I have never seen why Howard should have to carry the whole brunt on his shoulders," said Connie White.

Margaret Deachman continued to relay Penny's tidings.

"So Nesta is going to deal with the insurance company." Connie emitted a ladylike snort. "Well, her tactics should be interesting. Did I tell you about the cleavage she was showing in Chicago . . .?"

In the Community Medical Building, Pat Costello took advantage of his newfound intimacy with Jim Rojak to descend one floor for a consultation.

"We're next!" he wailed. "What are we going to do?"

Unlike most of his colleagues, Rojak had been thinking. "Now's the time for Giles Perrin to earn his keep. To hell with little statements to the subcommittee. The AMA has got to lay it on the line to Great Lakes. They negotiated the policy and they have to insist that all doctors be treated the same. Great Lakes can't single out scapegoats."

"Absolutely," said Costello fervently.

Little as the AMA approved, the HEW office was also part of Newburg's medical circle. Particularly when it came to subpoenas for billings.

Quentin Trumbull cradled the telephone receiver with a thump, then turned challengingly to his audience of one.

"I've had it up to here," he announced, guillotining his own throat. "You know what Fournier was asking? He wants HEW to join Great Lakes in a formal protest to the bar association. He thinks their ethics committee should discipline any lawyer who has the nerve to sue him!"

Charlene Gregorian gave a brief chortle of laughter, then sobered. "He must be hysterical."

"Of course he is. Great Lakes thought they were out of the woods when Karras was murdered. They'd make a modest settlement with his client and the trouble would be over. Now, out of the blue comes this second suit, and they realize that Karras had a partner who's sitting on the HEW files."

Charlene Gregorian gave it as her opinion that Lawrence Fournier had relaxed too soon.

"Well, he's paying for it now. Did I tell you that Deachman is the target this time? But what I'd really like to know is the basis of this second suit. That's why I asked you to check out the Kenneth Atkins file."

Charlene stared at him. "You mean that Fournier doesn't know? Why didn't he ask Deachmen?"

Until now Trumbull's face had been a rigid mask of disapproval, but at this question the frown began to melt. "Fournier didn't talk with Deachman. It was *Mrs.* Deachman who called." A full-scale grin appeared. "Haven't you heard the latest dirt? Deachman is hiding out in his own nursing home, pretending to have heart trouble, so he won't have to testify before the subcommittee. I suppose when the summons came he decided it wouldn't help his public image to come busting out and take charge himself."

"And so his wife is pinch-hitting for him."

Trumbull was still amused. "If you ask me, half of Larry Fournier's trouble comes from dealing with Mrs. Deachman. Apparently she's putting on an act as the admiring wife of a wonderful husband. Larry couldn't let loose at her with all the shots that Deachman has coming. So he bit down hard and just made sure it really was another malpractice action. He's flying in tomorrow to learn the grisly details."

"Well, I can do better by you than that. It stands out from the file like a sore thumb. This time it's appendectomies."

"What could be wrong with that?" Trumbull demanded. "Only a couple of days ago Congressman Martinelli was recommending it as damn near foolproof."

"Yes," Charlene agreed temperately, "but not three of them on the same patient."

"They never learn, do they?" Trumbull muttered. "At least that should make it simple to tell if the references to our files are accurate. You want to take a look?"

Charlene Gregorian accepted the subpoena he pushed across the desk, flipped to the list of documents demanded and began to compare it with her own notes. It didn't take long for her to render a verdict.

"Correct in every detail," she announced cheerfully.

"I didn't really expect anything else. And if Kenneth Atkins is a Social Security case, I suppose he'd be sympathetic to a jury. Is he over sixty-five?"

"No, he's blind," said Charlene absently. She was still studying the subpoena.

"Boy, that's another one that Fournier won't dare take into a courtroom. You have to hand it to Karras. When he set this thing up, he sure knew how to pick his files."

Charlene might not have heard him. "You've been concentrating on the wrong names in this thing, Quen," she charged, tapping the subpoena like a school teacher.

"What do you mean? There are only two names. It's *Atkins* v. *Deachman*."

"There also happens to be an attorney of record."

Trumbull snorted. "What difference does it make who he is? We already know it's some two-bit lawyer who went in on this with Karras. It hardly matters . . ." His voice trailed away as he realized that Charlene was authoritatively shaking her head. "No?" he asked weakly.

"No, it's not some two-bit lawyer. For God's sake, Quen, this is Michael Isham of—" She broke off to lower her voice impressively. "Of Briggs, Briggs and Isham."

Momentarily, Trumbull goggled. Then he gave a long, low whistle.

No small American city can boast the kind of giant law mill that exists in New York and Washington. In the hinterland most attorneys practice either alone or in partnerships of three or four men. But if the city houses a respectable amount of industry, if its banks and brokers and insurance offices provide financial services for a wide enough area, if there has been money around long enough to generate complicated estates, then there will be one law firm that towers above the rest in size, respectability and influence.

In Newburg that firm was Briggs, Briggs and Isham. Their letterhead listed eleven lawyers. Their offices needed a full floor of the bank building to accommodate legal file clerks, a law librarian and four paraprofessionals.

"And," said Charlene Gregorian with a snicker, "Duncan Briggs is president of the Newburg Bar Association. Someone might mention that to Larry Fournier before he organizes a march on the ethics committee."

But Trumbull was busy calculating the effect of this new element on his own position. "This changes everything," he remarked, scratching his head with the eraser end of a pencil.

"I don't see why. Ken Atkins' case is self-evident without a first-class lawyer."

"I'm not looking at it from Atkins' point of view. I'm looking at it from HEW's point of view. With Karras, we could assume that he filed the first suit as a show of force. Then he would have put the word out that he could be bought off. In view of what's at stake, the other six doctors would have coughed up and that would have been the end of it. HEW and the subcommittee would have stayed on top of the Medicaid situation without any of these end-runs."

"On top of the situation!" Charlene repeated derisively. "When HEW and the subcommittee were helpless to do anything? And don't talk to me about legislation in five years' time. I mean these particular seven doctors. Besides, I've never believed Theo Karras was on the take. You didn't know him, but he was one of those old-fashioned socialists still worrying about the Pullman strike."

Quentin Trumbull was not a man who shifted gears readily. "Then maybe he thought shaking down Rojak and the others was a primitive form of justice."

"You're missing the point. No matter what he felt about the doctors, he would never have double-crossed a Wanda Soczewinski or a Ken Atkins."

"What difference does it make?" Trumbull asked grumpily. "Karras isn't around anymore. And instead of returning to the old rules, we've got another outsider lobbing grenades onto the field."

Charlene raised her eyes to the ceiling in a parody of exasperation. "Oh, Quen," she reproached him. "Use your head. The minute Karras was murdered, the old rules went up in smoke. There are a lot of outsiders circling around us now, and, in case you haven't noticed, most of them are wearing police uniforms."

"Well, yes, there's that." Trumbull forced himself to consider this aspect. "I realize that if we end up with a murder trial against one of those goddamned doctors, that's going to raise even more Cain than a string of malpractice suits. But all of that's in the future. I'm worried about what I should be doing now. And there's no way to decide without knowing what Michael Isham plans."

"We could try asking him."

"Sure!" Trumbull bleated sarcastically. "And a fat chance we have for a nice informal huddle with anybody in that firm. They'll just tell us to buzz off."

"Oh, not with us." Charlene, her head bent studiously over her corner of the desk, was doodling furiously on a scratch pad.

Quentin Trumbull was not a native of Newburg. He had been deputy director in the Cincinnati HEW office before his promotion. But in three years he had learned a good deal about Newburg and even more about Charlene Gregorian. She was a walking encyclopedia about her hometown. She knew the names and the faces, she knew the current deals in the making and the past scandals that had been forgotten. And whenever she contemplated releasing a nugget of information, she doodled her way to a decision.

"Then with who?" he said softly.

"It's possible, just barely possible, that Isham won't say no to an off-the-record chat with Congressman Safford."

Past photographs from the *Newburg News* rose to haunt Trumbull. "But Wesley Briggs is on the Republican County Committee," he protested.

"All the Briggs are Republicans. But Michael Isham is a big contributor to the Democratic Party." Suddenly Charlene raised her face, revealing the wide smile that etched a dimple in her chin. "Briggs, Briggs and Isham has always played both sides of the street."

It was not just in politics that Briggs, Briggs and Isham covered the field. They offered a wide range of personal styles. Duncan Briggs conveyed an air of such mummified perma-

93

nence that it was worth money in the bank. Wesley Briggs was a pragmatic man of affairs—conservative by inclination, but willing to accept benefits from the right kind of government intervention. Michael Isham, who did the trial work, was the firm's rough-and-ready extrovert. He preferred the courtroom to the boardroom, frankly admitting that he enjoyed the opportunity for showmanship and combativeness.

"Hi, Ben!" he shouted from three tables away as he barreled through the lunchtime crowd in Corrigan's. "Sorry to be late. But I got held up at a hearing in Curryville."

Ben waved a welcome. Isham was one of his favorites among the party faithful. He could always be relied on to take two tickets to the fifty- and hundred-dollar-a-plate dinners. More important, any table that held Mike and Fanny Isham was so entertaining that it was worth—almost—the price of admission.

"There is no courthouse in Curryville," Ben pointed out as his guest finally thumped his burly form into a chair.

"This was a hearing before their Land Use Board." Isham leaned forward to pluck a breadstick from Ben's plate and, elbows on the table, began to chomp contentedly. There was a glint in his eye that told its own story. "And have I put the cat among the canaries!"

Ben considered what he knew of Curryville. Until fifteen years ago it had been a sleepy little community. Then a new road had brought it within commuting distance of Newburg and the town fathers had seen an opportunity to broaden the tax base. Discreet developments of expensive homes on substantial lots had been approved. Zoning variances had been granted for two private schools. The main shopping strip had been so artfully preserved that it was a jewel of old-time perfection.

"Somehow it doesn't seem like the right environment for you, Mike."

Isham's spirits were dancing. "I'm representing the develop-

94

er. We're applying for permission to put up low-income housing."

Ben had a strong suspicion that there was worse to come. "And they don't like it?" he asked warily.

"Today was only the first round. I explained to them that, according to Federal statistics, they owe the world 453 units of low-income housing and we're only planning for 218. They should be thanking me."

In spite of a football build, a mop of wiry dark hair, and bushy black eyebrows, Michael Isham contrived to look virtuous. Ben, however, had caught the significant word.

"Did you say *Federal* statistics?"

"That's right, Ben."

"Then they'll be on *my* neck. Thanks for the warning."

Isham waved graciously. "Any time," he said before turning to order a vodka martini.

Ben waited patiently for the drinks before introducing his main theme. "I can do without a lot of crazies from Curryville in my office right now. I have my hands full with these Medicaid hearings."

"I figured that was what you wanted to see me about."

"Naturally, I wouldn't ask you to disclose the contents of a confidential conversation between you and your client."

"Naturally."

Calmly Ben continued, "I wouldn't even ask you how you got your client's files from HEW."

"You'd better not," said Isham genially

"Because I don't care. But, Mike, we're trying to run some Medicaid hearings in this town. And if you're going to drive all of our star witnesses underground, I'd like to know about it. It's going to mean some replanning for us."

Isham twirled the stem of his glass as he considered his reply. When he looked up, he was serious. "I just don't know yet, Ben. For the record, I'd like to point out that I haven't driven anybody underground yet. Old man Deachman was in his fox-

95

hole long before I had him served. I expect the others are already digging theirs. For what it's worth, I'm willing to let you know once I make up my own mind. At the moment I'm just contemplating one malpractice suit. But I'll tell you something, Ben. This kind of case could grow on me."

Ben was too pleased to have won this much of a concession to press for more. "And you've got a sure thing. They tell me this is another perfect plaintiff."

"It's easy enough to say that. Hell, I said it myself before I got to know Ken Atkins. But there's such a thing as being too cynical. You know, Atkins is only twenty-four. There he is, a big, athletic guy who's always led a physical life. And two years ago he's blinded when his car goes off the road. His big problem now is that he's stir-crazy. He's got nothing to do, nothing to think about. Well, I intend to change all that. I admit that I like twisting the tail of insurance companies, just for the exercise. But, believe me, Great Lakes is going to change Ken Atkins' life. They're going to support his family while he goes to school, they're going to train him for a profession, if necessary they're going to set him up."

Ben laid down the menu and stared at his companion. "This is a new tune for you, Mike."

"What the hell, Ben? Most of us spend our lives not getting much done. I'll bet it's the same with you as it is with me. I may get a niggling change in the interpretation of the antitrust laws into the casebooks. Oh, I'm not saying that there isn't satisfaction to be derived from that. There's the satisfaction of having done a good, professional job, even of having seen right prevail. But it hasn't changed anybody's life. And I've come to the conclusion that there isn't much pleasure in the middle-sized jobs."

"Like the ones I spend my time on?" Ben asked politely.

Michael Isham was too intent to notice the jab. "That's right. Real satisfaction comes from the big jobs—like devoting your life to outlawing child labor—or from the little jobs that make a big difference to one human being, that are damn near life transforming."

Ben was so silent that Isham had to prod him. "Don't you agree?"

"Oh, I agree. I can spend days working on a fairly important amendment to some legislation and it doesn't give me the same bang as helping one constituent who's gotten into a tangle with the Veterans Administration. But I wasn't thinking about me. Look, Mike, how would you like to transform two lives?"

"What?"

"I've been trying to think of the right lawyer for her since Friday. It's a girl called Mrs. Wanda Soczewinski. . . ."

— 12 —

Nero believed in bread and circuses, and so has every government since. The skimpier the loaf, the grander the pageantry. Washington, D.C., is no exception. At inconvenient intervals, Congressmen and civil servants with better things to do are asked to drop everything and participate in spectacles.

Ben Safford knew his duty, and, having promised to be on the South Lawn of the White House at three o'clock on Tuesday afternoon, he was there. But he was seething at the futility of the whole performance. If Newburg was anything to judge by, soybean prices and OSHA rules were not driven from anyone's mind by flapping flags and Presidential cavalcades. Ben did not know exactly what could make Elroy Hackett forget the Curry River Flood Control Project; he doubted if it was within the capacity of the Federal government to lay it on.

Greeting the Prime Minister of Canada sure as hell did not fit the bill.

"I suppose they'll get over it in time," he said with desperate fair-mindedness to Tony Martinelli. "All the others have."

New administrations were always ceremony-happy. It was

part of the human condition. Nor were Chief Executives the worst offenders. It was the White House staff, the new Cabinet members, the most recent regulatory and diplomatic appointees—all pleased as punch to be young, powerful and in the public eye. They were going to change the world overnight and they wanted everybody to see them do it.

Normally, Ben was tolerant of this failing. But there was another force, besides Elroy Hackett, beyond the control of the Federal government. That was the weather. Over the weekend, when these proceedings were being planned, there had been fleecy clouds and blue skies in Washington as well as South Bend, Indiana. The master of protocol had extended himself—an honor guard to be inspected, the Marine band to play, speeches to be delivered. Unfortunately, Mother Nature had produced a steady drizzle, not bad enough to cancel outdoor activities but sufficient to delay flights, to drip from hat brims into collars, to turn the South Lawn into a soggy morass.

"It may be too late by then," croaked Tony, who was sadly watching his black patent-leather shoes sink deeper and deeper into the mire. "Do you think the Canadians will ever get here?"

They were already half an hour late.

"It's just low visibility delaying them, not a typhoon," Ben pointed out before continuing on a more positive note. "And once they get the welcome ceremony out of the way, there's a reception inside. Say what you want about the White House, at least it's waterproof."

"We'll probably all have pneumonia before we get there," predicted a strangely disembodied voice.

Val Oakes could be heard, but not seen. He was gallantly sheltering Elsie Hollenbach under the grandfather of all umbrellas. From Ben's point of view, the two of them were hidden inside a gleaming black tent.

"I do not wish to raise false hopes," said Elsie suddenly, "but I believe I hear the sirens."

As usual, she was correct. Within seconds the banshee wail was audible to all. The limousine with its escort arrived and, right on the dot, the Presidential couple emerged from the

White House and came forward under a sheltering canopy. The Chief Executives shook hands and clasped shoulders, the first ladies embraced, from nowhere a small child appeared with a bouquet of American Beauty roses. Then the company stiffened to attention for the band's rendition of "The Star Spangled Banner" and "O Canada!," the honor guard was reviewed on the double and the last lap of the ceremonies was at hand.

Smiling benignly from his dry podium, the President spoke for eight minutes about the United States' good neighbor to the north. By rights, the Prime Minister should then have used the same amount of time in eulogizing Canada's great neighbor to the south. Had it not been for his nation's peculiar internal problems, no doubt that is what he would have done. But at the eight-minute mark, with terminal phrases rolling off his tongue, he suddenly raised his voice and picked up speed. Those present had time only for a brief premonitory shudder before he plunged into a word-for-word repetition of his speech—in French.

At precisely that moment the drizzle became a torrential downpour.

The discipline of public life kept the ranks from breaking. Huddled in misery, they simply endured as water cascaded off canopies, trombones and raincoats. The Prime Minister, his eyes rolling in apology, discharged his polished Gallic sentences at a faster and faster clip until, after the final benediction, he was swept off to the private quarters. The lesser fry stampeded into the shelter of the public rooms set apart for their entertainment.

With soaked garments out of the way, with the first bourbon down the hatch, the guests reverted to standard operating procedure. Even in ordinary times Washington social events are mere camouflage for the sleepless political instinct to caucus, to cajole, to buttonhole. This emphasis on personal contact, however, becomes intensified in the first year of any administration. Legislative and executive personnel are both busy sending out cautious feelers to discover what manner of beings they are dealing with.

100

Legislators at least have the advantage of being able to recognize their quarry.

"Look," said Elsie, who could dispose of any number of martinis and still be the first to see what was going on. "Why do you suppose Lou is bringing Joseph Buckley over here?"

"Buckley? He's Secretary of HEW," Val Oakes rumbled accusingly.

"One of the Kennedy leftovers," Tony chimed in. "Always available."

Ben could have made the identification without all this assistance. Joe Buckley had been one of the last Cabinet appointees to climb aboard the Ship of State, and it was barely two months since his picture had been plastered all over front pages and television. In his publicity Buckley had been smiling and relaxed. Today, however, he looked strained and intent. Ben didn't make the mistake of suspecting a crisis in government. Buckley was merely trying to match the right face to the right dossier. That creased forehead, that tight jaw merely signaled the effort not to take Val Oakes for a Democrat from southern Ohio or Ben Safford for a Republican from South Dakota. It was not so long ago that an Under Secretary of Defense had somehow managed to identify Tony Martinelli as the elected representative of the Mormon Church from Salt Lake City.

"And this is Elsie Hollenbach," said Lou after the difficult hurdles had been negotiated.

"Mrs. Hollenbach, of course!" cried Buckley with genuine pleasure.

There were still so few women on the Hill that they stood out. For a man struggling to master over five hundred faces, they were oases in the desert.

Flecker didn't let them stray into small talk. "Joe here has just been telling me about an interesting proposition that was put to him. I thought you'd like to hear about it."

"It only happened this morning," said Buckley, taking up the tale. "The lobbyist for the insurance trade association called. Jackson started off by apologizing for taking up my time on such a small matter. He just wanted to bring to my attention a petty detail in paperwork that had been overlooked."

101

Val Oakes emerged from his glass suspiciously. "In this town when people describe one of their problems as petty, it usually means that they've got a real tiger by the tail."

"That's the way I figured it." Buckley had shed his unnatural tension and was becoming more buoyant by the moment. "Jackson went on to say that naturally HEW wanted to give the health industry the same protection that the airlines and most manufacturers get."

Now everybody was suspicious.

"All it took to set things straight was a simple change in our application form for Medicaid," Buckley continued. "Just before the signature line, there'd be a new clause establishing limited liability for the provider of any health service. In exchange for this, the applicant would waive all other legal remedies." He paused as if politely assuring himself of his audience's attention.

He could not have been in any doubt, Ben thought. Tony was breathing in and out like a steam engine. Ben, on the other hand, realized he had been holding the same breath for several seconds. And Val was enveloped by the unnatural calm of a placid elephant who is about to stop being placid.

"The limit that Jackson suggested was five thousand dollars," Buckley ended neatly.

"Jesus Christ!" snarled Tony before he was drowned out by the explosions of his male colleagues.

Elsie of course reacted differently. First she waited for the tumult to subside. Then: "And what was your reply to this outrageous proposal?" she asked with such icy precision that Ben expected the air to crystallize.

"Oh, I told him where he could put his petty detail," Buckley chuckled, then paused in horror at his choice of phrase.

"Splendid!" said Elsie warmly.

The whole exchange passed by Tony, who was still boiling. "I suppose this bastard never mentioned malpractice suits?"

"Hell, he never even mentioned doctors." Buckley was becoming hilarious. "To hear him tell it, we were discussing innocent misfortunes happening to hospitals—a power breakdown, an elevator accident, an ambulance skidding on a rainy night. When I pressed him about medical personnel, he did allow that a nurse might give a patient the wrong diet tray."

Lou Flecker believed in giving new Cabinet Secretaries congratulations whenever possible. In his experience, the occasion seldom arose after the first six months.

"This end-run by the insurance companies could have raised Cain. We're all grateful, Joe, that you quashed it right at the start."

Buckley was modest. "I might not have seen the implications if I'd come to it cold," he admitted. "But this regional director we've got out in Newburg seems to be on his toes. He sent me a memo just last week predicting that the insurance companies would have to try something. And when I called him today after Jackson tried his little game, Trumbull brought me right up to date on everything. Or at least everything that's relevant to HEW. I suppose you could say that we don't have a justifiable interest in the more sensational details."

The wistful note of his conclusion was not lost on his listeners. Joe Buckley yearned for an irresponsible gossip about the murder embedded in Newburg's Medicaid scandal. But, far away in Ohio, Quentin Trumbull was being understandably cautious in his dealings with this unknown quantity now heading up HEW. Ben glanced at his colleagues. Surely a Cabinet Secretary who could fend off marauders like this deserved some encouragement? The way Val Oakes lowered his eyelids was as good as a vigorous nod from another man.

"It just so happens that the Police Chief back home is an old friend of mine," Ben began. "We were talking about the Karras murder the other day and he said . . ."

Five minutes later they were all well away on a tide of discussion and speculation.

"So the timing of the murder wasn't simply a weird coincidence," Buckley marveled. "There really isn't any other motive for the shooting except that malpractice suit?"

"None that the police have been able to come up with," Ben reported. "But you have to remember that the motive varies a little from person to person."

"It sure does." Lou Flecker had every reason to recall how

Theo Karras had served his subpoena. "Howard White was the only one Karras had directly attacked."

Elsie Hollenbach was at her crispest. "Come now, we mustn't forget that Dr. Rojak was actually placed at the scene of the crime. Oh, I know it was hours after the murder, but surely that argues some kind of contact."

"And from what your friend Chief Jones tells us," Oakes said, "that Rojak has a reputation for meeting trouble halfway. Maybe he decided not to wait for his subpoena."

"He admits as much," Ben pointed out. "But, according to Rojak, it was bribery, not shooting, he had in mind. Besides, if you ask me, the doctor who did the murder took good care not to be found at the scene of the crime."

"If it was a doctor."

Everybody stared at Tony as if he had gone mad.

"Look, I just thought of this," he defended himself. "If Karras was gunning for all the doctors, who was going to be the big loser?"

As the incredulous silence continued, he became impatient.

"Well, who's having hysterics all over Joe Buckley's phone? The insurance companies, that's who! The doctors were only afraid that something terrible might happen to them. But Larry Fournier knew he was going to lose a bundle. Maybe Karras was shot to put a stop to seven malpractice suits, not only one."

Elsie was the first to recover. "But, Tony," she protested, "Lawrence Fournier merely works for Great Lakes. He isn't going to lose anything himself."

"Like hell he isn't! The day his division becomes a money-making machine for people on welfare is the day he's out on his can."

"Personally, I wouldn't put anything past that industry." The telephone call from Jackson had left an indelible mark. Secretary Buckley was now prepared to believe that no outrage was beyond the men who had dreamed up that limited-liability clause. But, like all government officials, he had to reserve most of his attention for the broader issues. "Leaving aside the question of who actually killed Karras, we can all see how the poor guy's actions stirred up a hornet's nest. The doctors thought they were going to steal from HEW with impunity. The insurance companies thought they could cover these jokers without getting dragged into the mess. The AMA thought they could protect any individual member because of their group clout. Suddenly it's a whole new ballgame, and they're all roiling around trying to relieve the pressure. A lot of crazy things are bound to happen, from murder to trying to pull a fast one on me. What I don't understand is why there haven't been headlines from coast to coast. I assume the main facts are common knowledge?"

As Ben Safford reviewed the headlines and the front-page stories that had rocked Newburg during the past two weeks, he came to a surprising conclusion. "Not as much as you might think," he said finally. "Of course, the Cincinnati papers already had a crusade going when the murder broke. They had cast the doctors as villains, so they were satisfied with the surface outline—phony Medicaid bills were filed, Karras was smart enough to use that fact for a malpractice suit, and the minute he did, he was shot. They certainly weren't going to muddy the waters by suggesting Karras was an extortionist. But, for all I know, they never got wind of Rojak's testimony. There sure as hell hasn't been one single word about outsiders having access to HEW files."

Buckley grimaced. "I'd be the first to know if there had. And, as a matter of principle, I suppose our files shouldn't be used in lawsuits." He paused as a wonderful vista opened before him. "Not unless we're doing the suing."

Flecker sternly reminded him of administration policy. "And we're all agreed that wouldn't be in the best interests of the country."

"Of course not," said Buckley, unable to hide his regret. "Although I'd sure enjoy hauling some of these doctors into court. And it makes more sense for the Federal government to put them through the wringer than some unknown blackmailer."

Elsie was still suffering the aftereffects of Tony's wide-ranging suspicions. "Speaking of blackmailers, there's another possible solution to Theodore Karras' murder. Presumably he had a confederate who actually stole the documents from HEW. Maybe the confederate decided it would be more profitable to

105

continue the operation singlehandedly."

"No, that won't hold water anymore. I haven't had a chance to bring you up to date on the latest wrinkle." Rapidly Ben told them about the Kenneth Atkins suit and the emergence of high-powdered legal talent. "So whoever is feeding evidence to Mike Isham is not out for personal gain."

The committee members naturally were concerned with the impact of this development on their own plans. Tony, who had not forgotten Nesta Deachman's Gray Lady impersonation, predicted that now her husband really would have a heart attack. Flecker began to fuss about the possibility of a new delay in his faltering schedule. Val and Elsie were convinced that wily old Ben must have extracted the provenance of Atkins' medical records from his good friend and political supporter.

Joe Buckley's attention, however, had been riveted by a familiar name. "Michael Isham!" he repeated. "According to Trumbull, he's the one who's turning the screw on Great Lakes."

"That sure was what he had in mind," Ben agreed.

"And now that Jackson hasn't gotten any change from me, I suppose he'll be canvassing the rest of Washington," Buckley predicted darkly. "I guess I'd better start warning some people."

He left them almost immediately to start the good work, and Flecker, watching his jaunty progress across the room, said: "Pleased with himself, isn't he?"

"And who can blame him?" Tony asked. "So far Buckley's been smart enough to take coaching from a regional director and to dodge a bean ball thrown at him by some lobbyist. That's not bad going for a rookie."

To a man, they agreed that they had all seen dumber Cabinet members. But they shared the legislator's ingrained distrust of non-elected officeholders. When Ben remarked that it was still early in the game, Val replied somberly:

"It sure is. Great Lakes may have to take a trouncing from your pal Isham this time, but they're not going to make a habit of it. They've got to do something. The only question is what."

—— 13 ——

Larry Fournier was way ahead of the subcommittee. When Michael Isham, baring his teeth in a wolflike grin, announced a decided preference for taking his case before a jury, the soul-searching began.

The law department at Great Lakes, far from being helpful, was affronted at the mere suggestion of a courtroom defense.

"We're not miracle workers, you know," they said testily. "Look what Isham has going for him. First, there's the policy-holder. Everyone knows he's defrauding the government to the tune of a hundred thousand a year."

By now Fournier was desperate. "Isn't that what we've got jury selection for? Can't you keep out the people who know that?"

"What's prejudicial about it?" they challenged. "All the papers did was print the grand total of his billings. White himself testified before the subcommittee that the amount just showed how hard-working he is. Besides, fraud is the least of your problems. Half of Ohio is convinced that he's a murderer to boot. That's your client. Now take a look at Isham's."

Fournier appreciated another distinction that was being made: Howard White was *your* client, not *our* client. The law department proceeded to elaborate.

"According to our reports, Wanda Soczewinski is young, pretty and worn to the bone trying to make a home for two small children and a dying husband. What's more, White knew all about her circumstances because when she came to him for anemia he insisted on talking with the specialist treating her husband."

"Does she say that?" Fournier demanded. "How do we know it's true?"

They looked at him as if he were six years old. "Because White charged for the consultation. You know, it's not just the plaintiff who can subpoena HEW records. *We've* looked at them, too."

Fournier had never been a last-ditcher by nature, but this seemed to be the time to start. "All right, all right. So White's an SOB and the Soczewinski girl is a saint. That doesn't change the facts. We all know that White couldn't have damaged her because he never operated on her."

"He couldn't have damaged her physically," said a legal precisionist. "But what about psychic damage from defamation?"

"Defamation?"

"Picture how it's going to look to a jury. There's Tommy Soczewinski in a wheelchair, trying to defend his wife with his last ounce of strength. There's Wanda Soczewinski looking young and frail and embarrassed. And there's Isham describing how she's working herself to death taking care of a husband who's been incapable of fathering a child for over two years when along comes White to tell the world—entirely for his own fraudulent purposes—that she has to have an abortion."

This aspect had never occurred to Lawrence Fournier. "Oh, my God!" he cried.

At that moment he abandoned all resistance to Michael Isham's claims in behalf of Mrs. Soczewinski. In his heart of hearts he knew that he was not going to contest the Kenneth Atkins case either. All that was so much spilled milk. Great Lakes could survive two settlements. But was there any end in sight?

There was no point in looking to allies. HEW, in the person of Quentin Trumbull, had flatly refused to endorse Medicaid fraud. The insurance industry, when alerted to the problem, had spurred its lobbyist into action that had failed. The AMA had not only rejected sanctions against embezzling members but had mounted threats of its own.

By the time that Lawrence Fournier was meeting with Michael Isham to exchange one large check for a battery of releases, he had reached a fundamental decision. Potential allies were either hostile or helpless. All the firepower was in the hands of that unknown X who, with such unnerving omniscience, raided HEW files at will, unearthed uniquely deserving plaintiffs, selected ideal lawyers. Maybe it was a signal of submission to X that was needed. Fournier was beginning to think of X as some primitive deity belching thunder and lightning unless propitiated with a sacrificial offering. And he knew just where to find the sacrifice.

He was already making his plans as he handed over the check and rose to say goodbye.

"No hard feelings I hope, Isham," he said producing a weak smile and a limp handshake.

Michael Isham patted the breast pocket where he had placed his haul.

"None in the world," he trumpeted joyfully.

Two hours later the scene was the same, except that Dr. Howard White was occupying Isham's chair.

"Now that you know the size of the settlement Great Lakes

has had to make with Mrs. Soczewinski," Fournier continued his introduction, "I'm sure you won't be surprised at our additional actions."

"Go on." White's shoulders were hunched as if prepared for the battering to come.

"We would, of course, be fully justified in seeking full monetary restitution from you."

White flapped an impatient hand. "I'd like to see you try," he grunted. But it was an automatic defiance. He was too intent on the blow that was coming to produce his usual outrage.

"But our directors have decided that under the circumstances they will forgo recovery." Actually the directors were trying to placate the AMA. "The one step they insist on is that your policy with us be canceled immediately."

White had never really believed it could happen to him. In spite of anticipation, in spite of calculation, in spite of financial preparation, he was so shocked he could not speak for several seconds.

"You can't get away with this," he said at last.

"Oh, yes we can."

"You don't understand." White licked suddenly dry lips. "It's not just me you'll be fighting, it's the whole AMA. You can't have thought of that."

There was no sympathy in Fournier's glance. "I have just had a very thorough discussion with the regional AMA outlining Great Lakes' proposed action."

"Well—what did they say?"

"They didn't like it, but what could they do about it?"

White stared in dismay. In his experience, the world always jumped through hoops for the AMA—the drug companies did, the insurance companies did, even Washington did. And now Lawrence Fournier was telling him that Great Lakes didn't give a damn whether the AMA was happy.

"That doesn't make any difference," he said doggedly. "I can still go to court and force you to insure me. Your agreement with the AMA obligates you to offer malpractice coverage to every licensed MD in the area."

Fournier might have been finishing his sentence for him. "Except where there has been fraud on the part of the policyholder."

"But that's in all insurance policies. It's supposed to protect you against people who lie in the application. It doesn't mean me."

"And against people who burn down their property to collect fire insurance or people who sell things and pretend they're stolen. A policy is not an invitation to steal from the company."

White was pleading now. "You call it canceling my coverage, but you know that you might just as well take away my license to practice. You can't do this to me."

Suddenly Fournier was tired of the whole exchange, tired of the stately phrases masking ugly realities. "Why the hell not?" he asked, almost conversationally. "Look, White, it's time you came down from the clouds. You've been robbing the government blind for years. Now, with the Soczewinski settlement, you've managed to rob Great Lakes. And still you think we're under some moral obligation to let you go on doing it. Well, we're not."

White had never heard his activities described so bluntly. It was as if the protective mantle of his profession had already evaporated.

"But it's not going to happen again," he stammered, sounding like a guilty adolescent. "That's all over."

"It could happen again tomorrow," Fournier said brutally. "You weren't just greedy with your rotten little schemes. That wasn't enough for you. You had to be lazy and stupid, too. You don't even know how much dynamite may be sitting in those HEW files. But, let me remind you, there's someone who does. And another Wanda Soczewinski out of your past could walk in here any time."

"Look, you're just trying to pressure me about the settlement, aren't you?" White assumed a ghastly parody of a smile. "Maybe I was over hasty about that. I could see my way to splitting the tab with you and then—"

"Forget it. There isn't going to be any deal. You're too hot to handle."

White was looking at an incomprehensible future. "But what am I going to do?" he asked.

"Look for a job."

There was a brief flash of the old White. "A job?" he gasped before stiffening. "That's out of the question."

"It's what quite a lot of us do." Fournier gave a harsh bark of laughter. "Maybe you could find an insurance company that would hire you."

White glared at him with something very close to hatred. "You don't know what I've done to get where I am and stay where I am. It can't all be wasted. It would be too unfair."

Fournier was not laughing anymore. "We've all made big mistakes," he said grimly, "and I guess we're all seeing the things we've worked for go down the drain."

"I didn't want you to hear it from anyone else, Connie," White told his wife almost humbly.

Connie White shook her head as if that simple action could somehow produce clarity from the tumbling kaleidoscope of her thoughts. Cut down on expenses! Sell the house! Move to another part of the country! It was all too much for her.

"They cut you off—just like that," she repeated dully. "Then it's all over with us."

"Oh, no, it isn't. Things could be even worse." Quickly he added: "You forget, doctors are always in demand."

She ignored his attempt to hearten her. "And I thought you'd taken care of everything," she said.

Sadly he shook his head. "So did I, Connie, so did I."

Patrick Costello was the only doctor who had taken Jim Rojak's reassurances about the future at face value. As soon as he learned the news, he dialed Giles Perrin at the local AMA, convinced there was some mistake.

"Giles, what's this I hear about Howard White? It can't be true that Great Lakes has canceled."

"I'm afraid it is, Pat." Perrin had the perfect voice for grave sympathy. In a pinch he could have substituted for an organ.

"But how can that be? I thought we'd agreed you were going to back him."

Perrin was gently reproachful. "We agreed that the medical association would remind Great Lakes that our agreement calls for coverage of all physicians."

"Then do it!"

"We have." Perrin, mindful that he was addressing one of the Newburg Seven, coughed delicately. "Unfortunately, it seems that there is a clause, a purely technical clause—you know what insurance fine print is like—that exempts the company in cases of fraud."

Perrin's tact was wasted on the raging Costello.

"You call that backing Howard? To hell with their fiddling technicality! Why don't you use some muscle on them? Tell them we'll all pull out of their plan and go someplace else. Remind them how much money they make out of us."

"That was exactly the line I took. I told them that this was no way for Great Lakes to keep us as friends."

"That's more like it. What did they say?"

Perrin choked at the mere recollection. "Fournier said: 'Who needs friends like you?'"

"What!"

For a moment the line buzzed as they both silently contemplated this blasphemy. Then Perrin completed his catalogue of woe. "And when I reminded him of our total premium payments, he laughed and said that Great Lakes would be losing money on us before these malpractice suits are over. He practi-

113

cally invited us to find another insurer. And really, Pat, if half the things he predicted come to pass, I don't know where we can go."

"Never mind about that. What are you doing for Howard?"

"What *can* we do? I've told you what they said to me."

"There must be plenty. After all, we contribute a mint to the AMA for just this sort of situation. Go to the national office. Make *them* do something."

Perrin was now on home ground. "Our contributions are used to lobby the government and educate the public. Well, Great Lakes isn't the government and it isn't the public. All they care about is dollars and cents."

He infused so much disgust into his final statement that a stranger would have found it hard to believe that he spent one day a week at his broker's, reviewing his stock portfolio.

Stubbornly Costello persisted in his assault. "Well, there must be some way to bring pressure to bear. Can't Washington force Great Lakes into line?"

"Apparently it's the other way around. HEW is simply handing out medical records to anyone who drops by with a subpoena. They're not doing a thing to protect us. Of course, I always said that it was a mistake to allow Medicaid to be administered . . ."

Pat Costello had already heard Perrin's speech on the iniquities of Federal intervention and he was not interested in a replay.

"So you mean you're just going to let poor Howard hang there, slowly twisting in the breeze?"

"I don't know what you mean," said Perrin, who did understand and did not care for the Watergate reference.

"Well, you're not doing much to help the poor guy."

"That is simply not so, Pat. I did everything I could. Even after Fournier started taking pot shots at the whole Newburg Medical Association, I hung in there. And I did manage to accomplish something. Great Lakes agreed not to make any attempt at reimbursement for its settlement with Mrs. Soczewinski."

"I thought Howard had already transferred everything into Connie's name."

"I wouldn't know about that," Perrin said loftily. "I merely thought he'd probably need the money."

This transformation of Howard White into overnight indigent startled Costello. "He's still a doctor," he said sharply.

After carefully examining this statement, Perrin accepted its accuracy. "Yes, yes, I suppose you could say that," he agreed slowly. "Of course, he won't be in private practice. And these MD's who go into research or work for companies, it's simply foolish to claim that they're the same as us. I always have maintained . . ."

Costello was not a sensitive man, but the detached nature of this observation sent a chill down his spine. Giles Perrin was making Howard sound like someone encountered a long time ago in a faraway land. How many weeks would it be before he was taking the same tone about Patrick Costello? "Oh, Costello," he would say, dredging up the name from the depths of memory, "yes, I believe I did know him once."

Pat gulped and barely listened to the organ notes still coming down the wire. It was a great mistake, he realized, to have adopted Jim Rojak's faith in the power of professional solidarity.

From now on, it was going to be every man for himself.

14

When Ben Safford had reluctantly left Newburg to take part in the extravaganza on the South Lawn, he had intended to remain in Washington long enough to record his vote on the farm bill, then return to his fence-mending in Ohio. These plans were scuttled when Lou Flecker, carrying a legal pad filled with scrawled notes, entered Ben's crowded office. He was too preoccupied for greetings.

"I've just been with the Speaker," he announced. "He's very upset about my adjourning the hearings in Newburg."

Three startled faces lifted.

"How can that be?" asked Ben. "We weren't getting anywhere. Did you explain to him that all of our witnesses are getting hit with malpractice suits?"

"That's when they're not getting grilled by the cops as murder suspects," Tony amplified.

Flecker shook his head. "He says it doesn't make any difference. The hearings have got to go on."

"Now, that's not like Gus," Val Oakes said comfortably. "I wonder what's biting him."

A martial voice spoke from the doorway. "Probably this irresponsible behavior by Gerry Ewell." Having said her piece, Elsie stalked into the room, sat bolt upright in a chair and impatiently waved away Ben's mute offer of hospitality.

Senator Gerald Ewell was a Democrat, and, by the rules, a fellow party member had to open the attack.

"What's Wonder Boy done this time?" demanded Tony.

"I was just coming to that." Lou squared his shoulders and resolutely carried on. "It seems that when Ewell was on *Face the Nation* last week he promised immediate action in clearing up the Medicaid mess. Then after Buckley talked to him at the White House yesterday, Ewell held a big press conference. He's proposing a bill that requires all HEW regional offices to isolate cases of fraud and immediately start criminal prosecutions. He wants to throw three or four hundred doctors in jail before year-end."

There was a horrified silence. Every member of Congress realized that the slow, steady seepage toward a national health program was reaching a critical point. There was not a single respectable body of opinion that condoned the current situation. Strange to say, this surface unanimity was the major obstacle to legislation because it blanketed at least a hundred different approaches. A complex process of synthesis was taking place whereby the hundred approaches were being reduced first to fifty, then to twenty and finally to a number small enough to permit conference negotiation.

Into this delicate web Senator Ewell had just thrust his big, heavy foot. He would distract attention from the real issues, force legislators into alliances they would later be stuck with and, incidentally, intensify the already serious shortage of doctors.

"You know," said Val Oakes reflectively, "I think the biggest barrier to running this country may be those nuts on the other side of the Hill."

Historically, relations between the two houses of Congress have always been tortuous. Recent elections have not helped, with too many successful candidates undergoing their political boot training on the Senate floor.

Lou Flecker, who would have enjoyed letting his hair down on this subject, made a misguided attempt to divert the storm. "I suppose we were all young and foolish once."

This piece of imbecility received the treatment it deserved.

"It is true that I was once as young as Gerry Ewell," said Elsie through clenched teeth, "but I have never been as foolish."

"Well, Gus is going to talk to the Majority Leader about it."

Flecker was answered by four heartfelt groans.

"And we all know how much good that will do, with the kind of party discipline they've got over there," he continued hurriedly. "So Gus wants all the medical hearings to be in action nonstop for the next couple of weeks. He figures that if we can't stifle Ewell, then we can drown him out."

"Back to Newburg, uh?" Tony Martinelli was unhappy.

"No, not Newburg," Lou said. "The mandate of the committee has been enlarged. We're staying in Washington and we're looking at the big, broad picture of Medicaid abuse, not just doctors charging for nonexistent treatment. We're going to call the bigwigs from Public Health, from the armed services—from Sweden, if we can get them. And Gus says the more headlines, the better."

Eugene Valingham Oakes had long been acknowledged as the supreme political realist by his colleagues.

"If that's what he really wants, Gus may be making a mistake not sending us back to Newburg," he rumbled. "Say what you want, a nice, juicy murder will get you headlines a lot sooner than some quack nobody's ever heard of."

118

Offhand, Ben would have agreed with Val—until he met Dr. Patrick Costello two days later.

"Costello? Dr. Patrick Costello?" Ben repeated doubtfully when Madge Anderson announced the visitor. "Say, wasn't he one of the . . . ?"

Madge proffered an old newspaper clipping. "This may refresh your memory."

Ben did not have to read very far. "That's what I thought. He comes after Deachman and Rojak. What do you think he wants? He sure wasn't seeking my company in Newburg."

Madge knew exactly what he meant. She raised an eyebrow in inquiry.

"Yes," he decided. "I'll want you to sit in on this. And bring your book with you."

Patrick Costello was so distracted when he entered that he did not notice Madge seating herself in a corner and poising a pencil. In fact, it took him some time to come to grips with Ben's presence. He began by stumbling over a small table, pushed himself away from it, managed to land successfully in a chair and then peered desperately around the room. After scanning the ceiling, the floor, the drapes, he allowed his glance finally to settle on Ben.

"It's hard to know how to begin," he said and stopped short.

Ben was deliberately formal. "Of course, Dr. Costello, I am aware that you have been subpoenaed to appear before the Subcommittee on Medicaid Abuse, and I assume you received our notice when we temporarily adjourned the hearings in Newburg."

"I know you left Newburg," Costello exclaimed petulantly. "But that hasn't helped things any. I tell you, I can't stand much more of this."

"The subcommittee's departure was largely due to lack of cooperation from the first three witnesses we called," Ben said stiffly.

Patrick Costello gave no indication that he had heard a word. He was continuing his lament.

"It was bad enough at the beginning, when the papers started all that lousy publicity. I can remember our discussing it at the hospital. We all agreed we'd never expected to see doctors smeared that way. Little did we know what was coming." Dr. Costello swiveled his head, inviting the world to share his wonder. "Say, what's she doing?"

"My secretary is taking notes of our conversation."

"Oh, no, she isn't. That way, you'd have me coming and going. We don't need notes to settle this problem."

"All right. Miss Anderson, would you put your book away?" Ben wanted a witness more than he wanted a written record. "Now, what's this problem, Dr. Costello?"

"My God, I want to get off the hook, that's the problem. I'm just as tough as the next guy, but things have gone beyond a joke. Do you know that the cops actually came to the medical building and questioned all of us? Now, how do you think that looks?"

Ben blandly returned his visitor's glare while he decided which question to answer. "No, I hadn't heard that."

"Well, you must have heard that yesterday Great Lakes canceled Howard White's malpractice insurance. For God's sake, if you don't know that, what do you know?" This was such an earth-shaking event in Dr. Costello's world, he never doubted it was receiving national attention.

The news did, in fact, interest Ben. He hoped that Great Lakes' action was the result of a gigantic settlement for Wanda Soczewinski. But at the moment inquiries on the subject would be tactless.

"Dr. Costello, I can see that you're upset at what the police and Great Lakes are doing, but I must remind you that none of this is the subcommittee's fault."

"You're the ones who are trying to put us out of business."

Ben's tone sharpened. "The subcommittee is a lot more in-

120

terested in encouraging doctors to behave responsibly and honestly than in putting them out of business."

"Oh, I know all about that system. You encourage the rest of the medical profession by making object lessons out of us." He narrowed his blue eyes and assumed a look of childlike cunning. "Well, Patrick G. Costello doesn't intend to be one of the whipping boys. It's not enough that you're yanking our insurance, now you want to throw us in jail. That's enough to scare me, and I'm not ashamed to admit it. I'm getting out from under, and I'm willing to pay for the privilege."

Ben could scarcely believe his ears. "Dr. Costello," he said warningly, "I am one member of a subcommittee that has five members. I am not even the chairman."

Patrick G. Costello was not the man to back down in the face of a little resistance. "Yes, but you're my Congressman, and it's your job to help me."

Ben was beginning to think that he didn't need a witness, he needed little men in white coats. Anybody who was foolish enough to offer a bribe in the face of a clear red light was foolish enough for anything. Across the room, Madge Anderson looked like one of the avenging furies.

In tones as portentous as he could manage, Ben said, "I think you may have been misled by recent political scandals. In spite of what you clearly believe, it is still not common practice to—"

Costello interrupted indignantly. "It's not just politicians, it's everybody. So why can't *I*? I began thinking of it as soon as I saw that Senator on *Face the Nation*."

Behind his left shoulder, Madge was violently semaphoring as she prominently mouthed the same set of syllables over and over again.

"Senator Ewell?" asked Ben, stalling.

"That's the one. I want you to keep him off my neck, and I'm ready to do the usual thing."

Suddenly light dawned. "Dr. Costello, do you mean that you

want immunity from prosecution if you testify?"

"Of course that's what I mean," the doctor snapped. "What else could I have in mind?"

"I can't imagine," Ben murmured absently. Who would ever have thought that Gerry Ewell's self-indulgence would bear such useful fruit? "Tell me, have you consulted your lawyer about this?"

Costello's eyes nearly started from his head. "Are you crazy? Look at the trouble that White and Deachman have gotten into with lawyers. I'm not going anywhere near one."

"I see." Ben nodded. It was not his job to explain the difference between lawyers working for you and those working against you. "If the chairman approves, it is possible, just barely possible, that we can provide immunity against Federal prosecution."

Costello folded his arms and struck a Napoleonic pose. "That's what I want, and I won't settle for less. Not one word do you get out of me otherwise. After all, I can always come down with heart trouble, too."

This remark erased the last of Ben's scruples. If the occasion should arise, there was plenty of time for Dr. Patrick Costello to learn that the murder of Theodore Karras was a matter for state prosecution. There was one point, however, that had to be raised.

"You do realize that any immunity granted by the subcommittee will not necessarily be a protection against Great Lakes?"

"Oh, yes, it will. I've thought the whole thing out." Costello hunched forward and explained his strategy. "If HEW can't prosecute me for fraud, there's no reason why I can't take the stand in my own defense and testify that I didn't perform any of those operations I charged for. So Great Lakes wouldn't lose a penny in a malpractice suit."

He beamed broadly, inviting congratulation.

"Always assuming the jury believed you," Ben said.

Costello was affronted. "Good God, why shouldn't they? I'm the doctor. I know whether I performed an operation. Besides," he continued buoyantly, "nobody's going to come after me, not now that I've changed sides. I'm going to be a voluntary, cooperative witness."

Many men have made this promise. Few have fulfilled it as completely as Patrick Costello did in the days that followed.

During the first few hours of the resumed hearings he behaved like any witness with something to hide. He weaseled, he hedged, he palliated, he justified. But when Elsie Hollenbach's turn at the microphone came, a miracle took place. It soon became apparent that, all his life, Costello had been looking for someone who found every tawdry detail of his existence as interesting as he did. In Elsie he recognized a genuine thirst for knowledge, in himself he discovered a genuine desire to instruct. A torrent of names, dates and facts began to pour across the subcommittee table. There were only a few newsmen in the room, but after twenty minutes with Mrs. Hollenbach at the helm they knew they had a front-page story.

"We call it ping-ponging," Costello told her chattily.

"I've never heard that expression before. Could you tell me what it means?" Elsie asked.

"You see, we all have offices in the same building. So when someone on Medicaid comes in to see me, I look him over and say he ought to see the internist across the hall. Then the internist sends him back to see the cardiologist, the cardiologist routes him to the neurologist and so on. By the time he gets to the end of the corridor, instead of just one billing, we've got eight or nine racked up. It really maximizes his visit."

"So it would seem." Elsie was devoid of all human expression.

Under these circumstances, Lou Flecker was far too shrewd to continue rotating the microphone. With silent unanimity the subcommittee delegated its tasks to one member, and the hearings became a dialogue. The success of these tactics was self-evident at four thirty when participants and onlookers spilled out into the waiting arms of television reporters eager to tape a few comments in time for the evening round-up. By six o'clock there were even headier signs of triumph.

"CBS has just asked Gus for permission to televise tomorrow's hearings." Flecker was so overcome he was whispering.

The next day was even better. In front of a packed gallery, Elsie Hollenbach made an incautious remark suggesting that she was now familiar with the depths of medical avarice.

"Oh, that's nothing. If you really want to clean up, you should try nursing homes," replied Costello, who seemed to have convinced himself that Elsie was on the brink of graduating from medical school.

Elsie cocked her head thoughtfully. "Of course, that way you get rid of the civilians, as it were," she reasoned. "You have a population consisting entirely of patients."

"That's only half of it. The big thing is to *own* the nursing home. And don't worry about the cost," he advised her earnestly. "The bank finances most of it. After all, why shouldn't they? It's a sure thing."

"Because the government is the ultimate guarantor?"

"Sure. A lot of people over sixty-five are already on Medicaid. So if a doctor decides a nursing home is a medical necessity, the tab just goes on their bill. And even if they're not on Medicaid when they go in, HEW picks them up when their money runs out. But the monthly fee is only the beginning. There are all the extras—examinations, tests, therapy, psychiatric observation."

Elsie was grim but determined. "And, as the patient's doctor, you have no competition in a nursing home. You decide on what services are necessary."

This was so obvious that Costello merely nodded. "But the real gold mine is prescriptions," he continued enthusiastically. "All you have to do is come to an understanding with a pharmacist. Then he can supply the stuff by the barrel, you okay it and the two of you split the take."

"And they all agree to this arrangement?"

"Well, naturally. Do you realize the mark-up on drugs? Besides," said Costello as if the thought had just occurred to him, "a pharmacist who didn't agree to the split would never get to fill a prescription for one of our nursing homes."

During the afternoon Costello regaled his audience with a further refinement on this scheme. It was possible for physician and pharmacist to set up their own drug house. Then the physician wrote brand prescriptions rather than generic prescriptions and the mark-up was even higher.

"All you have to do is make yourself into a company," Costello confided. "That's the way we handle the nursing homes. In 1972 we set up Rest Vale Homes, Inc. We just had to put in a hundred and twenty thousand, and in 1977, after all expenses, we made . . ."

That evening Gus sent more than congratulations; he sent reinforcements.

"We've got two full-time staff members now," Lou reported upon meeting Ben and Val on their way out to dinner. "They're going to winnow out some more witnesses for us. Gus doesn't want us to lose momentum now we've started rolling."

"That's fine for Gus, but what about poor Elsie?" Ben objected. "She's been on stage for two full days now and she's had about enough."

"It wouldn't be easy for me," said Val, wagging his head solemnly, "and I don't feel things the way she does."

Lou rushed to agree with them. "I know it's hard on Elsie. She's carrying the full load. But what can I do?" He raised his hands helplessly. "You saw what happened when I tried to spell her this morning. Costello clammed up, and then she had to work twice as hard as if I'd never interfered."

This was so true it needed no discussion. During the past forty-eight hours Lou had tried to introduce every single member of the subcommittee into the dialogue—to no avail.

"Elsie isn't the only one who's been in the spotlight," Ben said optimistically. "Maybe Costello will start to run down."

These hopes were dashed the next morning. Elsie arrived looking like an aristocrat on her way to the guillotine. Costello, on the other hand, came bouncing in, all boyish anticipation. Back in Newburg he had his own private gold mine and a certain status. In Washington, for the first time, he was tasting the sweets of fame. He could hardly wait to take Tony Martinelli aside and tell him that the headwaiter of a downtown restaurant had addressed him by name.

"And it was the first time I was there," he marveled.

Tony's reply was more a form of gargling than an attempt at human speech.

By eleven o'clock Elsie had decided on desperate measures. In an attempt to stem the flow of Patrick Costello's disclosures, she raised the hitherto banned topic of billing Medicaid for nonexistent services.

"I really don't know why we bothered with that," said Costello, willing to consider the subject philosophically. "After all, there are plenty of surgeons around who'll operate at the drop of a hat. You just shove your patient on to them for gallbladder or something, they give you the regular kick-back and everybody's happy."

"Everybody?" Elsie's control was beginning to weaken. "What about the patient?"

Dr. Costello defended himself. "Mrs. Hollenbach! I always make it a point to use a first-class surgeon."

After that Elsie pulled herself together and doggedly went on doing her duty, while Ben reflected that Wanda Soczewinski could be thankful that Howard White had confined himself to paper crime. He could have used a knife.

When Lou Flecker entered Ben's office six hours later with his daily ration of good news, it took him some time to realize that a mutiny was brewing.

126

"We've done it!" he said gleefully. "*Meet the Press* has scrubbed Gerry Ewell for this weekend. They want Elsie in his place. Gus says keep up the good work."

Lou had not expected the room to ring with cheers, but the total lack of response led him to examine his colleagues warily. Elsie Hollenbach was lying back in the most comfortable chair with her eyes closed. Val Oakes was examining the ceiling. Ben was looking for something in a drawer.

It was Tony Martinelli, who had his back to the room while he messed around with a small hotplate, who finally brought himself to reply.

"You want to know what Gus can do with his pep talks?" he asked with menacing calm.

"Oh, come on," Lou protested. "I know this has been a hard week for all of us, but Gus is just trying to get some results, Tony. He didn't invent Costello. Tony, what the hell are you doing over there, anyway?"

"I'm making tea," said Tony defiantly. "That's what Elsie wants and that's what Elsie is getting."

"And what Gus wanted was to have Ewell drowned out," Val said. "We've done it, and now we're through."

It was Ben's turn. "The whole thing is a circus. We're not Congressmen questioning a witness. We're an audience watching some kook act out a fantasy with a mother substitute."

Nervously, Lou cast a glance at the brooding, silent figure in the middle of the room. "If I'd only known you felt so strongly," he began and then could think of no conclusion.

"Here, Elsie," said Tony, tenderly offering a cup. "I think this stuff is dark enough to drink by now."

Given the personalities of the two principals, Tony, in spite of his office, did not resemble a ministering angel. He looked more like a second trying to get a punch-drunk fighter on his feet before the bell rang. What's more, he succeeded.

After an invigorating sip Elsie straightened and fixed a basilisk gaze on Flecker.

127

"As you know," she intoned somberly, "I am opposed to violence in all its forms on principle. But if I have to face that man for one more session, I shall not be responsible for the consequences."

"Attagirl!"

"But, Elsie! Tony!" Lou pleaded. "I'm on your side."

He had just made the decision. Like every chairman, Flecker spent his life alternately propitiating the party leadership and the members of his committee. Gus had just had three days' priority, and now, Lou realized, it was time to shift his weight to the other end of the seesaw.

"I'll tell you what," he cajoled. "We won't call Costello anymore."

"You'd better not."

"What's more, we won't even go public tomorrow. As a matter of fact, this fits in very well. You know Robarts, this staff man we've got now. Well, he's got a witness he wants us to see in executive session."

There were times, Ben mused, when Lou Flecker came apart under the pressure. "Now wait a minute," he said. "The whole point of our holding these hearings, Lou, is to attract publicity. If Robarts has decided this witness isn't appropriate for public hearings, then there's no point in calling him."

"But that's just it. Robarts refuses to make the decision himself," Lou replied. "He says that either this guy is exactly what we want or else he's too hot for anybody to handle."

— 15 —

"This guy" was Dr. Alexander Urquhart, and it took only ten minutes the next morning for the subcommittee to understand Robarts' quandary. Urquhart's credentials were overpowering. His illustrious career had included the Army Medical Corps, UNRRA, the World Health Organization, the U.S. Public Health and the Rockefeller Institute.

His paper record misled the committee. Of course, they knew that expert witnesses are never really unbiased. That, after all, is why special-interest groups hire economists, scientists and engineers to do the talking. What they are buying is the appearance of being above the battle. To a man, these professionals cultivate a veneer of scholarly detachment.

Compared to his colleagues, Alexander Urquhart might have been a bull in a china shop. He was a large, grizzled man of incredible vigor and passionate conviction. For his appearance on Capitol Hill he had chosen to wear a bright red shirt and a sky-blue tie under a disgraceful jacket. As he argued his case, the scrap of tissue he had applied to his chin after shaving waggled in rhythm to his speech. He freely characterized his opponents as a bunch of corrupt mercenaries or, at best, a pack of mindless idiots.

His platform was as startling as his personality.

"You want to know what to do with the present medical establishment?" he demanded, lowering bushy brows. "Well, I'll tell you. Sweep the whole damn thing away!"

The illustrative gesture accompanying this proposal toppled the carafe on the table. As Robarts rushed forward to mop up the stream of water, Urquhart continued, "You're not going to get anywhere with a lot of mincy-pincy little changes. The rot goes too deep. Now's the time to cut!"

At least three of the subcommittee members flinched at Urquhart's gusto. Only Elsie Hollenbach was unmoved.

"Perhaps you could be more specific, Doctor," she said composedly. "We would be interested in your detailed recommendations."

Urquhart grinned ferociously. "That *was* a specific recommendation."

Lou Flecker looked worried. A playful witness was the last thing the House leadership wanted as an encore to Patrick Costello.

"Come now, Doctor," he said impatiently. "We've been holding hearings for over a month, and we've learned a lot about some pretty nasty corners in modern medicine. But we do realize that there are many fine, dedicated men in the profession."

"So you think you know the worst," Urquhart said. "Oh, I've followed your proceedings in Bangor and Newburg, and I suppose they were all right. Although, if you ask me, you should have been able to have them without getting some poor lawyer gunned down. I even listened to that bastard Costello. Not that any of that even scratches the surface. When are you going to stop horsing around and get down to brass tacks?"

Tony Martinelli was stung. "Horsing around?" he repeated. "We've uncovered rip-offs wherever we've gone. What are you complaining about? That we haven't gone to every town in the country?"

"You're letting some petty thefts blind you to the big picture. Larceny doesn't have anything to do with medical care. Why, in Malaysia I had to protect the antibiotics with armed guards. But that didn't affect the real problem, which was a cholera epidemic."

Only Elsie was on top of the situation. "Granted that fraud does not directly relate to patient treatment, still it is a major defect in our present system." She narrowed her eyes. "Moreover, it diverts Federal funds that could be more usefully employed."

"I suppose you think that it's the crooked doctors who are a menace," Urquhart said. "Well, let me tell you, it's the *good* doctors who are imperiling decent health care!"

There was a moment's silence. Then Ben Safford cautiously ventured into the arena. "Would you care to expand that and explain to me why we couldn't use some more hard-working doctors?" he said, remembering good old Doc Yarborough cruising off Tahiti while sending in bills for long-dead patients.

"Sure." Urquhart was openly enjoying the subcommittee's reaction. "First off, you've got to realize that most doctors don't have the sense of a groundhog. How can they? From the minute they step inside a medical school, they start losing contact with reality. They're supposed to become high-powered specialists, to keep up with all the advances, to master the modern technology. So what happens?"

With a well-honed instinct for timing, he broke off to refresh himself.

"I'll make it easy for you. If you had a serious accident a hundred years ago, they'd cart you off to the nearest shelter. There some woman would run around stanching the blood, yelling for blankets, washing the dirt away. Her techniques may have been primitive, but she was addressing the right problem. She was trying to keep you alive. Now, suppose you got smashed up on the throughway in 1972 before my shock program."

Urquhart beamed at them as he prepared to reel off supporting evidence.

"They'd take you to a hospital. Someone would draw specimens for tests. The orthopedic man would want a lot of X-rays. The burns man would decide what skin grafts you'd need. The neural surgeon and the kidney specialist would get in on the act. In the meantime you would die. My shock program is the modern equivalent of that housewife who had enough sense to put first things first."

Elsie Hollenbach was beginning to take his measure. "As a matter of fact, the subcommittee is familiar with your shock program and the quite remarkable results it achieved," she said. "But we can scarcely scrap an entire system because it has failed in a special instance. We are concerned with medical procedures over a broad range of applications."

Urquhart's smile became even wider. "So it's general applications you're interested in. What about birth and death? Is that general enough for you?" he added with genial contempt.

Four of the subcommittee members looked as if they suspected a trap. The fifth stretched and, for the first time, assumed an air of wakefulness.

"I like the sound of that," Val Oakes said. "But where are you going with it?"

"Nowhere unless we agree on certain fundamentals. I proceed on the assumption that a human being is born, lives a certain number of years and then dies."

Oakes nodded approvingly. "That's what the Good Book says. Threescore and ten."

"Fine! You're already way ahead of most doctors," Urquhart encouraged him. "Take birth, for instance. In nine cases out of ten delivery is normal. But, Jesus Christ, have you seen what's going on in the maternity wings these days? The standard procedures are designed for the one-in-a-thousand genuine emergency. It costs a hell of a lot, it wastes resources and, above all, it's turning women off. Before we know it, they'll be having their babies at home, where they're unprotected against the one overwhelming danger, infection."

Lou Flecker always made an effort to see both sides of the question. "I can see how it's wasteful, but why should the women complain?"

"Horse water! How would you like it if you got a small cut and some nitwit shoved you into intensive care?" Satisfied that he had quelled all signs of revolt, Urquhart went on, "The minute you get inside a hospital, everybody acts as if you're sick. But if what you're doing is natural, you're *not* sick. A mother delivering a baby isn't sick. And if you really want to get down to the crunch, an eighty-six-year-old man who's dying isn't sick. But try telling that to most doctors. Medicine doesn't have any business waging war against death. It should be concentrating on providing maximum function and maximum comfort throughout a normal life span. And I'm telling you that when an establishment has lost its marbles about birth, about death and about any accident you have in between, then it's ready to be junked."

Val Oakes was not only staying awake, he was bandying words with an expert witness. Dr. Alexander Urquhart was the only person in the room who did not recognize the compliment.

"Now, that all sounds pretty God-awful, Doc," Oakes said. "Got any suggestions for improving the situation?"

"Ah, ha! What do you think I came up here for? There's no mystery in providing decent health care, not if you've got the guts to ram your program through." His gaze roamed the table, seeking those qualities. "Mrs. Hollenbach, the first thing you have to do is take the administration out of the hands of the doctors. They don't know anything about running large institutions and they can't handle financial problems. It's like expecting Picasso to run the Metropolitan Museum of Art."

Elsie was competently taking notes. "Of course, doctors are often notoriously bad executives," she agreed.

"If that were only the worst of it." Urquhart fanned out three large-knuckled fingers. "First, they run hospitals for their own convenience instead of the patient's. That's why you have unnecessarily radical surgery. It's not that they're all crooks, but it's a lot easier to overdo rather than exercise judgment. Second, they're patsies for the drug companies, handing out estrogens and tranquilizers like peanuts. Finally, they're indifferent to the policy implications of what they do. Look at any city with old people on Medicaid. Somewhere you'll find an operating theater where a whole team of surgeons is putting a pacemaker into a ninety-two-year-old who's going to die the next week of kidney failure."

Tony Martinelli nodded. "The action always follows the money," he said sagely.

"Well, it shouldn't do so by accident," snapped Urquhart. "Nobody in his right mind would allocate scarce medical resources to the dying instead of the living."

"Naturally, we realize there's a shortage of doctors, but—" Lou Flecker began.

"Of course there's a shortage. And there will be as long as you people let the AMA walk all over you." Urquhart was still ruffled. "We need to triple the number of MD's. And not with a lot of dermatologists and plastic surgeons. What this country needs is an army of GP's."

"Medical students don't want to be GP's!"

Urquhart was beginning to flail again. Silently Robarts rose and removed the carafe to a side table.

"To hell with that! There are probably a lot of boys at West Point who don't like their first assignment. You should establish a dozen medical schools, support the kids through their training and then make them spend five years doing what the country needs. Apart from relieving the shortage, you'd get

134

some ballast into the medical profession that way."

Privately Ben thought you were more likely to get a doctors' strike, but he understood that to get information from Dr. Urquhart, you had to play by his rules. "And just what do you mean by ballast?" he asked.

"In the old days when doctors were GP's they had some common sense," said Urquhart, who had never spent a single day in general practice. "That kind of experience wouldn't be a bad idea for young doctors today."

"Maybe not," Flecker conceded, "but the Army can send officers where it wants because it pays their salaries. How are these young doctors going to be taken care of?"

Urquhart bared white teeth. "Exactly the same way. The sooner these kids are weaned from the fee-for-service system, the better."

Elsie Hollenbach drew herself up. "I fail to see that. Doctors have traditionally charged on the basis of services performed."

"Why the hell should they? If your house is ablaze, the fire department comes and puts it out without sending you a bill based on the size of the fire or the amount of work they had to do. If you hear burglars breaking into the house, you call the police without haggling about how much it's going to cost you. Those are public services designed to protect human life. So is medicine. Why should doctors be handled the same way as electricians and plumbers?"

Elsie was caught on the horns of a dilemma. She regarded fee-for-service as the hallmark of the professional. Urquhart had just reminded her of its use on a lower level.

"But surely there is a reason," she argued. "Fire and police protection has to be institutionalized. But doctors—and plumbers, if you like—are individuals. Would the taxpayer be willing to salary individuals whose major effort in any time period may be for someone else's benefit?"

Urquhart raised his bushy eyebrows. "That's what they do with their Congressmen," he retorted. "Honest to God, I don't

135

know what ails you people on the Hill. You set up Medicaid so that the more services a doctor performs, the more money he gets. Hasn't it crossed your minds that the mess you uncovered in Newburg would never have occurred if the doctors had been salaried? Doesn't that recommend a change to you at all?"

"It depends on the changes," said Flecker. "You're coming up with the kind of overhaul I'd expect from the Baader-Meinhof gang."

"You haven't heard the half of it," Urquhart promised.

Three hours later Ben Safford reeled back to his office, his head ringing. Lou Flecker, after announcing he would defer consideration of Dr. Urquhart's future role, had scuttled off to the seats of the mighty. Elsie and Val had disappeared, arm in arm. Only Tony trailed in Ben's wake.

Madge Anderson needed only one look to realize that refreshments should come before questions. She waited until they had collapsed with glasses in hand before asking:

"Well, what was Dick Robarts' mystery witness like?"

"He's a wild man," said Tony uncompromisingly.

Ben expanded on this simple judgment. "Oh, he's a real expert, there's no doubt about that. But he hits his audience like a train going downhill without brakes. Anything in his way is just going to get smashed to smithereens."

In some ways Madge was as much a politician as her employer. "Yes, but is he for or against a national health plan?" she asked with lively interest.

"Oh, he's very much for," Ben reassured her.

"And with allies like him, who needs enemies?" Tony added.

Madge was backed against the desk, her chin resting thoughtfully on one fist. "You mean you're not going to call him in open session, even though he's an expert and he's on your side?"

"How can we? The guy doesn't know how to behave." Tony looked confidently toward Ben for support. When it was not forthcoming, he sat upright, a perplexed frown forming.

Ben was studying the contents of his glass. At last he raised his eyes. "What makes you think he can't persuade the American public, Tony? He hasn't done a bad job on the committee."

"The committee!" Madge had every right to be dumfounded. The last people likely to be influenced by expert testimony are those to whom it is addressed. The subcommittee included many political views. Ben and Tony were the standard-bearers for thoroughgoing reforms. Elsie, representing her affluent suburb, was concerned with skyrocketing medical costs. Val and Lou were the two fiscal conservatives.

Until today it had been assumed that this spectrum would remain unchanged throughout the hearings.

"Dr. Urquhart," said Ben, almost strangling over the name, "has persuaded Val and Elsie to consider a major government role in health care."

At first Madge gaped. Then she tried to look on the bright side. "Well, you were hoping to persuade Mr. Oakes to modify some of his opinions."

"Val hasn't modified his opinions. He's had a religious conversion," Tony sputtered. "A week ago he wouldn't even listen to a national insurance program. Now he's ready to draft doctors, put the Public Health people in charge of all inoculations, establish Federal licensing, Federal medical schools and Federal panel practices."

Ben joined in the chorus: "Val says Urquhart is the first person who's come up with a coherent program."

"What's more, he's carrying Elsie along with him."

Nobody could have worked on the Hill for more than one week without grasping the implications of this statement. And Madge had been there for five years.

"But that means the Republicans on the committee are running away with the whole ballgame," she gasped.

137

The silence that followed was mute agreement. Then Ben became philosophical.

"Well, that's the way we reopened relations with mainland China. Maybe it has to be the Republicans who pass a national health program."

Tony, who had been sweating blood in the cause for three terms, was so indignant he was stuttering.

"Who cares about China?" he demanded. "How the hell am I supposed to explain this to my constituents?"

— 16 —

Closed sessions were taking place elsewhere. In Newburg, Ohio, for example, there were private discussions going on all over town.

At the Riverside Manor Nursing Home, where Dr. Arnold Deachman was still recuperating, Graham Friend, the manager, sat listening.

"... put through the call and it turned out to be some damned reporter from the *Chicago Tribune* asking about Costello," Deachman complained. "People don't come here to be disturbed by nuisance calls, Friend. You tell your switchboard that."

Friend nodded wearily.

"And I don't want people just dropping in whenever they please. The desk should check with me before they let anybody in to see me—and I mean anybody."

"I'll make a note of it," said Friend absently.

"See that you do," Deachman told him sharply.

The nursing staff classified Dr. Deachman as a difficult patient—demanding, ungrateful and self-pitying. Graham Friend knew better. Deachman in bathrobe and pajamas was no different from Deachman reviewing the books.

"How long are you planning to stay here at Riverside?" he asked.

Deachman, sitting in a comfortable chair near the window, gripped the armrests. "What the hell kind of question is that? I'm staying here until my doctor decides it's safe for me to go home."

Graham Friend was professionally unctuous. His capable head nurse ran the nursing home while he soothed, sympathized and deferred. For fifteen fat years Friend had offered Newburg families everything a first-class undertaker provides, this side of the grave. To the doctor who made all this possible he was prudently obsequious.

But Friend knew that Arnold Deachman's lawyer was a more frequent visitor than Deachman's doctor. He knew every word of Patrick Costello's performance in Washington, too. And he was scared enough to be himself.

"I know you've got problems, Deachman," he said with a new inflection. "But right now I think you're making one big mistake drawing attention to Riverside."

While Deachman gasped, he continued, "You'd better talk to that lawyer of yours about our arrangement here. That's what *I'm* doing."

"Why . . . why . . ."

But before Deachman could pull himself together, they were interrupted.

"Oh, Arnold. Out of bed? Do you think that's wise?"

Nesta hesitated on the threshold. She was carrying an armful of packages. "Oh, hello, Graham. Do you think Arnold should be out of bed?"

Graham Friend was all too willing to slip back into his traditional role. "Well, now, I'm not the doctor, you know."

"Never mind about that," Deachman growled. "You'll be

140

interested to hear, Nesta, that Friend thinks I'm bad publicity for Riverside just now. He's going to his lawyer to review our arrangements."

Nesta paid no attention to the querulous tone in her husband's voice. Instead she cocked her head, inspecting Graham Friend thoughtfully. The brilliant blue eyes were very cold.

"Who needs a lawyer? You're simply on the payroll here, Graham. You can leave any time." She paused before delivering her final thrust. "Or we can throw you out."

"Now, wait a minute. I have a proprietary interest—"

But she wouldn't let him finish. "Ten percent!" she said scornfully. "That's just to give you a bonus when you do your job properly. Have you forgotten that I know all the figures? You made a damn good thing out of us last year. If you don't watch your step, there won't be a *next* year."

As if the conversation were finished, she turned away from him and busied herself unwrapping books, depositing a new pair of slippers, tidying away some dried flower petals.

Friend stared at her back for a moment, then shifted his attention to her husband. But Deachman had recovered his assurance during the counterattack.

"You'll remember those points I raised, won't you, Friend?" he demanded.

Graham Friend knew when he was beaten. "I most certainly will," he said, withdrawing.

Nesta dropped her pretense of aloofness the moment the door closed. "Little rat," she muttered.

"He's just the first. They've all heard about Howard White by now. They've all read what Pat Costello is saying. And you know what's going to happen next, don't you? Great Lakes will pull *my* insurance. God knows I've done my best, but it's all been wasted effort." He was deliberately whipping himself into one of his unreasoning, unrestrained rages. "Everything was supposed to be over by now. Karras was just some cheap lawyer on the south side trying a shakedown, you all said. He

141

was supposed to have a hundred enemies. The police would go haring off in some other direction and there wouldn't be any more lawsuits. Instead, look what's going on."

With a sickening lurch in the pit of her stomach, Nesta realized that he was now in that frenzied stage where he would lash out at her.

"It's all your fault," he suddenly charged, just as she had known that he would. "Look what I've done for you. Look what—"

Clapping a gloved hand over his mouth, she spoke urgently, pleadingly. "*Don't* say it, Arnie. Try to get a grip on yourself. You don't know who may be listening. Do you want to ruin your whole life?" Her voice was almost hypnotic. "Think of me for a change. Haven't I been a good wife? Haven't I been trying to help you?"

He thrust her hand away, but the moment of crisis was over. Almost sullenly he agreed with her. "Oh, you mean well. But it's money, money, all the time with you, Nesta. If it isn't a diamond bracelet, it's a mink coat. And I gave in to you. That's the real trouble. I should have put my foot down. None of this would have happened if I had."

She knew it was untrue, but she was all too ready to encourage this new line of thought. "That's all over, Arnie. We'll be more economical now."

"You'll have to handle everything," he insisted. "I'm a sick man, I can't take any more. I don't want to hear about lawsuits or malpractice or Howard White . . . or anything."

Out in Curryville, Dr. White was not reciprocating.

"I suppose they'll sue Deachman once he comes out of hiding," he said with satisfaction. "Then Great Lakes will pull *his* insurance too. And as for that little bastard, Costello—"

He and Connie were barricaded in his den, the only small room in their whole house. They sat as they had been sitting every day since Great Lakes had canceled. Unlike her husband, Connie could still face the children, the housekeeper, the delivery men and the neighbors. But, since she was loyal and supportive, they were huddled together.

"I don't care about Deachman and Costello," she said warmly. "I care about us."

"Then they'll go after Jim Rojak..I've never liked him," said White. "He's too damned smart for his own good."

They had spent long hours on nondialogue like this. By now White was corroded with bitterness. Connie still thought there must be a way out.

"Howie, I understand you can't practice in Newburg anymore. But what about moving to someplace new—someplace like Hawaii? It would be hard on the kids and I'd hate to pull up roots, but—"

Bluntly he told her again what his lawyer had told him: no malpractice insurance in any one of the fifty states.

Connie bit her lip. Then: "But isn't there any way you can practice without insurance?"

"I could join the Army," he said sourly. "Or I could take a job with one of the oil companies and go to some hellhole in Arabia. Or I could become a medical missionary."

"Oh," she said, deflated. She knew that medical missionaries, even oil-company doctors, do not run to yachts, expensive colleges and ocean frontage on Cape Cod. She took a deep breath and forged ahead. "Howie, tell me: how soon are we going to have to sell the house?"

"Soon," he said in anguish.

Straightening her shoulders, she said: "Well, you know how Phyllis is always saying that I'm really a born salesman. Maybe now's the time for me to ask her for a job in the real-estate firm."

"Oh, God," he moaned, burying his head in his hands.

She rubbed his neck. "Don't, Howie. Don't."

Raising his head, he peered at her blearily. "God damn them all to hell. That cheap little shyster. And that little slut of a Polack."

Mrs. Wanda Soczewinski looked around Charlene Gregorian's office with wide eyes. Usually the door was open and the throbbing life outside spilled in. Usually Mrs. Gregorian was yelling at somebody in the anteroom or answering the telephone while she looked up all the rules and regulations for someone. But today the phone was quiet by request. The door was shut. Mrs. Gregorian, her plump features crinkled into monkeylike concentration, was giving Wanda her undivided attention.

Wanda herself was bathed in the golden radiance of utter happiness. Otherwise, she would have been uncomfortable. But right then nothing could touch her.

"Two hundred and fifty thousand dollars," she breathed. "Mrs. Gregorian, we're never going to have to go on welfare again."

In the old days Charlene Gregorian would have been whooping with joy, rushing around getting the secretaries to congratulate Wanda, breaking out coffee and cookies. Now she said quietly, "You bet your sweet life you won't. Here, Wanda, you've got to sign this."

True, she looked immensely pleased. But it was an inner glow, not fireworks.

As Wanda Soczewinski carefully wrote, Mrs. Gregorian studied her benevolently, then said, "How's Tommy?"

With sunrise in her eyes, Wanda looked up. "He's down at Lundgren Ford—to see about getting a car that's all specially fitted out for a wheelchair."

"You're not going on a spending spree with all that loot, are you?" said Charlene with a fair assumption of severity. She didn't have to heed Wanda's earnest protestation. Michael

Isham had already been busy. The Soczewinskis were going to live on a modest income from an annuity tied up by the sharpest lawyer in Newburg. Wanda and Tommy were in no danger of spending sprees—or of fast talkers who had wonderful ways for them to invest their money.

" . . . kind of sorry for Dr. White because it's so much money," Wanda was saying, to Charlene's unconcealed horror. But she went on, "But Mr. Isham explained how it was the insurance company, not the doctor. And besides, he shouldn't have said those things about me."

"I wonder if he realizes that now," said Charlene, to herself rather than Wanda. "Well, that's his problem and good luck to him. Wanda, I'm awfully happy about this."

"I know you are, Mrs. Gregorian," said Wanda fervently. "You've been so good I don't know how I can thank you. I don't know what I would have done."

"That's what we're here for," said Mrs. Gregorian gruffly. "Now, Wanda, I've got a favor to ask you."

Unresentfully she watched the girl's struggle with sudden wariness. Wanda's life was a triumph and a tragedy. The goodness, the love, the gratitude were real; the innocence was gone forever.

"Anything you want, Mrs. Gregorian," said Wanda Soczewinski steadily.

More touched than she would admit, Charlene said, "I'd like you and Tommy to let me set up a press conference for you."

When Wanda looked blankly at her, Charlene said, "You see, we get so much flak about welfare, Wanda. I'd like to let everybody know that people do go off it."

"We-ell, it's okay for me," said Wanda honestly, "but I'll have to ask Tommy."

"Why don't I drop by tonight to ask, if that's all right?" said Charlene cunningly.

She had lit another candle. "Oh, that's wonderful," Wanda

145

exclaimed. "He loves talking to you. And I suppose it *is* a good idea to let people know how much we want to stand on our own feet."

Charlene Gregorian smiled blandly. She was using Wanda, but in a good cause. It wasn't going to be a media blitz, just a *Newburg News* feature. But before a lot of local sympathy built up for poor Dr. Howard White and his poor wife and his poor kids, Charlene Gregorian intended to remind the taxpayers about Wanda Soczewinski, former welfare mother. Tommy, she knew, would see what she was up to. But Tommy would be with her one hundred percent.

If they were reading about Pat Costello or Wanda Soczewinski at the Newburg Country Club, there was no sign of it. When Dr. James Rojak pulled into the parking lot, when he left his name at the switchboard, when he changed clothes in the locker room, he was met with exactly the same degree of cordiality that his visits always evoked. In many ways the club and Jim Rojak were made for each other. He might be contemptuous of the decorous Saturday-night entertainment, but he appreciated the excellent athletic facilities. He was a familiar figure on the tennis courts for eight months of the year and inside on the squash court during the other four. And when Rojak did something, he liked to do it well.

"That wasn't bad at all, Jim," said the tennis pro as they left the court after their hour together. "You're handling the follow-through on your volley a lot better."

"I've been working on it," Rojak admitted.

After approval came disapproval. "But if you don't do something about your base-line game, some chump is going to steal the tournament from you. You can't rush the net all the time."

This was another facet of the club that Rojak enjoyed. Like the flight room at the airport, like a sports-car rally, it gave him the illusion of participating as an insider in a totally different life—and a suitably virile one. The tournament they were

146

discussing was simply the club's annual event, but Wayne Milton analyzed technique and strategy as if he were coaching Rojak for Forest Hills. And Jim Rojak, who knew perfectly well that he could not pilot a Boeing 707 or tune up his own engine, was willing to abet the illusion.

"Got time for a drink, Wayne?" he suggested.

Milton consulted his watch. Here it was he who was the busy professional, and Rojak who was the patient.

"Glad to. I don't have to be back on the court for forty-five minutes."

Five minutes in the bar proved why Rojak, in his turn, was an ornament to the club. He made a habit of ordering lavishly, always choosing the top of the line whether it was whiskey or beer. He tipped everybody in sight. Unlike the brokers and real-estate agents, he was never guilty of touting for business. His conversation, rigorously confined to his hobbies, suggested not only that he was a man of leisure but that the other members were, too. And when his profession did obtrude—as it did now—it added immeasurably to the tone of the place to have the PA system request Dr. James Rojak to call Dr. Stephen Oldenberg.

"Don't have to leave, I hope?" said Wayne Milton when Jim returned to his seat.

"No, no. Just some test results." Rojak stuffed his notes into his pocket and returned to pleasure. "Now, about my backhand."

Milton was earnest. "You could improve it a lot in the next two weeks if you put in the time."

Rojak looked unconvinced. "Putting in time isn't going to change my nature."

"Oh, you're always going to play an aggressive game," the pro said in laughing agreement. "You'll still get nine out of ten of your points from your serve and the net. All I'm trying to do is stop you losing points at the base line."

Rojak produced his diary in token of surrender. "All right,

we'll try it your way. Why don't I have an hour with you this Thursday, then on Saturday and Tuesday? And I'll tell you what: if this scheme of yours seems to be working, I'm ready to put some real work into it, come spring. Then maybe I could blast out of these club games and get into some of the real amateur competition. Aren't there some sanctioned matches for the state playoffs?"

One of Rojak's many gifts was the ability to pick up a conversation at the same point where he had left it. This time he was forced to break off when Wesley Briggs paused at their table for a greeting. But after affable inquiries about a Briggs hunting trip in Michigan, he returned to his point.

"What do you think?"

"Well . . . I guess . . . that is, I mean to say it might work out."

It did not take a musician's ear to detect Milton's embarrassment. Another man might have ignored it. But that had never been the Rojak way.

"What's the matter, Wayne? You think my game's as good as it's ever going to get?"

"God, no! That's not it," Milton answered far too readily. Then, reminding himself that they were on his turf and Rojak was forcing the issue, he met the problem head on. "You see, Jim, the word's going around that you're next in line for one of those malpractice suits."

"So?" The challenge was unmistakable. "What effect is that supposed to have on my game?"

"I just didn't expect you to be making plans that far ahead," the pro answered sturdily. "If you want to know, we haven't seen a sign of the Whites or the Deachmans for over two weeks here."

All of Rojak's arrogance was to the fore. "You don't surprise me. They're probably shivering in their houses, waiting for the roof to fall in. But this is the last place I'd stay away from, it gives me a real sense of security. And hiding isn't the way I play the game, remember? I'm not hanging around the back court waiting to get clobbered. I'm going right in to make things happen my way."

The pro had long since realized that he was paid to help members straighten out their tennis, not their lives. He regularly disengaged himself from conversations about marital discord, sexual frustration, financial failure. The first step was to finish his beer.

"That's fine for tennis, Jim," he said after a mighty swallow. "Let's hope it works as well with this."

"Don't worry about me, Wayne. There are a lot of things worse than losing malpractice insurance, and I aim to avoid them all. You may not know it, but you're looking at a survivor."

The glass grounded with a thump. "I can tell that. And now I've got to get back to the courts." Milton was already on his feet. "Can you make it four o'clock on Thursday?"

"As far as I know. I'll give you a ring if anything turns up." Rojak's smile glinted defiantly. "But why should it? I'm not worried about a thing."

17

Nobody was tracking the activities of the Newburg Seven more carefully than the Newburg police.

They had followed Patrick Costello's testimony word by word, they had known about Howard White's cancellation within the hour, they had even had a little talk with Graham Friend about Dr. Arnold Deachman's profits from Riverside Manor.

"The whole thing gets crazier and crazier," Lieutenant George Doyle summarized for the benefit of Chief Owen Jones.

"You're not claiming those doctors don't have plenty to cover up, are you?" Jones asked. "If half of what Costello says is true, most of them should be up the river."

"Hell, yes. There's plenty of dirt to sweep under the rug. But I don't see how shooting Karras has helped anybody."

"It sure didn't do White much good. I hear he's closing his practice."

Doyle shook his head in baffled irritation. "And I haven't told you the latest on Theodore Karras. That makes less sense than the rest of it put together."

Momentarily Jones hoped that some interesting anomaly in the victim's private life might have emerged. "I told you to do more digging there," he congratulated himself.

"We dig any further, Owen, and we'll come out in China. I know more about Karras now than I do about my own wife. I've talked with his relatives, his neighbors, his clients, his oldest friends and everybody he routinely bumped into on his daily round. I've even had a session with the boys at the precinct house in his district."

"I thought Karras wasn't a criminal lawyer."

"He wasn't," Doyle replied. "But he was in the habit of obliging the people in his neighborhood. If somebody's kid got picked up on a first offense or somebody's husband got thrown in the drunk tank, Karras would roll around to do what he could. So he was no stranger to the precinct. When you get right down to it, it's surprising the number of fixes we can get on Karras. He was practically a regular at the Federal Building. In the old days they saw a lot of him in Immigration and Naturalization. Lately he's been spending more of his time at all the welfare offices. Only yesterday I was asking about him at HEW."

"Well, we already knew he had an inside contact at HEW. That must be how he latched on to the ammunition for his malpractice suits."

"But this time I was asking about Karras as a man. And everywhere you go, it's the same story. He was old-fashioned, he was small-time, he was a nut about social justice. But he was honest as the day is long. He was enough of an oddball, they all agree, to hanker after the idea of playing Santa Claus. He would have enjoyed dreaming up a scheme to defraud the insurance companies in order to benefit people like Wanda Soczewinski or Kenneth Atkins. But as for his taking a bribe from some doctor to double-cross his clients—no way!"

Chief Jones had good reason to distrust the judgment of ordinary Newburg citizens. Every time an embezzler at the bank was arrested, every time a lawyer was disbarred, his old friends were shocked and incredulous.

"Is that what the boys at the precinct say?" he asked skeptically.

Doyle let the words drop like individual stones. "That's what they say."

Jones produced a complicated sound—part grunt, part groan, part snarl. "All right, *their* word I'll take. But you can't just go around knocking perfectly good theories on the head, George. You've got to—"

Fortunately, the phone saved Doyle. The call wasn't long, but it diverted the Police Chief.

"Sure, send her in," he was saying. "George is right here with me. We'll both talk to her."

As he hung up, he looked inquiringly at his lieutenant. "Somebody called Charlene Gregorian wants to talk to whoever was at HEW yesterday. You know who she is?"

"Sure. I've never met her, but I've heard all about her. She's a bigwig at Social Security. You know the one I mean. She cleared things up for Duane's father."

Owen Jones was more than willing to be cordial to a lady who had helped the father of a policeman, but he never got the chance. Charlene took charge of the discussion while he was still drawing a chair forward.

"Somebody was with Quen Trumbull yesterday asking a lot of questions about Theo Karras," she said accusingly.

Doyle misunderstood. "I'm sorry I missed you, Mrs. Gregorian. I guess that was a real mistake. After all, Trumbull hasn't been at the agency for all the years you have."

"Never mind about that," Charlene flicked back. "It's not who you were talking to, it's the questions you were asking. Quen says that you've got some harebrained idea about Theo being an extortionist."

George Doyle suppressed a sigh. Not only was everybody he visited prepared to endorse Theodore Karras' character, now they were storming the police station with their testimonials.

"That's not quite fair," he said, using every ounce of control. "When a man is murdered, we have to look at all the possibilities. We've kept as much as possible out of the papers. But you know the HEW set-up, you must realize how it looks to an out-

152

sider. Karras had found some way to penetrate the HEW files and get the raw material for a bunch of malpractice suits. He was getting in touch with the doctors to put the pressure on. Of course, that doesn't necessarily mean he was out to line his own pockets. Maybe he was just trying to jack up the ante for his clients by getting the opposition nervous. But we have to be realistic: somebody blew his brains out because of what he was doing."

Charlene was aghast.

"There's another side to all this. We haven't forgotten that," Doyle pressed home his advantage. "Maybe Karras was honest and he had a partner who wasn't. But in that case you'd expect the shakedown attempts to continue."

"And this is the way you try to solve a murder!" It was an indictment, not a question.

Like all policemen, Owen Jones regularly modified his tone to suit the circumstances. If Doyle was going to be warm and sympathetic, then Jones automatically became harsh. "We have to work with what we've got. We still don't know how Karras arranged for Kenneth Atkins' file to surface. If we can't figure it out now, it's a cinch the murderer didn't foresee it."

"But Theo didn't bribe anybody at HEW. He never had any files until Wanda Soczewinski brought hers to him."

"Mrs. Gregorian, you knew Karras and we didn't. We respect your opinion, but there's no way anybody can know what he had and how he got it."

"Of course I know! I'm the one who rifled the Medicaid files. I'm the one who sent Wanda to Theo Karras!"

Both policemen froze into immobility and stared at their visitor. Charlene stared right back, her cheeks flushed with determination, her jaw cocked defiantly.

When Doyle at last found his voice, he spoke softly and slowly, as if to displace a minimum amount of air.

"Let me see if I've got this straight. You claim that you and Karras were in this together?"

Charlene shook her head so vigorously that the frosted blond

153

curls bobbed like corks. "There's no claiming about it, and Theo Karras didn't have the slightest idea what I was doing. I sent that file to Wanda Soczewinski and told her to take it to Theo. Then I repeated the operation with Kenneth Atkins and his file, but that time with Mike Isham."

"You got any proof on all this?" Owen Jones challenged.

"Well, that's a fine approach." Charlene was bristling with indignation. "I come here to straighten you out, and you're so hellbent on making Theo Karras out to be a blackmailer that you're not even interested in the truth. There's proof lying all over the place. For heaven's sake, I'm the one who did all the original work on those files, I'm the one who knows them backward and forward. The other five files I was going to send out are sitting in my apartment, so is the typewriter I used for notes to Wanda and Kenneth Atkins. My fingerprints are probably somewhere if you could be bothered to check."

"We've been interested in the truth all along," Chief Jones said gruffly. "What about you? How come you just got around to straightening us out?"

"That's because you're so proud of keeping everything out of the papers. All you've managed to do is mislead people. I knew Wanda would tell you what happened. That should have been enough. How was I to guess that you'd go tearing off in the opposite direction—until Quen Trumbull told me about the questions you were asking?"

"So you're just doing your duty in a murder investigation?"

"No." Charlene was looking at her motive for the first time. "I never thought twice about that. But I'm not going to have you smearing Theo Karras. God knows he had his faults. He could be completely unreasonable, and he liked seeing conspiracies around every corner. But the idea of extortion would simply never have crossed his mind."

"All right, all right!" This time the irritation was coming from Doyle. He had emerged from his bemusement, impatient to move the conversation along. "You're saying that Karras never had any file except the one relating to Dr. Howard White."

"Exactly." Charlene was relieved to see that the Newburg Police Department was finally taking it in. "The only reason he had that one was that I knew Wanda would be too timid to go to one of the flossy downtown offices. But she lived in the same neighborhood as Theo and she'd seen him around all her life."

Owen Jones belatedly saw where Doyle's reasoning would lead. He wanted to explore the possibilities, but not in front of an outsider. "Well, I'm glad you finally came in, Mrs. Gregorian," he said, placing his palms flat on the desk and hoisting himself upright. "I hope you realize that we may not be able to keep your activities to ourselves. As soon as we start checking out your story, somebody at HEW may get wise and—"

"That doesn't make any difference." In her attempt to be casual, Charlene was curt. "I told Quen Trumbull all about it before I came down here. That was only right."

Jones shrugged. "So long as you know what to expect. And if we find all this proof you've mentioned, we'll accept your story. But I'll be damned if I understand your reasons for starting this whole circus."

"You must have been crazy!" In spite of himself, Ben Safford could come up with no other explanation.

Michael Isham squeezed Charlene's elbow reassuringly. "Don't mind Ben," he advised her. "He's had a long, hard day."

Ben glared at the attorney even though his statement was undeniably true. The morning had been spent in Washington on the nagging question of natural-gas prices. The longer the debate continued, the more irreconcilable opposing viewpoints became. Then he had embarked on a jolting flight to Newburg and an endless taxi ride to Curryville, where he appeared as featured speaker to the Southern Ohio Soybean Conference.

155

There followed more taxis, more handshakes and another speech (this time to the Future Veterinarians of America). By the time he trudged up to the Lundgren front door, it was nine o'clock and he was dreaming of a hot tub and a rum toddy. Instead he was met in the front hall by his sister Janet fiercely whispering that she had her most tiresome in-laws in the living room and would he please make himself respectable at once.

Under most circumstances Mike Isham's arrival without the courtesy of a preceding phone call and with a wilting client tucked in his arm would have met a cool welcome. But half an hour listening to Martha Kirkland slander every living member of the Lundgren family had worked its familiar magic.

"Come in! Come in!" he had sung out joyfully. "We can talk privately over in *my* wing."

But somehow they had never got farther than Janet's kitchen. Partly this was because Charlene's blurted confession had halted Ben in his tracks. Partly it was because Mike had cast languishing glances at the electric percolater, which was just issuing its final thumps on the counter. Now, ten minutes later, they were established in the breakfast corner.

Ben had not revised his opinion. "Crazy as a coot," he repeated.

"I'm sorry for the trouble I'm causing Quen Trumbull. I'm sorry for using Theo and Mike." Charlene was pinkly defensive. "But I'm still not sorry that I did it."

"Good girl!"

Ben ignored this contribution from Mike Isham. "It's not as if you were some minor file clerk. You're a responsible Federal official."

"That's just the trouble. If I were a clerk, I might be innocent enough to think something would be done to those seven doctors. But I knew damn well they'd sail through the whole scandal and come out as if nothing had ever happened."

It was Ben's turn to be defensive. "I suppose it looks as if we're lying down on the job. Or, worse, that we just don't care."

156

"No, no," Charlene said swiftly. "It's not your fault or those other Congressmen's. Your job is to come up with a better health system, not to punish a few crooks. But you've got to remember that I personally know the people whose misery was enriching those doctors. I couldn't help contrasting the burning shame that Wanda Soczewinski felt at being on welfare with the total lack of shame with which Dr. Howard White used her Medicaid number every time he wanted a bigger boat."

Ben was finding it harder and harder to maintain a keen edge on his indignation. "I can see why you were mad," he admitted. "It's the next step that baffles me."

"At first, when I noticed that Wanda's file was the perfect material for a malpractice suit, it was just an academic observation." Charlene sounded almost nostalgic. "I told myself that if only the money were to come out of White's hide, I'd start something. But what was the point if an insurance company was going to protect him? I was really very stupid. It took me almost a week to realize that the insurance company wasn't going to sit down under that kind of loss. As soon as they saw what Medicaid fraud was costing *them,* they'd put a stop to it. If they didn't do it for one suit, they'd certainly do it for a whole series. And suddenly the whole ball of wax gelled. With a simple set of photostats I could get seven deserving people off welfare for life, I could give those seven crooks a kick in the groin they'd never forget and I could probably scare every other doctor in Newburg into being honest for at least a year."

Mike Isham beamed. "Beautiful, just beautiful," he murmured.

"I'm not denying that your motives were good. Hell, they were wonderful," Ben said in desperation. "But what about you? You've spent your whole life in Social Security. You'll lose your job. You may even lose your pension. And you're not a young woman."

"I thought about that. I knew it was a risk." Charlene was very dignified. "But my two girls have finished college. I decided I could always take care of myself. And then, when I went to see Mike to apologize, he said . . ." She trailed away in her first show of confusion. "You'd better explain that part, Mike."

Isham braced the fingertips of his right hand against those of the left and became every inch a counselor at law. "You may be leaping to conclusions, Congressman Safford," he said formally. "On what possible grounds could Mrs. Gregorian be discharged?"

"For God's sake, Mike! She raided confidential Federal files, she disseminated their contents to the public."

Isham's smile had thinned down to narrow legal specifications. "Any classification of 'confidential' implies that there are certain parties to whom distribution is proper. Are you aware that every document mailed by Mrs. Gregorian was simply a duplicate of information already forwarded to the same recipient?"

Ben knew more about Medicaid's budget than its method of payment. "Then why were her mailings such a bombshell?"

"Because the way HEW mails the information out, nobody can make head or tail of it," Charlene said bluntly. "I pruned."

Isham waved a magisterial hand. "Let *them* say that, honey, not you. And it doesn't change the legal position. Wanda Soczewinski already had everything you sent her. That makes her an appropriate person for distribution in the eyes of the Federal government. In addition, she has a statutory right-to-know that would have enabled her to get those documents. And, finally, Charlene did not disseminate anything to the public. It was Soczewinski and Atkins who chose to do that. When Charlene came to me with this story, I had no hesitation in offering myself as her advocate in the unlikely event that anyone at HEW contemplated action against her."

"Unlikely, is it?" Ben did not know whether to be outraged or hopeful.

"It sure is," said Mike, returning to normal. "How do you think the Cincinnati papers are going to play it when I tell

158

them that it was their investigative reporting that inspired Mrs. Gregorian's conduct?"

"You son of a B," Ben muttered in admiration. The message was clear as a bell. In the first place, any attempt to specify a charge against Charlene would stir muddy waters. Second, Michael Isham was expert at turning muddy waters into a strong current running in his client's favor. Third, with one phone call Mike was going to turn Charlene into a public heroine. "Under the circumstances, it probably *is* unlikely that HEW will make trouble. It's a cinch this Congressman will resist any such attempt."

Isham threw his head back with a bull-like roar of laughter. "I knew you'd see it our way, Ben."

Charlene, who had been anxiously watching first one man, then the other, gave a sigh of relief. "Then you really think I won't be fired? It sounds like a miracle."

"Hell, it's only simple justice. They ought to give you the Medal of Honor."

Ben decided somebody had to introduce a sobering note. "The question is, how many miracles do you need, Charlene? You may be out of the woods with HEW. But what are the police going to say about all this?"

"Oh, the police!" In Charlene's universe the men in blue came a long way behind HEW as upholders of social decency and compassion. "All they care about is that murder of theirs."

At that very moment Owen Jones and George Doyle were confirming Charlene's opinion of them.

"Okay, the squad car we sent says everything is in Mrs. Gregorian's apartment, just the way she said." The Police Chief was still disgruntled. "So we accept the lady's story as the truth. Where does that leave us?"

Doyle had been champing at the bit for hours. "The only file that Karras ever saw was the one that girl Wanda brought to him. He had no reason to expect to see any others. Nine chances out of ten, he thought Wanda had managed to get it out of HEW herself. Which means that Theodore Karras had no reason to see any doctor except Howard White."

"And in spite of that," said Jones, "we have Jim Rojak telling us that Karras called him out of the blue to try a shakedown."

"He was very careful to say that Karras didn't mention a shakedown specifically."

"What difference does that make? Rojak was lying through his teeth. Karras didn't call him and Karras wasn't blackmailing anybody."

Doyle was more cautious. "Rojak may not have known that."

"Holy Christ, George! We just proved he's lying."

"Sure he is. But don't forget the background. When Karras slapped that malpractice suit on White, he really shook up the whole bunch. All seven of them had a meeting that day, and they assumed he was out for what he could get."

"Why should they assume that?" Jones asked, genuinely puzzled. "Lawyers start suits every day without planning on extortion."

Doyle wondered if he could explain. "You haven't met these doctors, Owen. They're as crooked as corkscrews. Take Rojak. You should have seen him in Karras' shabby little office. He takes it for granted anybody that poor would do anything for a buck. Which means that if anybody tried to sell him a story about Karras' corruption, he'd swallow it, hook, line and sinker."

Jones rubbed his knuckles thoughtfully along his jaw. "If you've got something in mind, George, come on out with it."

"Try this on for size. White goes down to Karras' office to buy him off. Karras won't play, they quarrel and White kills him. God knows why. Maybe in his excitement White gives Karras more ammunition. Anyway, White beats it, and when he's back home, he realizes he left something behind. He considers his buddies and he decides that Rojak is the he-man in

160

the crowd. So he calls him, but he dresses up the story. He says Karras was the one who called, Karras was planning to fleece all seven of them, but he, White, has saved the day. In return for all this self-sacrifice he wants Rojak to go down the next morning and pick up his glove, his lighter or whatever it was. It's as safe as houses. If the body has already been discovered, Rojak simply walks away. If Rojak has to make the discovery himself, the body has been cold for hours."

"If it's that safe," Jones objected, "why doesn't White do it himself?"

"He's afraid of being recognized. That isn't a deserted street by evening. Say White parked in front of the newsstand or the drugstore. He doesn't want to stir anyone's memory." Doyle was growing enthusiastic. "And it explains one thing that's always bothered me. The reason Rojak went to the drugstore to phone in the murder was so that he could call White and tell him everything had worked out."

"I like it," Jones said slowly. "But you realize we don't have nearly enough to bring White in and question him."

"Hell, no! All we've got on White is logic. But we've caught Rojak in a couple of lies. That's plenty to start leaning on *him*."

Jones had not met Rojak, but he had heard enough to be dubious. A man who is not embarrassed by being exposed as an arrant thief has a thick skin.

"It's not going to bother him to be trapped in a couple of lies."

But Doyle was riding a crest of confidence. "It is if he thinks it opens him to serious suspicion of murder. Then he'll sink anyone else faster than you can spit. Believe me, when push comes to shove, Dr. James Rojak is looking out for number one!"

18

Within twenty-four hours the predictions of both Lieutenant Doyle and Michael Isham came to pass. When Dr. James Rojak was ordered to present himself at Police Headquarters the next day, he seemed to be expecting the summons.

"All right, then. Five-thirty." There was a pause, followed by a sound that could have been a sigh. "And don't get your handcuffs ready. I can clear myself without any trouble."

His lack of surprise might have been due to the fact that Charlene Gregorian's story was spread all over the front pages in Cincinnati, in Dayton, even in Chicago. The press corps had unanimously hailed her as a heroine.

At the Community Medical Building in Newburg, of course, she was viewed differently. There, only a thin veneer of normalcy remained. Patients still sat waiting, receptionists still granted appointments, doctors still appeared fleetingly. But, just below the surface, the Community Medical Building was riddled with dissension, fear and recrimination. This deterioration was amply evidenced by the early arrivals for a council of war.

Dr. Howard White chose to enter by the main entrance and

the public elevator. Using the private entrance would have shielded him, but he had decided that this was a gesture that had to be made. Nowadays his life consisted almost entirely of gestures. The substance had evaporated the day he became Great Lakes' sacrificial lamb. White nodded a greeting to his nurse, trying to ignore the fact that there were no patients in his waiting room. The whole rabbit warren of interconnecting cubicles was empty except for himself and Mrs. Blair, Miss Anstruther and the typist.

"You'll be glad to hear that we're holding a meeting this afternoon to discuss action," he announced with an eerie feeling that his voice was echoing through catacombs.

Mrs. Blair and Miss Anstruther had the inscrutable eyes of registered nurses. For the first time in many years White wished he could tell what they were thinking. Unconsciously he pressed for some kind of response. "Now that this woman at Social Security has come into the open—"

"Charlene Gregorian, Doctor," supplied Miss Anstruther acidly.

White did not know how to take this. "Charlene Gregorian," he repeated. "This announcement of hers has changed the entire picture. She actually admits using confidential medical records in a deliberate attempt to destroy me and other doctors. Obviously, there must be laws against that sort of conduct. And redress, too. . . ."

Groping for words with the right resonance, White did not notice their lack of attention until Mrs. Blair, after an exchange of glances with Miss Anstruther, said: "Doctor, since you're giving up all your appointments, you obviously don't need nurses anymore. Irene and I—and Leslie, too—have to start making plans." She saw his incomprehension and became more specific. "We have to start looking for new jobs."

While Howard White watched his world crumble, Arnold Deachman and Nesta were still fighting for theirs on the floor above.

"Yes, I'm feeling better, but I'm not up to seeing any patients," said Deachman to his junior associate, Dr. Garcia. There were still customers in these offices, although the receptionist reported some cancellations. "Mrs. Deachman and I have come in this afternoon for an important meeting. I don't have to tell you, Garcia, now that we know what's behind these so-called malpractice suits, we've got a real weapon."

Dr. Garcia's perfunctory interest drew a hostile glance from Nesta, who was restlessly lighting a cigarette. Charlene Gregorian's bombshell had blasted Deachman out of Riverside Manor Nursing Home, itching for a counterattack. But Nesta, who did not share his confidence, was assailed by apprehension. Usually she enjoyed sweeping into Arnold's office with a brilliant smile for the nurses and secretaries who had once been her co-workers. Today it had been an ordeal.

"Arnie says that we've been stymied until now because we didn't know who was doing this," she said, hoping for agreement. "But now it's a different ballgame."

Garcia merely nodded in silence. It was Deachman who grew enthusiastic. "Mrs. Deachman is sitting in with us because she has been dealing with Great Lakes while I was convalescing," he said weightily. "Not that there's any doubt about what line we should take with them. We have a right to demand that they stop this Gregorian woman in her tracks."

Nesta was wondering how long her husband could ignore Garcia's mask of impassivity when there was an interruption.

Jim Rojak, jaunty in a sports jacket, stuck his head in the door. "Somebody told me you'd left your sickbed to come down here and fight the good fight. How are you, Arnie? Nesta?"

Garcia muttered something about a patient and fled. Rojak looked after him appraisingly. "Poor guy thinks we're contagious," he said, apparently without ill will. "He should try going upstairs. Howie White is roaming around there pretending to be his usual cheerful self. I saw Eddie Cohen duck into the ladies' room to avoid him."

In the old days Nesta had claimed that a little of Rojak's insouciance would be a big improvement in her husband's colleagues. Today she was singing a different tune.

"Howard?" she gasped. "You mean someone was stupid enough to invite *him*? What in the world can he hope to gain by sitting in? He's already lost his insurance."

"He wants to get it back," Rojak told her bluntly.

Her jaw set. "At our expense. His being here could hurt the rest of us." She turned to her husband. "Can't you do something about it, Arnie?"

"I'm not sure that would be wise, although I agree that his presence may be an embarrassment," said Deachman. "Howard would have been wiser to stay away and rely on us to protect his interests."

Nesta was getting jolts from every direction. "Are you crazy, Arnie? We're going to have our work cut out protecting ourselves. Howard is already sunk. Of course it's too bad and all that, but it's not our fault he was at the head of the list."

All of Deachman's old pomposity seemed to have revived. "I refuse to concede that any one of us is sunk. And I shall certainly advocate that we stand by each other. We are all policyholders of Great Lakes. And now they have proof that these trumped-up charges are nothing but a cheap piece of malice, it is their clear duty to hold us harmless. Without regard to the fact that Howard White was number one on that list or—" he took a deep breath to go on—"or that I am number two."

Jim Rojak knew all about these numbers. "Arnie, do you really think this powwow is going to do any good?" he said with undisguised contempt.

Deachman flushed at his tone. "I wouldn't be here if I didn't."

"You and our buddy Pat Costello!" Rojak commented sardonically.

For a moment Deachman forgot his commitment to unity. "Costello!" he said indignantly. "Do you mean to say he has the gall to show his face—after what he did in Washington?"

"He's in the same mess we all are," said Rojak, dropping all pretense of amusement or detachment. "Isn't that what you just said?"

Arnold Deachman stared at him unblinkingly. "When we meet with the lawyers and Fournier at four o'clock—" his Rolex showed it was half past three—"I fully expect to find differences that will have to be ironed out."

"You certainly will if you go on insisting that we try to carry Howard White," Nesta burst out bitterly. "He's nothing but a dead weight now."

"Every man for himself, is that it, Nesta?" Rojak asked.

She refused to be intimidated. "Naturally, we have to look out for ourselves. And you don't have to act as if I'm pushing Howard White off the raft. The way I see it, he doesn't have a chance and it would just be silly to saddle ourselves with him when *we* still do."

"Oh, yeah?" said Rojak evenly. But he was looking at her husband.

Deachman set his lips stubbornly.

With a short laugh Rojak pushed himself off the corner of the desk. "What I need now is a good heart-to-heart with Howie White. I'll see you upstairs at four." And he strode out unceremoniously.

Nesta stared after him in bewilderment. "What was all that about?" she asked.

Deachman glared at her. "Can't you even put two and two together?" he demanded harshly. "My God, it was spread all over the front page."

"But that was all about the Gregorian woman and how she stole files from HEW," Nesta protested. "What are you suddenly so uptight for? You said that was a good thing, knowing who she was."

"A good thing for us and a bad thing for Jim Rojak," he instructed her flatly. "There are still murder charges pending. Or have you forgotten?"

She paled under her make-up. "But what does that have to do with us?" she stammered.

"It's what it has to do with Rojak that's important. He claimed Karras was trying to blackmail him, and we all accepted that. Then this woman comes along and blows his story sky high. Karras had no material with which to blackmail any doctor after Howard. Now that makes me start thinking." His death's-head grin made Nesta shrink. "And naturally it has the same effect on the police. They want to know why he really went to Karras' office."

"My God, Arnie, that's a terrible thing to suggest."

He lost all patience. "It's a lot better than what you've been doing. Here Rojak has just been ordered down to Police Headquarters, he's on the hot spot of his life, and you're prattling about how it's every man for himself, how we should stop standing by each other, how we should throw stragglers to the wolves. You can imagine how that all sounded to him. God only knows how much damage you've done, even though I tried to undo it."

She clasped a hand to her cheek. "Oh, no!" she cried. "But I didn't mean Jim, I was talking about Howard White."

"I think it was your general philosophy he was interested in," Deachman said with savage irony. "Why couldn't you take your cue from me? When you consider all that I have at stake—"

"You!" she snapped, getting to her feet with an energy that shook him out of his pose. "Why do you always think of yourself?"

"What are you doing?"

She was at the door. "I'm going to find Jim and tell him it's going to be all right."

"Nesta, for God's sake!"

But, whipped by emotion, she would not listen to him. "You've enjoyed this, haven't you, Arnie? Sitting there watching everybody at cross-purposes and feeling superior. You're the kind who cuts his nose off to spite his face. Have you considered how much this could cost? Don't you know there are other ways to handle people besides laughing at their misery?"

Deaf to his protest, she swept out.

Deachman sank back in his chair, clenching and unclenching his fists. Then, heavily, like a stricken old man, he forced himself to his feet.

— 19 —

The top floor of the Community Medical Building was a private lounge where doctors and their guests could drink and relax over a picturesque view of the Curry River. Traffic in and out was light most mornings, picked up as the day wore on, then peaked between five and six. Today, at four o'clock doctors were lining up for admission. So were lawyers and a delegation from Great Lakes Insurance Company.

Nesta Deachman, out of breath, hurried around the corner to join them. "Is Arnold here yet?" she demanded anxiously. "He's not in his office."

Somebody had seen him going inside earlier.

"Oh, that's a relief," she gasped. "He really shouldn't exert himself too much."

But even as she spoke, the line pressed forward with the mute impatience of all crowds. Nesta was too preoccupied to notice how many new faces had been added to the cast.

This was not lost on Jim Rojak. Hands in pockets, he surveyed the room. Arnold Deachman, pale and stone-faced, sat in an easy chair by the window, watching Nesta thread her way toward him. In the corner, at one of the tables, Pat Costello was alone but smiling hopefully. Howard White trailed in, ready to buttonhole any colleague he could. But also present were at least twenty Newburg doctors who had not, thus far, been part of a published list.

"What are you up to?" Rojak demanded of Lawrence Fournier, who was waiting for the group to settle. "I thought this was a business meeting. Calling a pep rally is a waste of everybody's time—including mine."

Fournier did not answer him directly. Instead, raising his voice commandingly, he addressed the room: "I think we're about ready to get started." When the buzz of individual conversations obediently died, he continued: "Dr. Rojak has just asked me to explain why we have enlarged the participation in this meeting."

"I think my client, Dr. Deachman, should have been consulted first," said a voice from the rear.

But before Fournier could reply, someone across the room yodeled: "Deachman's consulting days are over."

Arnold Deachman shrank at the taunt and the laughter it evoked.

His lawyer would have persevered if Howard White had not taken it upon himself to make peace. "We won't make any progress squabbling among ourselves. I vote to get down to work—that is to say, deciding how to neutralize this Gregorian woman."

He waited for applause. But most doctors were keeping their distance from White. With unkind frankness Jim Rojak said, "I don't think you've got a vote anymore, Howie. Me neither, if that's any consolation to you."

At this, lawyers and doctors began talking at once, their voices rising in agger, so that Fournier had to shout. "Quiet!" he bellowed.

Surprise, more than anything else, achieved the desired effect. Despite all that had happened, most Newburg doctors still did not grasp how the balance of power had shifted against them.

There was, however, one holdout. "Fournier, I demand to

know why you asked me here. *I* haven't been accused of Medicaid fraud. *I* haven't lost my malpractice insurance. *I* haven't been subpoenaed by a Congressional committee!"

"You were asked to join us, Doctor," said Fournier, equalizing with a vengeance, "because of your substantial Medicaid billings."

The chill that settled over the room satisfied him. At last the full implications of Charlene Gregorian's campaign were beginning to sink in.

"I'll ask our lawyer, Mr. Vail, to outline the current situation to you," he continued.

Vail, rising, presented the doctors with a succinct evaluation of Charlene's potential for further trouble.

"That's fine, Dave," said Fournier hastily when Vail showed a tendency to linger over Mrs. Gregorian's ingenuity. "So you see, gentlemen—and ladies—we have a real crisis before us."

He pronounced this death sentence, and waited. There was not a sound in the room. Then Nesta turned to her husband. "Arnie, why doesn't Phil say something? That's why you brought your lawyer—"

"Because there's nothing he can say," Deachman said bleakly.

A doctor in the front row was badly shaken. "But there's got to be some way we can reason with her so she won't just go on mowing us down, one after another."

Fournier had been expecting this. "That is exactly what Great Lakes hopes to do," he said. "Mr. Michael Isham, who is representing Mrs. Gregorian's interests, is due here in one hour—at which time we will try to persuade Mrs. Gregorian to drop these highly publicized tactics. Perhaps she can be convinced . . . er, that the sensationalism of her suits against Dr. White and Dr. Deachman has been sufficient for her purposes."

"Who are you trying to kid?" asked Jim Rojak. "You got us

together to say you're throwing all seven of us to the wolves, didn't you? Not just Howie and Arnie."

Fournier was stung. "We are trying to contain the damage. If this Gregorian woman stops hitting the headlines, it will be better for the medical profession—and for Great Lakes."

"You mean maybe she'll agree to sit on her other Medicaid files if you yank our malpractice insurance," Rojak said rudely.

Vail interjected himself: "We still don't know what Mrs. Gregorian's demands will be."

Rojak laughed in his face. "Oh, don't we? Come on! We're not kids. That woman is out to get us, and we know it as well as you do. The only question is how many it will take to satisfy her. Well, I'm putting an end to the pressure."

"But, Jim," somebody objected, "that's just guesswork. All that's actually happened is two lawsuits against—"

"Crap!" he shot back. "We've had a man murdered. We've got a woman who can blow us all sky high—and I don't mean just the seven of us. Well, you can sit around playing games, but I'm going to protect my own interests. And I'm going to start right now at Police Headquarters."

"Now, wait," Fournier began.

But with an insulting shrug Rojak ignored him, striding toward the door.

His departure was almost unnoticed in the babble triggered by his cold predictions.

"What was that? You mean they may yank *my* malpractice?"

"How can Great Lakes cancel if we're not sued?"

"Listen, Mueller, do something!"

With an effort Fournier tore his attention away from the door through which Rojak had vanished. "All right, let's all keep cool," he said abrasively. "Dr. Rojak is overreacting. Until we know what Mrs. Gregorian's demands are, we don't know what steps Great Lakes will be forced to take. At that time we

171

will inform you—and your attorneys—so that you can take any appropriate individual legal action you may want."

This unconciliating speech brought a howl of protest from all sides. Urgently, Vail tugged at Fournier's sleeve. "Larry, for God's sake," he said, "don't get them all steamed up again. We want some cooperation."

But the damage was done. Cooperation was now out of the question. Some doctors had followed Jim Rojak's example and stormed out. Others were consulting their lawyers in frantic undertones. The Deachmans sat still, as did Howard White.

Patrick Costello had formed a temporary alliance with fellow sufferers and was on his feet, hurling questions at Fournier.

"Goddam bunch of dummies," said Fournier without bothering to lower his voice.

Vail was getting alarmed. In twenty-five minutes the serious business of the day would begin with the arrival of Michael Isham. Between now and then Great Lakes needed a calm, collected Lawrence Fournier and some semblance of order.

"Larry," he said, recklessly assuming responsibility, "why don't you go take a walk? Let me sweet-talk this mob for a while and clear them out before Isham gets here."

He did not add that the original game plan, which had called for a disciplined delegation of doctors, was now blown.

To his relief, Fournier responded with a rueful smile. "Boy, Rojak really balled it up, didn't he?"

Vail nodded sympathetically.

Fournier looked at the scene before him. Then: "Okay, I'll fade for twenty minutes while you pick up the pieces. We'll have to play Isham by ear."

Vail was too experienced to show relief. "Okay, we play it by ear."

But Michael Isham, when he did arrive, had an innovation

of his own. Instead of confronting the doctors alone, he had re-
cruited an ally.

Accompanying him was the Honorable Benton Safford,
Member of Congress.

"Look, it'll be money in the bank," Isham had argued. "I
know just how Great Lakes will play this. Fournier's going to
have some doctors who don't cook their books. And he'll try to
break my heart showing me how much harm Mrs. Gregorian
can do to them.

"Ye-es?" Ben had replied without enthusiasm.

"So I turn up with the awful authority of the Federal government and it's a new horserace. We remind everybody that
we're not talking about Dr. Joe Blow. We're talking about a
major reform of the American medical system. That'll jolt
Great Lakes—and they'll be willing to cancel everybody that
Charlene even suspects of chiseling."

"I'm the muscle man?" Ben had suggested.

"That's right!"

As a result of this conversation, Ben found himself accompanying Isham into the enemy camp. As it happened, he had
never before visited the Community Medical Building, and he
was under no illusions about how welcome he would be. Assuming the gravity he usually reserved for Presidential visits to
the House of Representatives, he stalked in beside Isham, prepared to remind the doctors and Great Lakes of bigger forces
in the world.

They never got as far as the lounge. Their crowded elevator
stopped without incident at the second and third floors. But on
four the doors opened to reveal a near-riot. A milling crowd
filled the corridor, including many of the men Ben had expected to see upstairs. More compelling, however, was the woman
in a white coat who was sagging against a doorway, screaming
mechanically.

"Ai-ee!"

173

Without conscious thought, Ben pushed the hold button. As he did, Dr. Howard White appeared from nowhere, strode forward and slapped the hysterical woman.

With a ragged sob, she stared at him, then buried her face in her hands, moaning, "He's been killed! They've murdered him!"

The occupants of the elevator surged forward into the maelstrom of confused questions, aimless movements, feverish excitement. Ben, with Isham beside him, did not pause, but straight-armed his way through the human barrier to walk into a waiting room.

In the office beyond, Dr. James Rojak lay in a pool of vomit at the foot of the desk.

It did not take a doctor to see that he was dead.

— 20 —

When a patrol car radioed in the first news of Dr. James Rojak's death, Owen Jones responded with model efficiency. He issued careful orders to the patrol car, he dispatched a second unit to the scene and he then spent twenty minutes assembling his field team. By the time they arrived at the Community Medical Building, the situation was not only under control, it was developing along the right lines.

"I've got those doctors all penned up, just the way you wanted, Chief," the officer in charge reported. "And we got identification from everyone who left the building."

"Good," said Jones, preparing to pass on.

"But there's one more thing. I've got Steve Cella in with one of the nurses. She's giving him an earful."

"I told you not to start questioning anybody until I got here." Jones ran a tight enough ship to expect a good reason for this disobedience.

His subordinate grinned. "With her, it wasn't a question of starting. We would have had a hard time shutting her up. And so long as she was flowing, I thought we better keep her going until you could hear her yourself."

Jones nodded. Talking jags were notoriously unpredictable. Once the witness ran down—or was prematurely halted—the original impulse might not be recaptured.

"She really have anything to say?"

"Does she ever! You better take a look-see, Chief. They're in Room 207."

Jones signaled to George Doyle and the two of them broke off from the main party already on its way to the elevator. One flight of stairs and a short walk down the corridor brought them to a door which had been left ajar. They could see that Room 207 in its normal use was the waiting room of a pediatrician. The bright primary colors, the piles of comic books and wooden toys, the occasional piece of diminutive furniture all hinted at patients under the age of eight.

But the two people sitting on the sofa were oblivious to their surroundings. Officer Cella was perfect for his role. He was a grizzled veteran exuding fatherly wisdom and sympathy. At the moment he was saying: "It's no wonder you were upset, Mrs. Blair. He had no right to talk to you that way."

Mrs. Blair no longer had the inscrutable eyes of the registered nurse. Her cap had been flung off and her cheeks were flushed with color. She was formidably angry.

"Who does he think he is? I wouldn't take that from him even if he was still going to be paying my salary."

"No indeed." Having brought the conversation to the right point, Cella now decided to notice his superior. "Ah, here's Chief Jones. He'll want to thank you personally. It's because of Mrs. Blair's prompt action that we got here early enough to keep the scene from being trampled, Chief."

Cautiously Jones and Doyle moved forward with expressions of gratitude.

"When Mrs. Blair saw Dr. Rojak's body all contorted with the hypodermic lying right there, she went and called the police," Cella continued easily. "Now, you wouldn't think anyone would say that was wrong, would you?"

Jones murmured his agreement.

176

"But I'm sorry to say that Dr. White seems to have lost his head."

"He behaved like a madman," Mrs. Blair grated. "He claimed I was being paid to make trouble for him, he accused me of being in league with that Mrs. Gregorian and he threatened to blacklist me all over the country. Then he ordered me to call the police back and tell them it was a false alarm."

Cella shook his head. "As if it wasn't too late for that."

"It was too late right from the beginning. Imagine the nerve of it! He and Dr. Deachman were going to move the body, sign the death certificate and say it was a natural death."

"Oh, they were, were they?" growled Jones.

Retelling her story had relieved Mrs. Blair's emotions enough so that she now discarded the handkerchief she had been twisting and tearing as if it were some portion of Dr. Howard White's anatomy.

"They acted as if they were in control just because it happened in the medical building," she said on a calmer note. "Even though Nancy Diehl was making enough noise to bring people from all over."

"Nancy Diehl is the young technician who found the body," Cella explained in an aside.

"And she screamed the house down. Why, I saw Congressman Safford and Mr. Fournier crowding around the doorway. They certainly weren't going to join in any funny business. Particularly with Nancy yelling that it couldn't have been Dr. Rojak's allergy shot that killed him, that there must have been something else in the hypo."

"Silly, that's what Dr. White was," Cella concluded. "Just plain silly."

Along with her cap and her handkerchief, Mrs. Blair had abandoned the last shreds of professional decorum.

"He wasn't silly," she spat. "He was scared shitless."

The homicide squad was hard at work when Jones and Doyle arrived in Dr. Rojak's inner office. George Doyle took one look and whistled.

"This is some death to try and pass off as a heart attack."

Already chalk marks starkly outlined the body, the vomit, the hypodermic that lay with the other objects swept from the desk. A photographer was recording the overturned chair and the scars gouged along the side of the desk as if by flailing heels. A man crouched over the corpse, and a fingerprint specialist was awaiting his permission to approach. Dr. James Rojak still lay cramped in the tight arc of his final agony.

"It wouldn't have looked like this if White and Deachman had had their way," Chief Jones argued. "Rojak would have been laid out looking as peaceful as a baby, the hypodermic would have disappeared, the rug would be at the cleaner's. Do we have the story on the hypodermic yet?"

The photographer was the one who answered. "It's simple enough. Rojak was giving himself a series of allergy shots. That Nancy Diehl, the one who did all the blubbering, she says his nurse regularly put out the hypodermic and the ampule on his desk so he wouldn't forget."

Owen Jones' eyebrows rose. "I think I get the picture. There's a needle and some dope lying on the victim's desk for an unspecified period of time. Then he comes back to his office, shoots the stuff into himself and dies. What a set-up! That means we have a million unanswered questions. How long was the hypo there, who was on duty in this suite, was Rojak anyplace nearby, how many people knew about this allergy treatment of his? George, suppose you get the boys started on this. In the meantime I want some cooperation from the Coroner's office."

The man crouched by the body looked up alertly.

"Now, Pete," Jones continued, almost pleading, "just for once, will you forget you're a perfectionist? I know you're going to tell me that you've got to do a post-mortem and send the organs and the hypo for analysis before you can be sure of anything. So I'm not asking you to be sure, I'm not asking you to put anything in writing. I just want a starting point. Did Rojak die because of what was in that hypodermic? And if so, what was it?" His voice became a coaxing whisper. "Just an educated guess, that's all I'm asking."

Pete rose to reveal a wide grin. "It sure as hell wasn't an allergy shot. As for the educated guess, you can probably make one yourself—when you see what's in the wastebasket."

He led the way to the other side of the desk, which had been untouched by the havoc of Rojak's last convulsions. Pointing downward, he indicated an expensive, heavy, leather bucket. It was empty except for one crumpled sheet of paper and two small objects lost in the dark shadow.

Chief Jones peered into the depths. "Aren't those the little cartons for hypodermic ampules?" he asked.

"They sure are. And wait till you see what they contained." Pete was openly chortling. Normally, the Coroner's office does its detecting in the laboratory, not at the scene of the crime. "Say, Dave, shine your light in there, will you?"

Now, without disturbing the contents of the basket, the Chief could read the lettering. "Sodium pentothal," he breathed softly. "And is that compatible with the medical evidence so far?"

"Entirely compatible," Pete said. "If he shot that stuff directly into his bloodstream, he'd have been dead inside of seconds."

Owen Jones was plucking and releasing his lower lip. "There's one thing I don't understand. Rojak was thrashing around in here, knocking things over, falling on the floor and, if he couldn't manage to scream, he was at least groaning. How come nobody heard him?"

Pete was still enjoying his victory. "I thought of that one myself. In the first place, you've got to realize that the victim's movements would have been involuntary. He would have been strangling and vomiting and cramping. There wouldn't have been any rational activity like trying to reach the intercom. As for the rest, I'll let Dave tell it."

"I'd better begin by giving you Rojak's schedule today, Chief," Dave began as he flipped through several pages of his notebook. "His last patient was at three o'clock. He'd scrapped everything else to leave the afternoon free. First, he was attending this big meeting with the other doctors and their insurance company. Then he was going to do some errands before his appointment with you at Headquarters. So at three thirty he told his nurse and receptionist they could have the rest of the day off. They were out of here within five minutes. Well, you can see for yourself how these suites are arranged. There's a room between Rojak's office and the hall, and the sound-proofing in this building seems pretty good. He would have made plenty of noise, but there was nobody to hear him."

The Police Chief was seeing a good many things. Methodically he attacked them, one by one.

"All right, that means after three thirty there was no one on duty in this suite. And Rojak himself was tied up most of the time in a meeting. Do we know if his nurse put out his allergy shot before she left?"

"Yes, it was the last thing she did before leaving. I got her on the phone at her house." Dave decided to amplify this. "She said she even interrupted Rojak while he was talking to Dr. White to remind him of his shot."

Firmly, Jones refused to be distracted. "Let that go for a minute. Did you ask her if she told anybody that Rojak was letting her and the other girl go? That the suite would be empty all afternoon?"

"She didn't have to. Rojak was out in the corridor in front of a whole lot of people when he told her to close down the office. He made a big production out of it, said it was the last time he'd waste a whole afternoon on ancient history. He was even beefing because he had to detour out to the country club and rearrange his appointment with the tennis pro. Deachman and Costello agreed that it was a fine state of affairs when the police hassled a doctor that way," Dave concluded sardonically.

The Police Chief was too intent on the picture that was forming to appreciate sarcasm. "It's a beautiful set-up, isn't it?" he murmured. "First, everyone can figure out that Mrs. Gregorian's testimony has shot Rojak's story full of holes. Then Rojak himself tells the world that the police have stopped treating him with kid gloves and have ordered him down to the station. In addition, they all know that his offices are going to be vacant. And finally, as the cream in the coffee, there's a loaded hypo on his desk that Rojak is going to inject into himself without a second thought. Boy, if I'd wanted to shut him

180

up before he blabbed, I couldn't have asked for anything better."

Doyle, who had finished giving low-voiced instructions to two of his men, was modifying his earlier views. "No wonder they were trying to pass it off as a natural death. It was worth big risks for the six of them if there was any chance of avoiding this stinking mess. They must be sweating it out right now."

"Let them stew a little longer." Jones knew all about the softening process. "I want all the ammunition I can get before I talk to them. So far, we just know what Rojak was willing to say in public. Do we have anyone to tell us what went on in the lounge?"

"We've got that insurance guy, the one from Great Lakes," Dave offered. "He was in on the whole conference. I think Mike Isham and Congressman Safford came in after it ended."

"And they're still here?"

"Yeah, all three of them offered to stay. They're having coffee together down the hall."

Jones returned to more immediate problems. "All right, I'll see if they can tell me anything. In the meantime I want you to work on the source of the sodium pentothal. I know damn well we're going to find out that this building is full of it and that every doctor has access to it. Nonetheless, pin down exactly where it came from. And while you're at it, you can . . ."

Chief Jones joined the kaffeeklatsch five minutes later.

"I know you're all busy men and I appreciate your waiting here for me. Of course, we could have sent men to your offices, but this saves a lot of time, and just when it may make all the difference."

Ben Safford and Larry Fournier gravely replied that they were anxious to do all they could to assist the authorities.

Mike Isham chose a different approach. "Wild horses couldn't have dragged me away," he said with a gleam of white teeth. "My God, Owen, who would have thought a lousy little Medicaid fraud would pack so much dynamite?"

Ben had the grace to be shamed by Isham's frankness. He, too, had been motivated more by curiosity than by civic virtue.

181

"Anything we can do, Owen," he offered in vague expiation.

With the niceties out of the way, Jones became all policeman. "I want to know what went on at this meeting Rojak attended." He looked at Fournier. "Unless you figure it's confidential for some reason."

Larry Fournier was all too ready to talk. Because he had spent the last hour going over the scene in his own mind, he was able to deliver an almost verbatim transcript of what had been said upstairs.

When he finished, Jones expressed disappointment. "Then, except for Rojak describing his police appointment—to anyone who didn't already know about it—you just chewed over the insurance problem. The doctors thought Mrs. Gregorian's confession gave them a way out, and you told them it didn't."

Fournier nodded, but Ben Safford had an objection. "Wait a minute. There's more to it than that. From what Larry says, Rojak was the only one who included Theodore Karras' murder in the scenario, wasn't he?"

Mike Isham, who had been subjecting Fournier's narrative to step-by-step dissection, agreed with him. "You're right, Ben. Rojak saw a bigger problem than the rest of them. But for some reason he was confident he could handle it. And apparently he was going to begin the process down at Police Headquarters."

"You may be right." Larry Fournier was only partly convinced. "The one thing I am sure of is that he was confident to the point of arrogance."

Ben thought back to his encounter with Jim Rojak in the Federal Building. "Are you sure that wasn't just his style? Maybe it was all an act. Underneath he could have been as scared as everyone else."

"Maybe," said Fournier. "But he sure told all of us he was going to protect his interests."

"All of you?" Chief Jones narrowed his eyes as he saw the possibilities. "Or was Rojak talking to someone in particular?"

— 21 —

While Owen Jones was considering possibilities, his detectives were busy establishing facts. Armed with their findings, Jones entered the doctors' lounge half an hour later.

He wasted no time on preliminaries.

"Good afternoon. I hear some of you did your best to keep us from investigating Dr. Rojak's death. I want to know why."

Howard White rushed into speech. "I suppose you've been talking to Mrs. Blair. It's true that I took her to task for her hasty and ill-advised action in calling you. As a nurse, she should have remembered that is a decision for the attending physician."

"Maybe she didn't see any room for doubt," Jones suggested blandly.

"There is always room for professional judgment. Regardless of how simple the situation may look, there can be factors requiring skilled interpretation by a licensed medical doctor."

White had begun on the defensive, his words tumbling out, his eyes constantly gauging Jones' reaction. But the familiar phrases—*attending physician, professional judgment, li-*

censed medical doctor—soon worked their customary magic. By the time he paused for breath, he had regained much of his old confidence.

"Still claiming Rojak died of natural causes?" inquired Jones, curious to see how far White would go.

"Perhaps not natural in the strictest sense of the word," White conceded. "But still no occasion for a police investigation."

"You mean it was an accident?" Jones made no attempt to hide his incredulity. "Rojak mistook sodium pentothal for his allergy shot?"

White took a deep breath. "Surely that would be the kindest way to label Jim's death. Of course you can fault Dr. Deachman and myself for failing to follow the letter of the law. But can you really blame us?" All the organ stops were out now. "We were Jim's friends and we have a duty to that friendship. Would society be any better off if we were willing to smear a dead colleague, to distress his family, to destroy his memory?"

"So you're pushing suicide." It was a statement, not a question. Chief Jones had expected this gambit and had prepared himself to deal with it. But at the moment he was less interested in rebuttal than in Howard White's emergence as group spokesman. According to Larry Fournier, just two short hours ago White had been treated as little better than a hanger-on. Now the entire room was yielding him the floor. "Do the rest of you feel the same way?"

Nobody volunteered a remark.

"What about you, Dr. Deachman?" Jones pressed. "You seem to have pitched right in with Dr. White."

Arnold Deachman was lying on a couch while Nesta sat at his side, her eyes fixed on him with painful anxiety. He turned to face the Chief of Police, grunting as he shifted.

"Don't say anything, Arnie," his wife pleaded. "You know you shouldn't try and talk. Remember what it can do to you."

184

She turned on Jones. "Can't you see that my husband isn't well?"

Jones examined the couple. They both looked terrible. Nesta was pale and her make-up was blotched with tear streaks. Her breast heaved as if she were fighting to control herself. Arnold's reaction was quite different. His face was gray and haggard and he was abnormally inert, confining his movements to the bare minimum. There was no doubt he had received a shock, but his breathing was regular and his eyes focused clearly.

"Your husband has already refused medical attention once," Jones said for the record, "but the offer is still open. We can have the police surgeon here in a couple of minutes."

"He doesn't need medical attention," she retorted, her voice beginning to rise. "He needs rest and quiet. He should be back at the nursing home."

"Mrs. Deachman, there are six doctors in this room, counting your husband. Why are you the one writing prescriptions?" Jones recognized incipient hysteria and hoped to make use of it.

"I know Arnie, I know what's best for him." She caught her breath on a sob, and Dr. Deachman intervened.

"It's all right, Nesta, I can handle it," he said, his gaze still fixed on Jones. "What you say is true. I'm not ashamed of helping Howard White keep Jim's suicide from becoming public. Why should we have to go on suffering for what Jim did, with more headlines and more publicity? It's all over now, thank God. We can put it behind us and forget it ever happened."

The immense weariness in Deachman's voice made it easy to believe that he honestly wanted to put the past behind and never think of it again. That was about all Jones did believe.

"You really are a bunch of prizes, aren't you?" he said, deliberately challenging. "First you want to shovel Rojak out of here and pass him off as a heart attack. Then, when Mrs. Blair

185

gums that one up for you, you shift over to suicide for no good reason."

There was a spontaneous roar of protest and, for the first time, the doctors in the corner associated themselves with White and Deachman.

"What do you mean, no good reason?" Patrick Costello demanded, his round eyes bulging with indignation. "We all read about the Gregorian woman, and she blew holes in Jim's story about that murder."

"Sure, but was he bright enough to realize that?" said Jones, affecting skepticism. "He sounded pretty cool when we told him he'd have to come down to the station for further questioning."

They were all eager to correct him. Four or five voices were raised simultaneously. Jim Rojak always pretended to be cool, they said, but he had realized his danger, all right. In fact, he had specifically said so at their meeting.

"He put it even stronger than that. He said now the crunch had come, he was going to end the pressure. At the time I didn't realize he meant suicide," Costello babbled. "But it's clear now that's what he had in mind."

"No," protested a surgeon. "I'll bet it swept over him when he was about to take his allergy shot. Just seeing the hypodermic may have put the idea in Jim's head."

Jones was pleased with his tactics. Already he had extracted general agreement that Rojak's plans were common knowledge. Cautiously he inched down his list.

"What's all this about an allergy?" he asked innocently.

Obligingly they told him. Everyone knew about Jim's shots. He had tried converting the whole building to his new regimen.

"And even if he forgot about it, it didn't make any difference," the surgeon said, "because his nurse always put the stuff out for him."

It was too good to last. Jones was not surprised when his next question, aimed at the hour and a half during which Rojak's suite was empty, finally aroused suspicion.

"But why are you asking us all these questions?" said Costello, scenting danger.

"Well, there's another possibility besides suicide," Jones said.

"Nonsense!" Howard White exploded. "It's as plain as the nose on your face. Jim murdered Karras and thought he'd gotten away with it. He could afford to relax. Then, out of the blue, this Gregorian woman emerges. Jim must have been desperate from the moment he read her story. Finally you order him down to the station. He knows the end has come. There's nothing more he can do." White had fallen into a funeral cadence—slow, smooth, inexorable. "Finally he goes back to his office. He thinks of what lies ahead—notoriety, disgrace, jail. His eye falls on the hypodermic. He realizes there's an easy way out. The needle's right there and it's almost as if it were meant to be. He injects himself and dies."

Owen Jones' matter-of-fact tone broke the spell. "Having first wiped his fingerprints off the ampule container."

"Fingerprints?" Howard White sounded betrayed.

Systematically the Chief of Police continued to destroy the suicide theory. "What's more, the sodium pentothal didn't come from Rojak's drug supplies. It came from Dr. Barjian's."

"But Mark Barjian is in Europe." It was an involuntary objection from the surgeon.

Jones spelled out chapter and verse for them. "That's right. He's in Edinburgh for six months while his office here is closed. But someone opened the door to his suite with a key, smashed his drug cabinet and stole two ampules of sodium pentothal. No suicide behaved like that, particularly when Rojak's own office was filled with poisons that would have done the job just as well. Now, any of you people want to tell me who had access to Barjian's keys?"

187

Silence.

"All right. What about master keys? Keys that would open all the doctors' suites?"

There was still no verbal response, but the appalled glances exchanged by the doctors told Jones everything he wanted to know.

"Then I guess we're going to have to do this the hard way," he said menacingly. "Let's start with the order in which you arrived at the meeting and left the meeting."

The next hour proved to be a contest between witnesses and interrogator resulting in a draw. Everyone had had ample opportunity to lay a lethal trap for Jim Rojak. Nobody was cleared; on the other hand, nobody was pinpointed.

"And the keys aren't going to be much of a help, either," Doyle reported later as he and Jones headed for their car. "The whole pack of them has been in this building for over five years. I don't say they're casual about their keys with outsiders. But they go in and out of each other's offices enough so that the maintenance people say there are at least four master keys floating around."

"Just one big, happy family," said Jones. "Until they start knocking each other off. If you ask me, we're not going to get anything more here. They're all too familiar with the ground. We've established that they all had opportunity. And, God knows, we already knew that they all had the same motive."

"I wouldn't go that far, not about the motive," Doyle disagreed.

"For God's sake, George. Rojak *must* have been killed because of what he was going to spill."

Doyle nodded. "Sure. But I was talking about the motive for shooting Karras. It's all very well to say that he looked like a threat to all seven of them. But, by and large, people don't pull out guns until the threat is imminent. If you were the seventh man on that list, a lot of things could happen before Karras got to you."

188

Jones had no trouble translating this. "What you're really saying, George, is that you still like White as the murderer."

"You can't get away from the fact that Howard White was the one Karras was actually moving against. But I'll give you the fact that Deachman was next in line and, from what you say, Mrs. Deachman was pretty upset back there."

"She was so worried she was ready to flip. But that doesn't necessarily mean that she knows her husband is a killer." They had·reached the car. Jones waved his subordinate to the radio as he himself slipped into the driver's seat. Then he continued, "After all, she'd just seen the corpse. Probably it was a shock realizing just how deep a mess Deachman was involved in. Until then it had simply been talk and newspaper—"

Jones broke off because the radio was chattering a message at them. By the time it was over, George Doyle was grinning.

"Still want to go back to Headquarters, Owen? Dave seems to have found something interesting at Rojak's apartment."

But the car was already sweeping into a wide turn away from downtown Newburg.

"No wonder the lady was upset," Jones was saying fifteen minutes later, handing Nesta Deachman's letter to Doyle. "Her lover had just been murdered."

After a swift perusal, Doyle grinned. "He wasn't all that obliging as a lover. According to this, he'd just told her she was good enough to play games with, but he had no intention of getting married."

"He must have sugar-coated it some, because she was willing to go on the same as always. She says she'll meet him at the usual time on Labor Day. That means this letter is over a month old. Say, Dave," the Chief said, "are there any more of these things around?"

It almost needed a shout to reach Dave. Jim Rojak's apartment was actually a condominium that had been expensively remodeled. Most of the downstairs was one huge room, half of

189

it two floors high and half of it topped with a large balcony bedroom reached by a spiral staircase. In the back lurked a kitchen and a second bedroom converted into a study. As Dave loomed up by the railing and then came clattering down the stairs, Doyle allowed his glance to take in the sliding glass doors, the patio, the fireplace, the built-in hi-fi.

"Boy, this place must have cost a fortune," he said.

"Why should that bother Rojak?" Jones asked. "All he had to do was manufacture some fictitious Medicaid billings."

Dave's arrival brought their attention back to Rojak the victim, rather than Rojak the thief.

"No more pink love letters," he announced, "but there are some women's things in the bedroom and bathroom. The other stuff I wanted to show you is back here."

They followed him to the study. Even though it was a severely functional room, it bore signs of the Rojak penchant for spending money. The gun collection was housed in a custom-made cabinet, the desk stood on a handsome Oriental rug and the file cabinets were encased in solid walnut. One manila folder of correspondence was waiting for the Chief's inspection.

"Take a gander," Dave invited. "That line Rojak was shooting about toughing things out in Newburg was nothing but a bluff. He just didn't want anyone to know what he was up to."

The file had been systematically maintained. It began with a neatly clipped advertisement inviting applications for the post of medical director at an oil encampment in Kuwait. At a rapid clip there followed Rojak's application, an exchange about salary in which Rojak demanded all the traffic would bear, then a firm offer of the job. Dr. Rojak's acceptance had been written out yesterday.

"That sure spells it out," Jones sighed. "He knew he was in trouble from the minute Karras was murdered, so he started to open a line of retreat. But as long as there was a chance of riding it out, he wanted to keep his options open. Then when Mrs. Gregorian blew the whistle on him and we made it clear that we were really going to clamp down, he decided he didn't have a future in Newburg anymore and he took the job."

Doyle was willing to go further. "Rojak was no fool. He didn't think an oil company was going to harbor a murder suspect. So he wasn't planning a flit. He thought he could clear himself with us, finger the murderer and then take off for Kuwait."

"Which means it wasn't a simple case of his word against someone else's," Jones pointed out. "If he expected to leave town with our blessing, he had hard evidence."

"And we don't have a clue what it is," moaned Doyle. "Dave, haven't you come up with anything in this place?"

Dave was not sharing the general depression. "I don't know whether it helps, but I do have one last bit for you. It's real off-beat."

Like a magician, he whipped aside the leather-framed desk blotter to reveal an envelope lying beneath.

"There," he exclaimed. "What do you think of that?"

The envelope was empty, but nonetheless it packed a wallop. The letterhead in the upper left-hand corner was that of Theodore S. Karras, Attorney-at-Law. It had been addressed in handwriting to Jim Rojak at his home.

"For Christ sake! You mean Karras was writing to Rojak?" Jones cried in bewilderment. "But the whole point of Mrs. Gregorian's story was that the two of them didn't have anything to do with each other."

Dave beamed broadly. "That's what I thought until I went through the desk. Then I realized that the handwriting is Rojak's."

For a moment there was baffled silence. Then Doyle's mind began clicking on all cylinders. "Wait a minute!" he yelled. "Let me see that postmark." Without apology he snatched the envelope and held it to the desk light, squinting at the smudged figures. What he saw made him too excited for coherence. "I was right all the time! Except that I was wrong."

"You'd better explain that, George," Jones said patiently.

"I always said Rojak's leaving Karras' office to go to the drugstore was phony. But I thought he wanted to call somebody from a soundproof booth. That wasn't it at all. He needed an excuse to leave the building so he could mail this. The postmark is the day of Karras' murder. He picked up something in that office and wanted to get rid of it before we arrived—in case we searched him. So he raided the secretary's desk for a stamped envelope, addressed it to himself and then mailed it. I'll give you five to one there's a mailbox on that street before you get to the drugstore."

"And then what?"

"He gave it back to White just like I said all along."

They all stared at the envelope as if massive willpower could produce a picture of its original contents.

At last Chief Jones shrugged. "Not necessarily White. It could have been any of the others."

"All right then, Deachman. You say his wife was damn near hysterical. Maybe she knew her husband had just killed her lover."

"I doubt it. She was nervous as hell, but that could be explained easy enough by all this." A wave indicated the whole condominium. "She and Rojak may have been cautious enough for ordinary purposes. But if she's got any sense, she knows a murder investigation uncovers everything. She's probably terrified her husband is going to find out about her love nest."

Doyle was a stubborn man when it came to abandoning a theory. "Why should it bother her so much? A month ago she was ready to dump her husband."

"She was ready to leave a rich old man in order to marry a rich young man." Jones smiled sourly. "Nesta Deachman is an expensive woman and she wants to stay that way. She sure

192

doesn't want to be kicked out in the cold. Mind you, I'm not saying that Deachman may not be our killer. I just don't think that's what's sending his wife up the wall."

"Okay, then we're back to square one." Doyle hunched his shoulders in discontent. "Aside from telling us it was mailed for fifteen cents, this envelope doesn't do us any good at all."

But Jones was shaking his head with new confidence. "I wouldn't say that. If Rojak was planning to walk out from Police Headquarters—and from Newburg—with a clean bill of health, then he knew there was hard evidence he could put his hands on. And if he could find it, so can we!"

— 22 —

The murder of Jim Rojak put Newburg, literally, on the map. CBS, the *Atlanta Constitution* and *Newsweek* all showed the world southern Ohio, with large arrows pinpointing Newburg.

"'. . . where the second body was found,'" Quentin Trumbull read aloud from the Associated Press dispatch.

"'This prosperous community on the banks of the Curry River has been jolted. . . .'"

"That's pretty much what John Chancellor said last night," said Ben Safford. "Janet tells me that ABC is already talking about mass killings and a string of unsolved deaths."

The sensationalism of Newburg's sudden vault into national prominence was not what had prompted Trumbull's SOS. It was the inevitable context. Jim Rojak led back to Theo Karras, to malpractice, to Medicaid fraud—and to HEW.

"They're in a sweat in Washington," he told Safford. "I had three calls this morning before the office opened, including one from the Secretary himself. He wants a full report by noon, with special emphasis on Charlene Gregorian. . . ."

His sentence trailed off suggestively.

Ben knew that the Secretary of HEW was a different quantity to his regional directors than he was to an important Congressman. So Ben tempered his frankness.

"Don't let that worry you too much. Remember, everybody in Washington is publicity-conscious—especially a new administration. HEW is fielding questions from the networks, and the press corps is probably pestering the White House. They want to be prepared."

"Oh, I understand that," Trumbull said uneasily.

"Besides," Ben added, "when you get right down to it, HEW isn't getting the bad publicity. It's Mayor Wilhelm and Owen Jones who are taking the heat."

Although Quentin Trumbull did not look altogether convinced, this was substantially true. Newburg was attracting attention because the news accounts of Jim Rojak's murder were oversimplified, as well as lurid. To most of the media, fear stalked the streets and that was that. Trumbull and HEW were resolutely declining interviews. Arnold Deachman had ducked back into his nursing home, and his fellow doctors, including Howard White and Pat Costello, were lying low. Great Lakes, in the person of Larry Fournier, had simply fled Newburg. Only His Honor and the Chief of Police were available for public comment.

Mayor Wilhelm chatting with Barbara Walters had been a sight for sore eyes. What's more, this overnight notoriety had been less damaging than Ben had expected. Treatment of the Subcommittee on Medicaid Abuse was, he had been happy to see, perfunctory. Charlene Gregorian, when she was discussed, emerged as a public-minded woman.

"And even Owen and Wilhelm look good, compared to the doctors of Newburg," Ben commented with passing satisfaction. He found some poetic justice in headlines screaming:

Quentin Trumbull remained unhappy. "You may be right, Ben. But they're still flapping their wings in Washington, and that scares me. What if they decide that they have to make some kind of gesture because of these murders? Charlene could be disciplined—or even summoned before a departmental review board. That could mean dismissal or a reduction in grade. And any disciplinary action would affect her pension rights. My God, the way it sounds, this killer is going to go free. Well, I don't want Charlene to be the whipping boy."

Ben knew, better than Quentin Trumbull did, how the blaze of publicity affects official Washington. The strangest political contortions he had ever seen were the direct fruits of public-opinion polls.

"But I still think you're being overly pessimistic," he said. "Charlene is coming across like an angel of mercy. Still, if it will make you feel any better, I'll put in a good word. . . ."

Trumbull was embarrassingly grateful, and Ben had the grace to feel somewhat ashamed of himself as he left the Federal Building. He did not take Trumbull's bogey seriously, but he was going to use it anyway. What he wanted now was a phone where he could not be overheard.

"Ben said *what?*" demanded Congresswoman Hollenbach an hour later.

"He said that Buckley and HEW are planning to reprimand Charlene Gregorian," said Tony Martinelli without a qualm. Where Ben Safford could bend the truth in a good cause, Tony was ready to dispense with it altogether.

He was rewarded immediately. Elsie, who had dropped into his office on her way someplace else, plunked herself in a chair. More to the point, her draft proposal for a national health-insurance system was placed, temporarily forgotten, on the corner of his desk.

"What is this about Charlene Gregorian?" she said. "I was

196

pleased to see this morning's *Post* had a very strong editorial commending her. Good heavens, she's the one redeeming feature about this dreadful situation in Newburg. Have they lost their minds over at HEW? I thought better of Buckley—I really did!"

Martinelli did not hesitate to malign his fellow Democrat. Gazing out at the Mall, he said: "This second murder has scared him to death."

"Nonsense!" said Elsie.

"No, Buckley's all shaken up. That's got to be it, Elsie. I, personally, don't think the fact that his father and his brother are doctors has a thing to do with it."

If Elsie had not been convulsed with moral outrage, she would have smelled a rat. But, as Tony well knew, when incisive activity beckoned, she did not hesitate.

"This shall not be permitted. I insist that the committee go on record immediately, deprecating any such ill-advised action by HEW. Moreover . . ."

Tony leaned back and listened. Elsie insisting led to Elsie doing, which was exactly what he, Ben and Lou Flecker had in mind. While Elsie was busy championing Mrs. Gregorian, she was not going to be circulating her bombshell Republican national-health-insurance plan. And by the time the smoke cleared, Elsie's fervor might be channeled in the right direction.

The trouble with converts, Anthony Martinelli had always believed, is that they were too damned enthusiastic.

"Mighty convenient," said Congressman Oakes when he lumbered into the office a few minutes later with Lou Flecker.

"What's convenient, Val?" said Flecker. The House leadership was nagging him to cut Elsie Hollenbach off at the pass. The press was camped in his office, clamoring for revelations about Newburg. Flecker withstood the buffeting by living each moment as it came. He had no time for overtones, undertones or subtleties.

"I suspect you're setting a fire to fight a fire," said Oakes. He, too, was a convert, but nothing could make him a zealot. "Well, you may be wise."

Before Flecker could frame a tactful version of the majority opinion, Elsie evinced impatience with her colleagues' propensity to waste valuable time on nonessentials.

"I have asked Dr. Urquhart to join us," she said. "We have an appointment with Secretary Buckley at two o'clock this afternoon—"

"By which time there's likely to be another murder in Newburg, according to what I read. Poor Ben. Does he sound as if he's holding up, Tony?" asked Val.

Tony was a man who honored his obligations. "Ben sounds pretty tensed-up to me," he said gravely. "These murders aren't doing him any good. And if HEW smears Mrs. Gregorian, Ben's going to get it from both ends. He's caught in the middle, you might say."

"Ha!" said Elsie, rising. "I think it's time for us to leave."

As everybody obediently fell in behind her, Val Oakes offered Tony some advice: "Back home we always say that you can spoil a pie by putting in too many apples."

Unoffended, Mr. Martinelli promised to restrain himself.

Forty minutes later Joseph Buckley, Secretary of Health, Education and Welfare, surveyed his quarters with mixed emotions. There was the signed Presidential photograph. There was a vast rug with the department seal. Behind a distant door were a private dining room, a shower and a fully stocked bar.

Unfortunately, nearer at hand was the Subcommittee on Medicaid Abuse—minus Benton Safford but plus Dr. Alexander Urquhart.

"We are grateful you could meet with us at such short notice, Mr. Secretary," said Elsie meticulously.

"My pleasure," said Buckley, wondering how he could have avoided it. "Now, when you called this morning, you said it was in connection with possible disciplinary action against Mrs.

198

Gregorian in Newburg, Ohio. I did look into the file. . . ."

"Splendid," said Elsie menacingly. For all practical purposes, L. Lamar Flecker had yielded her the chair.

"I see that there have been protests from some members of the public," said Buckley, concentrating on his documents. "That was before this second murder—"

This time it was Dr. Alexander Urquhart who pounced. "What members of the public?"

"There seem to be forty-three names. . . ."

"My bet," said Urquhart ferociously, "is that they're all AMA—and probably a form letter at that. If HEW knuckles under to pressure like that—"

Buckley's tenure in office had been relatively brief, but he was already inured to undeserved attack. With a fixed, pained smile, he forged ahead.

"Now, I have been in touch with Trumbull to double-check on the facts. Undoubtedly we could press charges against Mrs. Gregorian—"

"But you won't!" Urquhart thundered while Tony evaded Mrs. Hollenbach's gaze.

Buckley had many good reasons to cooperate when the Congress descended on him. But he was human, too.

"We read the papers," he said indignantly. "If we went after this Mrs. Gregorian, we'd get lynched. God knows, what's happened in Newburg is bad enough. The last thing HEW wants to do right now is rock the boat any more."

"Hmph!" said Urquhart, only partly reassured.

Val Oakes then proved that there is such a thing as bipartisanship in the national interest. While his Democratic colleagues sat mum, he said, "That stands to reason. You want to lie low—at least until Congress sends a national health bill to the President, don't you?"

"Yes, we do, Mr. Oakes," said Buckley, ignoring the charged atmospherics. "Tell me, Congressman Flecker, do you have any predictions on when that's likely to be?"

Flecker manfully looked straight at Elsie. "If we don't get hung up with a lot of debate over last-minute bills, if we can hammer out a solid compromise in committee, if we can avoid one-man shows—well, I expect we may be able to report something out in two or three months."

"Not a minute too soon," said Buckley.

By common consent, no one replied until Elsie, with a grim little smile, spoke up: "I agree with you wholeheartedly."

She was not addressing the Secretary of Health, Education and Welfare.

". . . so we got things sewed up," Martinelli reported to Ben later that afternoon. "Elsie's back on the team. She's still out to revolutionize the health system, but she'll go along with us on starting at the beginning."

"That's one loose end cleaned up. I only wish we could do the same with the rest of them. You wouldn't like to come down to Newburg and look for some missing evidence, would you?" asked Ben, who had spent his lunch hour listening to Owen Jones' troubles.

"I've done my good deed for the day," said Tony. "What's all this about missing evidence?"

Ben described what the police had uncovered in Jim Rojak's apartment. Empty envelopes did not impress Tony Martinelli, and neither did love letters from Nesta Deachman.

"Not unless she was playing around with Karras, too," he reflected.

"Unlikely," Ben said.

But Tony liked his theory. "That way her husband just knocked off her boy friends, one by one. Try that on the cops."

Ben replied that the Newburg police were thinking along different lines.

"Thinking?" Tony scoffed. "It sounds to me as if they're chasing their tails. Look, Ben, you're not going to be stuck in Newburg until they come up with something, are you? We need you back in Washington for the conference committee on the tariff."

Recklessly, Ben promised to be back at work by Friday at the latest.

"Don't tell me, tell Madge," said Martinelli. "Every time I pass your office, she's sitting on the phone, canceling your appointments right and left. I think it's beginning to get to her. If you don't shake loose from Newburg, you're going to be missing one damned good secretary when you get back."

"Hmm," said Ben, idly visualizing Madge.

"Hey, I was just kidding," Tony protested.

But Ben was not thinking about Madge Anderson's loyalty when he hung up. He was thinking about something else Tony had said, something that touched off a sequence of random thoughts . . .

About a telephone call that Jim Rojak had not made . . .

About a threat more dangerous than blackmail . . .

About a diagnosis that was wrong from beginning to end . . .

— 23 —

Chief Jones was still at his desk when Ben marched into Headquarters. With him was George Doyle. A pall of blue cigarette smoke hung over them and Ben saw frustration and weariness reflected in their eyes.

"I won't disturb you for long, Owen," he said without preliminaries. "But I have an idea where Rojak hid whatever he picked up in Karras' office."

"Go ahead," said Jones indifferently.

Ben knew a tough audience when he faced one. Jones and Doyle had been grinding over the murders of Theo Karras and Jim Rojak for a long, profitless time. Ben decided to start strong, with the one inescapable question.

"Owen, why was Rojak planning to detour out to the Newburg Country Club the day he was murdered—just before he was due here at Police Headquarters?"

Jones studied him inscrutably. "To cancel his appointment with the tennis pro."

Ben glanced from him to Doyle. "When he could just pick up the phone?"

A sharply indrawn breath told Ben he had scored, and he

pressed his advantage: "You use the telephone to cancel appointments, especially if you've got other important things to do. No, Rojak was heading out to the club for a reason. . . ."

He had their full attention as he outlined his argument. Neither Jones nor Doyle interrupted him once.

"Look, we know Rojak was planning to march in here with a piece of hard evidence. That was his passport to security. Well, where would he keep it? His apartment? With at least one woman running in and out? His office? We've seen how well that could keep out another doctor. No, he wasn't stopping at the country club to cancel his appointment. He was stopping by to pick up that evidence."

Jones was still dubious. "You sound awfully confident about your theory."

"It's more than a theory," said Ben gravely. "I just called the tennis pro myself. That appointment was for the same time as the meeting with Fournier. Rojak had already canceled. And I know another good reason that Rojak hid his evidence at the country club. . . ."

Doyle was ahead of him. With a sudden access of energy, he rose to his feet. "If you're right," he said, "we haven't got any time to spare."

"Why?" Ben asked. "Everything will be where poor Rojak left it—"

"I wouldn't bet on it," said Doyle. "Dr. Deachman got out of that nursing home of his this afternoon."

Owen Jones was already heading for the door.

The drive to the Newburg Country Club was an experience. Jones ordered an unmarked car that was just pulling up as the trio emerged. Ben hurled himself into the back seat and waited for sirens and flashing lights, but they didn't come. What did was a display of speed driving bordering on the homicidal. The driver, a young uniformed man, followed Jones' commands joyously, gunning out onto Main Street with a roar. After they had avoided a head-on collision by inches, Jones hitched himself forward:

"Okay, Warren, stop showing off your reflexes. Get us out to the country club as fast as you can—but don't kill anybody on the way!"

Warren slowed to sixty and even stopped for one red light. It was a memorable trip for Ben, who did not expect to survive.

"And, Warren, when you get out toward the club, take the Frontage Road shortcut. We want the service entrance."

Ben, who had been visualizing a gravel-spattering arrival at the stately portico, glanced interrogatively at Jones, who smiled.

"We don't want to scare anybody when we get there. Warren, you stay with the car and make sure nobody sneaks out back. George, you get around to the parking lot and find out from the attendant if Deachman's car is there. Ben, you and I—"

"So I'm a member of the force, am I?" said Ben, interrupting this show of strength.

"You sure are," Jones told him. "You're in this up to your neck. If we end up with egg on our faces . . ."

"Okay," Ben said, "I'll take my chances. What's the drill?"

"First," said Jones with a wry twist of the lips, "we find out if this trip was necessary."

Warren had pulled up behind the country club, beside four large trash bins. Without a word, George Doyle scrambled out of the front seat and set off, dog-trotting toward the parking lot. Jones, followed by Ben, mounted the steps and pushed open the screen door.

There were three white-clad figures in the kitchen, busy with preparations for dinner. The chef, brandishing a chopping knife, froze at the sight of intruders. At the salad counter a golden-brown youth was startled into juggling a head of lettuce. Only the black-haired woman at the steam table ignored them completely.

Owen Jones discovered quickly that none of them spoke English.

Cursing under his breath, Jones pantomimed a futile request for the club manager. Meanwhile Ben stepped around him to take measures of his own. Punching buttons until he heard a protest, he gave orders into the intercom:

"Tell the manager the police want him here in the kitchen, on the double," he barked.

The manager came bustling through the swinging doors in

minutes. He was nervous about life in general and his kitchen staff in particular, toward whom he kept casting placating glances.

Jones silenced his dithering with a flip of his wallet. "Official," he snapped. "Is Dr. Deachman in the club?"

"Dr. Deachman? Yes . . . yes, I think I saw him."

"Where?"

"I believe he was heading for the locker room. But you can't—"

"Lead the way!" Jones ordered.

The locker room of the Newburg Country Club was down a long corridor which opened onto the putting green. Jones and Ben trailed the manager in silence.

"In there," said the manager, pointing to a large steel door. He seemed reluctant to accompany them.

Quietly Jones opened the door and stepped inside, with Ben at his elbow. They were assailed by the aroma of strong soap overlying the sweet-sour reminder of athletic gear and perspiration-soaked towels. Six stalls against the far wall stood empty. Before the rows of lockers were narrow wooden benches.

And near the showers was Dr. Arnold Deachman, surrounded by squash rackets, tennis sneakers and a duffel bag. He was rooting through an opened locker.

Jones, now directly behind him, asked, "Looking for something, Dr. Deachman?"

The man did not move. Ben saw his neck redden, but otherwise he might not have heard.

"That's Dr. Rojak's locker, isn't it?" Jones continued.

Slowly Deachman turned to face them. His mouth was distorted and there was a glitter in his eyes that reminded Ben of trapped animals. Then, as if a plug had been pulled, the tension drained out of him. Sagging slightly, he tried for his usual manner. "I have nothing to say. Nothing."

George Doyle, arriving late, flicked the folder from Deachman's nerveless fingers.

In it was a check for fifteen thousand dollars—made out to Theodore Karras.

Jones was remorseless. "You have plenty to say, Dr. Deachman. Where do you want to say it?"

205

Nesta Deachman opened the door when they arrived. When she saw her husband between Owen Jones and George Doyle, she turned white.

"What's happened?" she said, moving to bar the door.

"There's nothing to worry about, Nesta," said Deachman too loudly.

"Arnie!" she cried, her voice rising. "Are you all right? Oh, I knew you shouldn't have gone out so soon. I told you so. Oh, you should have listened . . ."

Deachman was shaking his head. "Nesta," he said imploringly.

She looked at him, then turned to Jones. "He's a sick man," she said as if Deachman were not present. "You shouldn't be bothering him now."

The tremor in her voice betrayed her.

Owen Jones, like a large, competent sheepdog, moved them all indoors.

"That's why we brought him home to finish our talk, Mrs. Deachman," he said, forcing her to step back. "We thought that was the best idea for all of us."

"What do you want to talk about?" she asked sharply. "Arnie, what have you been doing?"

Deachman's head jerked back as if he had been slapped, but Jones didn't allow him to reply.

"Your husband's been looking through Dr. Rojak's belongings, Mrs. Deachman," he said conversationally.

She bit her lip, and Deachman broke in. "Now, Nesta, don't get excited. Don't lose your head. They can't make you answer any questions until we get hold of a lawyer. . . ."

But as he spoke, George Doyle was carefully placing the check to Theodore Karras on the hall table.

Nesta drew a long, shuddering breath.

"And that's not all," said Owen Jones.

From his own pocket he drew out a letter on pink stationery.

Nesta Deachman could have been staring at her destiny. When she looked up at her husband, she spoke in a tone that froze Ben's blood.

"So you led them right home to me, didn't you, Arnie dear?

Once you found out about Jim and me . . ."

Deachman's mouth had fallen open. Almost groggily he stretched out his hand toward the letter. Obeying a nod from Jones, Doyle let him inspect Nesta's handwriting.

"You—and Jim?" he repeated dully. "You and Jim?"

Trembling, he began to read.

She watched him contemptuously.

"My God!" he said finally. "My God!"

He let the sheets fall to the table, to the floor. "You slut," he said in a monotone. "You cheap slut. After everything I gave you . . ."

"Gave me?" She laughed harshly. "You didn't give me anything. I earned it, baby, I earned it the hard way. God only knows how hard."

As he stared at her, she crossed her arms. "At least Jim was a man!"

"You—" But even in a rage Deachman remembered they were not alone. He bit down hard, his mouth a clamp.

"Afraid?" she taunted. "You're a terrible coward, in addition to everything else. Everything scares Dr. Arnold Deachman, from performing in bed—"

Deachman choked and would have lunged at her if Doyle had not crowded him into the wall.

"Oh, sure!" she crowed. "Hit me! That's all you're good for, hitting women. You don't know what else to do with them, do you, Arnie? And you're too much of a coward to hit anything but a woman, aren't you?"

He was struggling ineffectually against Doyle's bulk.

"Shut your mouth!" he yelled in a frenzy.

"Try and make me, Arnie! Try and make me! You couldn't, and you know why? Because you're a stinking little coward. Even too scared to do anything about Karras. You left the dirty work to me, didn't you, Arnie?"

He moaned and Nesta stopped, cupping her hand over her mouth.

But it was far too late.

"Nesta Deachman, I arrest you . . ."

24

"You mean it wasn't any of the doctors? Nesta Deachman was the murderer all along? And her husband didn't even know?" Tony Martinelli still could not believe it.

"Oh, Deachman found out pretty early in the game," Ben corrected. "But he wasn't in on it with her."

The members of the subcommittee had been pelting Ben with questions from the moment of their arrival at 8 Plainfield Road. The first news stories to reach Washington had merely reported that both Deachmans were in custody and murder indictments were expected. This, while it had not been nearly enough to slake the curiosity of Ben's colleagues, had been enough for the Speaker, who recognized a heaven-sent moment to resume hearings in Newburg.

On the surface, the gathering at the Lundgren home was an ideal coming-together of people who wanted to know something and people who had all the answers. Unfortunately, Ben had learned years ago that orderly discussion was impossible during one of Fred's famous barbecues. Janet, for some reason, could produce a five-course meal for sixteen people with no disturbance beyond the steady chug-chugging of the dishwasher. But when Fred was overcome by a desire to feed his friends with his own hands, the upheaval stretched far and wide.

Looking around the backyard, Ben recognized all the usual symptoms. Charlene Gregorian and Michael Isham, who had been invited especially to hear Ben's recapitulation, were nowhere in sight. Charlene was probably still chopping the immense salad due to receive a dousing of Fred's house dressing. It was fifteen minutes since Mike had volunteered to help Lou Flecker remove the piles of debris husked from the corn now roasting in the coals. As for Val Oakes, he had taken one look at the shambles and promptly created a makeshift bar. This necessitated frequent trips to the kitchen, and every time he padded off he sternly commanded Ben not to say one word until his return. Only Elsie and Tony had the good sense to join Ben in deck chairs and let the whirlwind rage around them. Elsie was apparently resigned to never hearing about the murders, but Tony was sending off sparks of impatience.

"Well, you could have fooled me," he kept saying. "I had that Deachman dame pegged as the kind who gets other people to take the risks."

"God knows that's what she wanted," Ben agreed. "But the people she knew weren't very cooperative."

Before he could develop this theme, there was an interruption.

"Now, there you go again, Ben," Val Oakes grumbled as he emerged from the kitchen door carrying an ice bucket in one hand and leading Mrs. Gregorian with the other. "And what about poor Charlene here, who has the most right to hear the whole thing?"

Charlene, of course, had been closer than the Washington contingent to the rumors and the speculations flying around Newburg for the last twenty-four hours. But, far from being better informed, she was suffering from additional misconceptions, and Ben had to start by shooting down all her ideas. No, he told her, Rojak had not been Nesta's partner in crime, Howard White had not tried to steal Rojak's body and pretend he had fled town, Costello had not . . .

"In fact," he concluded, "you don't seem to have heard one accurate detail. I don't know what's happened to your grapevine, Charlene, but there was no conspiracy or—"

"Wait a minute, Ben!"

This time it was Michael Isham, rounding the corner of the garage and dangling a redwood chair from one powerful fist as if it were a handkerchief. He planted it with a thud, straddled the seat and rested his elbows along the back.

"All right. Let's start at the beginning and go on from there," he suggested.

Ben glared at the assembly. "Look, I'm only going through this once. I am not going to start, stop, go back, fill in, every single time somebody wants to look at the coals or get ice. Now, first of all, is everybody here?" He spotted an absentee. "Where's Lou?"

Janet appeared. "That's all right. Lou said to go on without him. He's gotten a call from Washington." She preened herself slightly. "It's the Speaker, and he remembered me when I answered the phone."

Val was more than equal to the occasion. "Only natural he should," he said. "Gus knows where the real political talent in this family is."

Janet acknowledged the compliment. With a deft twirl she rearranged the tray of snacks she had brought so that the cashews were now in front of Val. Ben got the peanuts.

"And don't wait for Fred," she added, as if the Lundgrens had not already pumped Ben dry. "He's put the steaks on, and he's not interested in anything else."

"So we're all here and nobody is going to make a move," Mike Isham said threateningly. "Now, Ben, I suppose this mess started with Karras filing suit against White."

Ben realized that Isham was cueing him not to begin with the arrival of a packet of HEW documents in the Soczewinski mailbox. Charlene's ebullience had not been completely restored by the good news carried from Secretary Buckley by Elsie and Val. She still had moments of guilt when she blamed herself for having delivered Theo Karras into the hands of a murderess.

Nonetheless, Ben shook his head. "You have to go further back than that. Probably to the day that Nesta Deachman decided to have an affair with Jim Rojak."

"What's so special about *that?*" Tony argued. "Married to Deachman, she was bound to play around somewhere."

"It's not the situation that was special. It's the effect it had on a very cold, avaricious woman. Because Nesta Deachman wanted money and pleasure, and for a while it looked as if it was going to be a case of what Nesta wants, Nesta gets. She'd set her sights on Deachman and she'd made him divorce his wife to marry her. Then, when she got tired of simply spending money, she set her sights on Rojak and he obligingly became her lover. By this time she had delusions of grandeur. Once she had gotten her hooks into Deachman, she'd had no trouble converting that hold into marriage, and she thought it was going to be just as easy the second time around. But Rojak made no bones about telling her that he wasn't interested in wedding bells."

Elsie Hollenbach had been listening to the recital with pursed lips. On the one hand, she was the last woman in the world to encourage discussion of infidelity. On the other hand, she might well claim to be the group expert. The late Henry Hollenbach had been adept at letting his playmates go just so far and no farther.

"That is not an unusual occurrence," she said with a finality that nobody dreamed of questioning.

Ben hurried on. "Yes, but it was the first blow to Nesta's confidence. She had been pretty careful about her relationship with Rojak. But when he flatly refused to marry her, she realized how many risks she had taken. And I imagine there was no lack of people she'd antagonized who'd be happy to publicize any indiscretions they got wind of."

"And how!" Mike Isham proceeded to list some of Nesta's enemies. "You know, the Deachman divorce made big waves, and it isn't as if the family had moved away. Margaret Deachman still has plenty of friends who'd love to catch Nesta in the wrong bed, and Deachman's kids have always had their knives sharpened for her."

Ben had not known these points, but they came as no surprise. From what he had seen of Nesta, he could easily believe she had left a trail of ill-wishers. "Exactly. When Owen Jones found one of her letters to Rojak, he said that she was willing to trade in a rich old man for a rich young man, but she had no intention of losing them both. Well, Rojak's ultimatum made it important for her to consolidate her hold on Deachman's affections. Then she got her second shock. You may not remember that Great Lakes started to threaten cancellation the minute Karras filed suit."

"How in the world could we forget?" Elsie reproved him. "Lawrence Fournier mentioned it the first time we met him at the HEW office, and we know he told the Newburg Seven, because that's why the police regarded Howard White as a leading suspect."

"All right, Elsie. I didn't mean you. But you can see what happened next. The doctors spilled out their troubles to their wives, and Nesta faced the prospect of being stuck with the old man when he was no longer rich. That wasn't her style at all."

"For God's sake, Ben," Tony Martinelli said, "you don't have to tell us that. But how did she get from there to murder? A chippie like her, you'd expect her to pry as much cash and jewelry out of Deachman as she could and then take off."

"You forget she was still seeing Rojak. What's more, she was taking the time of day from him. On the afternoon before Karras' murder, Rojak told her that he wasn't waiting to be sued. He was going to buy Karras off. That impressed Nesta as the height of worldliness. She couldn't help comparing her lover's active approach to Deachman's passivity. Then, a couple of hours later, she had a brainstorm. She had the answer to all her problems. *She* would bribe Karras. Luckily, her husband had just deposited sixteen thousand in her account for a fur coat. When the whole transaction was over, she would tell Deachman, thereby earning his undying gratitude."

Janet shook her head in sisterly criticism. "You don't know much about Arnold Deachman, do you? He's not the undying-gratitude type."

Ben agreed that he might have overstated the case and would have gone on, but there were other objections from the floor.

"The little lady wasn't interested in gratitude," Val pointed out. "She just wanted her husband to be a money-maker."

"Sixteen thousand? For a license to practice medicine?" In his own way Michael Isham was shocked. "Was she cheap or plain crazy?"

"Do you want to hear this story or not?" Ben demanded. "I'll rephrase that. Nesta wanted to keep Deachman sweet and she wanted him making a medical income. So, once she had her brilliant idea, all she needed was opportunity. It came that very night when Deachman was called away from a party they were attending. Nesta knew he'd go straight home from the hospital and she could figure on an hour to herself. She called Karras and found out he was still in his office. Then she left the party, drove downtown and made her first big mistake. She took the gun out of the glove compartment and carried it with her."

Charlene stared at him. "You mean she thought Theo was going to attack her? Where in the world did she pick up a notion like that?"

"Oh, no—" Ben began before he was overcome by a spasm of coughing as a cloud of acrid smoke drifted across the lawn. The alarmists in the group looked wildly at the house and the garage. They expected sirens any minute.

"That's just Fred," said Janet on a note of long-suffering. "He must be turning the steaks."

Only Tony was bold enough to venture a comment. "Christ, Janet, you must have to have the house painted every year."

"Never mind about that," Charlene said impatiently. "I want to know why Nesta Deachman was packing a gun."

"Because she was wearing diamonds, carrying a wad of cash and driving an expensive doctor's car. When she had to walk a block in a rundown neighborhood at night, she wanted protection."

213

Michael Isham laughed jeeringly. "Come on, Ben. Act your age. She's just trying to establish there was no premeditation."

"Well, that's her story, and Owen Jones believes it. And it makes sense. Her only source of information about Karras was the doctors, and they all assumed that any lawyer who had the nerve to sue them must be out to feather his nest. Nesta says she didn't expect any trouble from Karras beyond his trying to jack the price up."

Things were worse than Isham had thought. "You mean she's *talking?*" he asked in horror. "All this stuff is coming from *her?*"

"She was until her lawyer got hold of her," Ben explained. "Anyway, according to her, she swept into Karras' office with a check for fifteen thousand dollars, flung it on the desk and told him he couldn't have more because that's all she had. That's where she had her second stroke of bad luck. Because Karras had gotten a telephone call from Rojak just before she arrived."

Tony Martinelli's bright eyes were gleaming. "I'll bet he thought it was some kind of badger game," he said knowledgeably. "That's how it would have struck me."

"More or less. Karras thought Nesta and Jim Rojak were trying to frame him on a bribery charge so they could have him disbarred or pressure him into dropping the Soczewinski suit. He went up in smoke. But he was an old-fashioned man. He didn't believe in fighting with the wives. Instead he said he was going to call Deachman and tell him what Nesta and Rojak were up to."

"Poor Theo!" mourned Charlene Gregorian. "In some ways he was awfully innocent. He probably thought of Nesta Deachman as a filthy capitalist, without ever noticing that she was a sex object."

"Well, you can imagine how his threat sounded to her. She thought he knew all about her affair with Rojak. She says she yelled at him not to do it, he simply reached for the phone and,

214

before she knew what was happening, she'd taken out her gun and shot him."

"Rooty-toot-toot!" Mike Isham chanted lustily. "Then what did this charming doll do?"

Ben shrugged. "What do you think? She rushed out of there and high-tailed it home. Owen Jones admits his boys flubbed it the first time they questioned the Deachmans. The police were so used to wives trying to cover for their doctor husbands it never occurred to them it could be the other way around. And when Nesta Deachman told them she came home from the party to find her husband already there and in his usual frame of mind, there was no outright deception. She was the one with screaming hysterics, and Deachman was doing the covering."

In spite of Medicaid fraud and other provocations, a certain sympathy for Arnold Deachman was surfacing.

"So Deachman knew everything that night," Tony concluded.

"No, Nesta was in no condition to talk coherently. When she shot Karras, he fell over the desk screaming and spouting blood. She was in shock by the time she reached home. Deachman had to sedate her before he could get anything out of her. Then he did what he could. After he packed her off to bed, he got rid of the clothes and cleaned the gun."

Tony goggled. "You mean, he didn't ask why she had committed murder?"

"She wasn't in any shape to answer questions until the next morning," Ben replied. "By then she'd heard the newscast and she'd had time to cook up her story. She sold her husband a bill of goods—about how Karras first tried extortion, then physical abuse, about how she was so scared she had to defend herself. Then she gift-wrapped it for him by pointing out that she had gotten rid of the malpractice menace once and for all."

Elsie was hewing to her own concerns. "Does that mean that Deachman did not go into hiding to avoid our subcommittee?"

"That's right," Ben told her. "Deachman had bigger problems than us. He was convinced that Karras had been a crook, and he didn't doubt Nesta's good faith. So he gave her the best alibi he could. But he didn't want to hang around for a second session with the police."

Mike Isham shook his head in wonder. "You mean he was hoping against hope that this would be an unsolved murder?"

"He wasn't the only one," said Ben grimly. "Look at Rojak. Of course, you could say he was in a worse pickle. He arrived the next morning to find Karras with his brains blown out—and Nesta's check lying there in plain sight. On top of that, the police have discovered that he'd already contacted his broker to see if he could raise a hundred thousand fast. We'll never know what went through his mind, but the upshot was that he mailed himself Nesta's check—and kept his mouth shut."

"He did more than that." Charlene's teeth closed with a click. "He lied about Theo, making him out to be some sort of criminal."

Here Ben was in no doubt about Rojak's mental process. "You have to remember that Rojak was no dummy. If he passed himself off as somebody willing to spend a half-hour and a few thousand dollars on a two-bit chiseler threatening him with a nuisance suit, he was almost a casual bystander. But if he admitted that he had called Karras, begged for an early appointment and started collecting big money to save his medical license, he would sound like a man desperate enough to murder."

"Wait a minute, Ben." Val Oakes was lying back in his deck chair, his hands cradling a frosty glass. He didn't bother to open his eyes. "If Rojak was so all-fired keen on being a bystander, he could have left that check for the police to find."

"I guess Rojak decided he could always do that. But he was already up to his ears in a fraud scandal. If Nesta was arrested, he knew everything would come out—the affair, his own plan to bribe Karras. There's a limit to how much a man can tough out. He did start to arrange an escape route. But Rojak didn't want to be exiled to Kuwait on a salary except as a last resort.

So he did what the other doctors were doing—prayed that Karras had enough sordid activities in his life to generate a bunch of suspects other than the Newburg Seven."

"Great," Mike Isham bleated sarcastically. "That left everybody pretending the pressure was off and they could go back to normal."

Suddenly Ben chuckled. "Everybody except Nesta Deachman. That woman has a real genius for rewriting history. In no time at all she forgot she'd gone hysterical and convinced herself she'd been man enough to do what Deachman or Rojak should have done. Considering what they both owed her, it was only right that they should go on protecting her."

Elsie Hollenbach had no difficulty recollecting the arrogant display by Dr. James Rojak in the Federal Building. "I don't imagine she had much success converting Rojak to that view. Wasn't she alarmed when he held on to the check?"

"Not really. It wasn't until her husband spelled out the implications at the Community Medical Building that she got worried. Deachman, of course, didn't know about the check, so he still didn't see what was coming. But Nesta promptly rushed off to Rojak for reassurance. He dumfounded her by announcing that the crunch had come. He was picking up the check at the country club and handing it over to the police."

Tony Martinelli knew this world contains very little hard-and-fast evidence. "Was the check good enough to nail her? Couldn't she claim she intended to take it to Karras the next day?"

Ben ticked off the damning points, one by one. "The check was signed by Nesta, it had Karras' fingerprints as well as hers, it was dated the day of the murder, it was numbered so that it came directly after a check Nesta gave to her hairdresser at five o'clock that afternoon. As a nice finishing touch, it even had a drop of blood."

"Wow!" Mike Isham whistled reverently. "No wonder she was willing to murder for that check."

"Rojak didn't help things any. Apparently he explained to

217

her how she, being a beautiful woman who had killed in a panic, would get off with a minimum sentence. Then he waltzed off to be the first one in the lounge while Nesta prepared a death trap for him."

"Good heavens!" Charlene startled everybody by slapping herself noisily on the forehead. "No wonder she was able to do it. I had completely forgotten that Nesta had worked in that building when she was Deachman's nurse."

Ben grinned. "It took Owen Jones a while to remember that, but I'm willing to bet it was the first thing Arnold Deachman thought of when Rojak's body was discovered. He was finally admitting to himself that there was something fishy in Nesta's story. That's why he helped Howard White try to pass the murder off as a natural death. Deachman still didn't know about the check or the affair, but he knew he was married to a tigress. This time when he fled to his nursing home, he really was feeling sick."

Tony looked at it from another point of view. "Well, Nesta must have been pleased that at least one of her men was still covering for her."

"Nesta was mad as hell," Ben corrected him. "As long as Deachman stayed in bed, she couldn't get at that check in the locker room. She finally stormed into Riverside Manor and abandoned all pretense with her husband. For the first time, he heard about the check. And she told him that they were in this thing together, so he had to stop taking tranquilizers and rescue her."

"But he was too late," said Janet with a sigh of satisfaction. "Just think, if he'd gone out to the country club twenty-four hours earlier, we still wouldn't know who the murderer was."

It was a daunting thought that Ben was able to dispel.

"Don't be so sure of that. Once Owen Jones found out about the affair, he was slowly zeroing in on Nesta. The police had finally realized that she was the one who had Deachman's car on the night of Karras' murder—the car with a gun in the glove compartment. And Owen never really bought the theory that Rojak secreted evidence incriminating some other doctor. Rojak didn't sound like the kind who'd protect anyone else unless there was something in it for him—like hiding a discreditable relationship. Then, when Owen had time to think about Rojak's murder, he couldn't miss the smell of intimacy. It's all very well to say that other doctors knew about the allergy shots, but how much did they know? Only that Rojak was enthusiastic about a new regimen. And having a nurse remind him not to forget his shot didn't help much. Only Rojak's office staff knew the details—and, of course, someone who was spending a lot of spare time with him. Nesta was in his apartment occasionally when a shot was due, she had even prepared his needle for him—just like his office nurse, she knew how many cc's he took."

Tony Martinelli was discontented. "You make it sound too easy, Ben," he grumbled.

"But the clincher was the hiding place for the check," Ben swept on heedlessly. "Even if the cupboard had been bare when we got there, that was a giveaway. Why would Rojak put his evidence in a locker room which all the other doctors visited? It didn't make sense unless the murderer was a woman—particularly a woman who had access to Rojak's apartment. Nesta was the only suspect who couldn't put her hand on that check without help. And it was her undoing."

"It sure was," Isham said with professional detachment. "They've got her cold now. And she can babble all she wants about not knowing what she was doing with Karras, the trap for Rojak was about as cold-blooded as you can get."

A momentary chill fell on the company at this reminder of Nesta's calm vigil as she waited in the doctors' lounge for Jim Rojak to deal out his own death. Then Val Oakes, seldom at a loss for the appropriate Biblical injunction, bestirred himself.

"Vanity of vanities—all is vanity," he intoned. "If that little lady hadn't thought her love affairs were as important to Karras as they were to her, two lives would have been spared."

Isham let a moment pass, then continued his review of the legal action to come. "And I suppose they'll drop the charges against Deachman. Any jury would sympathize with a husband in his predicament."

"They already have," Ben reported.

"And thanks to your efforts—" Isham bobbed his head in acknowledgment at Elsie and Val—"I can stop worrying about Charlene."

"Absolutely," said Elsie, unbending. "Joe Buckley ended by saying that a few more enterprising civil servants like Charlene and we'd have a better health system."

"Did he really call me that? Enterprising?" asked Charlene, blushing with pleasure.

She was too pleased for Ben's peace of mind.

"For Lord's sake, Charlene," he cried, "don't push your luck and get any more ideas."

She stiffened with offended dignity. "I have lots of ideas. But I could never do anything about them," she added regretfully. "Not after what happened to Theo Karras. Even if I could be certain that—"

Her further plans were drowned out by someone who had no attention to spare for murders, or Medicaid fraud, or national health plans.

"*Come and get it!*" boomed Fred Lundgren. "The steaks are ready!"

As they all rose and began drifting around the garage, Val Oakes paused at the bar for a fresh drink to carry with him. Under Elsie Hollenbach's dispassionate gaze, he felt compelled to justify himself with yet another injunction.

"Man does not live by bread alone," he told her.

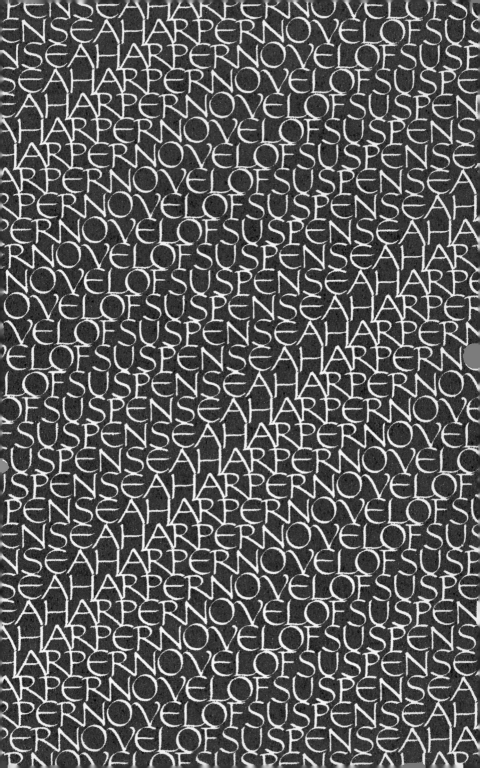